DEFENDER OF CANADA

C&C

CAMPAIGNS & COMMANDERS

GREGORY J. W. URWIN, SERIES EDITOR

CAMPAIGNS AND COMMANDERS

GENERAL EDITOR

Gregory J. W. Urwin, *Temple University, Philadelphia, Pennsylvania*

ADVISORY BOARD

Lawrence E. Babits, *East Carolina University, Greenville*
James C. Bradford, *Texas A&M University, College Station*
Robert M. Epstein, *U.S. Army School of Advanced Military Studies, Fort Leavenworth, Kansas*
David M. Glantz, *Carlisle, Pennsylvania*
Jerome A. Greene, *Denver, Colorado*
Victor Davis Hanson, *California State University, Fresno*
Herman Hattaway, *University of Missouri, Kansas City*
J. A. Houlding, *Rückersdorf, Germany*
Eugenia C. Kiesling, *U.S. Military Academy, West Point, New York*
Timothy K. Nenninger, *National Archives, Washington, D.C.*
Bruce Vandervort, *Virginia Military Institute, Lexington*

DEFENDER
OF CANADA

———

*Sir George Prevost and
the War of 1812*

BY JOHN R. GRODZINSKI

Foreword by Donald E. Graves

University of Oklahoma Press : Norman

Also by John R. Grodzinski
The War of 1812: An Annotated Bibliography (New York, 2007)

Publication of this book is made possible through the generosity
of Edith Kinney Gaylord.

Library of Congress Cataloging-in-Publication Data

Grodzinski, John R.
  Defender of Canada : Sir George Prevost and the War of 1812 /
by John R. Grodzinski ; foreword by Donald E. Graves.
      pages cm. — (Campaigns and commanders)
  Includes bibliographical references and index.
  ISBN 978-0-8061-4387-3 (hardcover : alk. paper)   1. Prevost,
George, 1767–1816—Military leadership.   2. United States—
History—War of 1812.   3. Generals—Canada—
Biography.   4. Generals—Great Britain—Biography.
5. Lieutenant-governors—Canada—Biography.   I. Title.
  E353.1.P74G76 2013
  973.5'2092—dc23
  [B]
                                                          2013015631

Defender of Canada: Sir George Prevost and the War of 1812 is
  Volume 40 in the Campaigns and Commanders series.

The paper in this book meets the guidelines for permanence and
durability of the Committee on Production Guidelines for Book
Longevity of the Council on Library Resources, Inc. ∞

1 2 3 4 5 6 7 8 9 10

CONTENTS

Illustrations

FOREWORD

This foreword was written in the opening months of the bicentennial of the War of 1812, perhaps the most embarrassing, misunderstood, and neglected event in the history of the English-speaking peoples. It was predictable, of course, that as the two hundredth anniversary of the conflict approached, we would be deluged with a shower of books about the war to mark it, many clearly written by authors who know little about the subject—and what they do profess to know, they often get wrong. A decade from now, very few books dropped on an unsuspecting public by this downpour of publication will be remembered, read, or consulted. Happily, that will certainly not be the fate of this book, which will remain for the foreseeable future the definitive biography of Lieutenant General Sir George Prevost, governor general and commander in chief of British North America from 1811 to 1815.

It is a much needed work because Sir George Prevost is one of the most neglected figures in North American history. Despite the fact that he was a senior military commander in the War of 1812—perhaps the senior commander on the British and Canadian side—Prevost is conspicuously absent from its hall of icons and heroes. Among others, Americans usually choose Stephen Decatur or Isaac Hull, William Henry Harrison, Andrew Jackson, Francis Scott Key, or Dolley Madison for inclusion, while, for their part, Canadians all too often choose the fabulous (and politically correct) four: Isaac Brock, Charles de Salaberry, Laura Secord, and Tecumseh. Britons

tend to either ignore the war completely or relegate it to the status of
a sideshow of the greater conflict with France. If they thought seriously about it, however, probably their choice would be either George
Cockburn and Robert Ross, the two men responsible for burning the
White House, or Philip Broke, the naval captain who brought to a
crashing end the string of American single-ship victories by capturing the frigate USS *Chesapeake* in less than fifteen minutes. Very
few American, British, or Canadian historians would put forward the
name of Sir George Prevost for inclusion in the hall of fame.

The failure by historians to accord Prevost the notice he deserves is lamentable. More than any other person, Prevost was responsible for the successful defense of British North America in
1812–1815, and it can truly be said that, after the Duke of Wellington, he held one of the most important commands in the British
Empire during the Napoleonic period. When historians have paid
attention to the man, it usually has been negative attention, and,
too often, they have made him the subject of particular obloquy.
This is partly due to the fact that he was recalled to Britain under a
cloud for the failure of the 1814 Plattsburgh expedition and partly
because many contemporaries, who had no idea of the responsibilities Prevost held or the pressure he was under, were extremely critical of his wartime leadership. In addition, Prevost's historical reputation has not been helped by the fact that he died at the young age
of forty-eight, ten months after the war had ended and before he had
an opportunity to reply to his detractors.

In the nearly two centuries that have since passed, very few
historians—certainly very few Canadian historians—have taken a
closer look at this much disparaged man. Most have been content
simply to follow what has become the party line to be critical of
Prevost or remain, at best, guardedly neutral (and I have to confess
that I am among them). A rare exception was the Canadian J. M.
Hitsman, who published a seminal article in 1962 on Prevost's conduct of the war and whose 1965 general history, *The Incredible War
of 1812*, furnishes an objective view of the man as a military commander and civil administrator. The author of Prevost's entry in
volume 5 of the *Dictionary of Canadian Biography*, published in
1983, is also sympathetic but concentrates more on Prevost's civilian administration, particularly in Nova Scotia in 1808–1811, than
on his wartime command.

In view of the fact that Sir George Prevost has generally been either ignored or criticized in the historiography of the War of 1812, the appearance of this book is therefore a matter of some celebration. What follows is the first extensive scholarly investigation of the life of Prevost, his wartime leadership and the circumstances that led to his removal. Its treatment of its subject is long overdue, and it will become a standard source for British strategic thinking during the conflict.

John Grodzinski thoroughly prepares the ground of his subject. He provides a survey of Prevost's family background and the course of his career up to the time he was appointed governor general and commander in chief of British North America. Born in New Jersey in 1767, Prevost received a military education in a private academy and was commissioned in the 60th Foot in 1779. Almost all of his military career was spent in North America, particularly in the disease-ridden West Indies, where he fought in a number of "island-hopping" campaigns in the last decade of the eighteenth century and the first decade of the nineteenth century. Prevost proved himself to be not only a professional soldier but also an effective administrator, and his reward was the governorship of Dominica, which he defended against a serious French attack in 1805.

In 1808, in the wake of the international tension caused by the *Leopard* and *Chesapeake* incident, Britain reinforced its Canadian garrisons and appointed military officers as colonial governors. Prevost was named lieutenant governor of Nova Scotia, replacing a particularly corrupt and unsavory predecessor, and again he was able deftly to balance the conflicting wishes of various interest groups while at the same time improving the colony's defenses. He took a brief sabbatical from his governorship to command a division in the attack on Martinique in 1809, performing flawlessly in a campaign that featured hard fighting in very difficult terrain. In 1811, when the British government was looking for a replacement for the ailing Sir James Craig as governor general and commander in chief of North America, Prevost was the natural choice.

Grodzinski devotes little space to Prevost's handling of civilian affairs when he was governor general, a subject that has been covered elsewhere. He does note Prevost's success in improving relations with the francophone population, which had been very bad during the tenure of his predecessor. The result was that the *Canadiens*, as the French-speaking people were known, supported the Crown during the war that shortly followed. Preparing for that conflict preoccupied Prevost during the first six months of 1812, and Grodzinski goes into some detail on the evolution of plans for the defense of British North America as well as the orders Prevost received from London immediately after the outbreak of hostilities in June 1812. Most of this book is concerned with Prevost's military leadership during the thirty-two months that followed the declaration of war, and the result is the most complete and balanced analysis of British strategic direction yet to appear in print.

As the commander in chief of British North America, Prevost bore a very heavy weight of responsibility. For the first two years of war, his objective was "to hold the line" and he held it well. Only in the spring of 1814, as the war approached its third year, did he receive the reinforcements necessary to carry out offensive operations, albeit limited ones, and it was the failure of one of these operations, against Plattsburgh in 1814, that led to his recall. This was not the only time Prevost faltered in the field—he was criticized for his performance at Sackets Harbor in May and Fort George in August 1813. Grodzinski does not gloss over these actions but provides an objective analysis of them that explains the decisions made at the time, and the results.

The failure of the offensive against Plattsburgh resulted from the defeat of the British naval squadron on Lake Champlain, and perhaps the most interesting part of this book is Grodzinski's discussion of the complicated relationship between Prevost and the Royal Navy in North America. The fact was that to obtain victory in the northern theater of war, a belligerent first had to attain and maintain naval superiority. This meant that Prevost's relationship with Commodore Sir James Lucas Yeo, the Royal Navy commander on the lakes, was both extremely important and also difficult because Yeo could report separately to his superiors at the Admiralty in London. Grodzinski rightfully invests much energy into discussing the problems Prevost encountered with his somewhat arrogant and certainly headstrong younger naval commander. It becomes apparent from Grodzinski's examination that Prevost has been blamed for many errors that more rightfully should be laid at the feet of Yeo, who tended to build up his own squadron on Lake Ontario to the detriment of the squadrons on the other lakes. The result was that the Lakes Erie and Champlain squadrons were starved of men, weapons, and equipment, and this led to an inevitable loss of control of both lakes to the United States.

Yeo became one of Prevost's worst enemies, certainly his foremost detractor. There were others. The anglophone population was annoyed by his sympathetic treatment of the francophone population. Many of the senior officers who arrived in 1814 were veterans of Wellington's army, and they disliked taking orders from Prevost and his staff, whom they regarded as rank amateurs. The business community disliked many of his decisions. Prevost's success in defending British soil during the first two years of the war held these wolves at bay, but when he was perceived to fail at Plattsburgh in 1814, they began howling for his blood. The home government, believing inaccurate reports from uninformed sources, decided to recall him, and this was done in early 1815. Once they were in possession of accurate information, however, many senior government members came to the conclusion that Prevost had been wronged and had a right to clear his name. His request for a court-martial was granted, but, tragically, worn out by the burden of command and the clamor against him, Sir George Prevost died in January 1816, a week before the court was to sit.

In effect, this fine biography is that court-martial. Through industrious research, John Grodzinski has amassed an extensive archive of evidence, sifted and weighed it carefully, arrived at a logical conclusion after lengthy deliberation, and communicated the results in a succinct and admirable fashion. Lieutenant General Sir George Prevost—long neglected and oft maligned—deserves no less.

Donald E. Graves
Maple Cottage, Ontario

October 2012

ACKNOWLEDGMENTS

I began working on this book nearly a decade ago. Historian Donald E. Graves, noting an important omission in the historiography of the War of 1812, convinced me to abandon writing my doctoral dissertation on the defense of Lower Canada and, instead, to examine the most misunderstood and neglected figure from that conflict: Lieutenant General Sir George Prevost, the commander in chief of British North America. The result is this book, which would not have been possible without the encouragement of a number of people.

Donald Graves was generous in his assistance, wise in his counsel, and limitless in his friendship. I am indebted to him and to his wife, Dianne, for their thoughtfulness and generosity in hosting me on so many occasions. Generous assistance in unraveling the nuances of the Prevost family tree came from Sir Christopher Prevost, who also provided access to family records. Dr. Carl Benn of Ryerson University in Toronto offered valuable advice and support, as did Jane Errington, Gary Gibson, Keith Herkalo, Donald R. Hickey, Roch Legault, the late Robert Malcomson, Rory Muir, Jonathon Riley, and the anonymous reviewers of the manuscript. The Society for Army Historical Research provided a generous grant that permitted me to undertake further archival research in Britain.

The staff at Massey Library of the Royal Military College of Canada readily processed my endless requests for interlibrary loan material and offered generous access to their special collections, including the journals of Major General Frederick Robinson. Brian Leigh Dunnigan and the staff at the William R. Clements Library of the University of Michigan provided copies of the papers of Major General Thomas Brisbane. Cheryl Desroches generously collected documents from the Public Archives of Nova Scotia related to Prevost's lieutenant governorship of that province. The recently created digital collection of War of 1812 documentation, containing 381 linear feet of British and Canadian documents, available on the website of the Library and Archives Canada, was of inestimable value in my research.

Charles Rankin at the University of Oklahoma Press, along with Emily Jerman and Robert Fullilove, patiently steered this book through the editorial process with calmness, while Tom Jonas turned my scribbled sketches into superlative maps.

To satisfy a promise made many years ago, I must also express my sincerest appreciation to Mr. Paul Keat, my high school history teacher who ignited within me a passion for history and for learning that has guided me through much of my life.

Finally, I offer a special measure of gratitude to my wife, Helga, and our children, Sylvia, Karl, and Natasha. Over many years, they have encouraged my studies; listened politely to my ramblings about Sir George Prevost, wartime strategy, and nuances of Napoleonic era naval, military, and logistical operations; and patiently endured the endless visits to historic sites and battlefields. This book would not have been possible without their encouragement and unfailing faith in me.

While a great many individuals helped me with preparation of this book, any errors within it are my own.

Note to the Reader

As certain British political, social, military, and naval terminology may be unfamiliar to American readers, a description of key terms is provided here.

General Terminology

Bateau and bateaux (pl.).   British records applied the term "bateau" to denote any rivercraft, including Durham boats, whaleboats, and Schenectady boats, that carried supplies. As the name suggests, the term originated with the French. In general terms, a bateau was a flat-bottomed boat, approximately thirty to forty feet long, with a beam of five to ten feet in the center, and having a movable mast with ten feet of hoist and lugsail. Bateaux were capable of carrying between six thousand and eight thousand pounds of cargo, while drawing only twenty inches of water.

British socioeconomic categories.   The socioeconomic structure of Great Britain during the Regency Era was far less rigid than is generally acknowledged. The wealth created by the industrial revolution led to increased social mobility, while the lengthy war with France necessitated the mobilization of a large portion of the British population. These factors resulted in the reordering of society and increased the participation of the landed gentry and middle class in certain roles, including commissioned service in the army and navy, that had been traditionally more restrictive in terms of recruitment. The emergence of a new "gentility" influenced conceptions of honor and duty that broadened the definition of a "gentleman," who now relied more on his professionalism than on birth or title for advancement.

While the categorization of social groups has varied over time and is subject to debate today, the main groups within the social hierarchy examined here include the peerage and baronetage, the landed gentry, and the growing middle class.

- The peerage, aristocracy, or titled nobility was the dominant force in British society. It included the highest-ranking members of society and consisted of those spiritual lords (archbishops of the Anglican Church) of England and English, Scottish, and Irish families headed by a duke, marquis, earl, viscount, or baron. Nonpeers, such as hereditary baronets, were also members of this group. The lengthy reign of George III, from 1760 to 1820, was noteworthy for the unprecedented expansion of the peerage. While many of the new peerages came at the pleasure of the Crown, the growing authority of Parliament allowed the prime minister to confer a large number of peerages as well.
- The landed gentry were a larger and more nebulous group of parish and country gentry marked by growing wealth, influence, and, of course, land ownership. Most members of this group were high-ranking individuals in their communities, and many held some form of political power, particularly in the countryside. The landed gentry were the main source from which the peerage was recruited.
- The merchant and professional class included a broad group with professional, clerical, trade, farming, and merchant connections. This group varied considerably in wealth and social status.
- At the lowest level were the "poor" of the town and country, who enjoyed few privileges and even less prospect of advancement.

Canadians and *Canadiens*. To ease differentiation between the major linguistic groups in Upper and Lower Canada, the term "Canadian" will be used to identify the English-speaking population (modern anglophones) and *Canadiens* for those people whose first language was French (modern francophones). It should be noted that limited use was made of the term "Canadian" before and during the War of 1812; it only came into regular use after that conflict.

Lower Canada.   From 1791 until 1841, the province of Lower Canada covered the southern portion of modern-day Quebec and part of Labrador, which is today part of the province of Newfoundland and Labrador. The city of Quebec was both the provincial capital and the seat of the governor of British North America. In 1841, Lower Canada and Upper Canada were incorporated as the province of Canada.

Upper Canada.   In 1791, the province of Quebec was divided in two: the western territory, settled largely by English-speaking Protestants, the Loyalist refugees from the United States, became Upper Canada, while the predominantly French and Catholic portion became Lower Canada. The capital of Upper Canada was originally established at Niagara, or Newark, on the Niagara Peninsula, until 1793, when fears of its proximity to the United States resulted in the seat of the government being moved to York (Toronto).

The Regency.   In late 1810, George III again fell ill and was unable to exercise rule. As a result, in February 1811, following passage of the Regency Act—which had in itself created a brief political crisis—his son, George, Prince of Wales, assumed many of his powers and became known as the Prince Regent. The terms of the act limited his powers and the Prince Regent allowed his ministers to take full charge of the government. In other words, power and prestige that the monarchy had lost were taken up by Parliament. In 1820, following the death of George III, the Prince Regent ascended to the throne as George IV.

MILITARY TERMINOLOGY

The British army.   The responsibility for the various elements that composed British field forces rested with various government departments or agencies. The division of responsibility was not always clear in the case of support services, and, in certain cases, several civil offices concerned themselves with the same service.

- *The Horse Guards.* This office was the headquarters of the army and was named after the site on which it was located. The Horse Guards included the office of the commander in chief and his staff, and commanded household, or guard, troops; line and foreign infantry; garrison units; reserve battalions; and fencible units based in Britain. Other boards within this organization oversaw the provision of medical care and barracks.

- *The Board of Ordnance.* The master general of the ordnance was a cabinet-level official responsible for the ordnance, or weaponry, provided to land and naval forces, and for the construction and maintenance of fortifications at home. The master general also commanded the Royal Artillery and the Royal Engineers and held responsibility for their recruitment and training.

- *Administration.* Several agencies supported forces in the field. The treasury oversaw the commissariat, which provided food, fuel, and forage for the army as well as ordnance and operated the transport service within theaters. Responsibility for the medical services, including a diverse range of supplies including drugs, surgical instruments, hospital tents, and bedding as well as the appointment of surgeons and their assistants, fell to the apothecary general, the purveyor general, and the medical board.

Artillery organization.   In 1812, the Royal Artillery was organized into ten numbered battalions, each comprising ten companies having 145 men each. The companies were designated by the name of their commander and on campaign were brigaded with the field, siege, or park artillery. The garrison artillery was intended for the defense of a fortified place, siege artillery battered forts, and field artillery accompanied the army on campaign. The more mobile horse artillery was not employed by the British in North America during the War of 1812. The term "battery" referred to the placement of the guns and was not a tactical organization. A complete artillery brigade with six guns had 145 gunners, 100 drivers (who moved the guns), 204 horses, several ammunition and baggage wagons, and a forge.

Regiment and battalion.   British infantry during the Napoleonic Wars was organized in more than one hundred numbered regiments of foot, each made up of one or more battalions. The term "regiment" applies to an administrative organization of the unit as a whole that never took to the field. The individual battalions of a regiment were employed overseas. This battalion system eased the expansion of the army during wartime; as additional battalions within a regiment were raised, they were designated by adding a number before the regimental number, hence 1/27th refers to the 1st Battalion of the 27th Foot. Many regiments were identified by the honorific or territorial designations they were granted, such as the 1st Foot, which was known as "The Royal Scots," or the 8th Foot, which was known as "The King's Regiment." The United States Army did not employ the battalion system, and all infantry units were designated as regiments.[1]

Naval Rating System.   Ships were the basis of naval power, and the arrangement of guns and decks determined the classification, or rating, of these vessels. The British practice of rating a naval vessel determined its position within the battle fleet and was not an assessment of its performance, although it did influence other factors, such as the rank of the commanding officer.[2] The largest ships, carrying 100 or more guns, were known as first-rates. Those with 90 to 98 guns were second-rates, while third-rates carried between 64 and 80 guns. Ships from these three ratings comprised the ships of the line that made up the battle fleet. They had three masts and two or three decks. Next came the fourth-rates, with 50 to 60 guns; fifth-rates carried 32 to 44 guns; and the most common sixth-rates had 28. Known as frigates, they were big enough to carry significant firepower and fast enough to evade the enemy. On the high seas, frigates were often given an independent role, whereas on the Great Lakes they were often grouped into squadrons with other rated or unrated vessels. The latter included smaller, (usually) two-masted vessels, such as sloops, brigs, bomb vessels, fireships, schooners, and cutters. While the overall size and armament of the respective naval squadrons on the lakes increased significantly during the War of 1812 to include ships of the line, the sailing conditions on the lakes and the ability to dispense with the holds necessary for long voyages resulted in their being much smaller and more shallowly draughted than the equivalent oceangoing ships.

DEFENDER OF CANADA

C&C

CAMPAIGNS & COMMANDERS

GREGORY J. W. URWIN, SERIES EDITOR

INTRODUCTION

The Untold Story of
Sir George Prevost's Leadership
in the War of 1812

Bidden to do his best without hope or money; and, though he [Prevost] received more of both than can be expected, he never received them at the appointed time, and thus was unable to lay his plans with any certainty of being able to execute them. . . . He had no naval force, but, for a few officers and men, that could be spared from England . . . and yet this war was to all intent a naval war inland. Hence his instinct was to husband his resources, to stand constantly on the defensive, and to welcome any chance of accommodation.

    —*John Fortescue*, A History of the British Army

Sir George, neither by his foresight, conciliation, example or impulse, called for the energies of the militia of either Province; and . . . the merit of preserving them from conquest belongs not to him.

    —*Veritas*, The Letters of Veritas

There was great excitement near the King's Wharf at Quebec on the morning of Friday, 13 September 1811. Crowded next to the structure were members of the provincial government, senior officers, British and Canadian soldiers, and many civilians all awaiting the arrival of Lieutenant General Sir George Prevost, the new captain general and governor in chief of British North America.[1] Prevost had arrived earlier that morning aboard the 36-gun frigate HMS *Melampus*, accompanied by the sloop of war *Rattler*. The riggings of both warships were now fully dressed with flags, while seamen lined the yards. Around 10:00 A.M., as the boat carrying Prevost began moving from the *Melampus* toward the King's Wharf, the guns of both warships fired a salute, which was replied to by the Grand Battery overlooking the harbor. Once Prevost was ashore, the field and staff officers of the garrison greeted him, and after returning the salutes and the playing of "God Save the King" by the band of the 8th Regiment of Foot, he rode in the company of several senior officers through the crowd-lined streets to the Castle of Saint Louis (or Saint Lewis as the British called it), which was the office and residence of the governor. In the castle's courtyard, Prevost passed through the two inward-facing ranks of a guard of honor comprising the grenadier company, color party, and band of the Royal Newfoundland Fencible Infantry. Prevost may have been impressed by the men from this regiment that had been raised in 1803 and stationed at Quebec since 1807. Members of the Executive Council of Lower Canada—the appointed body that advised the governor on the colony's public affairs—met Prevost as he arrived at the entrance to the castle and then escorted him indoors, where he was, exactly to the day, fifty-two years after the epic battle on the Heights of Abraham, officially sworn in to his new offices.[2]

When war broke out between Great Britain and the United States the following June, Sir George Prevost became responsible for defending a group of North American colonies that stretched as far as Paris did from Moscow, and he eventually commanded one of the largest overseas forces employed by the British during the Napoleonic Wars. By December 1814, the strength of the British army in Upper and Lower Canada numbered 31,000 British regular and provincial troops, several thousand embodied militia, and the most powerful naval force ever assembled on the Great Lakes. Prevost's wide range of responsibilities included overseeing affairs with Native allies, ensuring the proper management of logistical matters, monitoring the needs of naval construction and personnel requirements, supervising the conduct of colonial governments and their fiscal management, and commanding the defense of the Canadas. Prevost's authority was not limited to land operations. Each of these responsibilities had its own unique problems that, when combined with the instructions Prevost received from his superiors, added further complexities to an already challenging situation.[3]

Despite his successful defense of Canada during the War of 1812, Lieutenant General Sir George Prevost has been of little interest to historians. As Wesley Turner highlights in his study of generalship during the conflict, Prevost has emerged as the most criticized British general of the war. Turner observes that Prevost's critics complain "that he was an excessively cautious and weak-willed military commander, indecisive in the field, and as civil governor, far too conciliatory to francophone politicians."[4] While more recent studies, including one by Turner, have praised Prevost's "political approach as shrewd and his conduct as pragmatic, sensible, and effective . . . few defend his military conduct."[5] Historians generally use three wartime actions to support their conclusions: Prevost's decision to terminate the raid on Sackets Harbor, the American naval base on Lake Ontario; his similar decision to abort a reconnaissance of U.S.-controlled Fort George, at the mouth of the Niagara River, in 1813; and his leadership during the Plattsburgh campaign in northern New York in 1814. In doing so, however, these critics of Prevost move from the tactical to the strategic level of war without distinguishing between them, noting the relationships between them, or acknowledging the different professional qualities that each level demands. By their fixation on the tactical level, most historians of the War of 1812 have ignored or downplayed Prevost's operational and strategic successes.

This limited perspective of Prevost's leadership commenced in the spring of 1815 with the publication of letters prepared by his critics.[6] Montreal merchant John Richardson, a member of the English-speaking faction that despised Prevost for his apparent support of French over English interests, employed the nom de plume *Veritas*, meaning "truth," in a series of essays that criticized Prevost. These ten essays, which have become known as *The Letters of Veritas*, had a profound influence on the early histories of the War of 1812 and the interpretation of Prevost's wartime leadership. Veritas described Prevost's wartime strategy as a "timid defensive system" that attempted to "avoid irritating the enemy," but which backfired and only expanded popular support for the war in the United States.[7] The few instructions Prevost issued are said to have lacked energy, decision, and dash, while his indecisive conduct became evident during the early weeks of the war, a conduct that "unhappily Sir George so steadfastly adhered to during the whole course of the war."[8] It was Veritas who established that Major General Isaac Brock—commander of the forces in the upper province—working "without any written order or instruction," from Prevost, ensured the preservation of Upper Canada.[9]

In 1822, two articles appeared in the *Quarterly Review* written by an anonymous author, who was later identified as Major General Henry Procter, commander of British forces in western Upper Canada during 1812 and 1813. Aided by his nephew and the *Letters of Veritas*, Procter produced a lengthy article titled "Campaigns in the Canadas,"[10] which criticized Prevost for failing to prepare the defenses of Canada before the war, not providing Brock with detailed instructions once hostilities began, and agreeing to a ceasefire with the Americans during the summer of 1812. Above all, Procter believed "the most fatal and palpable error of the commander-in-chief was his neglect to preserve supremacy on Lake Erie and Lake Ontario," meaning Procter's command;[11] and he attributed blame for almost every setback of British arms during the war to Prevost. Following Veritas's lead, Procter claimed the successful retention of the Canadas was due not to Prevost, but to the exertions of his subordinates, who were forced to act on their own. Procter saved his most vicious attack for the end, where he questioned Prevost's loyalty to the Crown, as Prevost had come from a foreign family and had been born in the American colonies. Procter warned that "no man should be found in employ of the colonial government, whose connections bind him by the ties of interest or blood to the American republic."[12]

Another of Prevost's contemporary critics was Lieutenant Colonel George Richard John Macdonell, who had held several important tactical commands during the war. Macdonell developed a strong dislike of Prevost that grew to resentment over his belief that he was insufficiently acknowledged and paid for his wartime services. After the war, Macdonell regularly petitioned the War Office for further recognition of his services in defending Canada. His requests were refused and Macdonell chose to express his frustration in a series of letters attacking his nemesis written under the nom de plume *Philalethes*, meaning "lover of truth."[13] The letters appeared in several papers in Canada and England and in two issues of the *United Services Journal* in 1848.[14]

Macdonell admonished Prevost for his conduct of military affairs: Prevost appeared more concerned with the transport service between Montreal and Kingston than with attacking the Americans. Macdonell makes the unsubstantiated claim that Prevost gave secret orders to Brock permitting him to withdraw his troops from Upper Canada on the first sign of an invasion from the United States. Brock was so offended that he chose to "gallantly disobey the same secret order and thus save for England 'one ninth' of the globe, though he threw away his own most valuable life in the process."[15]

Criticism of Prevost also came from naval circles. In the 1827 edition of *The Naval Gazetteer, Biographer and Chronologist; Containing A History of the Late War*, J. W. Norie, a well-known hydrographer, writer on navigation, and publisher of naval books, claimed that the "gross misconduct or imbecility of Gen. Sir George Prevost" was responsible for the defeat of the British naval squadron on Lake Champlain and for the failure by the army to take Plattsburgh. Norie repeated Commodore Yeo's charges—which due to Prevost's death remained unchallenged—that Prevost "urged" Captain George Downie "to go into action" before his command was "fit state to meet the enemy."[16] By failing to keep to his promise and "take the enemy [land] batteries first," Prevost gave "decided advantages" to the enemy and caused the defeat of the British squadron and the death of Downie.[17]

The popular image of Prevost that has emerged in the historiography of the War of 1812—much influenced by these early writings—was of a leader who was overly cautious, who hindered his subordinates in the performance of their duties, and whose strategic leadership was flawed. By the early twentieth century, the established master narrative attributed the preservation of Canada to dynamic leaders such as Major General Isaac Brock; Lieutenant General Gordon Drummond, who from late 1813 until the spring of 1815 commanded Upper Canada; and Commodore Sir James Yeo, with Prevost's role often relegated to a footnote.[18]

As a result, most modern works on the War of 1812 do not enhance an understanding of Prevost's leadership and British wartime strategy. In 1965, Canadian historian J. Mackay Hitsman provided the first reinterpretation of Prevost, integrating his actions and decisions into a narrative of the war from the British perspective. Hitsman is the only historian who considered Prevost's actions based on the strategic environment he worked in, the defensive strategy he developed to defend British North America, and his wartime decisions. Hitsman concluded that Prevost should receive much more credit for the successful defense of the Canadas than he has traditionally been given.[19] American historian Harry L. Coles, who also outlined Prevost's responsibilities and some of the strategic limitations he faced, believed that Prevost's military leadership was competent but less able than Brock's, which was superb. In 1990, another American, Donald R. Hickey, introduced Prevost late in his general study of the war, limiting the discussion to a few brief points about Prevost's conduct during 1814. To his credit, Hickey provides a much more astute assessment of Prevost in his examination of the mythology of the war, concluding that Prevost's leadership has been generally underrated by British and Canadian historians. British historian Jeremy Black, who examines the war within the context of the wider struggle against Napoléon, also presents Prevost as being more competent than is generally accepted, but offers no evidence to support this claim. J. C. A. Stagg attributes the "superiority of the British military effort" during the War of 1812 to poor strategic decisions made by the United States and their "widespread incompetence in all aspects of the art of war," as much as he does to the British defensive strategy, which he believes proved "adequate for Canada's needs, even under the leadership of Prevost, who has often been condemned for fussy behavior and excessively cautious tactics."[20]

This work is a reassessment of the leadership of Sir George Prevost as Captain General, that is, as commander in chief of British North America during the War of 1812. It is hoped that this reexamination will restore him as a central figure in the history of that conflict. Prevost faced tremendous challenges. Far from home, with irregular communication and responsible for the defense of a massive and complex theater, he employed a mix of regular soldiers, sailors, locally raised forces, and indigenous peoples with prudence and economy that magnified the stresses on his opponents, defeating most of their plans and preserving British North America's existence. He also had to work within a system where despite the imperfect communications that existed, his actions were largely governed by a few orders and instructions from London, where the British global war effort was managed and the diplomacy that ended conflicts was controlled. Like other commanders in distant places,

Prevost found that distance sometimes provided advantages, including greater freedom of action—something that military commanders, whether in the early nineteenth century or today, always strive for—but the price of this independence could be high when serious difficulties were encountered.

1

THE MAKING OF A GENERAL, 1767–1808

He was not without reason selected by His Majesty's Government.
—*Edward B. Brenton, 1823*

When he arrived in Quebec to take up his new duties as captain general and governor-in-chief of British North America in September 1811, Lieutenant General Sir George Prevost had, in thirty-two years of commissioned service, amassed considerable experience in military operations and colonial administration. To understand the professional background Prevost possessed in military affairs, joint operations, and colonial government prior to his appointment as political and military head of British North America, it is necessary to examine his family background and career between his joining the army in 1779 to the end of his tenure as lieutenant governor of Nova Scotia in 1811.

George Prevost was the son of Major General Augustin Prevost, a Protestant Swiss who had found his way into the British army. The Prevost family were French Huguenots who originally came from Poitou, and by the late sixteenth century were established in Geneva, where Augustin's father became a jeweller. In 1756, Augustin became a major in the British 60th Regiment of Foot, also known as the Royal Americans, a four-battalion regiment raised principally from German émigrés living in Britain's North American colonies. Augustin's younger brothers, James and Marcus, who had settled in the New World, also joined the Royal Americans and together the three held considerable influence within the regiment from the 1750s until the conclusion of the American War of Independence in 1783. The Prevost brothers also amassed considerable wealth from investments, perquisites associated with lucrative appointments and land speculation in the colonies of New York and Nova Scotia. Through their service and fortune, the Prevosts also enjoyed the patronage of the British court, colonial administrators, and several officers who rose to high command in the army during the Seven Years' War and American War of Independence.[1]

James Prevost used his influence in London to obtain an important concession for officers serving in the 60th Foot, most of whom were foreigners. Nervous that this high proportion of foreign officers could create questions of loyalty, the British government had placed limitations on their commissions by stipulating that none could be employed outside of North America or rise above the rank of lieutenant colonel. James attempted to have these restrictions struck down by the New York legislature, and when that failed, in 1760 he made an appeal to the Parliament at Westminster. Any opposition was calmed by the euphoria following the *annus mirabilis* of 1759, the "year of wonders" that witnessed British victories in North America, Europe, and on the high seas. Charles Townshend, the secretary of war, supported James's petition and presented a revised bill to Parliament in 1762. The result was an ordinance naturalizing foreign Protestants after two years in the 60th Foot and guaranteeing their property rights in the colonies. James and Augustin benefited from their new status and became general officers, with James becoming governor of Antigua. Naturalization also meant that the Prevosts' offspring, including Augustin's son, George, were naturalized Britons, enjoying the same rights and privileges as anyone born in Britain.[2]

Following service with Major General James Wolfe's army at Quebec in 1759, Augustin Prevost was promoted to lieutenant colonel in March 1761 and given command of the 3/60th Foot.[3] The following year, he was involved in the capture of Martinique and Havana. At the conclusion of the Seven Years' War in 1763, he was sent to recruit for the 60th Foot in England. He afterward returned to North America and settled in Paramus, New Jersey, where he was joined by his brother James and his illegitimate son, Augustine. He entered into several successful land consortiums, but when the American War of Independence began in 1775, Augustin was sent to Europe to recruit for the 60th Foot. He was promoted to colonel and appointed commander in East Florida, and in April 1777, he became a brigadier general. Augustin managed to repulse a weakly pressed

American counteroffensive; this action led to the capture of Savannah and the restoration of royal government in Georgia in December 1778. He then undertook an incursion into South Carolina, where another brother, Jean-Marc, served as his second-in-command. In February 1779, Augustin was promoted to major general and successfully held Savannah against an attack by a superior Franco-American force. In 1780, after twenty-four years of active duty in North America, he returned to England and purchased an estate north of London, where he died in 1786.[4]

In August 1765, Augustin had married Anne-Françoise-Marguerite, née Nanette Grand. Unlike many of his fellow officers, Augustin did not marry into the colonial elite but chose instead the daughter of Viscount Isaac-Jean-Georges-Jonas Grand, a wealthy Amsterdam banker who resided in Lausanne.[5] Augustin and Nanette had two daughters and three sons. Of the two younger sons, William rose to be a major general in the British army and James a captain in the Royal Navy. The eldest boy, George James Marc Prevost, was born under the British flag in Paramus in the colony of New Jersey, on 19 May 1767.[6]

George Prevost was destined for a military profession and began his training in England when he was six years old. His father was determined that unlike the majority of youths, who had little or no professional education when they became officers, George was to receive preparatory instruction. In 1773, he was sent to the Lochée Academy in Little Chelsea, London, operated by Lewis Lochée, a naturalized Belgian émigré and self-described author of books on military subjects and education. At his school, the "sons of gentlemen intended for the Army learnt not only Fortifications and Tactics, but also Mathematics and Geography, History, Map Reading, Military Sketching and languages."[7] The curriculum was designed to correspond with the course at the Royal Military Academy, the training establishment for officers of the Royal Artillery and Royal Engineers, established in 1741. Once he had finished at Chelsea, George completed his education at another military academy at Colmar, in southeastern France, that catered to young Protestants, who were not permitted to attend the École Militaire, an academic college in Paris opened in 1760 to train cadet officers of the Catholic faith for the army.[8]

It was no surprise when George Prevost joined his family's regiment, the 60th Foot. On 3 September 1779, at the age of twelve, George received a commission as an ensign in the 4th Battalion of that unit. At this time, one of George's uncles, Jean Marc, was a major in the 1st Battalion and his half brother, Augustine, a captain in the 3rd, along with his cousin Ensign George William Augustine. The elder Major General Augustin Prevost was Colonel Commandant of the Fourth Battalion, and through family connections George would have been known to most officers of the regiment, including the colonel in chief of the 60th and future commander in chief of the army Lieutenant General Jeffery Amherst and Major General Frederick Haldimand, colonel commandant of the 1st Battalion. Haldimand had been recruited by George's uncle James when the regiment was first raised.

George's early career benefited from his mother's wealth, although not to the extent that some historians have claimed. Family connections were of even less significance. Commissions in the infantry and cavalry were governed by purchase, a system unique to the British army that in the period prior to the reforms implemented by the Duke of York, the commander in chief of the army, in the 1790s, was subject to many abuses. All ranks from lieutenant colonel downward were subject to purchase, whereas advancement to colonel and general officer was determined by seniority. Under this arrangement, blocks of officers of similar seniority were advanced to the next rank together, usually on the same day. A young man such as Prevost would buy his ensigncy, and as vacancies at the next rank appeared, whether due to retirement, the selling out of a commission (as a form of retirement fund), or transfer to another regiment, the vacancy was offered to the senior officer of the next lower rank. If he refused, the offer was repeated to the next senior man until it was filled. In an expanded, wartime army, however, upwards of 30 percent of the vacancies, normally resulting from the death of an officer, were filled without purchase. Active employment up to lieutenant colonel was subject to fluctuations in the army establishment between wars and peacetime when the number of senior command positions was limited, and a senior or general officer was never guaranteed active employment. Such was not the case with Prevost, who enjoyed continual employment, except for one brief period following the American War of Independence.[9]

Most of his father's estate went to his older half brother, Augustine;[10] therefore, George relied on the assistance of his mother to finance his early career. Fortunately for his mother's purse, the stationing of the 60th Foot in the disease-ridden West Indies made commissions in it more affordable than in a fashionable regiment, such as the Guards or the cavalry, which illegally charged purchase fees above official rates. Patronage, the influence exercised by family members and friends with senior officials, including the commander in chief of the army, could hasten promotion, but this was not the case with Prevost. His uncle James died in 1778, before George received his commission. Jean Marc passed away in 1781, and his father five years after that. By 1784, Haldimand was gone, and Amherst retired in 1795. Despite his apparent advantages, Prevost's advancement—at a time when rampant abuse of the purchase system brought swift promotions, leaving mere boys in command of regiments—was slow. George achieved a lieutenant colonelcy only after fifteen years of service, and his subsequent promotions proved no more rapid.[11]

George Prevost remained in England during the final stages of the American War of Independence. As was common at the time, he moved between different regiments, purchasing vacancies at the next higher rank as they became available. In 1782, he obtained a lieutenancy in the 47th Foot, but returned to the 60th as a captain in July 1783. This proved to be bad timing, for with the end of the American war, reductions were made to the establishment and the first two battalions of the 60th were reduced in strength and the other two disbanded. At age sixteen, Prevost was now one of twenty-three captains in excess of the regimental establishment's needs, and on Christmas Day 1783, he was placed on half-pay, an allowance or retainer provided when an officer was not in actual service. Fortunately for him, this period of enforced leisure did not last long, and in October 1784, Captain Prevost secured a vacancy in the 25th Foot and left England to join his regiment at Gibraltar, the important British possession guarding the entrance to the Mediterranean, which had recently been heavily besieged by France and Spain. The young Prevost not only found time for regimental duties at Gibraltar, he also courted and, in May 1789, married Catherine Anne Phipps, daughter of Major (later Major General) John Phipps of the Royal Engineers.[12]

The outbreak of the French Revolution in 1789 initiated a period of political and social upheaval in France. With the arrest of King Louis XVI in 1792, the Revolution gave birth to a republic whose excesses against its own people grew more violent while its policy of territorial expansion eventually caused a European conflict. Revolutionary France went to war with Britain in February 1793, and the government of Britain, having joined a coalition that included all the principal powers of Europe, deployed forces to the Continent while the powerful Royal Navy quickly secured command of the seas. Threats to British commercial and maritime interests in the West Indies, a group of islands that also held strategic and economic importance to France, led to the dispatch of an expedition to attack the French colonies. It was in the part of the island chain known as the Windward Islands that twenty-seven-year-old George Prevost would experience his introduction to combat, and through the course of several campaigns he established his reputation as a military commander and colonial administrator.[13]

In November 1790, Prevost was promoted to major, and the following year, he joined the 3/60th Foot at Antigua. This battalion had been reraised in October 1787 when increased tension with France brought an expansion of the army. In March 1794, Prevost became a brevet lieutenant colonel, an irregular form of wartime promotion that provided the status and authority, but not the pay, of the higher rank. He achieved substantive, or permanent, rank in August 1794, when he was appointed commanding officer of the 3/60th Foot. The battalion sailed for Demerara, a Dutch-held island, but when the governor, fearing French retaliation, refused them permission to land, they continued to Bermuda, from whence Prevost was ordered to St. Vincent, in the Lesser Antilles, or Windward Islands.[14]

The West Indies are an archipelago strung in a gentle arc that delineates the eastern and northern edges of the Caribbean Sea. The Windward Islands, situated at the southernmost end of the chain, are so named for their exposure to the northeast trade winds that propel sailing vessels westward. Threatened in the summer by hurricanes, exposed to earthquakes and volcanic eruption all year-round, the islands pose a variety of dangers. The hot, wet, mosquito-breeding summer months, which became known as the "sickly season," exposed Europeans to deadly yellow fever and malaria. These diseases

killed merchants, soldiers, seamen, and settlers by the thousands
regardless of social status and rank. It was the wealth these islands
offered that caused Britain, France, the Netherlands, Spain, and
other seagoing nations to dismiss these dangers and to compete for
control of the islands. During the eighteenth century it was found
that the West Indies had the ideal climate for growing luxury commodities such as sugar and coffee and for producing cotton and in-
digo needed by textile manufacturers. These products, which could
be easily accessed by merchant vessels, transformed the West Indies into the hub of trade and shipping in the Atlantic Ocean. The
potential disruption to an opponent's trade and economy made
these islands valuable military targets during the latter stages of
the American War of Independence and the French Revolutionary
War.

Britain's objective was to keep its trade with the islands open,
while halting the commerce of its rivals, France and Spain. In March
1795, the indigenous Caribs on the British possession of St. Vincent,
whose republican sentiments were fueled by French emissaries who
were "busy all over the place," rose in rebellion and gained control
of the windward half of the island.[15] St. Vincent is a rocky, mountainous island, eighteen miles long and eleven miles wide. The
mountainous terrain was believed to be impassable, thus restricting
movement to the shoreline. The island had been colonized by the
French in 1719 and acquired by Britain in 1763. About twenty thousand Europeans (mainly British and French) and Caribs lived on St.
Vincent.[16]

Rebel forces quickly drove the British garrison, consisting of in-
valids from the 4/60th and a weak company of the 46th Foot, into
the capital at Kingston, at the southern end of the island. Similar
uprisings took place on Martinique, while almost the entire island
of Grenada was lost. In June 1795, the British garrison at St. Lucia
was evacuated, and it appeared the British flag would soon be ex-
pelled from the Windward Islands.[17]

The fortuitous arrival of Prevost and the 3/60th at Kingston in
June 1795, in response to an appeal by Governor James Seton for reinforcements, strengthened the force on St. Vincent sufficiently for
the garrison commander, Colonel Baldwin Leighton, to attack the
insurgent forces deployed at Vigie ridge on the southeastern side
of the island. Seton also purged those members of the French

population supporting the rebellion by having them interned and later deported. Leighton organized the 800 men from his own 46th Regiment, a contingent of local levies, and Prevost's battalion into three columns. Two of the columns drove the insurgents from their position toward Prevost, who was positioned to cut off their retreat. Over 200 insurgents were killed and their commander captured for the loss of sixty soldiers, killed and wounded. Prevost's first action had gone well, and the entire force was directed to Mount Young, which commanded the road on the eastern coast. Patrols were then sent out to clear the region of rebels.[18]

The situation remained stable until July, when a 500-strong regiment of blacks from the neighboring French island of St. Lucia established a strong position at Morne Rhone, a hill near the British camp at Chateaubelair on the western side of the island, and reoccupied Vigie, shutting in the defenders at Kingston once more. Governor Seton directed Prevost—with a force of thirty men from the 60th, seventy local militiamen, and several sailors—to dislodge the enemy near Chateaubelair. Prevost's march from Kingston was conducted over extremely difficult terrain, and the enemy slowed his advance by "an incessant fire of small arms."[19] Reaching his objective, Prevost led an attack on the enemy position but the defenses were strong, supported by artillery, while the terrain channeled the British approach. The attack quickly bogged down in the face of fire from the more numerous opponents, and with twenty-three of his men dead and forty-six wounded, Prevost ordered a retreat.[20]

This failure left the leeward side of the island in enemy hands. Seton therefore recalled troops from the windward side, giving the British a strength of 200 men from the 46th and 60th Regiments, supported by 100 Native militia, which was still weaker than the 500 insurgents opposing them. Following a grueling night march through deep and wooded ravines, the column arrived near the enemy position at Chateaubelair and began preparations for an assault. When a party of forty enemy rebels attempted to dislodge one of the British posts, Prevost had his men hold fire and ordered the three 6-pounder guns and a mortar of his detachment to open up with caseshot, which effectively halted the attack, allowing Leighton to storm successfully the enemy position at Chateaubelair on the morning of 5 August 1795.[21] The situation remained stable until the first week of September, when the insurgents, again with French

assistance, were reinforced and renewed their attacks. In the meantime, Prevost briefly left the island and, in October 1795, was sent
to take temporary command of the troops at Dominica. He returned
to St. Vincent in January 1796 to find that the defenders had yet
again been pushed back around Kingston, the only corner of the island still held by the British.[22]

On the morning of 20 January, Prevost led one of three detachments that were to clear the enemy from redoubts they had established on Baker's Ridge overlooking the approaches to Kingston.
The ground Prevost and his 200 men traversed to get there was excessively steep, rugged, and covered with thick woods. The attack
began well when Prevost's men "surprised and cut their [the enemy's] picquet guard to pieces"—but enemy fire then intensified and
the momentum of the assault slowed.[23] Prevost continued urging
his men on, but "so strongly were the troops infected with panic
that but eight men would follow him."[24] Most of his men were recruits whose morale had collapsed due to the difficult conditions,
and "it became evident that the troops could not be relied upon in
any sustained effort."[25] Unable to inspire his motley force with the
necessary confidence, Prevost, who by now had been wounded twice,
ordered a retreat. He was pursued by the enemy to nearby Millar's
Ridge, where he established a hasty defense. The enemy made more
than twenty attempts to gain the summit of the ridge but failed,
and at nightfall, Prevost ordered his men, who by now were completely exhausted, to retire. The two other British assault forces
also failed, ending further operations until reinforcements arrived,
Vigie was finally retaken in June.[26]

Prevost's baptism by fire provided him with valuable lessons in
leading soldiers of mixed quality while campaigning under difficult
conditions. His superiors were generally pleased with his conduct,
and their reports followed him across the Atlantic.[27] In the meantime, he obtained leave to return to England to recover from his
wounds. Once his health improved, Prevost was appointed an inspecting field officer, responsible for overseeing the training of volunteers and recruits, and in January 1798, he received brevet advancement to colonel. In March 1798, at age thirty-one, he was
promoted to brigadier general and ordered back to the West Indies to
take command of the garrison at Barbados. This appointment quickly
changed as he found himself appointed instead as commandant at

St. Lucia, an island forty-five miles north of St. Vincent that Britain had gained from France in May 1796. Thus began his introduction to colonial administration.[28]

Prevost arrived at St. Lucia in the summer of 1798. The island's harbor, Castries Bay, was one of the best in the region, making St. Lucia of interest to both Britain and France. The end of the Carib revolt and the commencement of a trade struggle between France and the United States, known as the Quasi-War, allowed most British possessions in the West Indies to adopt a defensive posture, which meant military resources could be transferred to the Mediterranean and Europe. Prevost was left free to apply himself to his civilian duties. His first concern was to address the discontent of the French residents, who feared the loss of their legal and religious rights. Prevost adopted a conciliatory policy toward these concerns, reforming the law courts and securing guarantees for the Catholic Church that won the hearts of the populace. Due to the satisfactory manner in which he conducted the administration of public affairs and following representations by the Court of Appeal to George III, Prevost was appointed lieutenant governor of the colony in April 1801.[29] Unfortunately for Prevost, the climate aggravated his wounds, which seem not to have fully healed, and it was with much regret that in March 1802 he departed for England, just prior to the island being returned to France under the terms of the Treaty of Amiens, which temporarily ended hostilities between France and Great Britain.[30]

Prevost's exemplary conduct as governor of St. Lucia impressed Lieutenant General Sir Thomas Trigge, commander of British forces in the West Indies, who wrote the Duke of York, the commander in chief of the army, to express the "opinion with which he [Prevost] has impressed me, both in his civil and military capacities during his command in the island of St Lucie. . . . He has invariably conducted his command in the most satisfactory manner." Trigg saved the best for last, expressing that "it is my duty to recommend" so distinguished an officer as Prevost "in the strongest terms to His Majesty, and to the Commander-in-Chief."[31]

The government took notice of this strong recommendation, and when Prevost arrived in England in July 1802, he was offered the post of lieutenant governor of Dominica, an island ceded to Britain by France in 1783. His health restored, Prevost accepted and embarked in November, arriving at Dominica on Christmas Day. In June 1803, he learned that hostilities had been renewed with France and that plans were under way to take three French-held islands in the West Indies: Martinique, St. Lucia and Tobago. Prevost departed for Barbados to volunteer for one of the expeditions. Arriving thirty minutes before the transports for St. Lucia departed, he offered his services to Lieutenant General William Grinfield, who had succeeded Sir Thomas Trigge as commander in the West Indies. Grinfield gladly accepted and appointed Prevost as his second-in-command.[32]

Grinfield informed Prevost that he intended to use 3,100 men and an impressive array of artillery that included fourteen field and sixteen siege guns, along with a squadron under Commodore Samuel Hood, to reduce St. Lucia. On 21 June 1803, the fleet and transports arrived off the island, and landing commenced that afternoon, near Anse du Choc, just to the north of the island's capital at Castries. The British objective was the fortress atop Morne Fortuné, to the south of the capital. The French were quickly forced back from the beaches, and the governor, General Jean-François Xavier Nogués, was inclined to surrender, but duty prevailed and he continued to resist the attackers from within the fortifications on Morne Fortuné.[33]

Prevost went forward with the 64th Foot and drove in the French *piquets*. After being reinforced, he was then ordered to continue to Castries. Given the paltry resistance he faced, Prevost suggested to Grinfield that the French might be ready to surrender. He volunteered to deliver a summons to Nogués, but the French governor rejected it. Grinfield then organized his force into two equal-sized columns for a final attack on Mount Fortuné with Prevost receiving command of the first column, which included the 64th Foot and two companies of the 3rd West India Regiment. Brigadier General Robert Brereton commanded the second column, consisting of the 2/1st Foot and two companies of the 3rd West India Regiment. A third, smaller column under Lieutenant Colonel Theply was to conduct a feint, while Brigadier General Thomas Picton led the reserve, made up primarily of the 68th Foot.[34]

Prevost and Brereton advanced along separate routes for about two miles before joining for the attack. Prevost deployed his column with the regulars in the center, flanked on each side by a company of West Indian troops. His force reached the rendezvous first, and Prevost ordered his men to lie down. As Brereton's column approached, a challenge given by the 3rd West India Regiment led to a firefight in which five or six men were wounded.[35] Prevost rushed forward, reimposed order, and then ordered the combined force to attack. Within thirty minutes, the fort and its batteries were taken, and the island was returned to Britain. Most of the British troops reembarked on the transports and left for their next objective, Tobago, while Prevost was reinstated as lieutenant governor of Dominica. In his report on the operation, Grinfield praised Prevost's conduct, advice, and dispositions for the attack, noting that the "attack both in arrangement and execution" had been left to Prevost and that his "conduct and courage has been the means of so glorious a day."[36]

Aside from the birth of two of his children, Harriet and George, and the task of overseeing the implementation of legal and religious reforms to the satisfaction of the island's French population, the lieutenant governorship of Dominica proved to be uneventful for Prevost until 1804, when Napoléon, the emperor of France, attempted to recover French possessions in the West Indies. In December 1804, the emperor ordered Vice Admiral Pierre-Charles Villeneuve, commander of the Toulon fleet, to mount an expedition with 28,000 troops to reconquer the islands. In the event, only a single squadron, under Rear-Admiral Comte Edouard Thomas Bruges Missiessy, succeeded in evading the British blockade of Rochefort and sailed for the West Indies. Missiessy had ten ships with a total of 580 guns, and 3,500 troops led by General Joseph Legrange.[37] Their goal was to land military stores at Martinique and Guadeloupe, take Dominica, and then raid other British colonies.[38]

Dominica lay between the French-held islands of Guadeloupe to the north and Martinique to the south. The British were in a difficult situation as French privateers continually harassed British shipping, while widespread illness devastated the garrison.[39] Prevost, who had been promoted to major general in January 1805, commanded a 700-man garrison comprising 250 men of the 46th, fifteen gunners from the Royal Artillery, and a seventy-man detachment of the 1st West India Regiment, supported by several companies of militia and a contingent of sailors who manned the coastal batteries.[40]

After depositing stores and consulting with the governor of Martinique, Missiessy set sail for Dominica and arrived off the capital, Roseau, early in the morning of 22 February 1805. The French ships made their approach "under British colours," causing the harbor-master to believe the flagship was carrying a British commodore.[41] Meanwhile, ashore, Prevost concluded this was a ruse as "the frigates were ranging too close to Fort Young" and ordered the shore batteries to engage the French ships.[42] As the main body of the French squadron held its position, two elements maneuvered to cover the landing—one, three miles south of Roseau; the other, immediately north of it.[43]

Prevost instructed the light company from the 1st West India Regiment, the grenadiers of the 46th, and a company of the St. George's Militia, under Captain O'Connell of the West India Regiment, to drive back the lead assault boats as they approached the landing site south of Roseau. Fire from the fort was also directed against the ships and the beachhead, but two French ships moved in to provide additional fire support, forcing Prevost, who had moved to the landing site, to withdraw the defenders to a defile farther inland on the approaches to Roseau. He reinforced the position with regulars, militia and artillery while instructing Major Abraham Augustus Nunn, the local commander, "not to yield the enemy one inch of ground."[44] French naval fire intensified as another 2,000 French troops landed, but their advance was delayed by Nunn and his men. Prevost's selection of the narrow defile canalized the frontage by which the more numerous French could advance against the defenders, and in the afternoon they withdrew out of range.[45]

Meanwhile, to the north, contrary winds had slowed the French landings, and by 9:00 A.M., they had managed to put only 1,000 men ashore. They were initially opposed by 100 militiamen who retired under growing pressure, and the defense passed to a small body of regulars of the 46th, a handful of militia, and a 3-pounder gun. The defenders held out as long as possible but were eventually overrun, with Nunn being mortally wounded and his command passing to Captain O'Connell. The French then landed another 200 men midway between their initial two landing points. Seeing that the rear of O'Connell's position was threatened and that the civilians in the town were battling a blaze started by fire from the French ships, Prevost, "determined on one attempt to keep the sovereignty of the island," employed a ruse of his own.[46] During the midafternoon he ordered the white flag hoisted and the militia to stand fast. Leaving Mr. George Metcalfe, the president of the council, an appointed body that advised the lieutenant governor, to open negotiations with the French for the capitulation of Roseau, Prevost then collected the regulars and commenced a forced march on a trail that ran along the length of the island to Prince Rupert's Bay. He must have found this decision difficult, as his wife, daughters, and son became prisoners when the French occupied Roseau.[47]

As the surviving defenders and the wounded through made their way north through very difficult and thickly wooded terrain, Prevost went ahead with two staff officers, including his nephew, Brigade Major George William Augustin Prevost, and two companies of infantry. Aided by local inhabitants and the exertions of the Caribs accompanying the party, Prevost's contingent moved rapidly over the poor roads, covering much of the distance at night, and reached Prince Rupert's Bay in twenty-four hours, three days ahead of the main column. But the march was a great physical effort for Prevost, whose health suffered. He then ordered the defenses at Fort Shirley be prepared for a siege as the French could gain control of the anchorage only if the fort fell. General Legrange, who understood this as well, originally had planned to storm the fort by a coup de main but was overridden by Admiral Missiessy.[48]

The French ships arrived off the fort on 25 February. Lagrange immediately sent Prevost an ultimatum to surrender, which was refused, but Missiessy ruled out an attack on the fort once it was discovered there was no suitable landing beach in the bay. Owing to Prevost's clever tactics and well-executed plan, Missiessy was unable to satisfy Napoléon's emphatic command to take the island. He ordered all the French troops to reembark and remained offshore until 27 February before departing for Martinique. Prevost put his losses in the fighting as nineteen killed, twenty-one wounded, and eight taken prisoner, while reckoning 300 casualties for the French.[49]

Prevost returned to Roseau to learn from the captain of a Swedish ship he had sent to gather information on naval movements that a French fleet was nearby and that Dominica was still threatened. Prevost ordered improvements to the island's defenses, which were further enhanced by the arrival of reinforcements, and he also obtained information from neutral shipping that helped to clear up the contradictory official reports on French movements. Lookouts were also posted on the island's highest feature near Roseau. During a visit to this outpost in June, Prevost observed a large flotilla in the distance, but believing it was bound for Dominica, he ordered the alarm sounded. Fortunately for the British, the ships were headed elsewhere; what he had observed was a portion of the combined French and Spanish fleets as they shaped course for Europe. Vice Admiral Lord Nelson, who had arrived at Barbados with the Mediterranean fleet at the beginning of the month, had just missed intercepting this combined fleet and was now in pursuit. The two opponents would meet off Cape Trafalgar on 21 October, and the result would be Britain's most famous naval victory. As Missiessy had left for Europe at the end of March, the departure of the combined fleet removed the last threat to British possessions in the West Indies. Dominica was safe.[50]

The conclusion of the 1805 campaign brought to an end Prevost's successful governorship of Dominica. His conciliatory attitude toward the island's French inhabitants earned him their praise, while his successful defense of the colony was appreciated by all the English residents, including the planters and merchants whose interests were secured.[51] Prevost had also learned that a judicious deployment of forces could thwart the plans of a stronger opponent who enjoyed greater mobility and held the initiative due to command of the sea. With his health again in decline, Prevost resigned the governorship of Dominica and sailed to Tortola in the Virgin Islands, from whence he embarked for England in July 1805. When he arrived, Prevost received a new appointment as lieutenant governor of Portsmouth.[52]

PORTSMOUTH was the most important British naval base. Surrounded by a chain of forts, it had extensive wharves, anchorages, depots, medical facilities, an ordnance depot, and marine barracks, while other facilities lay beyond the limits of Portsmouth. A military camp and observation post occupied the crest of the hills north of the town, from which all ship traffic could be viewed. As lieutenant governor, Prevost was responsible for the arrangement of local defenses, the manning of fortifications, and the command of troops within the district tasked with protecting the naval facilities and harbor. More important, he became involved in managing the arrival and dispatch of army units for overseas service. Portsmouth was also a high-profile post, bringing Prevost into contact with many influential individuals, including the Duke of York and the Duke of

Kent, the former commander in chief of North America and fourth son of George III who regularly inspected regiments before they departed for overseas stations.[53]

At the end of 1805, Prevost received a baronetcy for his services in the defense of Dominica. Awards to British officers for meritorious service during the Napoleonic Wars were rare and usually included either investiture in the senior grades of orders of knighthood, a peerage, or a baronetcy. The first two were normally reserved for individuals holding larger, independent commands or for exceptional service. Prevost was created a baronet, which ranked above all orders of knighthood except the Order of the Garter. It was a non-noble distinction that granted him the hereditary title "Sir" before his name along with the postnominal letters *Bart*. Sir George Prevost, as he was now known, was one of only nineteen army officers to receive this distinction between 1805 and 1815.[54]

In September 1806, Prevost became the colonel commandant of the 5/60th Foot, the first of several honorary appointments he would hold. Such an appointment was usually granted to a general officer as the titular head of a battalion; the colonel commandant oversaw the institutional well-being of the battalion and also offered advice to the commanding officer on a variety of matters such as officer appointments. Prevost followed the exploits of the 5th Battalion, which had been raised in 1798 as one of the few British battalions armed with rifles, with great interest and corresponded regularly with the commanding officer.[55] He relinquished the post of colonel commandant in January 1813 as part of the regular rotation of officers holding this post, but through his association with the 5/60th, Prevost met two officers who would serve under him in North America. These were the German Francis de Rottenburg, the first commanding officer of the 5/60th, and Charles de Salaberry,[56] a Canadian who would gain fame in the War of 1812. Prevost also kept a close personal connection with the battalion, as his nephew James was to serve with it in Portugal.[57]

Prevost's duties at Portsmouth may have been varied and challenging, but he hoped for another overseas command. His appointment brought him into regular contact with many dignitaries, such as in March 1807, when he accompanied the Duke of Kent on an inspection of a battalion destined for the East Indies. There were also countless administrative responsibilities, involving the award of contracts for the supply of provisions for the garrison, and endless committee meetings to oversee the proper accounting of public funds. In May 1807, Prevost was considered for the post of inspector general of recruiting, whose duty was to inspect recruits for regiments abroad and make up their muster rolls. The appointment would have given him command over Chatham Barracks, where recruits were collected before going overseas, and the depot of the Isle of Wight, where reinforcements for most foreign regiments in the British army, including the 60th Regiment, were stationed. Reforms to the recruiting system led to the abolition of this office later in the year, leaving Prevost to wait for another appointment. It would not be long in coming.

Crises that occurred in Europe and North America during the summer of 1807 determined Prevost's fate. On the Continent, Napoléon's military victories and his alliance with Russia expanded France's hegemony over central and eastern Europe. With Denmark now a vassal state of France, British officials feared the Danish fleet would be combined with that of Russia against Great Britain. A joint expeditionary force was quickly mobilized to seize the Danish navy. Prevost was considered to lead one of the brigades until Anglo-American relations underwent a serious reversal following the *Chesapeake-Leopard* incident of June 1807, in which the British frigate HMS *Leopard* intercepted, fired on, and then boarded an American warship off the coast of Virginia. As Britain and the United States appeared to be on the brink of war, the British government decided, in light of Prevost's West Indian military and colonial experience, that he was more suitable for service in North America.[58]

In late 1807, British authorities decided to combine under a single person command of the civil government and the armed forces in Nova Scotia, in response to the poor state of its defenses. The colonial administration in British North America thus became increasingly military in character. This policy was implemented beginning in August 1807, when Lieutenant General Sir James Craig was appointed the captain general and governor in chief of British North America; in January 1808, Major General Sir George Prevost succeeded the aging Sir John Wentworth as governor and commander of the forces in the Maritime Provinces of North America with the local rank of lieutenant general. A brigade of regulars would accompany Prevost as a show of strength against the Americans.[59]

Three of the four battalions of infantry that had been hurriedly assembled in response to the crisis had recently returned from Denmark. The 1/7th, 1/8th, and the 1/23rd Regiments of Foot were just settling into barracks when they received orders for overseas service in November 1807, but an officer from the 23rd observed that conditions were "really too comfortable to last long."[60] The 13th Foot completed the brigade, and all units were quickly brought up to strength. Brigadier General Daniel Hoghton, also recently back from the siege of Copenhagen, was placed in command of the brigade. Delays in assembling the convoy at Portsmouth and the need for Prevost to depart promptly nearly resulted in his leaving for Nova Scotia ahead of the troop convoy.[61]

Before sailing, Prevost was guest of honor at a large farewell dinner "of the most profuse, sumptuous, and elegant kind"[62] at the Crown Inn in Portsmouth with more than ninety officers from the garrison attending the function. The next night, Lady Prevost was one of 150 guests at a supper and ball hosted by the naval captains in port. In early February 1808, the troopships, which had been loaded and ready since January, with Prevost and his personal staff aboard HMS *Penelope*—his family would follow in August—departed on the tide for Nova Scotia. Sir George would not see Britain again for seven years.[63]

2

NOVA SCOTIA, MARTINIQUE, AND QUEBEC, 1808–1811

An officer, who has so frequently proved himself worthy of commanding British colonies.
—*Address to Lieutenant General Sir George Prevost by the Clergy of Halifax, 15 August 1811*

The convoy carrying Sir George Prevost and the brigade of infantry to Halifax encountered rough seas and violent storms, making for a difficult passage. Vessels undertaking transatlantic voyages during the age of sail relied on winds and sea currents to move; thus a straight line was not always the quickest route between two points. Rather than sail directly from Britain to Nova Scotia, Prevost's convoy followed the trade winds diagonally across the Atlantic to Bermuda, from where it would use the Gulf Stream to take it north to Halifax. During March, the convoy was becalmed in midocean, a not unusual occurrence, whereby the northern and southern trade winds met creating an effect known as "the doldrums." After drifting for a few days, the ships caught a wind and arrived at Bermuda, the winter station of the North American squadron, at the end of the month.

The 13th Foot was left there, and the remainder of the force continued to Nova Scotia, which was sighted on 7 April 1808. Most of the transports arrived at Halifax within a few days. Prevost brought 2,300 soldiers to an important colonial port of some 9,000 souls. Their primary duty was to defend it, but they could be redistributed where needed, if the United States attacked British North America. There was also a plan, contingent on the normalization of Anglo-American relations, to employ Prevost and the brigade against French possessions in the West Indies. For the time being, the transports and the three battalions were to remain concentrated in Halifax, less three companies that were dispatched to Annapolis Royal, until their disposition could be confirmed. The arrival of Prevost and the brigade were reported widely in local newspapers to boost the morale of Nova Scotians and serve as a deterrent to the Americans.[1]

Prevost faced a difficult challenge. Since 1806, when its perceived right of free trade had become challenged by the economic struggle between France and Great Britain, the American government had followed a policy that relied on economic pressure to convince both powers, and in particular Britain, to respect the States' neutrality. Following Napoléon's Berlin Decree of 1806 that established the "Continental System" prohibiting trade with British ports and authorizing the seizure of goods from Britain and its colonies, the British government responded with the Orders in Council, a series of executive orders banning trade with any port controlled by an enemy of Britain and imposing duties and licenses on neutral merchantmen intending to trade with France or its allies. Its large navy allowed Britain to enforce these measures with more success than Napoléon achieved, and neutral trade with France declined, provoking outrage among many Americans.[2]

Nova Scotia was in the middle of this expanding commercial war as the British attempted to limit American trade with France, while seeking American produce to sustain their war in Europe. The Embargo Act of 1807 and subsequent Non-Intercourse Act enacted by the U.S. Congress forbade American trade with Britain and France, but failed miserably. In 1808, Britain retaliated by declaring the cities of Halifax and Shelburne in Nova Scotia and Saint John in New Brunswick as free ports: the elimination of customs duties served to channel most of the Atlantic seaboard trade through these ports while freeing up important supplies for the army on the Iberian Peninsula.[3]

While his primary task was to improve the military and naval defense of Nova Scotia, his orders also addressed Prevost's role in the succession of government in British North America, should the sickly governor, Sir James Craig, whose seat was at Quebec, die or become incapacitated.[4] Prevost was to be prepared to replace Craig— whose health was of concern, despite the fact that he had ostensibly recovered from a serious illness—as governor of British North America and also assume the appointment of commander in chief at Quebec.[5]

Prevost had received private and secret instructions from Lord Castlereagh, the Secretary of State for War and the Colonies, "which may be of use in exigencies" authorizing him to exploit American discord, particularly in New England, where many politicians, mercantile leaders, and inhabitants disapproved of the hostile measures against Britain.[6] Castlereagh directed Prevost to "gain Intelligence with regard to the projects of the American Government in General, and particularly those States bordering upon His Majesty's Territories."[7] In the event of hostilities, Prevost was authorized, if he found the "adjacent states indisposed to active Warfare, and willing to enter into any private arrangement for mutual convenience in point of Trade," to offer British commodities and goods, including fishing rights, gypsum from New Brunswick, or coal from Cape Breton.[8] Prevost also had permission to prepare and circulate "propaganda which will show the Americans that it would be unwise for their Government to engage in war with Great Britain."[9]

Prevost's first order of business was to implement changes in several civil and military appointments. A delegation consisting of Major General Martin Hunter, the commander of the forces, and Mr. Michael Wallace, the acting secretary of the provincial legislature, met Prevost on board his ship once it anchored in Halifax on 7 April 1808 before Wentworth received news of his appointment, and before the abrupt changeover of the colonial government created much surprise. Prevost went ashore at 6:00 P.M. under a salute from Fort George, the primary fortified point in the city, and was then escorted to Government House by the grenadier company of the 101st Foot. There he met Wentworth, who commenced providing Prevost with "the benefit of his long experience and personal influence"[10] in the province's affairs. On 13 April, Prevost assumed control of the government after his commission was read and he was sworn in; he also replaced Hunter, who took up the united offices of the civil government and military command of New Brunswick, as the commander in chief of the land forces in the Maritime Provinces. Prevost then sent a letter to the British minister in Washington that announced the change of appointments in Nova Scotia and detailed his plans for collecting intelligence from the United States, including a note in cipher about the codes to be used.[11]

Prevost next set about preparing the province for war. Every facet of the defenses fell under his scrutiny. He began by spending six weeks on an inspection tour of Nova Scotia accompanied by Lieutenant Colonel Edward Pakenham, who had been with him at St. Lucia in 1803 and who now commanded the 1/7th Foot.[12] Prevost ordered a series of reports to be prepared on specific aspects of the province's defenses, and the pace at which he acted was guided initially by intelligence reports privately compiled by Wentworth that were unclear about American intentions. More recent information highlighted border tensions, increased smuggling in the Passamaquoddy Bay region, and the American occupation of Moose Island, located between Maine and New Brunswick, which was claimed by both nations. The Royal Navy was monitoring the situation when "an act of violence" was reported at nearby Deer Island.[13] The navy had intelligence that an American sloop and six gunboats were to arrive off Moose Island in the near future. Prevost learned of improvements being made to the militias of the border states while the U.S. Army had been tripled in size—at least on paper—to almost 10,000 men in anticipation of war.[14]

During his three years in Nova Scotia, Prevost never committed to paper an assessment of its defenses. The best source for his thoughts on the subject is, therefore, a report he prepared in 1812, in which he laid out his strategy for defending British North America, as the concepts it contained about Nova Scotia would have been developed during his time there as lieutenant governor. Nova Scotia posed several unique problems for its defenders. In the Canadas, probable invasion routes could be identified, but since the peninsula of Nova Scotia offered an invading army many points where it could land, the establishment of "any precise Plan for the defence . . . [was] depend[ent] upon Contingencies in the event of invasion."[15] Prevost believed the security of Nova Scotia and New Brunswick "very materially"[16] depended on the Royal Navy, which required close cooperation between the forces to "remove the scene of Warfare to the American frontier."[17] Prevost, the Admiralty, and the commander of the North American squadron shared the belief that the most likely location of a landing would be in the Bay of Fundy, as had occurred in 1776, during the American War of Independence. Despite the establishment of regular patrols in the area beginning in 1808, Prevost could not convince the Admiralty to assign more ships for that task.[18]

The Royal Navy was simply not strong enough in North America for the role it would be required to play in defending Nova Scotia. Before Prevost's arrival at Halifax, the commander of the naval squadron based there, Vice Admiral George Berkeley, had delayed sailing for his winter station in the West Indies owing to the "defenceless state of this province."[19] The United States Navy was perceived as a threat, yet "no influential body of opinion" in London "believed that the United States . . . would launch a maritime war," and the Royal Navy was focused on operations in Europe.[20] High-level acceptance of this rationale allowed the strength of the Halifax squadron to steadily decline as ships were sent to other stations, despite the exertions of Prevost and successive squadron commanders. By 1812, the ships in the Halifax squadron were largely outclassed by the American heavy frigates, leaving it hard-pressed to undertake offensive operations if hostilities commenced.[21]

One of the first tasks Prevost embarked on was to organize the manpower of the province into a military force that could deal with any eventuality. The infantry brigade that arrived with him joined the other regular battalions of the garrison to become the backbone of the local defenses. There were still insufficient men, however, to protect the Atlantic Provinces, and Prevost partially overcame the manpower shortage with regiments raised locally and the militia. The units raised by royal warrant were regulars, subject to the same laws, regulations, and conditions of service as any other corps of the British army, with the distinction that their service was limited to North America. Several of these regiments were established throughout British North America in 1803, when war with France resumed. By 1808, the Atlantic Provinces of Newfoundland, Nova Scotia, and New Brunswick each had a regiment of fencible infantry that came under Prevost's authority. Prevost distributed the regulars and fencibles between New Brunswick, Nova Scotia, Cape Breton, and Prince Edward Island, based on the potential threat from the Americans. Over the next two years, this balancing act became more complicated as four of the regular battalions were transferred elsewhere. The reductions commenced in July 1809, when the 101st

Foot, which had arrived in Halifax in 1807, left for Jamaica. In 1810, Brigadier General Daniel Hoghton was posted to the Iberian Peninsula; in June the 1/7th left Nova Scotia for Portugal, followed by the 1/23rd in October.[22] The loss of these battalions was partially made up by bringing one of the units raised in North America by royal warrant, the New Brunswick Fencibles, into the line as the 104th Foot in 1810. The 1/8th was sent to Quebec in May 1810 and was replaced by the second battalion of that same regiment, which arrived from England in October. Thereafter the composition of the regular garrison remained steady until the outbreak of the war.[23]

Another source of manpower Prevost could call on to bolster the defenses of Nova Scotia was the militia, a force that fell under provincial jurisdiction. In 1808 the Nova Scotia militia included seventeen regiments and several independent companies of artillery and riflemen. Prevost concluded that the militia was lawless and inefficient and introduced legislation to convert it "into a more useful and less expensive part of the resources of this settlement."[24] He recommended revisions to replace the *levée en masse* with a smaller, better-trained volunteer force. The infantry was organized into twenty six regiments that were distributed between the province's seven counties, and the province was divided into several military districts, to enable the inspecting field officers to attend to the training. Prevost also used four "unattached and intelligent"[25] lieutenant colonels that were sent with him to Halifax to oversee training. They were to command brigades if hostilities with the United States occurred. As an inducement to serve, Prevost obtained approval for a maximum annual expenditure of twenty-eight days of pay and rations per man who had been trained and instructed for that period of time, rather than for merely being present, as under the old law. As arms were scarce, the provincial assembly also agreed to fund the purchase of 2,000 stands of new arms, while provisions in the new militia act improved the serviceability of weapons through a system of inspections and prohibition of their use for private purposes. Over a two-year period beginning in 1808, over £11,000 were spent on arms and accoutrements, and these funds were provided by a new levy on the importation of rum.[26]

The improvements in organization and training of the militia achieved the desired results and provided for a potential of 3,000 trained and equipped men capable of supporting the regular troops.

One thousand were called out at the end of 1808, with a similar number ready for service at short notice.

During his inspection tour of the province, Prevost found that the seaward defenses of Halifax were adequate, but the land fortifications, including the temporary works atop Citadel Hill, required strengthening. Five towers that had been constructed in and around Halifax between 1796 and 1798 were in ruin and desolation, and it would be less expensive to build new permanent fortifications than to maintain the old ones. Captain Gustavus Nicolls, Prevost's chief Royal Engineer, recommended the construction of another six towers in Halifax as "the cheapest, most permanent and effectual defence."[27] Prevost's efforts to improve the fortifications were limited by Lieutenant Colonel Ralph Bruyeres, commander of the Royal Engineers in Canada, who was reluctant to embark on a costly program of permanent works, a policy that also applied to Nova Scotia. Without these improvements, Prevost would have to place a greater reliance on the regular, fencible, and militia troops to defend the province. As he explained this to Castlereagh in May 1808: "I shall feel it necessary to augment the land defences" as "most works have been allowed to fall into such a state of ruin as to allow nothing short of total reform."[28]

The Native allies were another useful source of manpower, and Prevost worked toward improving relations with the Mi'kmaq. Several years earlier, Wentworth had discovered that the Mi'kmaq, whose hunting grounds were being lost to settlement, would welcome a French invasion of the province. In 1807, he ordered George Monk, the superintendent of Indians of Nova Scotia and Cape Breton, to "collect and secure the obedience of these people and their aid in case of necessity."[29] Prevost was alarmed to discover that little had changed and that if the province was invaded, the Natives intended to remain neutral until they could form an opinion of the strength of the enemy; then they would "join the strongest party."[30] Other reports indicated some bands would be neutral or merely seek plunder, while others were better disposed to the British. It was a difficult situation. Monk eventually recommended that arms, provisions, and clothing be offered to the Natives as a test of their fidelity, while those families wishing to farm their lands be given farm implements and seed. Prevost's support of both of these recommendations and his strengthening of the province's defenses may have contributed to the Mi'kmaqs' decision to announce their neutrality at the beginning of the War of 1812.[31]

For British officials, the need to gather exact knowledge of the political situation and military preparations in the United States was paramount. The steps taken to gather intelligence on American activities from Nova Scotia and Prevost's role in this activity are not well known. The first steps of the intelligence-gathering program were initiated by Sir John Wentworth and expanded by Prevost. They were based on instructions from the colonial secretary to use his "utmost endeavours to gain Intelligence with respect to the projects of the American government in General, and particularly those states bordering upon His Majesty's Territories."[32] Where Wentworth had employed William Girod, a lieutenant in the 101st Foot, for the task, Prevost informed the British minister in Washington in April 1808 that he had sent former Bostonian (and Loyalist) printer John Howe, "a respectable and intelligent Inhabitant of Halifax,"[33] and father of the soon-to-be-famous statesman Joseph Howe, to Boston, Washington, Norfolk, and New York to collect information on American preparations for war.

On Howe's return it was deemed desirable that further information be obtained, and Prevost requested that Howe make a second journey, which took place between November 1808 and January 1809. Howe was armed with a list of thirty-six topics prepared by Prevost on which to focus intelligence gathering that included government policy, internal political divisions and sensitivities, the proportion of federal politicians advocating war with Britain, the reasons for American hostility toward Britain, American apprehensions over the safety of Louisiana, foreign influences affecting Anglo-American relations, general military readiness and preparations, military activity along the frontier, trade, and attitudes on European affairs. Howe's visit took him to several states and while he was in Washington, he prepared several reports for Prevost, the most important of which was written in January 1809; it addressed all of Prevost's questions and included tables depicting the strength of the militia compiled from the latest returns and a complete list of naval vessels and their armament.[34]

Howe reported that the president and his cabinet wished to avoid disruptions to the economy and measures that would increase disaffection in the eastern states and that they "do not at present think it will be for their interest to be at War with Great Britain. They consider themselves as sure of their offices for the next four Years; and I am convinced from many circumstances, that they at present would prefer war with France, to war with England. They are satisfied they must have a contest with one or the other, and they seem to have become sensible that a friendly intercourse with Great Britain, will do them the most good, and that a War with our Nation will do them the most injury!"[35]

WHILE the economic damage a war with Britain would cause the Americans was understood, geographical practicability left only a single course open: "France is out of their reach and they cannot attack her,"[36] whereas Canada and the Maritime Provinces are within reach, and it is "against these Colonies therefore alone, all their Military Array is expressly pointed."[37] Howe found that members of all parties were in agreement that "an attack on Canada, New Brunswick and Nova Scotia would immediately ensue"[38] after an American declaration of war. Adding to the attractiveness of this option was the "ready welcome" the invading troops would receive "from a number of Americans who have of late years become Settlers in Upper Canada." Conquering Canada, "they contemplate," was "a matter perfectly easy,"[39] and a brief campaign would limit economic and political turmoil. The Americans were "more at a loss" about Nova Scotia, "so much surrounded by Water, to consider the best Mode of attacking it, but do not seem to doubt their ability to effect it."[40] For now, concerns about trade disruption and internal politics and recent British successes in Spain and Portugal, where American merchants hoped to gain markets, had placed the question of war in abeyance.

American military preparations were proving difficult as shortages of arms and equipment plagued compliance with a presidential order that 100,000 militiamen be readied for service. The federal government, Howe learned, "cannot easily raise in America any great body of regular Troops,"[41] and he had doubts that a proposed plan for Congress to authorize another 20,000 men for the U.S. Army would succeed given the experience at recruitment thus far:

The Common regular force of America Amounts to about 4,000 Men. This force has been chiefly employed since the

Peace in the Garrisons on the Frontiers, or in Forts situated at the entrance of the principal Harbours. Congress last Year passed an act to add 6,000 Men to the Regular forces of the Country; 3,500 of these Men have been raised. Recruiting Parties are employed throughout the States, endeavouring to raise the remainder. But they meet with no great success; and it is not probable that they will, in another Year raise the whole number. This 3,000 lately raised, are the great part quite undisciplined, and it will take much time to bring them into Military Order.[42]

Regardless of the state of their army, shortages of equipment and the protection of their economic interests, Howe considered the certainty the Americans had in their "Conquest of these colonies" posed enough of a threat to conclude his report with the warning that "Precautionary Measures of every kind are therefore highly necessary."[43]

The scope and detail of Howe's reports provided Prevost with a profound understanding of American politics and military capabilities that would help guide his decisions once he assumed command of British North America and during the opening stages of the War of 1812. The reports were forwarded to London in early 1809, and they may have made a lasting impression on the British government. When asked to ascertain what measure Britain could adopt to avoid war with the United States, Howe responded that reconciliation would be possible if the government revoked the Orders in Council; "if they do not we shall probably go to war."[44] The last-minute revocation of the Orders in Council by the British government in June 1812 and Prevost's hesitancy to undertake offensive operations against the Americans at the beginning of the conflict may have been influenced by Howe's intelligence. While this form of compromise might have achieved a settlement had it been attempted in 1808, it was not applicable to the conditions that existed in 1812.

Howe's reports also had an immediate effect on British military operations, the defense of British North America, and Prevost's future employment. It was clear that the crisis in Anglo-American affairs that had prompted the dispatch of Prevost and a brigade to Nova Scotia had now defused. Trade restrictions were loosened and

the new American president, James Madison, appeared more willing to seek a negotiated resolution to Anglo-American differences
than had his predecessor, Thomas Jefferson. The apparent accommodation between the two countries created conditions in which
British forces, including those in Nova Scotia, could be redeployed
to other regions. Tentative plans to push the French from the two
remaining islands they held in the West Indies could now be undertaken, and once completed, a portion of the troops employed on that
enterprise could be sent to Wellington as reinforcements rather than
remaining in Nova Scotia. Accordingly, Prevost was instructed to
commence preparations to participate in an expedition against
French-held Martinique.

Before turning to that campaign, a curious encounter experienced
by Prevost during the summer of 1808 must be discussed. On 16
June, Aaron Burr, who had been vice president during Thomas Jefferson's first term, made a brief stop in Halifax. Using the presumed
name of H. G. Edwards, Burr, whose political machinations and
conspiratorial activity against U.S. interests had led to his disgrace
and dismissal, was en route to London to solicit British support for
the independence movements in the Spanish colonies of Florida and
Mexico that, owing to Napoléon's occupation of Spain, were now
under nominal French control. Prevost received Burr and consulted
on his proposal with Vice Admiral Sir John Borlase Warren, commander of the Halifax naval station. Prevost felt unable to provide
official comment on Burr's proposal as the matter was outside his
jurisdiction. He offered Burr a letter of safe passage to England and
an introduction to Lord Castlereagh. During their meeting, the two
men presumably discussed family affairs as Burr had known Prevost's father, while in 1782 he had married the widow of Prevost's
uncle John Marc, Theodosia, and adopted her two children. Burr
arrived in London in July, but his appeals fell on deaf ears. Britain
had allied itself with its former enemy Spain and was preparing to
send an expeditionary force to the Iberian Peninsula. Burr next
tried convincing the French to establish a base in Florida and Mexico, from where they could, with the help of the United States, force
the British out of North America. That plan also went nowhere.[45]

By 1808, only two islands of any importance in the West Indies
were still held by the French, Martinique and Guadeloupe. Britain

wanted them, as the French occupation of these islands was tying down British forces that could have been better employed in Europe and it therefore seemed prudent to the government to provide temporary reinforcements to reduce those threats. As both attacks were not anticipated to be very costly and the reinforcements could be withdrawn before the sickly season arrived in the summer, approval was given in January 1809 to attack Martinique. Lieutenant General Sir George Beckwith, in command of the Windward Islands, learned he would receive troops under Prevost's command from Nova Scotia and from other garrisons to take Martinique and then Guadeloupe.[46]

In August 1808, Prevost had reported that his contingent, which included Prevost's staff, three battalions of infantry (1/7th, 2/8th, and 1/23rd Foot; a fourth, the 13th, would meet them from Jamaica), 21 men from the Royal Military Artificers, and a 167-man detachment of the Royal Artillery, could sail within three weeks. To protect Halifax, Prevost planned to leave 400 noneffective regulars behind, who were joined by the 101st Foot, which was moved from New Brunswick to Halifax. With 850 regulars remaining at Halifax and the twenty six battalions of sedentary militia at the peak of their training and placed under the immediate superintendence of the inspecting field officers, Prevost could tell Castlereagh that his measures had placed Nova Scotia "in a more respectable state than I found it."[47] By November, with winter approaching and the absence of military activity in the United States, Prevost was ready to leave for the West Indies.[48]

Prevost's pending departure received considerable interest from the press. In December 1808, the *Aberdeen Journal* reported that Prevost was waiting to sail on a "secret expedition,"[49] to Martinique. On 25 January 1809, the same paper printed an order of battle and stated that Prevost, who was being followed by journalists, had left Halifax with a large force of infantry for Barbados. These and other reports generated considerable interest in the United States, where several members of Congress expressed fears the expedition was destined not for the West Indies, but for New Orleans as a demonstration of Britain's opposition to the U.S. acquisition of the territory from France. The newspaper accounts proved more accurate in deciphering British intentions than the politicians. On 6 December 1808, the convoy carrying Prevost and 2,800 troops aboard twenty-six victuallers and transports, and escorted by the 36-gun frigate *Penel-ope*, departed from Halifax. By 29 December, they arrived at the expedition rendezvous point at Carlisle Bay, Jamaica, where they joined the ships of the naval component under Rear-Admiral Alexander Cochrane, the Royal Navy commander in the Leeward Islands.[50]

Beckwith organized the land component into two divisions, each comprising three brigades of infantry, with Prevost being given command of the larger First Division of 7,000 men. The brigades were led by Major General Daniel Hoghton, Major General Charles Colville, and Lieutenant Colonel (acting Brigadier General) Robert Nicholson.[51] The smaller 2nd Division, with 3,700 men, was led by Major General Thomas Maitland. The latter division included three companies of the 8th West India Regiment under Lieutenant Colonel William Augustus Prevost, the son of Prevost's half brother, Augustine.[52]

Preparations proceeded slowly, or so it seemed to the officers and men. On 7 January 1809, Beckwith conducted what seemed to be an unnecessary review of both divisions that caused considerable activity, as the men had to be unloaded from the transports. Even after receiving the additional troops under Prevost, Beckwith was concerned his force was still too small and at one point considered canceling the expedition. Beckwith turned to the newly arrived Prevost, who was the next most senior officer, for advice; Prevost convinced Beckwith that, with 10,000 men and a strong naval force, the attack should proceed. Beckwith yielded to Prevost's counsel, and following another review on the 18th in honor of the Queen's birthday, he announced his decision. Final planning and preparations began in earnest, and on 27 January orders were issued that further hastened the preparations, eliminating any possibility for rehearsals. The combined British naval and land force then left Barbados the next day and arrived off Martinique on 30 January.[53]

The island of Martinique is approximately fifty miles long and between twelve and twenty miles wide. The terrain is mountainous, with an indented coastline. About halfway down the western side of the island was the island's capital, Fort de France, located on the north shore of a bay that took its name from the capital. A number of batteries ringed the bay, but just north of the capital in the rugged hills was Fort Desaix (renamed by Napoléon from Fort Bourbon), armed with 100 guns. Robert Harbor lay about midway down the eastern side of Martinique. Admiral Villaret de Joyeuse was the governor of Martinique and commanded 2,400 regulars of the 26th and 82nd Regiments, two companies of artillery, and six battalions of National Guard militia totaling 2,600 men, plus 290 guns of various calibers. Three warships, two having eighteen guns each, and a forty-gun frigate were anchored in three different harbors around the island. Despite the efforts of the Royal Navy to blockade the island, the French had landed reinforcements and matériel as late as December 1808.[54]

Prevost was ordered to land his 1st Division, under the direction of Captain Phillip Beaver of the Royal Navy, in Robert Harbor and then make a rapid twelve-mile march across the island and seize Morne Bruneau, from where he could observe Fort Desaix, three miles to the south. At the same time, Maitland's division would land at two points on the southwestern end of the island and then advance north, taking the batteries on the southern end of Fort de France Bay before securing the capital.[55] This would give Beckwith control of the harbor, allowing the navy to bring in the stores necessary to begin the next stage of the operation, the reduction of Fort Desaix. Both divisions would then be combined for the siege.[56]

During the afternoon of 30 January 1808, Prevost's 1st Division commenced landing in Robert Harbor. Its approach was observed by the French, who chose to withdraw away from the numerically superior First Division. The surf made it difficult to get men and stores ashore, forcing Prevost to delay the advance inland until later that night. He had intended to advance in stages along his route halting at estates that could be turned into defendable positions; in preparation he placed the 1st Brigade under Hoghton in the vanguard. Recent rains and the poor state of the tracks slowed the advance, and after several hours of strenuous marching, the troops had covered only seven miles. With his troops fatigued and unsure of the terrain, Prevost ordered a four-hour rest stop at an estate on the Lezard River, which also allowed time for the remainder of the division to move up.[57]

The march resumed the next morning, and after pushing through several more miles of difficult terrain, most of the division halted at another estate, while the 7th Foot and the grenadier companies of the 1/23rd and the 1st West India Regiment pushed forward against the enemy, who continued to observe but not interfere with Prevost's movements. Occasional sightings of the enemy were made, but no fighting occurred.[58]

At daybreak on 1 February, the troops set out again. Prevost accompanied the advance party as the 1/7th and the battalion companies of the 1/23rd and 1st West India Regiment continued to the heights of the tactically important feature of Morne Bruneau. Prevost then ordered Hoghton to make a flanking move with the remainder of his brigade and link up with the advance force on the far side of the mountain. From there, Prevost would continue to the next objective, Mount Sourier, the highest feature on the island. However, the artillery could not be moved forward, as the few horses brought from Halifax were still unfit from the sea journey.[59]

The French decided to delay the British advance from Morne Bruneau to Mount Sourier. The British column had scarcely set off when it discovered a body of enemy troops, on the crest of a hill, their front protected by a mountain torrent that flowed into the Monsieur River. They also had deployed one or two guns on their position. Determined not to lose momentum, Prevost conducted a reconnaissance of the enemy position, then ordered Hoghton to clear it. Hoghton's men forced their way through the dense vegetation and rushed forward in a frontal attack. The well-placed French troops took advantage of the tall sugarcane to hide their numbers. The first French volley was so intense that, according to one participant, it "visibly shook the British troops," who replied with "poorly coordinated fire."[60] The British scrambled ahead, regrouped, and eventually closed on the enemy; using their bayonets, they drove the defenders from their position, despite their being reinforced.[61]

The French regrouped on Mount Sourier. Prevost pressed the attack toward the heights, forcing the enemy to flee to several nearby redoubts. Prevost had gained the important ground to the north of the fort. British casualties numbered 250 men, while the French lost some 300 men. Beckwith then ordered a pause to build scaling ladders for the next stage of the campaign, the assault on Fort Desaix. By this time, the second brigade had come up, and the men halted under the guns of one of the fort's redoubts.[62]

On 2 February, Prevost ordered an attack against two strongly entrenched enemy redoubts outside the fort. Each was held by a detachment of regulars supported by three 12-pounder field guns. Fierce fighting continued through the day. As a consequence of the persistent British assaults and the loss of National Guardsmen, or French militia, who slipped out of fortifications and returned home, the senior French officers held a council of war and decided to concentrate their resources at Fort Desaix. Fort de France was abandoned, and the frigate in the harbor was destroyed. Prevost then moved his men closer to Fort Desaix.[63]

Meanwhile, Maitland's division had made good progress, and by 3 February was approaching Fort de France Bay. French resistance crumbled when the local militia agreed not to resist the British advance. The defenses protecting the entrance of the bay were cleared, and Pigeon Island, which covered the southern entrance to the bay, was taken on 4 February, leaving the bay open for the fleet. Beckwith could now consolidate his troops for the reduction of Fort Desaix. On 5 February, the Second Division joined Prevost north of the fort and the siege commenced.[64]

Fort Desaix was a formidable work defended by sixty heavy guns, forty field guns, fourteen mortars, six howitzers, and a garrison of some 2,000 men. Prevost oversaw the development of the siege lines and the placement of artillery within his sector covering the northern and eastern sides of the fort. With few horses, almost no roads, incessant rain, and difficult terrain, the besiegers were challenged to move their artillery pieces into location and bring supplies up from the beaches. The immense labor of landing the ordnance, shot, rations, and engineer stores was left to the fighting troops. The enemy attempted to interfere with the progress of this work by launching several minor sorties against Prevost's positions. These were easily repulsed. Despite the aforementioned difficulties, five batteries totaling forty-six pieces were emplaced in less than two weeks. The bombardment of Fort Desaix commenced during the afternoon of 19 February, and over the next five days, 4,000 shot and 10,000 shells were fired into it. Another five battery positions were to have been ready by 26 February, but they would not be needed. Casualties in the fort were mounting, and on 23 February, the French commander offered terms of surrender, which Beckwith rejected. The bombardment was resumed, and the next morning a terrific explosion occurred after a shell penetrated one of the fort's magazines. Shortly afterward, the enemy offered to surrender unconditionally, and that night Prevost witnessed the signing of the formal terms of capitulation. The reduction of Martinique was an immensely successful operation, completed in twenty-eight days, and with the fall of the island, Guadeloupe remained as the sole French possession in the West Indies.[65]

Admiral Villaret de Joyeuse and his aides were provided passage to France, while the garrison—155 officers and 2,069 other rank—marched out with the honors of war.[66] Another 600 French troops were found in the hospital, along with large stocks of food and ammunition in the fort. The British had suffered more than 550 casualties, with three officers and 116 soldiers killed. This was a comparatively light casualty rate and, as Beckwith acknowledged, was noteworthy for the low loss to disease, especially given the hardship and fatigue the troops had been exposed to throughout the operation. The losses to Prevost's division were the smallest known on such service in the West Indies: sixty-one were killed or died of wounds and another twenty-five succumbed to illness.[67]

Prevost had performed ably throughout the Martinique operation, displaying decisiveness and aggression; he was also well served by his brigade commanders and several excellent battalion commanders. He had commanded the senior division in the campaign, and divisions were a type of formation that had only recently been adopted by the British military.[68] A division combined infantry and artillery and sometimes cavalry and engineers under one officer and was capable of securing a major objective, either by itself or in conjunction with other divisions. Before 1809, the largest formation fielded by Britain was the brigade, and it was not until June 1809 that Wellington structured the largest British field force of the time, the Peninsular army, into four divisions. Prevost's division was comparable in size and structure to those under Wellington, which afforded him experience he would make use of in the future, albeit in a very different context.[69]

For Beckwith, whose task in the West Indies was not yet concluded, the departure of Prevost and the brigade he had brought from Nova Scotia was a heavy loss; yet their success could not have occurred at a better time, as it did much to restore public confidence in Britain. This was because details of this victory followed on less welcome news, including the recent evacuation of British troops from Spain after the Battle of Corunna in January. The furor in London over the 1808 Convention of Cintra, which obliged the Royal Navy to return defeated French troops to France from

Portugal, had just barely subsided, while a scandal over the sale of army commissions had led to the resignation of the Duke of York as commander in chief . The only major achievement in 1809, aside from the victory at Martinique in which Prevost played a key role, was the consolidation of the British hold on Portugal.[70]

In early March 1809, Prevost and his troops embarked for their return voyage to Halifax. Before the ships sailed, Beckwith praised his brigade and expressed "his obligations to Lieutenant General Sir George Prevost, for his general exertions, and to the fine and efficient corps led by him from North America."[71] On 15 April, the convoy reached Halifax, where early on that Saturday morning the signal telegraphs announced "the approach of a Frigate and a fleet of transports; it was soon ascertained that the Frigate was the *Penelope*, and that his Excellency [Prevost] was on board—at nine she passed the wharves, and was successively cheered by the crowds of inhabitants—at ten Sir George Prevost quitted the *Penelope*, when a salute of seventeen guns was fired from her . . . he landed at the King's wharf. . . . The Soldiers, on board the Transports, as his Excellency passed in the barge most heartily cheered him."[72]

Prevost and his men were welcomed as heroes and feted by the residents of Halifax. Almost two weeks later, on 28 April 1809, they were hosted to a ball at the Masonic Hall, where the bands of the 1/7th and 1/23rd Foot provided dancing music that continued until midnight, after which toasts were drunk into the early morning. Prevost hailed not only the king's health, but also "the soldiers who did their duty," to the delight of those in attendance who repeated the toast heartily.[73] Particular attention was paid to the 1/7th Foot, with Prevost assuring Lieutenant Colonel Edward Pakenham, the unit's commanding officer, and "the officers, non-commissioned officers and soldiers that he . . . will not fail to lay their meritorious exertions before the King." Prevost was proud of his men, and he himself found pleasure in the relaxed atmosphere and gaiety of balls, especially when they were, as his daughter Anne Elinor recalled, "enlivened with the band."[74] A splendid dinner included a huge "pastry figure of Fort Bourbon [Desaix]."[75] While the guests ate, the bands played popular tunes.

Sir George and Lady Prevost liked to entertain, and officers from the garrison were invited to the many balls, dinners, and card-playing evenings held at their residence. Many of the guests at their table were familiar friends, including Major Thomas Pearson of the 1/23rd Foot, a veteran of Martinique who had presented a pony to Anne Elinor; Lieutenant Colonel Pakenham; and Lieutenant Colonel Henry Ellis, the commanding officer of the 1/23rd Foot. Prevost had high regard for Ellis, an "intelligent, active and zealous officer," whose humane treatment of his soldiers was admirable.[76] Sir George extended every courtesy to those serving with him. Pakenham wrote his mother of "the exceeding kindness of Sir George Prevost, [who] has made this Station [Halifax] most palatable to me."[77] Prevost's sincerity also impressed the future commander of the British expedition to New Orleans, after Prevost had fulfilled the promise made after his return to Halifax and "acknowledged the service of many deserving officers relating to their actions in the West Indies or the Canadas" in his official dispatches.[78] Amateur theater was also a popular pastime, and Prevost encouraged his officers to attend theatrical amusements as it "broke up long sitting in the Mess Rooms and gave young officers an employment for their leisure time far better than many others to which they might have recourse."[79] Officers often performed in plays presented at the Theatre Royal, where in May 1809 the proceeds from two performances went to the "relief of the Widows and Children of soldiers who fell at Martinique."[80]

Prevost always paid close attention to the affairs of his family. During 1809, he enjoyed a reunion with two of his American-born nephews in Halifax. James was a captain in the 60th, and Henry a lieutenant in Pakenham's 1/7th Foot. James quickly became infatuated with a Halifax belle, and Prevost, knowing his "young and extravagant" nephew "had nothing in the world but his pay," meaning he could not support a family, "thought the kindest thing he could do for him would be to send him to his regiment in Spain."[81]

Prevost's tenure in Nova Scotia nearly ended during the summer of 1810, when a powerful French invasion of Portugal threatened the evacuation of Wellington's army to England. In London, Robert Dundas, the president of the Board of Trade and the minister responsible for India, hoped that if Wellington was freed from his Iberian command, he could be appointed governor general and commander in chief of India. Dundas also needed a new commander in chief in Bengal, one of the three presidencies in India, and considered offering

the post to Prevost. Nothing came of the scheme as the French offensive in Portugal was blunted by Wellington's punishing defeat of
their army at the battle of Busaco in September 1810, while the government wished Prevost to remain in North America, as relations
with the Americans had worsened yet again.[82]

Trade continued to dominate the political differences between
Britain and the United States. In May 1810, Congress had restored
trade between both countries by replacing the Non-Intercourse Act
of 1809—which forbade American trade with Britain and France
and their colonies and which proved impossible to enforce—with
Macon's Bill No. 2, named after Nathaniel Macon, a former Speaker
of the House of Representatives. Then, in August 1810, France promised to withdraw its trade restrictions against the United States if
Congress would reimpose nonintercourse with Britain. In November, however, despite the announcement that the United States
would issue a revised Non-Intercourse Act in the new year, France's
trade restrictions remained in place. The British responded by declaring that the U.S. nonintercourse policy was unjustified; they
threatened further retaliations on American trade, unless Madison
provided proof that the French decrees had been lifted. This demand placed Madison in a difficult situation, as any response would
have amounted to an admission that he had been tricked by Napoléon. Furthermore, it became clear to Madison that until Napoléon
was defeated, the Orders in Council would remain in force, which
was an unacceptable condition. In July 1811, Madison chose instead
to call Congress into an early session in November, which "amounted
to no less than a decision to prepare the United States for war with
Great Britain."[83]

Prevost continued to improve the defenses of Nova Scotia, complaining to London that the outlying fortifications and the defenses of
Halifax "were falling into decay."[84] He also considered reoccupying
and refurbishing Fort Cumberland guarding the overland route to the
Bay of Fundy, which had been abandoned since the 1780s. The attention Prevost gave increased attention to the defensive measures for
the Maritime Provinces in the autumn of 1810, when Major General
William Balfour arrived at Halifax, accompanied by the 2/8th Foot,
to take military command of Nova Scotia. The defensive situation
facing Prevost grew even more acute after the British sloop *Little Belt*
limped back into Halifax Harbor following an encounter with the

American frigate USS *President* on 16 May 1811. Any opportunity Prevost had to consider these matters ended abruptly at the end of July, when a packet arrived at Halifax carrying orders instructing him to proceed immediately to Quebec to replace Sir James Craig as the governor in chief of British North America.[85]

By early 1811, it had become evident that Craig's illness had advanced to the point where he was unable to continue in his post. In January, Craig wrote to the prime minister and Earl Liverpool, the Secretary of State for War and the Colonies, to explain that "his failing health will compel him to give up the Governorship and leave Canada at the first opportunity."[86] Given the impasse with America, Craig's inability to discharge his duties necessitated prompt replacement. Craig's condition had been one reason for Prevost's posting to Nova Scotia, and by the spring of 1811, the government in London believed it prudent to have a plan ready to ensure a smooth and timely transition of power "without waiting for instructions from home."[87] Fortunately for Prevost, he had earlier been warned to be prepared "to assume the Government of Quebec" should Craig die or become incapacitated.[88]

Threatened by a possible war in North America, the government considered it preferable to appoint a military officer as head of the civil administration and military forces of British North America. Events then moved quickly as communication passed between Halifax and Quebec with London. In July 1811, Prevost received instructions from the government, dated 31 May, "to hold himself in readiness to proceed without delay to Quebec upon the first intimation he may receive from you [Craig] of the intention to relinquish" the government.[89] Prevost had by now commenced preparations to hand over the government and command of the forces in Nova Scotia as Craig had resigned in June. Lieutenant General Sir John Sherbrooke was to replace Prevost in Halifax. Prevost also directed Major General Martin Hunter to return from New Brunswick and resume the military command of Nova Scotia and ordered Balfour to replace Hunter as the military and civilian commander at Fredericton.[90]

Following the conclusion of his official business, farewell entertainments, balls, and levees, Prevost—accompanied by his wife and children; his civilian secretary, Edward Brenton; Commissary General William Robinson; and his personal staff and their families—departed Halifax on 19 August 1811 on board the 36-gun frigate HMS *Melampus*.[91] A large party of well-wishers lined the wharf as the frigate sailed. En route the ship's captain, Captain Edward Hawker, decided to mark the honor of having the new governor and a host of women aboard by holding a shipboard dance and "the quarter deck was covered with flags and lighted up."[92]

Prevost arrived in Quebec on 13 September 1811, the anniversary of the 1759 battle. Lady Prevost noted in her diary that this was "an auspicious omen."[93] A new phase in Prevost's life was about to begin. His career to this point had been successful, but little did he know the challenges, triumphs, and difficulties his service in Canada would bring in the coming years.[94]

3

PLANNING THE DEFENSE OF BRITISH NORTH AMERICA, SEPTEMBER 1811–JUNE 1812

All ill concerted attacks . . . can be resisted or repulsed.
  —*Prevost to Bathurst, in Report on the Defence of the Canadas,*
  18 May 1812

Prevost's first priority as the new governor and commander in chief of British North America was to determine the overall state of colonial defenses. The reports prepared by his predecessor, Sir James Craig, were pessimistic about the outcome of a war with the United States. Craig believed that, with only 5,500 British regulars to defend Upper and Lower Canada against a much larger American army, the forces in Upper Canada would at best achieve only a momentary check against invading troops while little would be retained of the lower province. If hostilities took place, he was convinced Quebec could be preserved only by reinforcements from Britain. Craig had mixed feelings toward those living in the two Canadian provinces. Treason, he suspected, was rife in both provinces and would hinder the defenses. In Lower Canada, much of the blame for this situation rested with Craig as his harsh treatment of the French-speaking population as a conquered people through restrictions on their political and religious freedoms caused much unrest. Craig did believe that reform of the militia and the raising of Canadian units could provide useful augmentation to the regulars. Craig also looked to the revival of aboriginal alliances that lay in ruins in the wake of the American War of Independence and to reinforcement of British positions along the frontier, especially in the western reaches of Upper Canada. As far as he could see, the only advantage that the British had, for the moment at least, was undisputed control of the inland waters.[1]

In his new position, Prevost faced a daunting challenge. His record in the West Indies and Nova Scotia brought predictions, however, that he would undo the harm caused by Craig in the lower province and prepare Canada's defenses sufficiently for a war that now seemed certain.

Although Prevost was officially "Captain General and Governor-in-Chief in and over the Provinces of Upper and Lower Canada, New Brunswick, Nova Scotia and the islands of Prince Edward and Cape Breton, and their several dependencies";[2] the realities of this span of control, the distance between British North America and London, and the time it took correspondence to pass led the government to designate the Maritime Provinces of New Brunswick, Nova Scotia, Cape Breton, and Prince Edward Island as a semi-independent command under Lieutenant General John Sherbrooke, Prevost's successor in Halifax. This allowed Prevost to focus his attention on the defenses of Upper and Lower Canada, the most threatened provinces of British North America. Prevost, who was commander of the forces and head of the civil administration of the lower province, confirmed Major General Isaac Brock to similar offices in Upper Canada.[3]

While Prevost was in theory ultimately responsible to the Prince Regent, who was little more than a figurehead, he primarily reported to two officials in Britain. The first was the Secretary of State for War and the Colonies, a member of the cabinet.[4] This secretary administered reports and addressed problems from every colonial governor, including campaign plans. He coordinated with various offices, such as the Board of Ordnance, the government department responsible for the Royal Artillery and the Royal Engineers; and the Transport Board, which handled movement of troops, ordnance, and supplies. Most important, he communicated with the Horse Guards, the headquarters of the British army; and the Treasury, which exercised fiscal policy and held several military responsibilities as well. Finally, he transmitted the orders and instructions of the government to the colonies. Until June 1812, the post of Secretary of State for War and the Colonies was held by the Earl of Liverpool, a man of great ability who later became prime minister. He was succeeded by Earl Bathurst, a competent and sensible minister, who remained Prevost's superior in military and civil matters throughout the War of 1812. These two men, along with Foreign Secretary Viscount Castlereagh, formed the inner group of ministers responsible for the day-to-day administration of Britain's global strategy and military effort. The second key official with whom Prevost had regular dealings was the commander in chief of His Majesty's forces, whose office was in the Horse Guards. Between 1811 and 1827, this appointment was held by the Duke of York, the second son of George III. For a variety of reasons, the management of military matters was divided between several government departments, leaving the Duke with an impressive title but with responsibilities restricted to matters related to discipline, organization, training, and promotion in the infantry and cavalry. This meant that, on occasion and depending on the requirement, Prevost had to correspond with other departments and agencies.[5]

The most important were the Board of Ordnance and the Commissariat, or Commissary Department. The board functioned somewhat like a ministry of supply and was responsible for land and naval ordnance and fortifications at home and abroad. It was also responsible for several corps supporting the army, including the Royal Regiment of Artillery, the Royal Engineers, the Field Train of Ordnance, and the Royal Sappers and Miners. Prevost had representatives of the Board of Ordnance on his staff, and Major General George Glasgow, the commanding Royal Artillery officer, was the senior ordnance officer in British North America. Glasgow reported to Prevost on matters of administration and control of ordnance assets. He also represented the interests of the Board of Ordnance and could speak directly to Prevost on behalf of junior personnel, or correspond on ordnance matters with the master general of ordnance in Britain, a prerogative shared by the chief Royal Engineer for British North America. Lieutenant Colonel (later Colonel) Ralph Bruyeres held this post from 1806 until he died of illness in May 1814. His replacement was Lieutenant Colonel Philip Hughes, who was followed by Lieutenant Colonel Gustavus Nicolls in the autumn of 1814.

For Prevost, the effectiveness of logistical arrangements was essential to the successful outcome of a war with the United States. In the early nineteenth century, British North America lacked the means of producing ordnance, weapons, ammunition, and most military supplies, and such matériel had to be obtained from Britain or from depots in the West Indies. As we have noted, the provision of supplies was divided between several departments of the government, such as the Board of Ordnance, while other agencies including the Medical and Purveyor's Department provided medical services; and the Quartermaster General's Department handled field equipment and clothing. Prevost and his staff had regular dealings with each of these departments, yet Prevost's biggest interest lay with another organization, the Commissariat.[6]

The Commissariat was a civil department under the Lords of the Treasury that was responsible for two essential services: the procurement, transport, and issue of food, fuel, and forage for the army; and the storage, transport, and issue of most other supplies. The head of this service in British North America was Commissary General William Henry Robinson. From his base in the city of Quebec, Robinson controlled a number of officials, including deputy and assistant commissaries, storekeepers, and clerks, who were scattered throughout the North American colonies. Like the army, the Commissariat suffered from having too few officials spread over too large a territory—in 1811, Robinson had only sixteen officers to manage a supply line 1,700 miles long.[7] Another logistical requirement that occupied Prevost was securing adequate foodstuffs and forage to meet the ration requirements of the army. A result of the outbreak of any war is often an immediate shortage of food, and the method Prevost employed to deal with this problem will be addressed below.[8]

To assist him with the execution of his duties, Prevost had two separate staff organizations. One of these handled civilian administration; the other, military and inland naval matters. The military staff comprised a small group of officers who served in two branches: the adjutant general and the quartermaster general. As adjutant general of the forces in British North America between 1807 and 1814, Colonel (later Major General) Edward Baynes was Prevost's primary staff officer. Baynes was responsible for issuing orders, supervising personnel matters, collecting intelligence, and preparing reports and returns. The other key staff officer was the quartermaster general, whose function was troop movement and quartering. Three officers held this post between 1812 and 1815: Colonel Edward

Macdonnell, Colonel Christopher Myers, and Major General Sir Thomas Sidney Beckwith. There were also other, more specialized departments responsible for logistics, field engineer tasks, medical services, barracks, and pay. Like the artillery and engineers, each was responsible to Prevost for the activity it conducted but also answered to offices in London, such as the Board of Ordnance, the Medical Board, or the Treasury, on technical matters related to its functions. Rounding out this group was Prevost's "family," or personal, staff at the center of which were the aides de camp, field and junior officers he personally knew and selected.

These personal staff officers were important because they provided Prevost with timely information independent of the reports from his subordinate commanders, which for various reasons might be delayed, inaccurate, lost, or missing critical information. The presence of one of these aides at a subordinate commander's headquarters also added gravitas to Prevost's written instructions, which may otherwise have been ignored. Aides were therefore an extension of his command authority and a valuable source of information.[9] For example, in January 1812, when Prevost was convinced the situation between America and Britain could no longer "be confined to paper and commercial warfare,"[10] he sent one of his aides, Captain Foster Coore, to collect "a correct account of the disposition and news of the American Government"[11] from British diplomatic officials in New York and Washington. Two of Prevost's aides also served as assistants to Colonel Baynes when he led the raid on Sackets Harbor in May 1813. The only instance where Prevost dispatched more than one aide to the same place occurred after the fall of Fort George in May 1813. Captain Robert McDouall and Captain Henry Milnes were both dispatched to Brigadier General John Vincent's headquarters at Burlington Heights to gain an appreciation of Vincent's intentions. McDouall also carried a letter from Prevost authorizing Vincent to withdraw to Kingston if the situation warranted it. Both officers later accompanied the attack on the enemy force at Stoney Creek in June 1813. During the Plattsburgh offensive in 1814, Prevost also maintained communication with his naval commander through an aide.[12]

Prevost also oversaw intelligence work. In 1803, the British army had created an intelligence staff within the Quartermaster General's Department, and while some progress had been made in creating a professional organization to support military operations, the intelligence service was still in its infancy by 1812. Nonetheless, commanders understood the need to obtain details of their opponent's movements, unit identification, numbers, equipment, and disposition, along with topographical information on where their own forces were operating. It is unfortunate that the role of intelligence during the Napoleonic period—that is, the gathering and interpretation of this data—has received only cursory attention from scholars.[13]

The War of 1812 was unique in that most Americans, Britons, and Canadians generally shared the same language and culture, which eased movement across the frontier and allowed individuals to pass as locals to gain information. Additional points of access were provided by Native settlements that straddled the boundary, such as the Mohawk territory at St. Regis, near Montreal. Prevost's immediate intelligence interests lay along the boundary between the Canadas and the United States, but he also gathered information from other locations either by sending agents, as he had when he was lieutenant governor of Nova Scotia, or in reports received from subordinate land and naval commanders. Intelligence was also gained from a wide variety of sources including newspapers, civilians, smugglers, Natives, and prisoners of war. Finally, Prevost had to identify American spies and sympathizers operating in the Canadas and develop measures to counter their efforts.

IN addition to his royal commission, the government issued Prevost specific and detailed instructions that placed strict limitations on his authority in foreign affairs and military operations. Prevost did not, "By colour of any power or authority" given him, possess the ability to "commence or declare War without [the government's] knowledge." Furthermore, if war should come, Prevost had been expressly restrained from striking offensively, "except it be for the purpose of preventing or repelling Hostilities or unavoidable Emergencies wherein the Consent of Our Executive Council shall be had and speedy notice given thereof to us by one of our Secretaries of State."[14] This important passage, appearing toward the end of the lengthy set of instructions, limited the options available to Prevost during the final weeks of peace and guided his actions in the early stage of the conflict.

Like most commanders, Prevost did not share with his subordinates the details of the orders and instructions he was given. He was directed to have them read to the Executive Council of Lower Canada, a nine-member appointed body that advised the governor; however, the members' attention may have waned after hearing sixty pages of text, and they likely missed the significance of these instructions or had little inclination to discuss its details with others. As Prevost did not inform his principal subordinates of these important details, they were never aware of the restrictions placed on him, and this may have fueled their impressions that Prevost was a too cautious commander. In the historiography of the War of 1812 (which now spans two centuries), only two historians have referred to this important passage from the government's instructions, using an even shorter excerpt.[15]

Prevost's preparations for the defense of British North America were limited by strategic priorities that were centered elsewhere. Recent British successes in the West Indies and Indian Ocean had eliminated all major French bases outside of Europe, allowing the government to focus "on the primary field of British military endeavour in the [Iberian] Peninsula."[16] Since 1810, the campaigns in Portugal and Spain had become the principal—and also the largest and most expensive—British military operation. Lord Liverpool made this clear in an 1811 letter to Wellington, the commander of the Peninsular army: "No government could attach more importance to the continuation of it [the Peninsular War] than the present, or be more disposed to direct the whole disposable Effort of the Country to this one object. . . . When I accepted the seals of the War Department, I laid it down on Principle, that if the war was to be continued in Portugal and Spain, we ought not to suffer any part of our efforts to be directed to other objects."[17]

The implications of this policy are important to understanding Prevost's actions from 1811 onward. British economic, military, and diplomatic power was focused on the Continent, and Wellington's army had priority for reinforcements, armaments, supplies, and money. In 1810, the only battalion available for overseas service had been sent to Portugal, where it had joined two of the battalions originally deployed to Nova Scotia with Prevost in 1808. The need for personnel to replace losses in the Iberian Peninsula fully con-

sumed the recruiting system, while that theater's rapacious requirement for supplies and stores left little for Prevost.[18]

It was evident that until Britain defeated Napoléon, any
"war with the Americans would be a sideshow for the Cabinet."[19]
Aside from Spain and Portugal, important developments were taking place elsewhere in Europe. In the Mediterranean, troops and
money were required for diversionary attacks against eastern Spain
during 1812. In 1813, a force was to be cobbled together to establish a
British presence in the recently liberated Netherlands, and in 1814,
additional units were required in the Mediterranean. Fortunately for
Prevost, the government was able to free up some reinforcements.
During 1812, it sent Prevost 2,800 soldiers, while another 700 were
assigned to the Maritime Provinces. Even with the fencible units
that Prevost raised, however, his overall strength was still insufficient, since the U.S. Army expanded more rapidly, giving the Americans the advantage in numbers until late 1814. This strategic reality forced Prevost to adopt a defensive strategy, designed to protect
the territorial integrity of the Canadas while avoiding a major loss
to his strength.[20]

Strength restrictions placed a significant constraint on Prevost's
actions during the war and limited his strategic and operational options. Application for reinforcements required foresight, as gazing
into the future to discern the probable course of the next campaign
season required considerable professional acumen and luck. Ideally,
forecasts for a coming campaign season, which normally occurred
between April and November, were made in the autumn of the pre-
ceding year so that needed troops could arrive in the spring. There
were several reasons for this. Correspondence with London took
time. Normally replies to letters could be received on either side of
the Atlantic in as little as three weeks, if sailing direct, but this was
not always the case.[21] In early February 1812, Liverpool wrote a dispatch to Prevost that he did not receive until mid-May, granting
approval for the construction of fortifications and barracks at Quebec. The dispatch of men and supplies took longer as, once requests
were received in London, they had to be coordinated between several departments. Units had to be brought up to strength and then
dispatched to a port of embarkation, where they were loaded onto
transports and then moved by convoy to Canada. Poor winds and

storms could delay sailing, cause losses to a convoy, or divert it to another port. Once at Quebec, the troops had to recover from the effects of their voyage before being moved west to the area of active operations.

Even when this system operated efficiently, Prevost was usually uncertain as to when promised reinforcements would arrive and whether they would be in condition to fight. Long voyages in the cramped spaces of the transports often resulted in the troops being sick and weakened when they arrived. Once the troops were in the field, Prevost had to exercise care with their deployment because if a campaign resulted in heavy casualties, his effective strength would be reduced, giving an important advantage to the Americans since replacements would not be available until the following year. There were no ready reserves, save perhaps the garrisons of Montreal and Quebec, although the forces stationed in Nova Scotia and New Brunswick could be called on in an emergency. In the autumn of 1811, in preparation for the possibility of having to transfer troops from Halifax or Saint John to Quebec, Prevost ordered two officers to test a canoe and portage route across New Brunswick to Rivière-du-Loup on the St. Lawrence River. Limitations in manpower also required Prevost to expand the role of the militia, sometimes using them in active operations. These considerations restricted the tactical and operational options actually open to Prevost and limited the level of risk he could accept in battle. Prevost was not a defensively minded general, but the wartime conditions he faced in North America forced him to become one.[22]

Prevost was short of troops, and with no immediate help expected from Britain, he was forced to look to the resources of British North America to augment his regulars and improve the militia of Lower Canada—Brock would do the same in the upper province—a goal that required his gaining the support of the populace. He also had to integrate naval power into his defensive plans, as it not only supported military operations but was crucial for the logistical support of his forces. Finally, Prevost had to secure aid from the Natives and the support of pro-British civilians operating in the American Northwest whose specialist skills might be of aid to the defenders.[23]

Prevost was fortunate in that he was able to retain two experienced regiments, the 41st and 49th Foot, which were slated to leave

Canada in 1812. In April 1812, he learned that the 1st Battalion of the 1st Foot was being sent to Canada from the West Indies. Still, with only six battalions of regulars to defend a large area, Prevost decided to redress the shortage of trained regulars by raising fencible units in each of the Canadas, despite a failed earlier attempt to do so. Establishing these units that would be required to serve only in British North America increased his regular strength without the commitment of additional regiments from elsewhere in the empire. Unlike militia units that received minimal training and were called out only as needed, fencible units were raised by royal warrant for the duration of the war. In December 1811, Prevost submitted the terms of recruitment for the Glengarry Light Infantry Fencibles, a provincial unit intended for service in Upper Canada, to the War Office. He received authorization to raise the 376-man unit and to expand recruiting to include men from Lower Canada and the Maritime Provinces. Beating, or recruiting, orders were issued in January 1812.

He also ordered the creation of a battalion in Lower Canada. This unit had the same status as a regular regiment, but as it was raised and paid for by the provincial government, it was not, like the Glengarry Light Infantry, placed on the British army establishment. The Provincial Corps of Light Infantry, or *Voltigeurs Canadiens*, was established with a strength of 538 men, under the command of Lieutenant Colonel Charles de Salaberry, a prominent French Canadian who, since 1794, had held a commission in the 60th Foot. The service of this battalion was to have been restricted to Lower Canada, but it eventually saw extensive combat in the upper province and even in New York State.

Prevost had other fencible units as well. Three regiments had been raised in the Atlantic Provinces in 1803, one of which became a line regiment (the 104th Foot) in 1810 and was still stationed in New Brunswick; in May 1812, Prevost ordered the Royal Newfoundland Fencible Infantry to provide marine detachments for the Provincial Marine on Lakes Ontario and Erie. Another unit, the 600-strong Canadian Fencible Infantry, was authorized in 1803 but not raised until 1805; it was based in Lower Canada. Finally, Prevost could call on a unique unit, the 10th Royal Veteran Battalion, which had been recruited in Britain from discharged or time-expired soldiers who wished to immigrate to North America for service in the outlying posts. It was sent to Canada in 1808 and was posted to the important fort at St. Joseph's Island on Lake Huron.[24]

Prevost's military preparations in Lower Canada, which included improvements to the province's militia and its defenses, required his gaining the support of the civilian population. As chief executive of the government of Lower Canada, he was successful in securing legislative support for military preparations, while also obtaining the confidence of the French-speaking populace. Prodded by instructions from Liverpool and relying on his own experience, Prevost attempted to balance the inequity in the English- and Protestant-dominated Legislative and Executive Councils in favor of the majority French and Roman Catholic population. He also wanted to resolve the legal status of the Catholic Church within the British colony, which was a source of continual French complaints against the colonial administration and a major obstacle in securing the support of the church for wartime mobilization of the male population. Craig had completely ignored the status of Catholic interests. The shift, subtle or not, was enough for the English camp to interpret Prevost's actions as an abandonment of its interests, and the response laid the foundation of bitterness toward Prevost that would lead to future problems for him.[25]

The reality was that little could be achieved in Lower Canada without the support of the Catholic Church—Prevost reported that the province was "in the hands of the priests."[26] But he was desperately in need of manpower, and the only means by which he could expand the role of the Lower Canadian militia in the defense of the province was to court the Roman Catholics. His handling of the manner was consistent with his quiet, diplomatic way of not confiding closely in anyone, including his personal staff. The key questions were the status and authority of the Roman bishop of Quebec, the appointment of priests, and the collection of tithes.[27]

Prevost was assisted by the tolerant attitude of the Prince Regent toward Roman Catholic interests. At the heart of the matter lay the constitutional position of the Catholic Church; recognition of the Roman bishop of Quebec, including his authority to regulate the clergy; the question of loyalty to the Holy See; and relations with the Vatican. As the Catholic bishop lacked official recognition, the function of his office depended much on the pleasure of the governor. In the spring of 1812, Prevost told Bishop Jean-Octave Plessis that he wanted to reach an understanding that would place the Catholic leader "upon a more respectable footing,"[28] including increasing his government salary as befitted his rank and office. Prevost's goal, as he explained to Bathurst in November 1812, was that such a move would "serve more firmly to attach not only the Catholics of the country to His Majesty's Government than any other measure that could be adopted" and would "be attended with the best effects of enabling me to carry on the Public Service."[29] In a short time, Prevost managed to enhance the Roman bishop's prestige and authority.

The results were twofold. Prevost immediately gained the enmity of two men: George Mountain, the Anglican bishop of Quebec; and Herman Ryland, Prevost's civil secretary, who would soon be replaced due to his opposition to the governor's initiatives. The anger and humiliation of these two powerful men festered during the course of the war, with the result that both openly complained about Prevost to the British government. Prevost's actions renewed the optimism of Bishop Plessis, however, resulting in his issuing instructions that greatly aided the widespread response of the province's militia when war broke out.[30]

Prevost also proved successful in securing provincial political support in the service of military preparation. He did suffer a setback when the Legislative Assembly, the elected fifty-member lower house of Lower Canada's legislature, refused to approve a temporary suspension of habeas corpus, but he was able to secure amendments to the Militia Act that authorized him to embody—to call out on full-time service for a fixed period—2,000 bachelors aged eighteen to thirty for ninety days during the next two successive summers. The normal six-month period of active service for the militia was extended in 1812 to a maximum of two years, with half the men being replaced annually. By May 1812, four battalions of select embodied militia had been called up, while additional battalions would be raised during the war, and they would serve continually during the war until they were disbanded in the spring of 1815. These units provided a valuable augmentation to his strength and secured Prevost's "first object" of preserving Lower Canada. These men received the same pay as British regulars and were promised that once their terms were completed, they would not have to serve again until the rest of their entire age group had been called up. The assembly also voted a significant increase in militia expenditure from £2,500 to £12,000 for defensive measures in Lower Canada, while another £30,000 would be made available to the governor once hostilities commenced.[31]

Military operations and logistical activity were based on the inland waters of the North American continent. Circumstances had caused Prevost's authority to be extended to the Great Lakes. Previous conflicts had demonstrated that with the undeveloped condition of land communications, dominance of this system of lakes and rivers that provided the main transportation routes to the interior was very important. Whoever controlled these waters gained the initiative for offensive operations, amphibious landings, logistical activity, troop movements, and the disruption of enemy economic activity. While the Royal Navy had operated on Lake Ontario, Lake Champlain, and the St. Lawrence River during the Seven Years' War and the American War of Independence, peacetime reductions had diminished its presence. In 1778, the Marine Department had been transferred to the army's Quartermaster General's Department and renamed the Provincial Marine. As commander in chief, Prevost held executive authority over the Provincial Marine.

Before continuing with a discussion of naval affairs, it is necessary to clarify the authority Prevost actually had as "Vice-Admiral of British North America."[32] This title did not give him executive authority over Royal Navy operations, vessels, or personnel. Instead, it was related to the power given to him over the local vice admiralty court, which had jurisdiction over trade and revenue laws, dealing mainly with wrecks, prize powers, letters of marque, and reprisals against privateers; this court provided local resolution of such matters according to the Navigation Acts, the maritime laws of Great Britain. The Provincial Court of Vice Admiralty in Lower Canada itself held authority over the District of Quebec, which included the section of the St. Lawrence River east of Three Rivers to the west end of Anticosti Island. Adjudication of cases before the court was conducted by judges nominated by Prevost.[33]

Prevost was no stranger to naval affairs. Campaigning in the West Indies had provided him with firsthand experience in joint army-navy operations, while his service at Portsmouth and in Halifax had exposed him to the broader issues of arranging troop transport and naval victualing. As lieutenant governor of Nova Scotia, he had gained an appreciation of the use of sea power in colonial defense. From his headquarters in Quebec, Prevost could call on Vice Admiral Herbert Sawyer,[34] commander of the North American Station at Halifax, or officers of the Provincial Marine for advice on naval matters. Time and distance did not always allow Prevost the luxury of this consultation, however, and he typically relied on the staff officer responsible for marine affairs within the Quartermaster General's Department, who understood the difficulties within the Provincial Marine. That service's military character had diminished as its discipline and training declined—by 1812 it was more a transport service than a military force—and it desperately needed to be reformed. In early 1812, Prevost appointed Captain Andrew Gray, an infantry officer who had reported on the Provincial Marine since 1811, as acting deputy quartermaster general and assigned him the task of reorganizing and improving the Provincial Marine.[35]

According to a December 1811 report, the Provincial Marine had suffered from a decline in the number of vessels and the quality of its men, forcing it to limit its operations to transport for the army and provincial government on Lakes Ontario and Erie and to use the North West Company vessels to serve the upper lakes. Two of the three vessels on Lake Erie were in poor condition, and the report stressed the need to build a new schooner to preserve control of the lake. The four vessels on Lake Ontario were in better condition, although their timbers were in decay. In Lower Canada the Provincial Marine operated a "formidable" schooner and six gunboats from its run-down base at St. John's. The service also suffered from a shortage of men, and many of its officers were too old to be effective.[36]

Prevost's staff expressed concern that the naval base at Kingston was vulnerable because of its proximity to the United States. During winter, it became icebound and was susceptible to land attack. Lieutenant Colonel Alleyne Pye, who headed the staff section responsible for the marine and was responsible for this 1811 report, recommended that the naval establishment be moved from Kingston to York, which was less exposed. Prevost supported the relocation of the Provincial Marine base to York, which was "a position well adapted for a Citadel and a deposit of Military Stores for the

Land and Lake Service."[37] Bathurst was reluctant to approve the project, as no estimate had been made of the cost of the move, and recommended that, for the time being, nothing be done. Prevost thought otherwise and authorized the move to be conducted incrementally as time and money permitted. If hostilities with the United States commenced, then it could quickly be completed.[38]

Prevost also agreed with the recommendation to replace seventy-five-year-old John Steel, the senior naval officer on Lake Ontario, with Hugh Earl, a much younger officer, while a similar change in commanders occurred on Lake Erie.[39] For now, none of the other officers would be replaced. Prevost approved the building of new schooners at York and Amherstburg, to be launched in June 1812.[40] While he was unable to find additional men for the naval service, he eased the manpower problem by ordering five companies of the Royal Newfoundland Fencible Infantry be employed as marines.

Prevost paid little attention to the Provincial Marine post at St. John's (modern Saint-Jean-sur-Richelieu, Quebec) in Lower Canada. In his estimation, naval operations would be concentrated on Lakes Ontario and Erie, and operations on Lake Champlain would be of minor importance. He chose instead to focus on the land approaches to Montreal, since the naval station at St. John's could be bypassed by new roads leading from the United States.[41]

Prevost's interest in the waterways incorporated the logistical function of the transportation and movement of personnel, food, and stores from the depots at Montreal to points in Upper Canada. Transportation could be provided by waterborne craft, such as bateaux or small sailing vessels, or overland by wagons or, in winter, by sleighs.[42] The road network in British North America was limited, however, due to the sparse population, and those roads that existed were subject to seasonal disruptions brought on by inclement weather. There were also too few wagons and draught animals to operate a truly effective military transport service. As a result, the most efficient means of moving supplies and personnel was by water, but therein lay further difficulties. The many cataracts and rapids along the 180-mile-long stretch of the upper St. Lawrence between Montreal and Kingston—particularly between Montreal and Prescott—limited movement to smaller, less efficient low-draught craft that had to be portaged several times along the route. This waterborne transportation service required a labor force to operate it and skilled pilots familiar with the river. Prevost's solution would be to call on the North West Company, one of two major fur trading firms in British North America, to form a corps of voyageurs in 1812, not only to conduct supplies between Montreal and Kingston, but also to crew the gunboats protecting them.[43]

The safety of the bateaux moving on this route would also be threatened by American forces, and occasionally by civilians, at various places along the 100-mile portion of the upper St. Lawrence that lay contiguous to the United States. The potential threat to the line of communication during war, as Prevost identified, necessitated the creation of a flotilla of gunboats and shore defenses to protect shipping, which raised further demands for manpower. The problems of river communication occupied much of Prevost's time, bringing criticism from several of his subordinates who did not share a similar interest in the preservation of this vital lifeline. On several occasions, provincial commanders in Upper Canada weakened its defenses by assigning resources farther inland, in contravention of Prevost's orders.

Was there an alternate route available for Prevost to use that afforded greater security to movement than the upper St. Lawrence? West of Montreal, the Ottawa River branched from the St. Lawrence, eventually meeting the Rideau River, which led to the Cataraqui River and Kingston. In 1783, brief consideration had been given to using this route since it was planned to settle Loyalists on the banks of the Ottawa. During the 1790s, its advantages as a more secure line of communication were noted, but there was little interest in developing that route or in improving the way along the St. Lawrence by building canals. Although several surveys were made and reports prepared on the practicality of the alternate route, Prevost was unable to develop it as the government was unwilling to invest in such a potentially costly venture. Prevost did give the Ottawa River route serious consideration in 1814, as part of a contingency plan should the Americans undertake a major effort to disrupt or cut the main route in 1815, but again nothing came of it until after the end of hostilities.[44]

Prevost's attention to the line of communication did not end at Kingston. From there, men and supplies were transported using a route from Lake Ontario, up the Niagara River, westward along Lake Erie and the Detroit River, and then into Lake Huron to the British posts in the American Northwest. Although most of this route bordered the United States, British naval supremacy on the lakes meant that, for the present, the Americans were unable to threaten it.[45]

Prevost understood that Britain's aboriginal allies would play an important role in the coming conflict, especially as the warriors would provide an important augmentation to the regulars, aid in maintaining outposts, and provide an important psychological boost to the defenders of British North America. A diverse group of Native peoples living in both Canadas, the Old Northwest (then the state of Ohio and the Indiana, Michigan, and Illinois Territories of the United States), and further afield were generally allied with Britain, while other groups in New York, Pennsylvania, and Ohio were principally aligned with the United States. An accurate estimate of the combined military strength of these nations is difficult to determine as the records are not complete, while the changing status of several nations as they shifted allegiance or became neutral also affected the total. Recent estimates, based on period documentation, have determined that approximately 1,600 warriors were available in Upper and Lower Canada and about 8,500 in the Old Northwest. The latter figure helps explain British interest in that region as it could provide access to a large source of aboriginal manpower.[46]

Relations with the Native nations were the responsibility of the army and a separate agency known as the Indian Department, which was established in 1755. Over time, suspicions grew within the army that the civilian Indian agents were corrupt and self-serving, causing army officers to have to take on a greater role and deal directly with chiefs. Distrust and competition between both groups sometimes led to their working at cross-purposes in pursuit of similar goals, such as when they unsuccessfully attempted in 1807 to calm a rift within the Grand River community so they could recruit warriors, with the result that there was a decline in British influence over the Grand River tract. Responsibility for the conduct of Native affairs in Lower Canada rested with Prevost as governor general and in Upper Canada with the officer holding the combined offices of lieutenant governor and provincial commander.[47]

In the wake of the American War of Independence and the withdrawal from the northwestern outposts in 1796, British aboriginal policy had suffered several setbacks.[48] Sir James Craig had tried to revitalize the Native alliance from late 1807 to 1811. Indian Department officials arranged a series of meetings with delegations from several Native groups and successfully renewed alliances with many of the nations around the Great Lakes. Prevost inherited this improved state of relations that complicated the delicate state of affairs between Britain and the United States because several nations that renewed a military alliance with Britain were located in American territory. Conflict between the United States and the nations of the Mississippi River valley and upper Great Lakes in 1811 led to claims that Britain was interfering in American domestic affairs. Prevost was therefore forced to manage a delicate balance between the aspirations of his Native allies and the need for them to exercise restraint as London attempted to avoid war and seek a diplomatic solution with the Americans.[49]

The situation vis-à-vis the Native populations was just as delicate in Lower Canada but was handled in a different manner. The Akwesasne community near Montreal straddled the international border along the important lifeline of the St. Lawrence River, and the British and Americans competed for its favor. Neutrals among the Natives also attempted to avoid a commitment to either side in order not to jeopardize the continued delivery of presents, which was conducted annually to reaffirm alliances and allowed officials to meet with the Native councils. Prevost believed an open declaration of support for Britain by any group would prompt the Americans to occupy their village and thereby threaten the St. Lawrence lifeline. Therefore, he chose to support the neutrals and to continue issuing presents to keep the Akwesasne favorable to the British.[50]

The Natives were not the only group in the Northwest that could be of assistance to the British. Prevost sent Captain Andrew Gray, from the Quartermaster General's Department, to meet with officials from the North West Company and the South West (or Michilimackinac) Company to solicit their assistance. These commercial organizations operated transportation networks that maintained regular contact with the Natives, and the North West Company controlled the King's Posts, the former French fishing bases, and posts extending from the St. Lawrence River to Hudson's Bay.[51] The bateaux the company operated on the major water routes from Montreal to the upper lakes would prove useful in the event of war. The heads of both companies were grateful for Prevost's interest in protecting their trade and agreed to join "with zeal any measure of Defence, or even offence, that may be proposed to them."[52] This support included the use of company vessels on Lakes Superior, Huron, and Michigan and a promise that their personnel would at short notice reinforce the meager garrison on St. Joseph's Island.

The fur traders also offered to use their influence to encourage the Natives, who were dissatisfied with the American government, to commence hostilities against the common enemy whenever necessary. During the first half of 1812, Major General Isaac Brock communicated with Robert Dickson, the foremost British mercantile trader on the upper Mississippi, and Dickson gained agreement from the western Natives to meet at St. Joseph's Island by June 1812. Thus, the support of Native peoples in the Northwest was secured before the war and would prove to be an important British asset in the early months of the conflict.[53]

ONE final consideration that weighed heavily on Prevost was the American preparations for war. He should not have been so concerned. Despite the experiences of the Seven Years' War, the American War of Independence, internal rebellions, and recent campaigns against Natives in the Old Northwest, the armed forces of the United States were poorly organized, and their plans were not well defined in the spring of 1812. The secretary of war was responsible for all matters of military administration, but he was inundated with the management of the entire army; he and his handful of clerks had little time to devote to strategic questions. The various departments in the U.S. Army became overwhelmed by administrative confusion and overlapping responsibilities. There was no general staff or any professional officer to advise the secretary on military matters, leaving him to develop plans largely on his own.[54]

In the spring of 1812, the Americans contemplated no fewer than four offensives against the Canadas using a mix of regular troops and state militia. The main offensive would be directed against Montreal in order to cut the St. Lawrence supply line. A diversion would be created by sending forces from Sackets Harbor against Kingston and across the Niagara and Detroit Rivers into Upper Canada, in order to divide the defenders in the province and undermine their ability to offer effective resistance at all three points. The army that would execute this plan was small. In 1811, the U.S. Army had 5,200 NCOs and enlisted personnel distributed between seven infantry regiments, one rifle regiment, two regiments of artillery, and a regiment of light dragoons. Five of the infantry regiments were scattered among posts along the frontier of the Louisiana Territory, another was on the Mississippi and only one was in the north, while detachments of the remaining units were spread throughout the United States. In anticipation of war, Congress approved the expansion of the army to more than 35,000 men, but recruitment did not begin until May 1812. Little progress in mobilization had been made by the time war was declared, when 12,000 men had been recruited.[55]

The only field force that was concentrated and ready for operations was in the Northwest. The Americans were interested in settling Native unrest there and feared continued British intrigue might lead to the loss of the region. Open warfare between the U.S. Army and Natives had been frequent in the Northwest since the 1790s. One thousand regulars, volunteers, and militia had recently fought in a campaign known as Tecumseh's War, and the readiness of this force, renamed the North West Army, under Brigadier General William Hull, a distinguished veteran of the American War of Independence and former governor of the Michigan Territory, became the focal point of American preparations. By the summer of 1812, it was in fact the only military force of any significance ready for operations.[56]

The United States Navy was small and highly professional, but it offered little threat to the Canadas. In 1812, its high-seas fleet had fourteen sea-ready vessels, and 5,700 sailors and marines, with half of the personnel serving on shore stations. Three of the five frigates were laid up in Ordinary—in reserve with all their masts, ordnance, and stores removed—being readied to sail, and flotillas of gunboats protected many coastal harbors. Like those of the Royal Navy, the officers of the U.S. Navy had little interest in the inland waters. Requests to provide vessels for the Great Lakes were routinely ignored, and there was only the 16-gun brig USS *Oneida* on Lake Ontario, while the U.S. Army transport *Adams*, built in 1799 and armed with six 6-pounder guns, was the sole vessel on the upper lakes. Fiscal accountability seemed to outweigh operational concerns, leaving the secretary of the navy with four clerks, while the naval accountant had a staff of seventeen. The navy was only partially ready for the war, and the first of its oceangoing vessels began leaving port on the declaration of hostilities.[57]

In general, the preparations undertaken by the American armed services during the final months of peace were made with little urgency and failed to keep pace with the aggressive foreign policy of the U.S. government. Even on the eve of war, few details—including the date when operations were to commence—had been settled. Only one of the four field forces had been concentrated, recruiting was a shambles, and the navy was only partly ready for sea. This situation was in sharp contrast to widely held British fears that the Americans would strike decisively and in large numbers.

Intelligence reports and his own experience gave Prevost some understanding of American preparations, but none of it revealed the inner workings of President Madison's cabinet or the difficulties his administration was experiencing. He received reports on the movement of regular and militia reinforcements to positions on Lake Erie, Lake Ontario, and the St. Lawrence River. But he would also have recognized that with the waterways under British control, American offensive capability would be limited to operations along the most likely avenues of access—namely, across the rivers bordering Upper Canada, and the approaches along the frontier into Lower Canada. What Prevost feared most was the chance that the Americans might quickly field a large army and overwhelm his forces, much as had happened to British forces at Boston following the initial skirmishes at Lexington and Concord in 1775.

PREVOST'S own ideas regarding the defense of British North America are contained in a report that Liverpool asked him to prepare in February 1812. Despite the previous war scares, London was largely ignorant of the state of the defenses in North America. In order to make them more cognizant of local problems and conditions—and given the importance of the North American colonies to Britain— the government instructed Prevost to prepare a report that would advise on "the measures which it might be prudent to adopt in the event of Attack, the degree of Confidence which can be placed in the Militia force, the means of resistance which are afforded by the fortifications of Quebec and other places"; Prevost was assured that his "observations will be received with great interest by His

Majesty's Confidential Servants."[58] In essence, the government wanted Prevost to develop a strategic defense plan.

In response, in May 1812, Prevost sent a memorandum titled "The Military position of His Majesty's North American Provinces and the means of defending them" to London.[59] It was organized geographically, beginning in the west with Upper Canada, as the province was the "most contiguous to the Territory of the United States . . . which renders it, in the event of War, more liable to immediate attack," and concluding with Newfoundland in the east.[60] Each section included a general survey of the fortifications and garrisons within each province, followed by a general outline for the conduct of the defense in each province or region.

Prevost began by highlighting the challenge that distance posed for the defense of the Canadas. The westernmost fortified point was at Fort St. Joseph on the St. Mary's River which drains Lake Superior into Lake Huron, 1,500 miles from Quebec, about the same distance from Paris to Moscow. The country in between was sparsely populated and had few roads. The only permanent fortress was at Quebec, while all the other fortifications were temporary in nature and in need of repair. Fort St. Joseph was an important assembly point for friendly Natives, and its possession provided protection for the Northwest fur trade. Fort Amherstburg at the southwestern end of the province on the Detroit River and Fort George on the Niagara Peninsula were both in a ruinous state. Even if repaired, the resistance these forts could provide against an attack in force was limited. A naval dockyard at Fort Amherstburg provided the marine arsenal for Lake Erie and the upper lakes, and the fort also provided a rendezvous place for Natives in that part of the country. The position of the provincial capital at York, which was distant from the American frontier, and its good harbor was an excellent location that Prevost believed should be further developed as a naval and logistical installation.[61]

Prevost's appreciation of the defense of the Canadas borrowed ideas from earlier strategic military calculations, including one submitted by Craig, but it also offered a departure from previous thinking. Like his predecessors, Prevost believed that Quebec would be the Americans' ultimate goal. In his opinion, Quebec "was the Key to the whole and must be maintained";[62] however, Prevost was not proposing—as is believed by many historians—to abandon

Upper Canada so he could concentrate his meager forces at Montreal and Quebec. Despite the many weaknesses he found in the defenses of Upper Canada, Prevost was determined to hold it. He did observe that Kingston, located at the head of the navigation of the St. Lawrence River and close to the American frontier, was "exposed to sudden attack, which if successful would cut off the communication between the Upper and Lower Province, and deprive us of our naval resources."[63] In the event of hostilities, "it will be indispensably necessary for the preservation of a communication between the Lower and Upper Province, to establish some strong Post for the Regulars and Militia to secure the Navigation of the St. Lawrence above the Rapids to Lake Ontario."[64] Prevost saw the need to reinforce or establish fortified posts at Kingston; at Prescott, where the end of the rapids allowed cargoes to be transferred from bateaux to larger vessels heading west; at Coteau du Lac; and on the south shore of Montreal, where a flotilla of gunboats would command the river. Rather than abandoning Upper Canada, Prevost planned to overcome its greatest weakness by ensuring the uninterrupted flow of reinforcements and supplies into the province.

Prevost was also concerned about communications farther inland. Fort George, which had been built as a depot rather than a major defensive position, was in such a dilapidated state that it could not withstand a determined attack, making it a weak link along the line of communication between Lakes Erie and Ontario. This line was supported by three fortified points along the Niagara River: Fort George, Chippawa, and Fort Erie. Prevost believed it would be highly advantageous to gain possession of Fort Niagara, which lay on the shore opposite Fort George in New York State, should hostilities break out. By recommending this course of action, Prevost was, in effect, proposing to secure navigation on the Niagara River. He also wanted to improve the communication line to the upper lakes by making improvements to Fort Amherstburg. Finally, Prevost concluded that the Provincial Marine on Lake Ontario needed a more secure base since Kingston, despite having a good harbor, was vulnerable because of its proximity to the United States. The provincial capital at York also offered a suitable harbor and, more important, a location distant from the American frontier that made it a more difficult target than Kingston.[65]

Prevost concluded by reviewing what was possible with the forces he had against the opposition he might face. If a determined, large-scale attack were launched, Prevost recognized he would have few options: "If the Americans are determined to attack Canada, it would be in vain the General should flatter himself with the hopes of making an effectual defence of the open Country, unless powerfully assisted by Home."[66] Prevost "considered the preservation of Quebec as the first object, and to which all others must be subordinate"[67] because, as defective as the fortifications of Quebec were, it was the only stronghold he considered to be tenable against a substantial attack, and also the most necessary to defend. "The preservation of it [Quebec] being of the utmost consequence to the Canadas, as the door of entry for that Force The King's Government might find it expedient to send for the recovery of both, or either of these Provinces."[68]

He acknowledged another possibility, one in which the Americans, for various reasons, might experience difficulties in raising armies, formulating strategy, or executing their plans. In this case, Prevost anticipated that "all predatory or ill concerted attacks undertaken presumptuously and without sufficient means can be resisted or repulsed."[69] The significance of this realistic assessment by Prevost, which guided his efforts throughout the war, has eluded most historians, who have believed he would rapidly abandon Upper Canada at the first instance of an American attack. Rather than withdraw from Upper Canada precipitously, Prevost was actually proposing to enhance its defenses to secure communications throughout the province and to improve the naval forces that would be crucial to connect its defensive posts. By controlling the inland waterways, Prevost would be able not only to have freedom of action but also to provide security and sustainment for his land forces.

Prevost actually said little about the naval defense of the Canadas. His only comment was of the potential loss of naval resources if communication between the two provinces were cut. Nonetheless, he recognized that whatever steps he took to improve the lines of communication into the interior of Upper Canada, or to find bases that offered better security to the Provincial Marine, control of the inland waterways would be a significant factor in determining the outcome of all operations. In May 1812, he considered the placement of troops at key points as being sufficient to protect ports and the navigation of the St. Lawrence and other rivers. No one at this juncture, however, foresaw the massive expansion that would occur with the naval forces on the lakes and the effects that growth would have on logistics, personnel requirements, and offensive capabilities, and no one, certainly, saw the need to bring the Royal Navy onto the lakes. Prevost's silence on naval matters may be due to the assumption that despite its faults, the Provincial Marine was sufficient to guarantee British supremacy on the inland waters, or at least maintain parity with American naval forces in time of war.

To summarize, defending the Canadas posed innumerable challenges and difficulties. Prevost had few troops and promises of little more, but while his quasi-naval force dominated the waters, it was small and rife with problems. He had a vast territory to protect, a territory that was threatened at widely distant points. Montreal, Kingston, the fortified posts between Fort George and Fort Erie on the Niagara River, and Fort Amherstburg were directly threatened as they lay along the best avenues of approach. The loss of any of them would threaten the safety of posts to the west, which once isolated, could easily fall. Given a sufficiently disorganized opponent, Prevost was certain Upper Canada could be retained within its present boundaries. To help ensure this outcome, he proposed to enhance the protection on the upper St. Lawrence River, relocate the Lake Ontario naval base from Kingston to York, send more troops into the interior, and raise an additional provincial regiment. As we shall see, several of these assumptions would prove to be incorrect; nonetheless, Prevost's commitment to Upper Canada and his employment of an active defense, making judicious use of the limited resources at hand and launching local counteroffensives to rebalance the situation as necessary, would prove correct. None of his prewar plans remotely considered invading the United States or acquiring territory, as either action would stretch the defenders and the logistical system even further.

INVASION was, however, in the mind of the American government. During 1811 and the first half of 1812, the American president and several members of the cabinet and of Congress became convinced that war with Britain would provide a more suitable resolution of Anglo-American differences than diplomacy. As the summer of 1812 approached, officials in London, who until then had given American complaints little attention, were surprised by the war rhetoric in Washington and began to worry about the effect a North American conflict would have on their affairs in Europe. The British government made a last belated attempt at appeasement, while encouraging Prevost to continue with his military and naval preparations. It also kept Prevost informed of its late-hour diplomatic efforts to seek reconciliation with the United States.

Prevost was not helped by London's unyielding responses to American complaints between 1807 and 1812, and in its last-ditch attempt to avert war, unfortunately, both he and the government misread American resolve. In May 1812, Liverpool wrote him expressing the hope that an understanding might be reached with the United States. He also repeated warnings that Prevost could not "expect that the Forces under your command can receive any considerable addition by the detachment of troops from home."[70] Prevost was therefore forced to walk a fine line, for, on the one hand, he was told that in "the event or the apparent certainty of hostilities," he was to consider himself "vested with the same General Discretion in taking measure for the defence of the North American provinces as given to your predecessor Craig";[71] on the other hand, he also had to avoid any act that might accelerate the American government to resort to hostilities against Britain.[72]

Prevost did not receive Liverpool's May directive for several weeks. In the interim, he relied on conflicting intelligence regarding U.S. intentions from the British Minister in Washington. In March 1812, Prevost shared with Major General Isaac Brock, the commander in Upper Canada, reports that "there prevails throughout the United States a great unwillingness to enter upon hostilities."[73] In April, however, the tone changed: "the American Government affect now to have taken every step incumbent on the executive as preparatory to war, and leave the ultimate decision to Congress."[74] The diplomatic situation was in the balance as the Americans were awaiting the arrival of the latest proposals from Britain, contained in letters being carried aboard the USS *Hornet*, which was en route to North America.

Some historians argue that at this time Prevost demonstrated undue caution, revealing a characteristic that would be later repeated. Prevost had already carefully informed Brock that, while there were "advantages which may result from giving rather than receiving the first blow,"[75] the reports of supposed American military weakness at Detroit "might be but bait to tempt us to an act of aggression, in its effects, uniting parties."[76] Such an act, Prevost wrote, could cause the Americans to raise additional men for the army, and "afford the Government of the United States a legitimate pretext to add to the clamor artfully raised by it against England."[77] These instructions given to Brock are often used as evidence of Prevost's timid leadership and the tight restraint he supposedly placed on Brock, who saw the early occupation of Detroit as necessary for defending the upper province and to cement support from the western Natives. In fact, not only had Prevost anticipated Liverpool's dispatch of 15 May 1812 that warned of the delicacy of the situation, he was also acting under very specific instructions from London.

Whatever omissions Prevost might have made in passing on the government's orders, he was clear in his own directions to both Brock and Sherbrooke. In March 1812, both commanders were ordered not to adopt "any measure bearing the character of offence, even should a declaration of war be laid on the table of Congress by the President's influence."[78] Prevost may have been willing to await the results of the last round of diplomacy but he was not being passive. He told Brock and Sherbrooke to continue such preparations as would, "upon a change of affairs, enable you to carry any disposable part of your force against the common enemy."[79] These instructions received the "full approbation of His Royal Highness The Prince Regent," Prevost assured them, and were readily endorsed by the government.[80]

The military and legislative problems that occupied Prevost restricted his presence to Quebec and did not permit him an opportunity to journey into Upper Canada before the outbreak of war. Given his resolution to defend that province, an inspection visit and opportunity to confer directly with Brock should have been a priority, but such a visit proved impossible in 1811 or during the final months of peace in 1812. As a result, contact between Prevost and Brock was restricted to correspondence and communication by staff officers. Despite the potential for misunderstanding that is inherent in written communications, both officers shared similar opinions regarding the need for improvements in the Provincial Marine and the defense problems of Upper Canada. It would appear that, for now, they enjoyed a unity of effort.

Sir George Prevost's concern that a miscalculation on his part, or a skirmish initiated by his forces or Native allies, might provide the American government with a reason to declare war proved groundless. The question of peace or war would not be decided by his actions, but by those of the American and British governments. By June 1812, President James Madison had decided to pursue resolution of American differences with Britain not by diplomacy, but by war.

4

DECLARATION OF WAR AND MILITARY OPERATIONS IN 1812

The enemy would again be foiled in any further attempts they may make to invade the province.
—*Prevost to Brock, 14 September 1812*

P revost's preparations for war came to an abrupt end in the spring of 1812. During May 1812, President James Madison became convinced that further negotiations were useless. At the beginning of June, he therefore presented Congress with four charges against Great Britain—the impressment of American seamen, the violation of neutral rights and territorial waters, the blockade of American commerce, and the trade restrictions imposed by the Orders in Council—as sufficient grounds for a declaration of war. Congressional support was not unanimous, but following a close vote, both houses gave their approval. On 18 June, a proclamation was issued declaring that "war exists between the Kingdom of Great Britain and Ireland and the dependencies thereof, and the United States of America and their territories."[1]

The news of the outbreak of hostilities arrived at Montreal on 24 June and was immediately relayed to Quebec. Sir George Prevost was not surprised by the declaration, as throughout the spring he had received intelligence indicating that Madison was pressing for war.[2] By 25 June, he had obtained a copy of the American proclamation, even before official confirmation arrived from the British minister in Washington. He wrote Liverpool that he had no doubt that the news was true and that war had commenced, and shortly thereafter, he moved from Quebec to Montreal to "be nearer the scene of operations."[3] Any offensive plans he may have entertained were tempered when the British government learned of the outbreak of hostilities and reminded Prevost of the Prince Regent's instructions that "owing to the extended warfare in which Britain is engaged, the means for defending Canada must be limited."[4]

The British government, which had placed great hope in its last-minute attempt to reconcile American complaints, was surprised by the U.S. declaration of war, and it now had to support yet another theater of war. The government was also confident, however, that the forces under Prevost's command would prevail. The Earl of Harrowby, the lord president, or presiding officer, of the Privy Council (a powerful body mostly made up of former parliamentarians that advised the government), who was never shy in his dislike of Americans, told Bathurst that he hoped the "American army may advance far enough to enable Sir G[eorge] Prevost to give them a beating."[5] Most historians, however, have not shared the same enthusiasm toward Prevost and have attributed British successes in the early months of the conflict to his subordinate Major General Isaac Brock.

In Canada, Brock has emerged as the iconic figure of the War of 1812. He is often portrayed as a "brilliant strategist" whose loss caused irreparable damage to the British war effort.[6] Traditionally, historians have been gentle in their criticism of Brock and generous in their praise. They have described him as the most significant British commander of the war and the man who prevented the American conquest of Upper Canada. They claim it was Brock's leadership that overcame both overwhelming odds and Prevost's ineptitude to change the entire course of the war. To many, Brock provides the yardstick by which other War of 1812 generals should be measured. This Brock hagiography has reversed the roles of the two commanders, creating the impression that it was Brock and not Prevost who set operational plans and priorities and who led British forces to victory during the early months of the war. Only a handful of historians have attempted to turn the tables and give Prevost credit over Brock.[7]

Brock's ideas regarding the defense of the Canadas evolved between 1806 and 1811, as he gained detailed knowledge of the two provinces. Unlike Prevost, however, Brock had only seen limited active service. Born in 1769, he obtained his commission in the infantry in 1784. In 1791, he was in the West Indies, but illness forced him to miss an expedition against French-controlled Hispanola in 1793. He then commanded a battalion of the 49th Foot during the Anglo-Russian campaign in the Netherlands in 1799 and 1800. In 1801 his assignment to lead an amphibious attack on Copenhagen turned into a passive role on the heels of the British naval victory over the Danes. In 1802, Brock took the 49th to Canada, and in 1805, he was promoted to colonel. After taking leave in his native Guernsey, he returned to Canada the following year as the acting commander in chief of British North America. It should be stressed that Brock agreed with the traditional view that retaining Quebec was the key to maintaining a British presence in North America and that its defense might require abandoning Upper Canada. When the *Chesapeake-Leopard* incident increased tensions with the Americans in 1807, Brock confirmed his views on the defense of the Canadas by ordering the garrison at Quebec strengthened and giving little consideration to deploying troops elsewhere, particularly in Upper Canada.[8]

In 1811 Brock was sent to take command in Upper Canada. Brock had a good reputation with officials in London, and this brought him promotion to major general and promises of an appointment with Wellington's army in the Iberian Peninsula. As he gained familiarity with his new command, he grew to dislike any idea of abandoning the province and decided on a more vigorous defensive stance. The reasons for this change are open to speculation as Brock never provided a satisfactory explanation for this volte-face. Brock's attention and the disposition of his forces were fixed along the Detroit and Niagara frontiers of the province and also focused on securing the assistance of the local Natives, especially in the western district of Upper Canada. This goal would be enhanced by taking Detroit and the American outpost on Mackinac Island at the opening of hostilities.[9] Not all of Brock's ideas were original. For example, in early 1808, following an exchange with his civil and military staff on the means of defending Upper Canada, Sir Francis Gore, the lieutenant governor of Upper Canada, had recommended to Governor General James Craig that by destroying Detroit and Fort Mackinac, "many Indians would declare for us."[10] Brock adopted Gore's strategy. Brock also wished to expand the Provincial Marine to guarantee

British supremacy on the lakes, improve the defenses on the Niag-ara Peninsula, and employ militia to augment the regulars. Com-pared to Prevost, he paid less attention to the important line of communication between Montreal and Kingston; although he knew it would be subject to predatory excursions by the Americans, he believed it could be adequately protected along its entirety by local militia forces supported by a handful of regulars.[11]

It is one of the great ironies of the war that Prevost and Brock never met. Because Brock was Prevost's most important subordi-nate commander, it was crucial that both officers understood one another and shared a common view on strategy. When Prevost ar-rived at Quebec in 1811, Brock was already in Upper Canada and Prevost's duties kept him from undertaking a planned inspection visit of the province. Once hostilities commenced, they were lim-ited to correspondence, which was a less than satisfactory method of developing plans and conducting operations. Even the briefest verbal exchange might have established a basis for common under-standing, a solid working relationship, and trust. As a result, Brock was not fully aware of the restrictions placed on Prevost, nor did he appear to comprehend the latter's plan for the defense of Upper Canada—perhaps thinking that Prevost was simply following the earlier plan put forward by Craig—and Prevost's decision that he would only withdraw from the province if confronted by a large-scale American attack. The misunderstanding between Prevost and Brock widened when Brock implemented his own ideas.

Nonetheless, the strategy Brock proposed for Upper Canada was consistent with that outlined by Prevost as it was intended to im-prove the security of the province. There were, however, important differences. Prevost's instructions from London were clear regard-ing offensive operations, and he was, for now, reluctant to support Brock's plan to reduce American posts, such as Detroit, along the frontier as it might cause the Americans to retaliate in force. Pre-vost also feared exploiting Native aspirations in the Northwest as the Americans might interpret this policy as a threat that would lead to war. For his part, Brock believed that a defensive emphasis in the west could divert the Americans from objectives farther to the east. As events would demonstrate, this was a false premise be-cause the Americans proved unable to mount more than one major offensive at a time and the only American army that was ready at the opening of the war was not in the east, but in the west near Detroit.[12]

Once war was declared, however, Brock's seemingly aggressive stance did not result in his immediately undertaking offensive operations, nor was Prevost altogether timid in the first weeks of the conflict. Brock soon decided his force was too weak to go on the offensive. This decision pleased Prevost, who still thought the war declaration might be rescinded. Like his superiors in London, Prevost knew that American opinion toward the war was divided, particularly in New England, and there was still hope that a last-minute diplomatic solution might end the war before it really began. Prevost was "inclined to let these sentiments take their course" as "our present plans are all defensive."[13] Critics of Prevost cite his caution as costing the British an opportunity to strike decisively at the Americans, but this restraint was not of Prevost's making.

Prudence was also exercised by the Royal Navy. In May 1812, Foreign Secretary Castlereagh had told the Admiralty, the headquarters of the Royal Navy, to await the outcome of diplomacy before commencing hostilities at sea. The warships stationed in the North American waters were allowed "to repel any hostile aggression," were "at the same time to take especial care that they commit no Act of Aggression" against American shipping, and were, for now, to "exercise all possible forbearance."[14] The constraints imposed by London made such an impression on Vice Admiral Herbert Sawyer at Halifax that, in late June, he released three American prizes taken by a British ship after an encounter against the American frigate USS *President*. It was not until October, after Admiral John Warren had replaced the cautious Sawyer, that a more aggressive stance was taken and the Royal Navy (and the holders of letters of marque) established a wider, albeit still limited commercial blockade of the United States. The only exemptions to these restrictions were American merchantmen carrying grain to the Iberian Peninsula, which were to be left alone.[15]

Prevost continued with military preparations in case late-hour diplomacy failed. His meager military budget could not support raising two provincial units, so he gave the Glengarry Light Infantry, intended for service in Upper Canada, the priority in recruiting over the *Voltigeurs Canadiens* in Lower Canada and ordered the strength of the former doubled to 600 men. Prevost also ordered improvements to the defenses of Montreal and assigned Colonel Robert Lethbridge to command the important post at Kingston. Prevost supported Brock's application to employ Natives and to use whatever funds or supplies were available to secure their support, and he asked Liverpool to post additional general officers to Canada. As there was a shortage of specie, Prevost called on the legislature in Lower Canada to create paper money as a substitute for bullion to help pay for his initiatives.[16]

In July, the situation changed when regular U.S. troops reached the American side of the Niagara and Detroit Rivers and appeared ready to invade Upper Canada. Brock informed Prevost that the Americans were parading their forces daily as a show of strength, but Prevost cautioned him to exercise forbearance until hostilities were more decidedly marked, which happened on 11 July 1812 when Brigadier General Hull's North West Army crossed the Detroit River, virtually unopposed, into Canada. Hull's immediate objective was Fort Amherstburg;[17] afterward he was instructed to "extend your conquests as circumstances may justify."[18] When Prevost learned of Hull's invasion, he could not at first provide any reinforcements for Brock but instead sent Major General Roger Sheaffe to assist him as his second-in-command. After receiving additional reports that Hull had 2,500 regulars and militiamen in his army, Prevost sent Brock more than 400 soldiers to augment his 1,400 regulars and militia and 400 Natives, including field equipment and funds for the soldiers' wages. Some of the newly arrived regulars were employed on the warships of the Provincial Marine and assigned to escort the bateau service. Anticipating that the Americans might move against Lower Canada, Prevost next deployed regulars and militia to protect the approaches to Montreal.[19]

Meanwhile, in the Northwest, the fate of Fort Mackinac was decided. During the summer of 1812, Captain Charles Roberts, commanding the British outpost at Fort St. Joseph, received conflicting instructions regarding the disposition of that place. In late June, Brock first ordered Roberts to take the fort or, if attacked, defend his outpost to the utmost. Brock then countermanded his instructions two days later, but then changed his mind once more in early July. The weak state of the garrison at Fort St. Joseph may have played on Brock's concerns as did his flagging confidence in Roberts's chances of success. The final order provided Roberts with the freedom to

choose whether or not the attack should proceed. Colonel Edward
Baynes, the adjutant general for British North America, also wrote
Roberts on 25 June advising him that war had been declared and
instructing him to maintain vigilance and cooperate with the
North West Company to preserve their interests and ensure the
protection of Fort St. Joseph. Baynes authorized Roberts to retreat if
necessary. This order, drafted on behalf of Prevost, made no mention of Fort Mackinac and therefore did not, as has been suggested
by some commentators, rule out an attack against that post. The
day after he received Brock's letters, but before Baynes's message
could have arrived, Roberts, judging that "the natives who had been
collected would soon abandon me if I had not made the attempt,"
decided to attack the American fort. He assembled a force of forty-
six soldiers, 180 fur traders, 400 Natives, and two 6-pounder artillery pieces and departed for Mackinac Island on 16 July.[20] After
paddling nearly fifty miles in less than twenty-four hours, they
landed the next day, and following a summons by Roberts, the
American commander surrendered and the fort fell without a shot
being fired.[21]

Prevost and Brock did not learn of the success at Mackinac for
more than two weeks, and in the interim, they both continued with
military preparations. From his position on the Niagara frontier,
Brock was afraid that his forces would be overwhelmed by American strikes across the Detroit and upper St. Lawrence Rivers. Prevost's response to Brock's pleas for reinforcements was less than
requested but all that could be provided. He sent two companies of
the Royal Newfoundland Fencibles, a small detachment of the 10th
Royal Veteran Battalion, materials to clothe 2,000 militiamen, a
variety of stores, and four 6-pounder artillery pieces. He also directed the Commissary Department to provide 1,500 pairs of shoes.
News that transports carrying the 1st Foot were nearing Quebec led
Prevost to begin sending another battalion into Upper Canada, and
he ordered three companies of the 49th Foot at Montreal to Kingston. He informed Brock that he could deploy these troops as he
"may find necessary."[22] Brock acknowledged that Prevost's support
had "in some measure supplied the deficiency"[23] of men and supplies needed and, in combination with measures he had taken within
Upper Canada, contributed to the overall improvement of conditions within the province.

Prevost's own frustration with equipment and manpower short-ages was evident in his reaction to the recent arrival of the 103rd Foot, a 750-man battalion from England that was actually made up of "very young Soldiers and Boys." Prevost informed Brock that this "scanty reinforcement" was destined for his command but would not "add materially" to it as the battalion was provided to "support to the utmost your [Brock's] exertions for the preservation of com-munication between Upper & Lower Canada."[24] Shortages notwith-standing, Prevost saw no need to alter his overall strategy. The com-mander in chief remained resolute in preserving the upper province and chose to improve the defense of the exposed communications between it and the lower province. Prevost established a cordon of troops in "the space between the Saint Lawrence and Richelieu Riv-ers to prevent eruptions into this Province and to secure Montreal from the effects of a predatory war"[25] the Americans had now initi-ated on the upper St. Lawrence.

Prevost also had to contend with the fragile state of his lines of communication with Britain. Following the loss of 6,000 muskets destined for Canada that went down when the transport carrying them sank during a gale, he was forced to order Sherbrooke to send him half of the arms in store at Halifax. Elsewhere in the Atlantic, the loss of 160 officers and men of the Royal Scots was narrowly avoided when the master of their transport and the lieutenant com-manding the detachment convinced their captor, the captain of an American frigate, to release them by paying a ransom of $12,000 and delivering up their small arms and ammunition.[26]

As the garrison of the Canadas grew, the demand for foodstuffs increased. The remedy to shortfalls in provisions required careful planning, particularly in Upper Canada, where local resources could not feed the expanding military forces, the civilian population, and Native allies all at the same time. Poor harvests would bring fur-ther shortages, and both Prevost and Brock agreed that the embodi-ment of militiamen for service had to leave enough men for plant-ing and harvesting. Prevost had requisitioned additional foodstuffs from Britain for delivery in the spring of 1813, and arrangements were also made to exchange surpluses with British colonies in the West Indies. Prevost even sent agents to advise the residents of New York, Vermont, and the New England states that their produce was welcome in the Canadas. The response was enthusiastic and a system of trading licences that offered good prices for provisions was quickly established. The inadequacy of Canadian resources ensured a constant need for American flour and livestock that developed into a flourishing trade in defiance of American government efforts to suppress it. This illegal trade freed up Canadian grain for domestic use as American merchants also agreed to provide grain for the British forces in Iberia. Another beneficial result for Prevost was that the personal contacts established by this cross-border traffic provided further sources of intelligence.[27]

In early August 1812, Prevost welcomed the news of Roberts's success at Mackinac. Not only had this victory occurred after the American incursion under Brigadier General William Hull in southwestern Upper Canada, but Prevost anticipated that the occupation of Mackinac Island would bring increased support from the aboriginal peoples. More important, it would threaten Hull's flank, "compelling him to retreat across the [Detroit] river"[28] back into U.S. territory. Prevost could also be satisfied that, despite his being distant from the main theater, his commanders were following his instructions. For his part, Brock had shown restraint and refrained from issuing his first order for Roberts to take Fort Mackinac until after he learned of the American declaration of war.[29]

Prevost was correct in his assessment that the loss of Mackinac would have a profound effect on Hull. The British victory made it impossible for Hull to form an alliance with the powerful Wyandot nation, and he feared his army would be overwhelmed by the Native forces supporting the British. Despite the number of Canadians who offered him their support following his occupation of Sandwich, Hull was convinced that he needed more regulars for an attack on Fort Amherstburg. He requested reinforcements and additional supplies from Washington and from several local governors, which were only partially received. A column of regulars, militia, and women and children from Fort Dearborn, located on the Chicago River, was nearly wiped out by Potawatomi and Winnebago warriors as it left for Fort Detroit. In August, Hull's supply situation became more desperate after defeats at Brownstown and Maguaga, which cut his supply line. Britain's Native allies were also responsible for an intelligence coup when Hull's personal and official papers were found in a schooner, seized in early August; they revealed important details regarding the size and state of his army.

With few supplies and facing encirclement by British forces and Native allies operating to his rear, Hull concluded he could not remain in Upper Canada and began falling back to Detroit in early August. Late on 13 August, Brock arrived at Fort Amherstburg from the Niagara Peninsula with a strike force of fifty regular troops and 250 militiamen and Grand River warriors whose service he had recently secured. After securing further assistance from the Natives, Brock concluded that action, rather than restraint, as his officers proposed, was necessary and crossed the Detroit River with his army, ready to assault Fort Detroit. Hull initially refused a request to surrender, but on 16 August, 1812, he capitulated with barely a shot fired. The terms of the capitulation included the surrender of two other detachments and the entire Michigan Territory to Great Britain. A great quantity of weapons and stores also fell into British hands and were immediately sent to Fort Erie for the defenses of the Niagara River.[30]

Upon cursory examination, it would appear that it was Brock's plan for the defense of Upper Canada and not Prevost's that had proven successful. This is not the case. Brock's aggressiveness was tempered initially by insufficient British forces, but it was the ill-concerted military preparations of the United States that allowed these forces to be unleashed. Once American weakness was revealed, Brock exploited British control of the inland waters to concentrate against Hull, which fit with Prevost's strategy. For his part, Prevost funneled what few troops and equipment were available into Upper Canada for Brock's use, while also preparing to deal with a possible American strike against Montreal. Prevost was willing to accept that the two victories achieved thus far, which had occurred on American territory, did not breach the orders given him by the Prince Regent, as the capture of Mackinac and Detroit eliminated bases from which the Americans could strike into the Canadas, improved the security of British communications, and enhanced Native support in the Northwest. Both successes occurred without a fight or heavy losses. Roberts's coup largely resulted from the American commander's ignorance of the declaration of war, but Detroit was a more significant victory, although it did not cause Prevost to deviate from his overall strategy. This sequence of events revealed to him that his fears of an easy American victory were unfounded: rather than facing large-scale coordinated offensives against the Canadas, his forces had defeated a series of ill-considered and poorly executed attacks.

One factor that had not been considered in Prevost's prewar plans was the acquisition of American territory. The surrender of Michigan offered the British both advantages and dangers. Winning the support of 9,000 warriors in Ohio, the Michigan and Illinois Territories, and adjacent areas would provide a formidable obstacle to any subsequent American invasion of Upper Canada. However, the British threat that resulted prompted the first significant American military enterprise. Following the loss of Detroit and the massacre at Fort Dearborn, Washington took decisive steps to deal with the consequences. Thus, the U.S.-Indian struggle that had commenced in the Northwest in 1794 merged with the Anglo-American war in 1812 resulting in an American strategy intended to oust the British from Michigan and regain control of the Native populace. The purported shift of American attention to the West is often attributed to Brock, but the reason had less to do with him than with American interests; meanwhile, as shall be shown, the first major American offensives in the following year would occur farther east than in 1812.[31]

THE campaign against Detroit coincided with a new attempt to end the war by diplomacy. At the beginning of August 1812, Prevost received an express letter from Augustus Foster, the former British minister to Washington. Foster was in Halifax awaiting transport back to England, when he learned that the Orders in Council had been withdrawn in June, and he sent an armed vessel under a flag of truce to New York City to deliver dispatches with the news for onward transmission to Washington. Foster believed this development might induce Madison to suspend hostilities and entertain peace negotiations, and he encouraged Prevost to order a ceasefire. Prevost agreed and on 2 August 1812, he sent Colonel Edward Baynes to discuss a ceasefire with Major General Henry Dearborn, the American commander in the northern theater. Prevost suggested to Dearborn that an armistice would provide the American government with time to consider the latest development. Baynes reached Dearborn's headquarters at Greenbush, New York, on 8 August, just as Hull was withdrawing from Upper Canada to Detroit. Dearborn immediately saw the advantages that a ceasefire would offer to his own preparations. He lacked authority to enter into an agreement, however, so he advised Baynes he could only order his subordinates to confine their actions to defensive measures. If the British took any offensive action within Dearborn's jurisdiction, which did not include Hull's command at Detroit, the agreement would be void. The ceasefire was nearly undone, however, by Major General Roger Sheaffe, commanding at Fort George, who, against Prevost's instructions, agreed with the American commander on the Niagara frontier to extend the original terms by including movement by water. Prevost immediately repudiated this revision to the agreement and instructed Sheaffe to respect the original terms.[32]

As it happened, Madison and his cabinet were unmoved by the British announcement, since it addressed only one of their grievances, and the war continued. In mid-August 1812, Dearborn received orders not only to terminate the armistice, but to waste not a moment "in gaining possession of Niagara and Kingston, and cooperating with General Hull in taking Upper Canada."[33] Dearborn passed Washington's decision regarding the ceasefire to Prevost, and both men formally agreed to its termination on 4 September.

The historiography of the War of 1812 maintains that the Prevost-Dearborn armistice was more advantageous for the United States than for Britain. This is not entirely the case, as it momentarily halted American offensive action, which left Brock, who did not learn of its terms until he returned to the Niagara Peninsula after the fall of Detroit, free to focus on Hull. Between 8 August and 8 September 1812, Prevost sent 650 regulars into Upper Canada, 400 of which went to the Niagara Peninsula. Brock was also able to send the flank companies of the York militia, a number of Grand River warriors, and additional artillery to join his forces that were deployed at various points along the river. He transferred soldiers from Fort Amherstburg to Fort George and made a visit to the defenses at Kingston. As the armistice came to an end, the Americans appeared ready to mount an assault across the Niagara River, but hesitated for more than a month. Their preparations were not as complete as Brock had believed. Intelligence that first indicated "an intention of commencing active operations" once the ceasefire ended, Brock reported, now "tends to different measures,"[34] as the American army was rife with sickness and desertion. Active American preparations for an offensive across the Niagara River would not begin until September 1812.[35]

While the truce was in force, the Americans moved three small merchant vessels and an armed schooner that were under blockade at Ogdensburg to Sackets Harbor. The U.S. Navy purchased these vessels and converted them into gunboats that began to contest British naval supremacy on Lake Ontario. As unfortunate as this setback was to the British, it was the appointment of Commodore Isaac Chauncey as the U.S. Navy commander in chief on Lakes Ontario and Erie in August 1812 that proved decisive. His experience as commandant of the naval dockyard at New York City made him the perfect choice for the task of building a naval force to challenge Britain on the lakes. Chauncey demonstrated the advantage in resources enjoyed by the Americans as he arranged for the delivery of guns, seamen, and a vast array of equipment to Sackets Harbor. He then increased the armament of the sole American vessel on Lake Ontario and converted four merchant vessels, purchased in October, into warships. This work was conducted without interruption from the Provincial Marine. By early November, Chauncey felt ready to raise a challenge, despite the fact that he faced unfavorable odds as the Provincial Marine squadron was still more heavily armed than his command.[36]

IN September, the scene shifted to the Niagara frontier. To meet any possible contingency, Brock had dispersed his 2,300 regulars, militia, and Natives at four posts along the Niagara River, but as they lacked mutual support, Brock proposed to establish a central reserve that could reinforce any one of them. He intended to create this reserve by transferring the garrison of Kingston to the Niagara Peninsula, and he also requested another 1,000 regulars from Prevost. The commander in chief rejected any reduction of the troops at Kingston, reminding Brock that they guarded the key logistical and naval base in Upper Canada. Nor could Prevost provide any reinforcements, since he had none to give. Instead, Prevost suggested Brock form the reserve with units from the Detroit frontier. The essential difference between their views, based on the problem of limited resources, was that Brock was interested in retaining the gains made in the west while augmenting the center in the Niagara Peninsula, yet leaving his eastern wing along the upper St. Lawrence River exposed. For his part, Prevost was willing to risk the British position farther west but refused to jeopardize his center and the logistical lifeline that allowed Upper Canada to be defended.[37]

In September 1812, Prevost proposed a contingency plan to Brock, which called on him to create a diversion by crossing the Niagara River into New York State if the Americans advanced into Lower Canada and threatened Montreal.[38] Brock tersely rejected this plan:

> I have perused with every possible attention Your Excellency's instruction "that whenever I was informed that the enemy have made an attempt to penetrate into the Lower Province I am to concentrate all my disposable force, and immediately make such a diversion as shall indicate a disposition to operate on his rear and upon his lines of communications." My force is so scattered, and so immediately required for the defence of the different posts at which it is stationed, that I am at a loss to know in what manner I possibly can act so as to produce the effect expected.[39]

Brock's attitude is puzzling, since he had, at times, previously concentrated and dispersed forces around the province depending on the military situation. As with the debate over the formation of a central reserve, Brock was again at odds with his superior. On the very same day that he rejected Prevost's plan, Brock boasted in a letter to his brother Savery that "I firmly believe I could at this moment sweep everything before me from Fort Niagara to Buffalo."[40] The difference between Brock's public and private correspondence during the summer and autumn of 1812 reveals that he either did not understand Prevost's strategy or, worse, was acting in defiance of it. Prevost seemed more confident than Brock—whose appreciation of the situation fluctuated—that Upper Canada could be held. With the enemy now expected to attack across the Niagara River, Prevost assured Brock that his present strength would allow him to hold his "position at Fort George, and that the enemy would again be foiled in any further attempts they may make to invade the province."[41]

The last American offensive against Upper Canada in 1812 ended at the Battle of Queenston Heights, on 13 October. This engagement is then considered Brock's greatest victory, but this is not really the case. The American assault on Queenston was a hastily conceived attempt to recoup the loss of Fort Detroit before the New York state militia was released for the winter, and its objective was limited to

seizing the village of Queenston to "get excellent barracks and winter quarters"[42] that would provide a base for a subsequent campaign.
Brock had taken great care to ensure that early warning of an American crossing would be provided, against which he would direct
his forces, which were distributed between four key points along
the thirty-five-mile length of the Niagara frontier. He demonstrated poor judgment during the battle. On learning of the American attack, he left his headquarters at Fort George for Queenston
without giving any orders or briefing his subordinate Sheaffe on
the steps to be taken in his absence. There is contradictory evidence
as to whether Brock had ordered the troops at Fort George and
Chippawa to reinforce the defenders at Queenston and whether he
made too hasty an evaluation of the situation when he arrived
there. By ordering a company to withdraw into the village from the
heights, Brock contributed to the American occupation of these
same heights and the capture of an important artillery position
overlooking the American crossing site. His rash decision to lead a
charge to retake the battery was tactically unsound—and he paid
for it with his life.[43]

Instead of rallying the defenders at Queenston and organizing
his forces to contain the Americans on the riverbank and then halt
the flow of reinforcements across the river, Brock acted prematurely
in attempting to recapture a well-defended battery midway up the
heights. His death during his first action in more than a decade
came as the British and Canadians were losing the battle. Their final success is in part due to Brock's second-in-command, Major
General Roger Sheaffe, who proved less impulsive and ordered regular infantry, artillery, militia and warriors to proceed to the west of
Queenston before he mounted a deliberate and successful attack
against the Americans later that day.[44]

As tragic as the loss of Brock was, British arms had prevailed. The
victory at Queenston signaled the end of major operations in 1812. In
November, one final effort by the Americans was made to capture
Montreal. Dearborn sent 2,000 regulars and 3,000 militia into Lower
Canada, and on 20 November a short, sharp battle occurred at Lacolle
Mill when the American advance guard of 600 men was defeated by
a slightly smaller group of British regulars, Canadians, and Kahn-
awake warriors. Dearborn ordered a retreat, and once back in New

York State, his regulars went into winter quarters, while the militia was sent home.[45]

DURING the autumn of 1812, the United States did achieve one small but telling victory, which stemmed from Chauncey's efforts at Sackets Harbor. On 10 November 1812, the commodore chased the flagship of the Provincial Marine Lake Ontario squadron into Kingston Harbor. Another vessel suffered the same fate the following day, and the Americans then blockaded Kingston for several days. News of Chauncey's successes reached York, where the other two British warships remained at anchor. With his main opponent cleared from the lake and British merchant shipping disrupted, Chauncey could report that he had achieved "command of The Lake and that we can transport Troops and Stores to any part of it without any risk of an attack from the Enemy."[46] He also informed the senior American commanders in the northern theater that he was "ready to cooperate with them in any Enterprize that may be deemed practicable, against the enemy."[47] Expansion of his squadron continued as additional merchantmen were converted to warships and a new corvette was launched at Sackets Harbor. In just eleven weeks from receiving his orders to take command at Sackets Harbor, Chauncey had created a small but effective squadron that had wrested control of Lake Ontario from the British, and the Americans would exploit this naval advantage in the coming 1813 campaign season.[48]

For Prevost, this latest setback suffered by the Provincial Marine conclusively demonstrated the ineffectiveness of that service. His confidence in the service had earlier been shaken in July, when an attack by four ships on Sackets Harbor was defeated by a single American vessel, while an encounter with an American schooner off Prescott at the end of that month demonstrated the poor state of British gunnery. Furthermore, in October a raid against an American sloop anchored in the Genesee River could not be exploited due to the lack of men. In a series of reports to Prevost and Sheaffe, Captain Andrew Gray, the staff officer in the Quartermaster General's Department responsible for the naval service, offered a bleak analysis of the state of the Provincial Marine. Gray believed there was a "lack of energy and spirit" among the officers and men, shortages of seamen "who were capable of doing their duty";[49] the advanced state of American preparations at Sackets Harbor, where the Americans were about to launch a new frigate and commence building another, meant that "nothing could save our navy from destruction the moment navigation opens in the spring."[50]

To prevent this from happening, Gray recommended that the defenses of Kingston and York be improved and that three new vessels be built at Kingston, York and Amherstburg "to keep pace with the enemy."[51] Gray had nothing to say on how the deficiencies of the officers were to be resolved, and his only comment on the shortage of qualified seamen was to encourage the procurement of "officers to command and seamen."[52] His most daring proposal to rectify the naval imbalance was to recommend the destruction the American naval force and base at Sackets Harbor using a force of infantry and artillery, which would march from Montreal over land and the frozen Lake Ontario to their objective and back.[53]

Prevost supported most of these proposals. One vessel each was to be built at York and Kingston, and a superintendent to administer the dockyards was sent to Upper Canada with 120 shipwrights and carpenters to do the work (Gray had asked for only fifty or sixty). The Quartermaster General's Department was also instructed to provide thirty-four seamen for service on Lake Ontario. Five artillery pieces were forwarded from Lower Canada for the protection of the naval bases at York and Kingston, and a company of the 49th Regiment and a detachment of artillery were ordered from Kingston to reinforce York; they would be replaced at Kingston by a company of Glengarry Light Infantry and artillery from Montreal. Ordnance for the new vessels was also being readied for transport as was the necessary iron, anchors, and naval stores.

Prevost was less satisfied with the proposal for a raid on Sackets Harbor. To him, the execution of the attack depended on "the force which I may have at my disposal at the time when you think it might be accomplished"[54] and on the state of enemy defenses along the frontier. Critics of Prevost have used his reply as another example of his cautiousness and reluctance to reduce the forces around Montreal and Quebec; yet Prevost had no doubt that "the object" of attacking Sackets Harbor "is certainly highly important,"[55] and as bold as Gray's proposal appeared, it was merely an initial outline and not a plan. The movement of a battalion of infantry with a detachment of artillery and supplies on a mission that expected to take ten days to march thirty-one miles into enemy territory during the dead of winter was dangerous. The weather had to cooperate. There were few details of the enemy's dispositions at Sackets Harbor, the terrain was unfamiliar, and risking 500 men or more on such an adventure was militarily unsound.[56]

Prevost also had ideas of his own. During the autumn, he decided that the problems of the Provincial Marine could be rectified by employing a professional naval officer to lead it and suggested that his brother James, who was a post captain in the Royal Navy, be "appointed for the purpose of organizing such a marine establishment as His Majesty's Government may deem sufficient for the Canadas."[57] Faced by the growing strength of the United States Navy on Lake Ontario, Prevost subsequently decided a major revamp of the naval service was necessary and in December "made the strongest representations to His Majesty's Gov't . . . of the necessity of the immediate supply of officers and men for the ships now on the lakes and those to be built."[58] Admiral John Borlase Warren, the commander of the united North American and West Indies Station based at Halifax, agreed with Prevost. Once the correspondence caught up with Warren, he sent three commanders, six lieutenants, and two gunners to Prevost to oversee the preparation of guns, rigging, and stores for an inland naval force. Warren hoped this detachment would be the first of a larger Royal Navy contingent and recommended to the Admiralty that 550 seamen plus ordnance and equipment be sent to the Canadas, along with an "Intelligent, steady, Active Master and Commander as Commodore"[59] on the lakes. Warren later explained to Prevost that he encouraged the Board of Admiralty to appoint "his friend Sir [James] Lucas Yeo," whom he knew to be "an excellent and gallant officer, as well as a man of resources in danger or difficulty" for this service.[60]

Prevost's appeal and Warren's recommendations found support in London. In December 1812, Bathurst informed Prevost that a detachment of 200 seamen with an appropriate number of officers would be sent to him. At this juncture, Lieutenant Colonel Sir Howard Douglas of the Royal Artillery, who had recently returned to Britain from the Iberian Peninsula, intervened. Douglas, the son of a rear admiral with considerable service in North America, and a student of navigation and naval affairs, had resided in the Canadas and Nova Scotia during the 1790s. His skill at seamanship was evident as he had gained familiarity with the Great Lakes, the St. Lawrence, and the waters off Nova Scotia, and as an artillerist he had a keen interest in naval gunnery.[61] Douglas, who was later appointed lieutenant governor of New Brunswick, was a figure familiar to the government, and he wrote Bathurst of the importance naval power could play on the Great Lakes. He emphasized that "the possession of the upper and the protection of the lower province depended upon our maintaining a decided superiority on Lake Ontario."[62] Douglas echoed the recommendations that the Provincial Marine "should be put on a better establishment" and encouraged the posting of "regularly bred naval officers"[63] for the inland waters. Armed with this letter, Bathurst succeeded in increasing the number of sailors destined for Canada to 425, and shortly thereafter, the Admiralty confirmed Captain Sir James Lucas Yeo as commodore to command the naval forces in British North America.[64] Prevost was pleased to learn that experienced officers and able seamen were expected to arrive in the spring of 1813.[65]

The results of the first six months of hostilities were surprising. The prewar assumptions held by both sides that Upper Canada would fall quickly were never realized, and a combination of factors was responsible for this outcome. The preparations Prevost undertook in both provinces on the eve of the conflict and his emphasis on defending both Canadas allowed an effectual defense. American mismanagement and poor leadership at the strategic and operational levels prompted a series of shoddily conducted enemy offensives that were repulsed. The renewal of the Native alliance resulted in great dividends as Natives made important contributions to the outcomes at Mackinac, Detroit, Queenston, and Lacolle, permitting the extension of British influence with nations in the upper Great Lakes district and the Mississippi country. Prevost's leadership, while not perfect, had achieved an effective balance among the political, economic, military, and naval pressures that he faced. His faith in achieving an end to the war through diplomatic action during the summer of 1812 was due not to a lack of resolution but to Prevost's having weighed the prospect of war in North America against British strategic goals. Once it was evident that war was coming, he set himself to it, directing Brock in Upper Canada, his key staff officers, the Commissariat, and the Provincial Marine toward the goal of defending the Canadas. As operations progressed, Prevost realized that a key component of his command was flawed and that action to rectify that problem was necessary. His request to bring the Royal Navy onto the Great Lakes would prove to be one of the most important decisions he made during the war.

5

OPERATIONS AROUND LAKE ONTARIO INTENSIFY

January to May 1813

To shield that Province from those evils.
—*Prevost to Bathurst, 21 April 1813*

In January 1813, as he prepared for the opening of the campaign season, Prevost learned that in addition to a naval contingent, he would receive reinforcements from other British garrisons. This augmentation included a company of artillery, a regiment of light dragoons, seven infantry battalions, two Swiss regiments in British service, and reinforcement drafts for the existing units in Canada. Experience had taught Prevost that the movement of troop convoys was subject to many disruptions that could delay their arrival at Quebec to the late spring or summer. In addition, transatlantic voyages in crowded troopships often left soldiers sick and weakened, requiring them to undergo a period of rest and recuperation before they could be employed. These units would then have to be moved an additional 350 miles to Kingston, from where they could be distributed to posts farther inland. The Royal Navy also needed time until it was ready to commence operations in 1813. Unwilling to gamble on the timely arrival of the troopships and faced with evidence of American preparations for an offensive against Upper Canada, Prevost looked within the North American colonies for additional manpower to "shield that Province from those evils."[1] Six companies of the 104th Foot, based at Fredericton, New Brunswick, and a detachment of artillery were ordered to march overland to Quebec. Two more companies of the 104th would follow by ship later in the year. Nineteen men were lost during the difficult winter journey, but by mid-April, most of this 800-man regiment was concentrated at Kingston.[2]

Prevost also expanded the role of the militia in the defense of both Canadas. The terms of service were renewed for 900 men serving in the five battalions of select embodied militia in Lower Canada, and a sixth battalion was raised. Three troops of light dragoons and a corps of artillery drivers were recruited, and small volunteer units were attached to the *Voltigeurs Canadiens*. Prevost estimated that these initiatives would provide him with 5,000 men. Between March and June, the legislature in Upper Canada approved the formation of a 350-man volunteer Incorporated Militia Battalion, three troops of cavalry, two artillery companies, and a corps of artillery drivers. Bounties were increased to make provincial service more lucrative, and the newly raised units in both provinces were engaged to serve for a minimum of eighteen months or for the duration of the war. The number of transport bateaux was also increased to satisfy the growing requirements of the army in Upper Canada, while the security of the convoys on the St. Lawrence was improved by the construction of additional gunboats.[3]

Prevost appointed Robert Dickson as "agent for the Indians of several nations to the Westward of Lake Huron."[4] Following the capture of Mackinac, Dickson, a fur trader, had journeyed to Lower Canada on his own initiative, to present a plan to the commander in chief to exploit British successes in the upper Mississippi Valley. Prevost directed him to encourage the aboriginal nations in that region to resist American encroachment beyond the Greenville Treaty line, the boundary between American and Native lands in the Ohio country established in 1795. In ordering the creation of this potentially sizable force, Prevost acknowledged the effect that further atrocities, such as the deaths of American soldiers and civilians at the hands of Native warriors near Fort Dearborn in August 1812, might have on American policies and advised Dickson to restrain the warriors "by all means in your power from acts of Cruelty and inhumanity."[5] Dickson, whose authority included the appointment of officers and interpreters to assist him, moved quickly, and within weeks, Native contingents were moving eastward to join in the defense of Upper Canada, while other war parties struck American outposts along the frontier. The British owed their continued influence with the Native peoples to Dickson and his officers, whose efforts contributed to the collapse of American authority in the upper Great Lakes.[6]

In January, Prevost departed Quebec for a tour of the upper province. Key among his concerns was to gain an appreciation of "the naval force to be employed on Lake Ontario in the spring," to review the "proceedings in the dockyards at Kingston and York," and to inspect the defenses.[7] Prevost left Quebec on 17 February and, averaging about seventy miles a day, arrived in the Niagara Peninsula nine days later. During a halt to change horses at Burlington Bay, he had a brief meeting with Sheaffe, the commander of Upper Canada. As there is no record of their conversation, one can only speculate it centered on topics they had discussed in correspondence, including the state of the provincial defenses, potential American actions, manpower needs, and changes to the militia. Prevost's whirlwind visit continued to Fort George and Fort Erie. In March, from temporary headquarters at Fort George, Prevost issued a series of general orders confirming the appointment of several officers to the provincial staff and announcing changes to the militia, including the formation of the provincial units described above. During his return journey to Quebec, Prevost visited York again in early March to meet with local dignitaries, to inspect a new warship under construction, and to observe firsthand the many shortages that plagued work at the dockyard. The problems he observed led to his decision to terminate plans to relocate the Lake Ontario naval base to York, and to instead concentrate it at Kingston. By the spring, Prevost, now back in Quebec, reported to Bathurst that much had been achieved but cautioned that these preparations could go only so far given the limited resources at his disposal.[8]

While he was on the Niagara Peninsula, Prevost had to resolve a disciplinary problem between the senior officers in Upper Canada. He explained to Bathurst that he had "to check a disposition that had manifested itself in that province in a cabal against the person administering the government in it" and to restore "order to the militia force."[9] Major General Sheaffe, whom Prevost had appointed as Brock's deputy in 1812 and confirmed as commander of Upper Canada later that year, was at the center of this dispute. Like Prevost, Sheaffe had been born in the American colonies and attended the Lochée Academy in London. He had served under Brock in the 49th Foot and arrived in Canada with it in 1802. In 1811, Sheaffe became a major general on the staff and was briefly considered as a replacement for Brock when it appeared the latter would be posted to Europe in 1812.

As the spring of 1813 approached, Prevost's confidence in Sheaffe, already weakened by the liberal and unauthorized concessions he had extended to the Americans during the ceasefire of the previous summer, was shaken further by reports of his difficulty in correctly deploying his troops for the final attack on the American positions at Queenston Heights. Further reports indicated problems with the measures Sheaffe had taken to defend Chippawa and Fort Erie in late 1812. Even more disturbing were murmurs questioning his leadership and advocating his resignation that circulated among officers stationed along the Niagara frontier, some of whom were appalled by Sheaffe's lack of resolution and his tendency "to weaken his exertions against the enemy."[10] Prevost put an end to this affair by censuring Sheaffe's detractors for their conduct. At York, Prevost also met with members of the legislative council, who assured him of their support. Finally, to improve the distribution of weapons and uniforms to the militia, he appointed several officers to the Quartermaster General's Department and issued instructions for the incorporation of several militia units. Prevost believed these initiatives ensured that "a proper understanding is restored in that Province."[11] While recent events had created doubts in Sheaffe's abilities, Prevost believed there were not sufficient grounds to remove him from command.[12]

During the early stages of his reconnaissance, Prevost was also involved in an event that ended predatory American attacks against settlements on the Canadian bank of the upper St. Lawrence River. From their base at Ogdensburg, a company of American riflemen had been attacking Canadian villages on the border and terrifying the civilian inhabitants. Prevost had anticipated these strikes would continue once the river froze, since it would be easier to cross at any point; therefore, in January 1813, he sent units to "strengthen the line of communication between Montreal and Kingston."[13] Other protective measures were adopted to reduce the chance of being surprised at night, including the restriction of nighttime movement and an increase in the number of sentries.

A recent raid at Brockville had resulted in American prisoners being freed and fifty-two Canadian militiamen and 120 stands of arms being captured. At Montreal, uncertainty over the security of the St. Lawrence prompted the delay of a convoy of forty sleighs carrying ordnance, naval stores, and several guns destined for Prescott until an escort could be mustered. Lieutenant Colonel Thomas Pearson, the commander at Prescott, then sent his second-in-command, Major George Macdonell, across the ice under a white flag to negotiate a suspension of the raids. The American commander was uninterested. Pearson decided to end the depredations by attacking Ogdensburg, but Major General Francis de Rottenburg, his superior in Montreal, refused him permission to do so. When Prevost arrived at Prescott on 21 February 1813, while on his way to Kingston, Pearson asked him for authorization to clear the American troops from the frontier. Prevost also refused, however, and then ordered Pearson to accompany him to Kingston, to take command of the garrison there, while Macdonell replaced him at Prescott.[14]

That evening, Macdonell repeated Pearson's request adding that Prevost's safety might be threatened as two soldiers had recently deserted to the Americans, who now probably knew of his presence at Prescott. Macdonell suggested Prevost continue his journey the next morning while he created a diversion out on the ice.[15] Prevost agreed and departed early on 22 February accompanied by Pearson. On reaching Brockville, Prevost felt it necessary to remind Macdonell not to exceed his authority and advised him "not [to] undertake military operations against Ogdensburg without previous communication from Major General de Rottenburg, unless the imbecile conduct of your enemy should offer you an opportunity for his destruction and that of his shipping, batteries and public stores."[16]

As it happened, after Prevost had departed Prescott, Macdonell immediately implemented the plan devised by Pearson and led a force of nearly 500 men onto the frozen river. Once formed, they marched across the ice and snow to Ogdensburg, where they forced the last regular American garrison on the entire upper portion of the St. Lawrence to flee to Sackets Harbor. Prevost, elated by the success, overlooked Macdonell's disobedience and praised him in a general order, issued on 25 February, for his leadership and for proceeding with this "just and necessary retaliation for that which was recently made on the British settlement of Brockville by a party from Ogdensburg."[17]

Prevost's reluctance to authorize the raid on Ogdensburg is another example offered by his critics of his supposedly cautious and

uninspiring leadership. This negative assessment is partly attributable to Macdonell, who after the war authored a series of letters,
under the nom de plume "Philalethes" (meaning "lover of truth"),
that criticized Prevost's conduct of military affairs.[18] Philalethes
claimed that after dithering over the proposed raid on Ogdensburg,
Prevost concluded the only course of action was "to send for Lieut-
Colonel Macdonell," whose success, by Macdonell's account (and
forgetting the plan was originally Pearson's idea), "saved the upper
province."[19] Macdonell's unabashed self-promotion also presented
his role in the success against the Americans at Châteauguay later
that year as a victory that was "one hundred times more of political
importance than Nelson's victory at Trafalgar."[20] Macdonell portrayed himself as a tragic hero, forced into insubordination by his
superior's ignorance and passiveness, claiming that his temper and
desire for retribution from the American officers who insulted him
during the negotiations at Ogdensburg may have been a factor. The
source of the verbal exchanges between Prevost, Pearson, and Macdonell at Prescott is anecdotal and incomplete, whereas the intent of
Prevost's letter is clear: it was not, as Macdonell claimed, a "mandate
of prohibition";[21] rather, it reminded him of his chain of command
while granting him the discretion to act on his own if conditions
warranted it. Rather than restricting Macdonell's options, Prevost
made room for Macdonell's zeal, which he later acknowledged while
expressing his own faith in his subordinate's judgment.[22]

Aside from his personal reconnaissance of Upper Canada, Prevost also sent Lieutenant Colonel Ralph Bruyeres, commander of the
Royal Engineers in Canada, to survey the principal posts throughout the province to develop plans for their improvement and to identify requirements for new fortifications. To counter the threat of
small, but irritating and disruptive raids by enemy forces against
communities along the upper St. Lawrence River, the fortifications
along the entire line of communications were strengthened. Prevost approved the construction or enhancement of fortifications at
a dozen sites between Coteau du Lac and Kingston. Gun positions
were established, defensive works built, and a fort begun at the important post of Prescott. Other work was ordered to improve the
defenses at York and the posts along the Niagara River.[23]

The most important change to the composition of the defenses
of the Canadas came in the spring of 1813 when the Royal Navy

replaced the Provincial Marine. In early May, Commodore James Yeo and his detachment of officers and sailors arrived at Quebec. Prevost greeted Yeo at Montreal and informed the commodore he would accompany him to Kingston. The journey provided an excellent opportunity for Prevost to discuss plans with Yeo and to establish a good working relationship with him. Cooperation between service commanders in the nineteenth century was, as it is today, largely a function of personality. Familiarity and understanding between commanders often eased the potential for misunderstanding, as had occurred between Prevost and Brock. Admiral Warren may have attempted to quell any doubts that Prevost might have of Yeo by writing him that "I think you will like him."[24] There is no record of their discussions, and one can only surmise that Prevost and Yeo spoke of the importance of regaining naval superiority on Lake Ontario and retaining control of the other lakes. Their exchange may also have touched on the command arrangements between them, naval support to the army, naval personnel, and the logistical requirements of the navy. Prevost undoubtedly learned more about Yeo's career during their journey.[25]

Yeo was well respected in the Royal Navy for his bravery, intelligence, and energy. He had joined the service in 1793 and established a reputation for audacity and bravery by leading several actions against enemy shore batteries and dockyard installations in the Mediterranean and on the Portuguese coast. He received command of the 22-gun *Confiance* in June 1805 and then gained considerable fame and honors for taking Cayenne in French Guiana in 1809.[26] He was knighted the following year and then given command of the 32-gun frigate *Southampton* in 1811. In early 1812, while on the Jamaica station, Yeo captured three French vessels before suffering a setback in November when his ship and an American brig he had seized ran aground on an uncharted reef in the Bahamas. Both vessels sank, however, and Yeo was exonerated at a court-martial for the loss of his command.[27]

For Prevost, the arrival of the Royal Navy solved his problems with the inefficiency of the Provincial Marine, but it also meant that control of naval affairs became complicated since the commodore's appointment brought subtle changes to the conduct of maritime warfare on the lakes. Prevost no longer had the superintendence of the Naval Department, and communication on naval affairs was now between Yeo, Admiral Warren in Halifax, and the Admiralty in London. However, since the Lords Commissioners of the Royal Navy and Warren had no means of communications into the Canadas, there would be no changes to the arrangements for storing and victualing the vessels on the lakes, which remained under Prevost's authority. Furthermore, as there were not enough seamen to crew all the vessels completely, Yeo would have to call on Prevost to make up the shortfalls. After distributing the able seamen he brought with him among the different vessels of the squadron, Yeo would then draw on most if not all of the Provincial Marine personnel. Any vacancies would have to be made up from the army. Yeo was thus required to develop a manning scheme with Prevost.[28]

In anticipation of Yeo's arrival, Prevost had ordered the Quartermaster General to prepare a plan for the employment of Provincial Marine officers, a proposed distribution of naval and military personnel on the vessels, and a comparative assessment of British and American naval forces on the lakes. Prevost and Yeo studied these details to ensure that "every facility may be afforded" to Yeo "in the accomplishment of the important object for which he has been sent from England"[29]—namely, the "great necessity of maintaining naval superiority on the lakes."[30] Prevost's plans would have appealed to a daring officer like Yeo, who, like the commander in chief, realized that achieving these goals would require aggressive action. For his part, Prevost was anxious to satisfy the needs of the navy because it was an important and powerful augmentation to his strength and provided the only resource he had that could guarantee control of the inland waters and achieve the ultimate security of the Canadas. The Prevost-Yeo command relationship would therefore prove the most important British command relationship of the war.[31]

Yeo's instructions from the Admiralty, the center of naval administration, stated that "the first and paramount object for which this Naval Force is maintained" was "the defence of His Majesty's Provinces of North America."[32] He was directed to cooperate with Prevost and to not undertake "any operations without the full concurrence and approbation of him" and "on all occasions conforming yourself and employing the Force under your command according to the Requisitions which you may from time to time receive . . . from the said Governor or Commander of the Forces."[33] These instructions were reinforced by orders from the first secretary of the Admiralty, John W. Croker, who instructed Yeo to consult with Prevost and arrange "all the various particulars of the important Services to which our joint efforts will be directed."[34] This was not all. Yeo was also expected to respond to direction from the Admiralty, and he was also under the supervision of Admiral Warren. The language of command arrangements in the early nineteenth century was not as precise as it is today, yet the intent of the Admiralty and its first secretary is clear: Yeo's operations were to conform to those of Prevost; the difficulty, however, was that he also had two other distant superiors, and if he wanted to, Yeo could play one against the other, or ignore all of them and do as he wished.[35]

In addition to his overall responsibilities, Yeo was authorized to "hoist a distinguishing Pendant as Commodore on Board such one of His Majesty's Ships as you might select"[36] and hold tactical command of the Lake Ontario squadron. It was usual practice for fleet and squadron commanders to base themselves afloat, rather than on shore, but Yeo's situation was unique in that he was responsible for not one but several bodies of water, with each respective command independent of the others.[37] Geography made it impossible to shift vessels between Lake Ontario and Lake Erie or combine them into a single squadron. Yeo chose to hoist his pennant on Lake Ontario, strategically the most important lake within his command, and he appointed as acting commander over the squadron on Lake Erie Robert Barclay, who was given a detachment of three lieutenants and twenty-two other personnel. Administratively, the entirety of the Royal Navy forces serving on the Great Lakes was subordinate to the army, and personnel were assigned en masse to one set of books rather than against a fixed establishment for each vessel. This arrangement left Yeo with absolute authority to assign personnel to each lake without any regard for the approved manning strengths for individual vessels, and he had the power to refuse appeals for more manpower from his subordinates on Lakes Erie and Champlain.[38]

Yeo's arrival in early May 1813 brought new energy to the naval squadron as he set about preparing his ships and men for action. He ensured that his personnel were properly placed and noted any shortfalls that still existed. He redistributed guns throughout the squadron to allow a more even firepower. These initiatives created much excitement at the dockyard and in Kingston, as it was apparent the navy was going on the offensive with new vigor. Yeo's energy masked his concerns regarding the relative weakness of his squadron and the advantage on Lake Ontario that Chauncey currently enjoyed, but he counted on the benefits new construction would bring. However, he feared that expansion of his squadron would be limited by a shortage of trained seamen. He also realized that if Chauncey's building program was not checked, the American squadron would soon be too formidable for him to fight.[39]

IN April 1813, when the campaign season opened, the United States immediately exploited their control of Lake Ontario. Plans were made to attack three objectives around the lake—Kingston, York, and Fort George on the Niagara Peninsula—with a joint attack force that included 5,000 regulars and militia assembled at Sackets Harbor. As American intelligence indicated the defenses at Kingston were formidable—an assessment that was fueled by Prevost's passage through there earlier in the year—it was decided to attack York first and then hold it until a relief force was detached from Fort George to reclaim it. The Americans would then make a lightning move across Lake Ontario, reduce that fort, and, aided by an army that would cross the river, secure the Canadian side of the Niagara; and afterward, a blockade was to be established at Kingston to contain the British naval squadron. Commodore Chauncey would then proceed "with all the officers and men that could be spared direct to Lake Erie" and then "destroy" British "naval power as soon as possible, attack and take Malden and Detroit, & proceed into Lake Huron and attack & carry Machilimackinac [Mackinac]."[40] This plan was complex in design and offered many challenges in execution. It was also dependent on the British responding in a particular manner.

The American object at York was to destroy naval stores and weaken British naval strength by capturing two 18-gun brigs under construction at the dockyard and the Provincial Marine schooners *Prince Regent* and *Duke of Gloucester* (reported to be carrying eighteen and sixteen guns, respectively), which, according to Chauncey's sources, were wintering at the provincial capital. The attack on York, which occurred on 27 April 1813, demonstrated the power of Chauncey's squadron and growing American amphibious capabilities, which in this case allowed them to transport 1,700 men, under the overall command of Major General Henry Dearborn, across Lake Ontario. At York, Major General Robert Sheaffe could muster only 413 regulars, 477 militiamen, 50 Native warriors, and about 100 miscellaneous personnel comprising his staff, town volunteers, and members of the Provincial Marine, while the town's main defenses included a fort, four battery positions, and several unarmed works. The process of establishing a post of defense at York had begun prior to the war when it had been decided to move the naval dockyard from Kingston, but by 1813, little had been done. Sheaffe actually anticipated a determined attack on York would likely succeed and hoped to finish *Sir Isaac Brock*, the sole vessel being built at the dockyard, before the Americans could sail. He had sent the *Prince Regent* to Kingston once the ice had cleared. Completion of the *Brock* was delayed, however, by supply problems and difficulties between the shipbuilder and government officials.[41]

During the morning of 27 April 1813, the Americans commenced landing a large body of troops to the west of the town. Sheaffe, who had been overseeing the preparation of the defenses, sent a detachment of regulars, militia, and Natives to meet them, but the direct route to the landing site was interdicted by American naval fire, forcing them to take a longer inland approach that prevented their arriving before the Americans were ashore. The delay in reaching the landing site forced Sheaffe to commit his reserve to support the Native warriors who were engaging the enemy. Superior numbers and fire support from Chauncey's squadron overwhelmed the defenders, who began to withdraw to York, with the Americans in pursuit. Sheaffe twice rallied his men, but they were unable to slow the attackers. By the time he reached Fort York, Sheaffe realized the battle was lost and ordered the *Brock* and the naval supplies burned. He then prepared to withdraw to Kingston, leaving the militia, which had arrived too late to influence the outcome, to surrender the town. In addition, he ordered the detonation of the grand magazine at Fort York, which occurred just as the Americans approached the fort. The debris from the explosion caused 250 American casualties, including Brigadier General Zebulon Pike, commander of the assault force. Contrary winds and poor weather forced Dearborn and Chauncey to remain at York for several days, and once they left, fatigue and sickness had weakened their men so much that Dearborn canceled plans for a direct assault on Fort George, and the squadron returned to Sackets Harbor to rest and refit. The Americans had gained a partial triumph with the destruction of the *Brock*, which it completed would have added a 30-gun frigate to Yeo's squadron and given the British the advantage on the lake. Furthermore, the loss of the naval stores would also have a detrimental effect on fitting out the Lake Erie squadron. Chauncey's intelligence had been false, however, as there was no vessel being built at York other than the *Brock* and the *Duke of Gloucester* proved to be a condemned schooner that was towed to Sackets Harbor, where it was renamed *York* and employed as a floating magazine.[42]

After the Americans left York, several prominent citizens of the town complained to Prevost that Sheaffe had been indecisive during the attack, withdrew prematurely from the action, and then hastily abandoned the town. Prevost concluded that Sheaffe had lost the confidence of the population and had to be relieved "for the good of the public service."[43] On 26 May 1813, he ordered Major General Francis de Rottenburg to assume command of Upper Canada. Sheaffe arrived at Kingston on 2 June 1813. Prevost joined him two weeks later, then held several interviews with the defeated general, undoubtedly touching on the attack on York and his dismissal. The decision to replace Sheaffe became public in early June when he was instructed to meet de Rottenburg at Cornwall and conduct a handover, after which de Rottenburg was to be in Kingston no later than 20 June.[44]

Historian Robert Malcomson believes that Prevost dismissed Sheaffe to deflect responsibility for the U.S. occupation of York away from himself. As American interest in the provincial capital was sparked by the construction of the *Sir Isaac Brock*, the presence of the *Prince Regent*, and the stockpiling of naval and military stores, more should have been done to ready the defenses. Warnings of a pending American attack against the dockyard went unnoticed. Across the lake, Chauncey concluded that "the exertions of the Enemy to create a force this winter superior to ours" required "corresponding exertions on our part to defeat their plans and destroy their hopes."[45] Fears that the addition of the ships at York to those in Kingston would give the British naval dominance led Chauncey to propose attacking Kingston and York to prevent that from occurring.

The fact is that Prevost cannot be blamed for the outcome at York. Assessments regarding the relative strengths of the Kingston and York garrisons resulted from exaggerated intelligence reports and the perceptions shared by Commodore Isaac Chauncey and Major General Henry Dearborn, who inflated the estimated figures even further. In reality, the strengths of the two garrisons during April 1813 were similar. There were 413 British regulars and 477 militia at York, while Kingston had 584 regulars and about 450 militia. It was faulty intelligence that led Chauncey to recommend striking York instead of Kingston, and he boasted to the secretary of the navy that the destruction or capture of "the *Prince Regent* of 18 guns, the *Duke of Gloucester* of 16 guns and two brigs building calculated to carry 18 guns each," would give him "complete command of the lake."[46] The British naval presence at York, however, was not as impressive as Chauncey believed. The *Prince Regent* had returned to Kingston days before the assault, and the unrigged *Duke of Gloucester* proved to be of little value. The two brigs said to be near launching did not exist, and charred timbers marked the spot where the *Brock* once stood. The destruction of the naval dockyard was unfortunate, but the loss of a vast quantity of stores to the Americans was of greater significance. Far from crippling the British Lake Ontario squadron, the attack on York proved disappointing to the attackers and with more than 300 casualties, the Americans had to delay their attack on Fort George and return to Sackets Harbor.[47]

Prevost took several lessons from York. Expansion of U.S. naval power, improvements to their regular army, and their naval control of Lake Ontario had provided the Americans with the capability to strike anywhere on the British shore, as had been demonstrated to great effect at the provincial capital. The scale, complexity, and boldness of this action were unlike anything that had been attempted thus far during the war, and Prevost found his opponent challenging the British with increasing confidence. American naval strength and operational flexibility threatened British outposts around the lake and outstripped Prevost's ability to defend all important localities adequately or to shift resources between them in response to changing threats, as had been done during 1812. The destruction of British naval power and the subsequent American dominance of Lake Ontario might have given the United States a decisive victory in the war but it did not. The attack on York did not affect the British squadron, now safely concentrated at Kingston, and kept the Americans away from the important Kingston–Montreal corridor. The Americans had also demonstrated that York was not the safe haven the British believed it to be, while at the same time fears of Kingston's vulnerability dissipated. Provost could take satisfaction in the conclusion he had reached in March that Kingston would be the primary naval base on Lake Ontario.

While Prevost dealt with the results of the raid on York, the enemy struck again and on 27 May 1813, following a two-day bombardment of Fort George, an American army landed on the Niagara Peninsula. Its objective was to encircle and capture British forces in the area of Fort George, but Brigadier General John Vincent, commanding in the Niagara region, had anticipated that the Americans might be too strong for his own forces and implemented a contingency plan to withdraw his command to the safety of Burlington Heights.[48] The following day, two American brigades, totaling 3,000 soldiers, set out in pursuit. Heavily outnumbered, and with Chauncey commanding Lake Ontario, the British found themselves in a difficult situation.[49]

Prevost was in Kingston, where, on 26 May, after studying reports that Fort George was under a tremendous bombardment that had begun on the previous day, he concluded this was a prelude to an enemy assault on the fort and proposed a bold plan to relieve pressure in the Niagara Peninsula and to divert American attention. He would attack the enemy naval base at Sackets Harbor. Prevost first conceived this idea on 22 May, when an American spy confirmed that Chauncey's squadron was at the western end of the lake. He ordered Yeo to reconnoiter Sackets Harbor during the night of 26 May, and at noon the next day, Yeo confirmed that Chauncey's squadron was absent and that the garrison appeared to be weak. Once he knew that Fort George was under heavy bombardment, and that Chauncey was supporting the assault on the fort, Prevost appointed Colonel Edward Baynes to command the raid and began planning in earnest. Prevost was "determined in attempting a diversion in Colonel Vincent's favour by embarking the principal part of this small garrison of this place and proceeding with them to Sackett's Harbour."[50] During 27 May, units were mustered and the squadron readied for departure.[51]

If Prevost's critics are accurate in portraying him as a cautious, defensive-minded commander, the raid on Sackets Harbor provides considerable evidence to the contrary. Prevost was proposing to mount a joint attack against an enemy naval base while the American squadron was still on the lake in strength. There were many unknowns. Yeo's officers and men were about to sail on Lake Ontario for the first time and knew little of the nautical conditions—the lake had not yet been charted—or the handling of their ships. The prospect of this operation would have appealed to the audacious commodore, yet one wonders if his subordinates shared the same confidence. Few details were known about Sackets Harbor, other than that a new ship was being built there. The British would find that the recently expanded defenses included two forts and several batteries mounting at least seventeen guns. There was no clear indication of enemy strength, and nobody in Kingston was aware that they would be facing 1,500 American regulars, plus New York state militia, and naval and marine personnel, totaling about twice the strength of the British attacking force.[52]

The 900-man assault force included most of the Kingston garrison and Yeo's Lake Ontario squadron. It was drawn from the light companies of eight different regiments and included two field artillery pieces and forty warriors. Less than one-third of the regular troops had seen any action at all. Yeo's squadron included 800 sailors distributed between five ships, a merchantman, thirty-three bateaux, three gunboats, and several canoes, with his warships mounting a total of 82 guns. With only a single civilian transport to carry part of the infantry and the two field guns, most of the soldiers were crowded on the open decks of the warships, leaving little room for the crews to do their work, and the extra load carried on each vessel affected its handling. An unfortunate few were also carried in the bateaux, which were towed behind the ships, for the thirty-six-mile journey. Just before sailing, a canoe delivered Prevost and his staff to Yeo's flagship, the *Wolfe*.[53]

The squadron got under way at night on 27 May and made good progress until early the next morning when the wind died. During the night, an American schooner spotted the squadron and fired a shot to warn the garrison at the harbor before returning to base. By 4:30 A.M. on 28 May, the squadron was within sight of the harbor, about ten miles away. At dawn, Captain Andrew Gray made another reconnaissance, while the troops made preparations to land. Upon his return at 9:00 A.M., Gray reported the welcome news that the American base appeared weakly defended. Elated by the report, one officer actually ordered his troops into the bateaux and began heading for shore, only to be called back by Prevost. An hour later the flotilla was still seven miles from its objective when the wind faltered. Yeo then decided to make a personal reconnaissance, and when he returned at 3:00 P.M., he and Baynes agreed to call off the attack, and the squadron turned back toward Kingston. Shortly thereafter, the wind shifted against the British again. Meanwhile, a detachment of thirty-seven Natives and a number of regulars that had been sent out from the squadron in three canoes and a gunboat captured 115 American reinforcements en route to Sackets Harbor. Encouraged, Baynes and the other senior officers now decided that the ease by which fifteen boats from the American convoy had been captured—most of the 130 survivors in the remaining boats had landed at Stoney Point and scattered into the woods and only a single boat made it safely to Sackets Harbor—meant that the troops at Sackets Harbor were of poor quality. It was agreed to proceed with the attack, and Prevost gave his consent.[54]

It is not clear to what extent Prevost influenced any of these decisions. An account by Midshipman David Wingfield, who was serving on Yeo's flagship, and who recorded his views many years afterward, stated that the cancellation order "emanated from the Governor General of the Provinces . . . and . . . Sir James was obliged to obey though much against his will."[55] Other sources offer conflicting evidence. Edward Brenton, Prevost's civilian secretary, accompanied the expedition, and he would have remained close to Prevost and been privy to many important discussions. Just after the raid, he recorded that Prevost "had not been a little surprised" that the senior officers previously entertained doubt of the raid "being undertaken."[56] The decision to cancel was, as Brenton wrote in 1823, the "unanimous opinion of the principal officers of the expedition under Colonel Baynes . . . together with Sir James Yeo."[57] Clearly, Prevost would not have sat quietly by while this discussion was in progress. Could it have been that while the senior officers debated the merits of continuing, Prevost intervened in Baynes's favor? Or did Prevost simply seek to end the "altercation"[58] between Baynes and Yeo, which Wingfield interpreted as Prevost having made the decision himself? Brenton claims that the "first time" Prevost intervened to give a direct order was after the landing, following the failure of the initial assault.[59] Prevost is said to have told Baynes to regroup and attack again. As a civilian, Brenton may have not fully understood the nuances of military decision making, whereas Wingfield may have been overly supportive of Yeo, his commander. Despite the lack of clear evidence to indicate whether Prevost intervened or not, his presence must have had a powerful influence on those present, and by virtue of his rank and position, he would almost certainly have been consulted.[60]

In any case, the decision to continue with the raid came late in the day of 28 May, and as the squadron was still some distance from the proposed landing site, it was forced to remain outside the harbor that night. Several participants claimed that this added delay allowed the Americans time to muster the militia and take up their defensive positions; which might have been avoided had Yeo's recommendation for an immediate assault been acted on. This is not true, however. Had the landings been conducted on the late evening or night of 28 May, the attackers would have found the defenders already in position, with the coming darkness in their favor.[61]

The defenses of Sackets Harbor were considerable. Colonel Alexander Macomb, the officer who commanded the garrison in early 1813, had correctly anticipated the British would avoid a direct descent as the approaches were well covered by the guns of two forts. Instead, they would establish a foothold on Horse Island about a mile west, cross a narrow channel to the mainland, and then advance toward the village. Even if the British overwhelmed the troops defending Horse Island, they would still have to negotiate a massive obstacle constructed from hundreds of felled trees, known as an abatis, that encircled the town and dockyard. No attack materialized, but in early May, concern for the safety of the dockyard began to mount, following Chauncey's departure for the Niagara frontier, which left the naval stores and the *General Pike*, the new ship under construction, a tempting target. The defenders, now reinforced by regulars, relied on the expectation that the British would come ashore at Horse Island, and a force of nearly 800 state militia and two guns were positioned there and on the mainland shore to resist the landings and maintain pressure on the British until they reached the main American defenses, which were centered on two log barracks. Here a regiment of dismounted dragoons and elements of three regular infantry regiments, equivalent in number to the entire British assault force, were expected to defeat any attack. Behind them was Fort Tompkins, surrounded by a stockade and armed with a powerful 32-pounder gun; farther beyond that, in the low ground, was Navy Point, a peninsula covered by six guns ranging from 12- to 32-pounders manned by experienced sailors. Overlooking the harbor from the high ground to the east was Fort Volunteer, which was armed with six or seven guns. Altogether the strength of the defenders amounted to 1,500 men and sixteen or seventeen pieces of ordnance, which outnumbered the attacker's ground force and also enjoyed an eight-to-one advantage in artillery. To reach the naval base, the British would have to sweep aside the militia protecting the beachhead, get through the abatis, and then overwhelm the regulars in the main defensive area. Even this was no guarantee of success, for the Americans were prepared to destroy the naval warehouses and their ship rather than let them to fall to the British.[62]

The British commenced their landings on the morning of 29 May. It is unlikely that Prevost played any role in the landings, the consolidation of the landing site, and the initial move inland. He and his staff would only land once a beachhead was secured on the mainland. Baynes then divided his force into two groups. One column under Colonel Robert Young advanced toward the naval dockyard using the shore road, and a second group under Major William Drummond (who had received a light wound during the landing) took a route farther inland, to the right of Young. Prevost likely marched with Young's column. The two artillery pieces that had been brought could not be unloaded from the merchantman, so artillery support was limited to fire from the gunboats and HMS *Beresford*, whose captain ordered the use of sweeps to row his vessel into the inlet.[63]

About an hour later, the two columns reunited with Young on the left and Drummond on the right. Before them were three barracks buildings. Baynes ordered "an impromptu attack"[64] against the barracks, but it was beaten back "with heavy loss."[65] Meanwhile, Colonel Young, who had been ill when he embarked at Kingston, was unable to continue and returned to the landing site. Major Drummond then suffered a second wound, but he continued leading

his element. By this point, the supporting fire from the British gunboats ended, as the line of fire was masked by a rise in the ground.
Baynes was now in a difficult position: he faced a strong, entrenched
enemy with clear fields of fire and artillery support, while his infantry were in the open with no artillery support and his force had
been reduced by this time to some 300 men.[66]

Prevost now intervened and ordered a second attack. The right of
the British line faced overwhelming fire and was rebuffed, but the
troops on the left cleared one of the barracks buildings. An attempt
to cross the open space to the next barracks was met by heavy fire,
however, and more casualties were suffered. Among the wounded
were two senior officers, Major Robert Moodie of the 104th and
Major Thomas Evans, commanding the companies from the 8th
Foot. Another key officer, Captain Andrew Gray, who had helped
plan the landings, was killed. Major William Drummond took a
message to the Americans demanding their surrender, which was
refused. Baynes, who had limited command experience, was uncertain what to do next and consulted Prevost. The commander in
chief intervened a second and final time, ordering the force to withdraw and reembark.[67]

It was the correct decision. The British attack force had been
ashore for five hours at this point and while they had advanced inland more than 1,200 yards nearly unmolested and were now at the
last obstacle before the dockyard, this progress proved deceptive.
The infantry had taken casualties of approximately 30 percent, and
three of the key officers—Young, Evans, and Drummond—were unable to continue. The attackers were unable to break through the
Americans' main defensive position, where the protected defenders
enjoyed artillery support. Many soldiers were running around aim-
lessly and in confusion. To some observers, it appeared that the
Americans were fleeing from Fort Tompkins, while other witnesses
believed the columns of dust near the village signaled the approach
of enemy reinforcements.[68]

At this critical moment, Prevost directed his attention back toward the stationary British squadron and considered where the
American fleet might be. If Chauncey's squadron arrived, it would
be disastrous—the combined British force might be captured in its
entirety, or intercepted as it returned to Kingston. In a possible naval engagement, the British squadron would have difficulty

maneuvering against the trimmed enemy vessels as the British decks would have been filled with soldiers and equipment. At no time did Yeo, however, express any concern. Rather, he left his squadron and, instead of supervising naval support to the operation, went ashore where he was seen "running in front of and with our men . . . cheering our men on."[69] The result was that most of the squadron and its powerful guns remained out of the battle, several miles away. The only British vessels to participate in the battle—gunboats armed with a single 24-pounder carronade each and the 12-gun schooner *Beresford*—did so on the initiative of their commanders and not from an express order by Yeo.

Prevost's fears of a sudden appearance by Chauncey were never realized—in fact, the American commodore did not learn of the raid until 30 May. He departed from the western end of the lake on the morning of the 31st and, when he returned, decided, after a period of "mature reflection," to remain in Sackets Harbor to await the completion of the *Pike*, which would give him command of the lake.[70] However, the new ship would not be ready until mid-July, which delay gave Yeo control of the lake for two months.[71]

Prevost was strongly criticized for his decision to withdraw. Various firsthand comments, largely from junior personnel, have been subsequently used by historians in their critical assessments of the commander in chief.[72] A junior officer, Lieutenant John Le Couteur of the 104th Foot, termed the raid a "scandalously-managed affair";[73] moreover, he believed Prevost was misguided in his decision to withdraw as he "mistook the body of three thousand Americans . . . I saw in retreat for fresh reinforcement."[74] Le Couteur claims that he was not the only disappointed member of the expedition and that, during the return to Kingston, "the murmurs against Sir George were deep, not loud."[75] Members of the Royal Navy had similar feelings. Yeo, who had landed with the troops during the assault, wrote that "the troops after gaining decided advantages were reluctantly ordered to re-embark."[76] Ship's Master James Richardson recorded a comment made by an unidentified senior officer: "Oh, if he [Prevost] would but give me my own regiment, I would land again, and take the place."[77] Midshipman David Wingfield called the raid a "disgraceful affair," as "the place would have been taken without the loss of a single man had things been conducted as they ought."[78] Wingfield believed that the failed attack affected the relationship between Prevost and Yeo: "this disgraceful affair caused a coolness between the Governor and Commodore, and at length broke out into an open rupture."[79]

Historians are almost universal in their condemnation of Prevost's decision to withdraw. Wesley Turner writes that Prevost had little to show from the raid as he "failed to capture Sackets Harbor or even inflict much damage."[80] Turner questions Prevost's decision to place himself at risk by accompanying "what was simply a quick raid" rather than a "carefully planned and powerful invasion of enemy territory."[81] According to J. Mackay Hitsman, Prevost showed "poor judgement" against the "few American regulars and militia" that opposed him.[82] William S. Dudley believes Prevost's indecision while crossing Lake Ontario delayed the operation and provided ample warning for the defenders to strengthen their defenses and rally the troops. Historian Patrick Wilder, author of the only book-length study of the Sackets Harbor operation, uses the first-hand accounts quoted above to convey the idea that "in the eyes of many, Prevost was to blame" for the failure.[83]

British historian John Fortescue offers a different perspective. He observes that Prevost lacked the professional skill to lead an amphibious operation. This was not a particular fault attributable to Prevost since within the British Army there were "very few men who are qualified to direct the joint operations of a squadron and an army, and unfortunately Prevost was not one of them."[84] George F. G. Stanley opines that Prevost failed to appreciate the importance the Americans attached to their base at Sackets Harbor and should have used a larger assault force and pressed the final "attack regardless of the risk and sacrifice involved,"[85] although Stanley fails to suggest where those additional troops could have been found in so short a time. Stanley concludes the outcome demonstrated that Prevost was a "fumbling, indecisive commander, lacking in leadership and firm resolution."[86]

Not all historians have shared these views. In an unpublished study of the raid prepared for the Canadian Department of National Defence, historian Donald E. Graves highlights the "inescapable conclusion that the British commanders exhibited indecision, poor judgement and a lack of resolve,"[87] and acknowledges that the "attack had very little to show for the over 200 casualties it suffered."[88] Graves believes, however, that while "Prevost has borne the brunt of the criticism that arose out of the operation," it was Colonel Edward Baynes, the nominal commander of the expedition, and Yeo, the naval commander, who "made all the major command decisions until very late in the operation," and who therefore must bear responsibility for the defeat.[89]

Fortescue's claim that Britain lacked experience in amphibious operations is not supported by the operational record. During the course of the French Revolutionary and Napoleonic Wars, the British conducted sixty-eight major amphibious operations and dozens of minor landings, though few of these landings were made against a defended shore, such as at Sackets Harbor. The main French islands in the West Indies were captured twice in this fashion, and several Dutch-held islands were also taken. In March 1801, the landing of 15,000 soldiers at Aboukir Bay in Egypt was an achievement that demonstrated the importance of careful planning, preparation, rehearsal and harmonious cooperation between the army and naval commanders that contributed to the French surrender in August. The navy delivered an army of 19,000 men to Walcheren in July 1809 and opened the Peninsular Campaign by landing a combined army of 30,000 men at Mondego Bay in Portugal during the following month. A fleet also rescued 26,000 men from General Sir John Moore's army at La Coruna in January 1809. No general doctrine seems to have existed at the time, and legally there was no provision for placing the forces of one service under the other. In other words, success was dependent on a variety of factors, including cooperation between admirals and generals, training, good decision making, management of resources, an understanding of people, and the ability to defeat the opponent's plan. Institutional experience, as the British enjoyed in 1813, does not necessarily translate into such success as the Americans, whose introduction to amphibious warfare really came only in the spring of 1813, demonstrated at York and Fort George.[90]

The essential truth is that the Americans had anticipated where the British would land and had prepared their defenses accordingly. They developed an effective, layered defense that used obstacles to wear down the British. The struggle reached a crescendo at the main American position at the cantonment, where the buildings aided the defenders. The British field pieces could not be landed, and contrary winds limited naval participation in the battle to the guns of the *Beresford*, brought forward by using sweeps on the initiative of its captain, while the remainder of the British squadron remained motionless several miles away. The gunboats under Commander William Mulcaster supported the advance from the beachhead, until the rising shoreline masked their fire. The final British assault was unsupported. There is no real evidence that success could have been achieved had the attack continued and every reason to believe that British casualties would have mounted. The raid was one of the most costly actions the British conducted in the northern theater; the casualties suffered were greater than those at Queenston Heights, York (regular casualties only), Stoney Creek, Châteauguay, and Crysler's Farm. Prevost's decision to withdraw was prudent, especially given his uncertainty as to Chauncey's movements.[91]

One key outcome of the raid on Sackets Harbor is undisputed—that is, Chauncey's decision, following the attack, to withdraw naval support for the American army at the head of Lake Ontario (which he had desired to do since the fall of Fort George) and then to remain in port to protect his new ship. This decision was a major turning point of the war because it allowed control of Lake Ontario, which had been held to such advantage by Chauncey since November 1812, now to pass to Yeo. Prevost immediately exploited this turn of events by sending the commodore to deliver 220 men of the 8th Foot along with much-needed supplies to Vincent's army at Burlington Bay. Commodore Yeo sailed on 3 June. Meanwhile, Vincent approved a plan put forward by Lieutenant Colonel John Harvey to attack the American camp at nearby Stoney Creek. During a night action on 5–6 June 1813, 700 British troops confronted more than 3,000 Americans, captured their two generals, and left the defenders in disarray. On 7 June, the Americans withdrew eastward to Forty Mile Creek.[92] By this time, Yeo had arrived and worked out a plan with Vincent to cut off the American force, but Dearborn, the U.S. commander at Fort George, fearing this might occur, ordered it to withdraw to the fort. This movement was hastened by pressure from Native warriors, British infantry, and bombardment by Yeo's squadron.[93] By the second week of June, all American forces were back at Fort George and by and large remained there for the summer. Encouraged by these successes, Yeo next ranged around Lake Ontario ferrying troops, bombarding shore targets, landing raiding parties and even preparing another assault on Sackets Harbor—which was canceled once the element of surprise was lost—before anchoring off Kingston at the end of June.[94]

The first American offensives of 1813 had been blunted, but the British had not defeated their enemy. With the Americans checked in the Niagara Peninsula and with Yeo's squadron growing in strength, the time seemed right for the commodore to engage Chauncey directly and secure control of the lake once and for all. But the enemy had similar designs on Lake Ontario and were about to strike elsewhere. The campaign of 1813 was far from over.

6

THE CANADAS SURVIVE REPEATED INVASION

June to December 1813

His Majesty's forces continue proudly to maintain their respective
positions against the efforts of a greatly superior numerical force.
—*Prevost to Bathurst, 22 September 1813*

As we have seen, the Americans had ambitious offensive plans
for 1813—plans that would exploit their control of Lake Ontario by attacking three objectives in Upper Canada: York, Fort
George on the Niagara Peninsula, and Kingston. On 27 April, the
second campaign season of the war opened with the attack on York,
which proved only partially successful. Intelligence that the Provincial Marine warships were based there proved to be incorrect,
and the death of the capable Brigadier General Zebulon Pike was a
serious loss. In May, the Americans landed on the peninsula, and
following the retreat of Brigadier General John Vincent's Center
Division to Burlington Heights, they took Fort George. Two brigades
were then sent in pursuit of Vincent, but in early June, the Americans withdrew eastward to Forty Mile Creek, after an attack by British troops on their camp at Stoney Creek. Meanwhile, at the other
end of Lake Ontario, Prevost ordered an attack on the U.S. naval
base at Sackets Harbor; though failing to achieve its objective, it
ended U.S. naval support of the land forces on the Niagara Peninsula. Commodore Chauncey withdrew to Sackets Harbor, remaining there until his new warship, the USS *Pike*, was completed. The
planned American attack on Kingston was put in abeyance until
Chauncey had regained naval control of Lake Ontario. With the lake
now in British hands, Prevost sent Yeo, along with reinforcements

and supplies, to join Vincent at Burlington Heights, and together they harassed the American force, forcing it to withdraw from Forty Mile Creek to Fort George. With the situation on the peninsula stabilized, Prevost and Yeo agreed conditions warranted an attempt by the latter to gain control of Lake Ontario through a classic naval action. During August and September, the Royal Navy met the U.S. Navy in four engagements that proved inconclusive as neither naval commander dared to risk his force in a major battle. Disappointed with the results, Prevost instructed Yeo to concentrate on supporting the army, while he dealt with mounting evidence of a new threat to Upper Canada. Growing U.S. naval strength on Lake Erie was threatening the line of communication to Major General Henry Procter's army at Detroit and the Royal Navy squadron based at Amherstburg under the command of Robert Barclay.

In contrast to 1812, when Prevost moved no closer to the scene of the fighting than Montreal due the demands of the civil government, he spent much of 1813 in Upper Canada. Reports and instructions could be passed faster from Kingston, and being at the naval base afforded Prevost the opportunity to supervise the distribution of stores and troops to where they were needed and coordinate the activity of the navy with the army. These were the primary means Prevost had, as a commander in chief, to influence the operational situation. Prevost regularly ventured farther west to gain an appreciation of the military situation and to consult with subordinate commanders. During most of 1813, he dealt directly with three officers: Major General Francis de Rottenburg, the commander of Upper Canada; Major General John Vincent on the Niagara Peninsula; and Major General Henry Procter on the Detroit frontier.[1] For Prevost, communication with Vincent was simplest and fastest as he could be reached by marching around or sailing across Lake Ontario. Detroit lay at the end of a line of communication more than 350 miles in length that required marching around or sailing across Lake Ontario, then moving by land across the Niagara Peninsula to Lake Erie, and finally traveling along the northern shore of that lake and then across the river to Detroit.[2]

Following the April 1813 debacle at York, Prevost had appointed Major General Sir Francis de Rottenburg to replace Major General Roger Sheaffe as the administrator and commander of Upper

Canada. Polish by birth, de Rottenburg joined the British army in 1795 and gained a reputation as a light infantry specialist. He had commanded a brigade of light troops during the Walcheren expedition of 1809 and arrived in British North America the following year. He served on Prevost's staff until he was placed in command of the Montreal district in 1812. As he was the next senior general officer in North America after Sheaffe, de Rottenburg was the logical successor to the outgoing commander, but his appointment also reveals the limited choices Prevost had to fill senior command positions. Aside from Lieutenant General John Sherbrooke, commanding in Nova Scotia, Prevost had only one other officer, de Rottenburg, of high enough "character and established reputation" to whom "he could entrust with the responsibility."[3] At fifty-five, de Rottenburg was older than the other generals in Canada, including Prevost, and this has led some historians to suggest that he was too elderly for the rigors of command.[4]

If his age was a factor, de Rottenburg's appointment was intended to be a temporary one. Prevost's complaints to the Horse Guards of having too few experienced generals had yielded results. In June, Prevost learned that a senior officer was being specially selected to command in Upper Canada and a second for the important Niagara Peninsula territory, but for various reasons, they were not due to arrive until October. These men were Lieutenant General Gordon Drummond and Major General Phineas Riall. London informed Prevost that Riall would be sent to Canada and that "orders will be transmitted to you for the return of Sir R. Sheaffe and M. Gen de Rottenburg to this country with a view to other employment."[5] In October, however, de Rottenburg was told he "was to remain in the command of Upper Canada"[6] until the arrival of his successor, which possibly indicates that de Rottenburg was not relieved due to unsatisfactory performance. Prevost never seriously faulted any of de Rottenburg's military decisions or reprimanded him in any way, and he employed him in other capacities after his replacement as commander in Upper Canada.[7]

In late June 1813, Prevost sent de Rottenburg to assume command of the Center Division at the head of Lake Ontario in place of Vincent, who was ill. The Americans continued to occupy Fort George, which interfered with British communication to Lake Erie, while the growing American naval strength on Lakes Ontario and Erie further interfered with British logistical support to both land and naval forces. The situation on Lake Erie was acute as the British naval squadron under Commander Robert Barclay was short of ordnance, supplies, and men. Prevost hoped that even temporary control of Lake Ontario would ease the logistical difficulties and allow the Center Division to force the enemy away from Fort George and permit the reduction of Fort Niagara. If this proved impossible, Prevost contemplated ordering de Rottenburg to occupy some defendable point between Fort George and York, and if the Americans achieved command of Lake Ontario, he was to retire with his command to Kingston. Farther to the west, Procter would be prepared to withdraw to Burlington Bay, and if upon arrival at that place he found that the Center Division had vacated the post at Burlington Heights, he was to make his way back to Montreal via Lake Huron and Georgian Bay, where he could gain the assistance of the North West Company to transport his force by canoe on the fur trade route to the Ottawa River.[8]

Earlier in June, British countermoves and the lack of naval support had signaled an end to the American offensive on the Niagara Peninsula as the U.S. commander, Major General Henry Dearborn, decided to concentrate his troops at Fort George, near the mouth of the Niagara River. Vincent pursued cautiously, sending detachments forward to maintain contact with the Americans as they moved into the fort. The sight of retreating Americans served to reinforce the resolve of the Six Nations and other aboriginal nations to support their British allies, an alliance that would soon pay dividends.[9] In mid-June, Vincent requested Prevost's permission for an immediate assault on Fort George. If Yeo cooperated, Vincent believed he would succeed, given the poor state of the fortifications and reports of sickness among the American troops. By vetoing the plan, Prevost appeared to have thrown away an opportunity to gain a significant victory, thus reverting "to the defensive form of warfare that characterized his war strategy."[10] This criticism ignores the fact that the Americans had 6,000 men around Fort George, while Vincent had about a third as many.

Nonetheless, the British noose around the fort tightened, in part owing to the Native victory over American troops at Beaver Dams in late June. A probe of the American lines in early July by British troops and warriors led to a vicious skirmish that allowed the

British to further extend their blockade into the close vicinity of the village of Newark, where British patrols continually harassed the defenders. By this time, de Rottenburg, who had assumed command in the region on 1 July, had determined that the uncertain naval situation on Lake Ontario and the stalemate around Fort George warranted increasing the garrison of the stronghold at Burlington Heights against a coup de main, while pickets maintained watch over Fort George.[11]

De Rottenburg's concerns regarding his exposed flank proved valid as, at the end of July, the enemy attempted to compromise his position around Fort George by undertaking an amphibious attack against Burlington Heights. Unable to determine a way to storm the heights, the 500 soldiers and sailors under Colonel Winfield Scott reembarked and were transported by Chauncey's ships to York, where they succeeded in taking possession of the town and destroying several public buildings before carrying off four hundred barrels of food and other supplies. The Americans landed in the area of the Don River on 1 August, searching for stores that had been hidden upriver by members of the garrison. Unable to find anything of use, the Americans reembarked and departed for Niagara. The trifling "plunder obtained by the enemy upon this predatory expedition" was of minor concern to Prevost, whose attention was fixed on the Niagara Peninsula, "the tidings of our own squadron under Sir James Yeo,"[12] and the supply situation along the Detroit frontier. In early August he ordered a redistribution of forces around Montreal that freed up a detachment of the 100th Foot for employment on the Niagara Peninsula.[13]

In August, circumstances caused Prevost to consider attacking Fort George. By this time, the British had 2,800 men surrounding the fort and nearby Newark; however, they still faced almost twice as many Americans. Prevost reached the British lines on 21 August. His visit was prompted by the worsening situation on Lake Erie and around Detroit, where reinforcements and supplies were desperately needed. Since he had taken command of his flagship *Queen Charlotte* at Amherstburg, Commander Robert Barclay had struggled to obtain matériel to outfit his squadron and sufficient seamen to complete his crews. Prevost, anxious to reestablish the flow of supplies to Procter and Barclay, wanted to eject the enemy from Fort George so as to free up troops to reinforce Procter and provide manpower for the Lake Erie squadron. Before he ordered a general assault, however, he deemed it necessary to determine the extent of the "enemy's position and strength";[14] he thus ordered a reconnaissance of the enemy's defenses on 24 August.[15]

The reconnaissance, made by British troops and allied warriors, drove in the American pickets and even entered Newark, just north of the fort. British officers made a careful survey of the main defenses, and their examination revealed that it would require a complicated plan, involving a battering train of artillery and the cooperation of Yeo's squadron, to take the fort. In addition, a second attack would have to be directed simultaneously at Fort Niagara, across the Niagara River and within supporting range of Fort George. Yeo was unwilling, however, to expose his squadron until Chauncey had been defeated. In late August, Prevost had himself studied the American defenses from the deck of one of Yeo's warships, during which a brief exchange of fire occurred with the American batteries. Once again, Prevost concluded a successful attack on Fort George was impossible until naval control of Lake Ontario had been secured, allowing joint naval-land operations to resume. The additional manpower needed for Procter and the Lake Erie squadron would have to be found elsewhere.[16]

Some historians have criticized Prevost for ordering this reconnaissance-in-force. They claim the information on American dispositions collected during an earlier reconnaissance at the end of July could have sufficed. That intelligence had become dated, however, by the end of August as the Americans had made considerable improvements to their positions. At the cost of two men killed and six wounded, with seventy enemy soldiers taken prisoner, Prevost's decision, when considered from an operational perspective, was reasonable and likely saved the army from serious losses for no purpose. His reconnaissance revealed that Fort George could not be taken under existing conditions, and Prevost decided it was better to avoid the risk of losing troops from the central part of his position while continuing with an "economy of force" operation that would contain a large American army on an insignificant part of British soil to prevent it being employed elsewhere.[17]

PREVOST knew that until the naval control of Lake Ontario was decided, Upper Canada would remain vulnerable. After nearly a month of Yeo's raiding American outposts and supporting army operations on the Niagara Peninsula, Prevost considered that conditions were right for the naval commander to engage Chauncey in a decisive battle. He authorized Yeo to seek out the American commodore. Prevost had high hopes of victory and wrote Bathurst that this departure from his general defensive strategy was "a necessary measure for the preservation of the advanced positions of the army"[18] because continued American domination of the lake would "eventually endanger the safety of a large proportion of troops in Upper Canada and convert the heart of the Province into the seat of the war."[19] The presence of enemy troops in the Niagara Peninsula was also disrupting the line of communication to Lake Erie, Detroit, and Mackinac. It is "scarcely possible," Prevost believed, "that a decisive naval action can be avoided."[20] All hopes now rested with Commodore Sir James Yeo and his squadron.

Yeo sailed from Kingston at the end of July, and the opposing squadrons came in view of each other a week later, northwest of the mouth of the Niagara River and within sight of the armies of both nations. During the morning of 7 August 1813, the two squadrons cleared for action as they maneuvered toward one another, but this first encounter between the Royal Navy and the United States Navy on the inland seas was brief, indecisive, and disappointing. Neither commodore was able to gain an advantageous position due to the differing armaments possessed by the squadrons, which limited the tactical options available to each commander: Chauncey possessed more long guns, capable of engaging a target more than 1,000 yards away, while most of the British ordnance consisted of short-barreled carronades, which had a shorter range, but which packed a devastating broadside at 500 yards or less. Chauncey therefore favored a long-range engagement, while Yeo hoped to maneuver in closer; and as neither could achieve an advantageous position, they withdrew. A second encounter three days later lasted longer but proved just as inconclusive. Following a meeting with Yeo, near the end of the month, near Ten Mile Creek on the northern end of the Niagara Peninsula, Prevost, who was visiting Major General Sir Francis de Rottenburg's headquarters near Queenston, was still confident the commodore would prevail. Prevost then joined Yeo on board his flagship on 27 August. After depositing Prevost at York later that day, Yeo returned to the southern part of the lake. The two squadrons met a third time off the mouth of the Genesee River on 11, September and the results proved as frustrating as the earlier engagements By mid-September, Prevost was becoming impatient with Yeo's apparent restraint and complained to Bathurst that "I cannot disguise from your Lordship that I feel some disappointment at the return of our squadron after being so many days in sight of the enemy's squadron without having obtained a decided advantage."[21] With control of Lake Ontario in a stalemate, Prevost, deciding the indecisive cat-and-mouse movements of the squadrons could not continue, instructed Yeo to return to supporting land operations.[22]

Prevost's frustrations with the naval commander continued. In mid-September, he sent Commander Richard O'Conor to relay verbal orders to Yeo, who was anchored in the mouth of South Bay on the southeast edge of the Prince Edward County littoral to return to Kingston and escort a supply convoy to the Niagara Peninsula. In a written reply to Prevost, Yeo said he did not think he was "justified in giving up watching the enemy," based solely on a verbal communication;[23] he therefore ignored Prevost's instructions. When Yeo returned to Kingston on 16 September—all the while keeping watch on Chauncey, who then quit the lake the following day—he was confronted by Prevost, who provided written orders to escort a convoy containing stores and supplies for the army at the head of the lake. Yeo was also directed to provide the army on the Niagara Peninsula with whatever support he could and to continue protecting the supply transports moving between Kingston and the head of the lake until the end of the campaign season. When Yeo sailed from Kingston with six vessels on 19 September, he carried out Prevost's instructions. However, after landing stores at Burlington Bay, and concluded that nothing more could be achieved by supporting the army, he went off again to hunt his American counterpart.[24]

Chauncey and Yeo met for a fourth time on 28 September, about fifteen miles to the south of York, in an encounter that has become known as the "Burlington Races." Chauncey caught sight of Yeo at dawn, and by the early afternoon, both squadrons were completely within view of each other, Yeo tacked to meet Chauncey, and the American commodore brought his line onto a parallel course and opened fire. Yeo's worst fears came to pass as a broadside from the *General Pike*'s powerful 24-pounder guns brought down the main and mizzen topmasts of HMS *Wolfe*. The flagship staggered, and then, as the enemy gun crews prepared to finish Yeo off, the *Royal George* under Commander William Mulcaster moved between both flagships, firing repeatedly at the American warship, forcing Chauncey to give way, and allowing the *Wolfe* and the British squadron to tear away for Burlington Bay, fifteen miles distant. Chauncey pursued his enemy, but fearing an approaching gale might force him into the British batteries along the shore, he quit the chase around 4:00 P.M. The much surprised but relieved Yeo brought his squadron to anchor in Burlington Bay, where several days were spent making repairs before sailing.

On the heels of this humiliation, Yeo suffered another embarrassment in early October, when Chauncey captured seven of eight small transports carrying 252 troops plus supplies from York to Kingston.[25] Yeo's excuse that the blame was attributable to a junior officer's failure to maintain his post was dismissed by Prevost, who questioned how such a loss could have happened while Yeo was on the lake. Prevost later learned that Yeo had put in at the Burlington Bay anchorage on 4 October, where he was erecting a temporary battery for the army, after learning that it was withdrawing to Burlington Heights. The following day, Yeo continued his search for Chauncey, confident that the armed escort provided to the convoy was sufficient. He did not anticipate the convoy encountering Chauncey's squadron, although Prevost feared it would, which is why he insisted on Yeo using his ships to protect it. After learning of the capture of the convoy, Prevost expressed his displeasure to the Horse Guards, from whom he now had to request replacements. He added that the convoy's movement had been well planned and that "it was expected the necessary protection would have been afforded to them by Sir James Yeo's fleet."[26]

THE difficulties between Prevost and Yeo continued. In mid-October, as Prevost puzzled over whether the movement of most of the U.S. Army at Fort George to Sackets Harbor indicated that the next American objective would be Kingston or Montreal, he ordered Yeo to post vessels at both ends of Wolfe Island, off Kingston at the entrance of the St. Lawrence, to guard against either eventuality. Yeo, reluctant to divide his squadron, replied that he would keep four vessels at the eastern end of Wolfe Island, while the other two would remain at Kingston. In reality, Yeo ignored Prevost's orders. Suspecting the American army at Sackets Harbor might attack York, where it would be joined by another force from the west, Yeo kept all of his warships at Kingston until the end of the month. While Yeo's conclusions regarding American intentions were not based on any evidence, Prevost actually had received several reports, including one from an agent sent to Sackets Harbor, that the Americans were planning to attack Montreal.[27]

The arrival of winter brought to an end the first six months of the Royal Navy's service on the Great Lakes. Anticipation of several decisive victories had greeted its arrival, but the results were mixed. While Prevost's superiors had supported his request for regular naval personnel, the force that had been provided proved inadequate for the task at hand. The U.S. Navy was constructing feverishly on both Lakes Ontario and Erie. In conjunction with American strikes at many points between the Detroit River and the boundary between the two Canadas, the American naval presence stretched British resources to the limit and nearly resulted in a strategic defeat for Prevost. He relied on naval power to transport troops, provide logistical support for his armies, and keep the sea lines of communication open on both lakes and on the upper St. Lawrence River.

Prevost and Yeo had had the advantage of discussing these requirements in the spring, but as the year progressed, their relations became strained as each commander, facing shortages in personnel and equipment, focused on his immediate objectives. In many ways, their goals were similar. Prevost could not defend the entire province, so he ensured that his center—that area around the northern shore of Lake Ontario to Montreal—was held; Yeo could do little better than attempt to hold that lake. A wrong move by Yeo or the defeat of his squadron would cause a serious setback, as nearly happened during the "Burlington Races." A better option, which Yeo appears to have realized following his final 1813 encounter with Chauncey, was to marshal his squadron, support the army, and interdict his opponent's shipbuilding plans by striking at his logistical line. This strategy was more in concert with Prevost's requirements and would have served British interests better than the independent actions Yeo favored on occasion. A good working relationship between the commander in chief and his naval commander was crucial in achieving their war aims, and although their relationship had been strained during 1813, it had not been destroyed.

AT the end of October 1813, the Americans commenced preparations for their next operation by moving troops northward from Sackets Harbor to a rendezvous point at French Creek on the St. Lawrence River, just to the east of Wolfe Island. This movement signaled the beginning of the largest American offensive of the war, directed against Montreal. Based on the intelligence he received from various sources, Prevost, who was monitoring developments from Kingston, repaired to Montreal in order to prepare its defenses. Once there, he learned that a 7,300-man army under Major General James Wilkinson would move down the St. Lawrence River, while a 4,000-strong division under Major General Wade Hampton would invade Lower Canada from eastern New York State. Their object was Montreal. Prevost concluded that the most dangerous threat came from Hampton, who was moving directly against the city; therefore, he concentrated a considerable body of troops to protect it. He was concerned that Hampton "has it in his power to molest the communication with the upper province and impede the progress of the stores required there for the navy and army."[28] Fortunately for Prevost, on 26 October, Hampton's advance was stopped on the Châteauguay River by 1,770 Canadian soldiers and Native warriors under the command of Lieutenant Colonel Charles de Salaberry. The Americans retreated.[29]

Meanwhile, at the eastern end of Lake Ontario, the parade of boats moving American troops to French Creek caught Yeo off guard, and he decided to implement the contingency orders issued by Prevost to stop the enemy's flotilla as it sailed down the St. Lawrence River. Yeo detached two ships and four gunboats under Captain William Mulcaster, whom Yeo had recently promoted in recognition of his service in the "Burlington Races," that joined two other vessels previously sent to the northeastern end of Wolfe Island. Mulcaster's orders were to attack the American camp at French Creek. A running battle was fought in difficult conditions on 1–2 November but, owing to intense fire from American shore batteries, interfered little with American troop movements. Mulcaster returned to Kingston, and on 5 November, Yeo moved his squadron up the river, anchoring near the American squadron. For his part, Chauncey cleared his vessels for action, expecting battle the next day, but for reasons that remain unclear, Yeo returned to Kingston without firing a shot.

By this time, Prevost's concern was not with Chauncey's squadron in the St. Lawrence River, but with Wilkinson's army advancing on Montreal. Based on orders issued by Prevost earlier, two regiments under Lieutenant Colonel Joseph Morrison left Kingston to pursue Wilkinson, while Yeo detached two schooners and seven gunboats under Mulcaster in support. Wilkinson's advance by boat down the upper St. Lawrence was slowed by British and Canadian troops, who enjoyed good intelligence and communication, while Wilkinson's logistical situation only worsened.[30] The campaign ended in November, following the British victory at Crysler's Farm. With the rear of his column hounded by British troops, his rations running low, and facing a large garrison defending Montreal, the strength of which was "equal, if not greater than our own,"[31] Wilkinson went into winter quarters at French Mills (now Fort Covington), New York, ending the last major U.S. offensive of the year. Mulcaster's flotilla provided fire support and transport until the middle of November, when weather conditions forced him to retire to Coteau du Lac in Lower Canada. By the end of the month, both Lake Ontario squadrons had moved into winter quarters. Prevost's defense of Montreal in the autumn of 1813 had been well planned and executed, but operations in western Upper Canada had resulted in two major defeats on land and sea.[32]

WHILE Prevost was able to retain central Upper Canada, from Kingston to the Niagara Peninsula, and thwart the American offensive against Montreal, the British position in the western end of the province was becoming tenuous. During the summer of 1813, the U.S. Army of the North West under Brigadier General William Harrison began to assemble in Ohio, and a large shipbuilding program commenced at Presque Isle, Pennsylvania. The American objective was to reverse the setbacks of 1812, retake Detroit, and seize control of Lake Erie to reestablish the security of the Northwest. The attainment of these objectives would undermine the British-Native alliances in this area and crush any hopes of creating an aboriginal homeland as a buffer between British North America and the United States.[33]

The ensuing campaign of the autumn of 1813 has raised questions about Prevost's leadership and accusations that he did not adequately support Major General Henry Procter, the commander of the British Right Division based at Detroit. Historian Sandor Antal, author of a study of this campaign, contends that due to a deep personal grudge, Prevost withheld support from Procter and ignored his warnings of growing American naval strength on Lake Erie, resulting in the loss of control of that body of water and the near destruction of Procter's army. Antal believes that Prevost refused to accept responsibility for these defeats, choosing instead to blame Procter. Antal contends that by criticizing Procter in general orders and through other alleged misrepresentations, Prevost influenced the outcome of the court-martial Procter requested to clear his name, ensuring he would be found guilty.[34]

These are serious accusations, but they isolate events in the western theater from the broader context of the overall military situation. This region lay at the extreme southwestern end of Prevost's lengthy defensive line. It was an important area because communication on Lake Erie provided access to the Detroit River and, from there, to Lake Huron and other posts in the Northwest and because retention of Lake Erie also allowed access to Native allies and their warriors. However, in face of the American land and naval threats, Prevost's defensive line was difficult to maintain; it was 560 miles long, from Montreal to Detroit, and had little depth. Once cut, access to the Northwest using alternate routes was difficult or impossible. The survival of land and naval forces along this line was dependent on unhindered communication, which ran along the lakes and rivers. Procter's force along the Detroit frontier and the naval squadron based at Amherstburg were supported by one of two routes. The principal route, by way of the Niagara River and to Lake Erie, was lost in May 1813 when the Americans cut off navigation of the Niagara. An alternate supply line was then established, extending overland from Burlington Bay to the Grand River to Long Point on Lake Erie, but it was less than ideal as it could not support the movement of heavy guns or equipment needed for the naval squadron. Waterborne movement along the northern shore of Lake Erie was also threatened once American warships appeared on the lake in strength in early August. The disruption of communication to the west caused the gradual depletion of supplies, stores, and foodstuffs; contributed to an overall decline in the health and effectiveness of Procter's army; and limited the completion of naval warships. If this situation persisted or the communications were permanently cut, British forces in the Detroit area would wither away.[35]

During 1812, as British dominance of the waterways and the Americans' problems with strategy undermined Brigadier General William Hull's campaign, Detroit fell, allowing Brock to annex the Michigan Territory. In 1813, the situation was far different. Forced to contend with large-scale offensives at several critical points, the evacuation of the Niagara Peninsula on two occasions, and growing American naval power on Lakes Ontario and Erie, Prevost needed to deploy his forces very judiciously. The result was that for much of 1813, he focused his attention on or around Lake Ontario, which became the key objective for both opponents. If the United States gained superiority on Lake Ontario and Prevost was forced to vacate the region from the Niagara River to Kingston or even points farther east, Upper Canada would fall.

During the spring and summer of 1813, Prevost sent what troops and supplies he could to Procter. He also encouraged Yeo to send men, ordnance, and equipment to Barclay. The latter's squadron required 250 to 300 men to render it effective, but Yeo consistently refused requests to provide that number since "the exigencies of the service on Lake Ontario will not admit of his sending many seamen."[36] Yeo's reluctance was of course due to manpower shortfalls within his own squadron—he had 860 men on his vessels, a quarter of whom were infantry serving as marines. Facing them were Chauncey's 1,300 men, most of whom were seamen. In August 1813, however, another 300 sailors arrived at Kingston, but Yeo kept most of them for his own squadron, sending only forty men to Barclay, giving the naval commander on Lake Erie a complement of sixty Royal Navy personnel, 110 men from the former Provincial Marine, and 230 soldiers provided by Procter. As the struggle for the control of Lake Ontario was still undecided, Yeo was unwilling to widen any disadvantage he might have had vis-à-vis Chauncey.[37]

Prevost, despite the presence of the Royal Navy, retained responsibility for naval manpower and did what he could to aid Barclay.

In July 1813, he advised Barclay that an interim solution to his difficulties was to "gain your Ordnance and Naval Stores from the Enemy," adding that he had "strongly pressed" on Yeo "the necessity of sending forward to you immediately a supply of Petty Officers & Seamen."[38] Prevost shortly learned from Lieutenant General Sir John Sherbrooke and Rear-Admiral Edward Griffith, Warren's deputy in Halifax, that with the overall naval manpower situation desperate, no men could be spared from the North American squadron. Unable to transfer seamen from Lake Ontario or the Atlantic, Prevost believed the British position on Lake Erie would be dependent "almost entirely on the exertions of soldiers belonging to the 41st Regiment and Royal Newfoundland" and what few sailors Barclay had under his command.[39]

These factors contributed to a shifting naval balance on Lake Erie, which, by the late summer of 1813, favored the United States. The American quest for dominance of that lake had begun in 1812, when Chauncey sent Lieutenant Jesse Duncan, U.S. Navy, to select a site for a dockyard. On the advice of another officer, the government intervened and selected Presque Isle or Erie, Pennsylvania, as the navy's base. Progress was hampered by logistical problems and animosity between Chauncey and Lieutenant Jesse Elliot, who had replaced Duncan. It was only following the arrival of Master Commandant Oliver Hazard Perry at Erie in March 1813 that matters improved. On the British side, in the spring of 1813, there were five vessels in Barclay's squadron that had been commissioned before the war, and his powerful new flagship, the *Detroit*, with nineteen guns, was expected to be completed by July. In contrast, the growth of the American naval presence on Lake Erie was astonishing—of the nine ships that eventually joined the American squadron, six were launched during May and June 1813 alone. Once completed, Perry's squadron enjoyed almost double the broadside firepower and weight of metal (1,528 pounds versus 883 pounds) despite Barclay having a slight advantage in the number of guns.[40]

Barclay kept abreast of American progress at Presque Isle during the summer. He chose not to exploit an opportunity that was presented to him on 4 August when, during a patrol, he observed several American warships being laboriously moved over a sandbar from their anchorage at Presque Isle Bay to open water. Rather than engage the vulnerable vessels, some of which were unarmed, Barclay exchanged fire with the enemy but, perhaps fearing shore batteries, then sailed away. It was at that moment Barclay surrendered control of the lake to Commodore Perry. The American commander then interdicted the British supply route from Long Point to Amherstburg, and a new threat appeared with the arrival of Major General William Harrison's Army of the Northwest, which began preparations for the invasion of Upper Canada. Harrison's cautious method of concentrating his army around fortified points as he advanced reduced the effectiveness of aboriginal guerrilla warfare, and in May, an attempt by Procter to halt Harrison at Fort Meigs failed. Tecumseh, the leader of the western Indian confederacy, then pressured Procter to try again in July, but the attempt proved fruitless. In August, an attack on American-held Fort Stephenson also failed after heavy fighting. The Native alliance then fell into jeopardy as Tecumseh and other chiefs grew critical of Procter's cautious leadership and several nations, including the Wyandot, Shawnee, and Ottawa, threatened to end their partnership with the British. The intervention of other chiefs dissuaded Tecumseh from abandoning the British, but they were unsuccessful in halting the departure of many western warriors, who saw no reason to continue after the recent setbacks. Prevost could do nothing to reverse this situation.[41]

By September 1813, Procter and Barclay had concluded the only means of reopening the supply route was to fight Perry for control of Lake Erie. Few other options presented themselves. Blockading Perry at his new anchorage at Put-in-Bay, Ohio—as Barclay had done earlier that summer at Presque Isle—was impossible. Both British commanders placed their faith in a decisive stroke on the lake that would improve their supply situation, reduce the threat from Harrison, and restore confidence in their Native allies. On 9 September, Barclay exploited a favorable wind and sailed toward Put-in-Bay. The battle opened before noon on the next day. After two hours, it appeared the British would win, but then, suddenly, the struggle shifted in the Americans' favor. Barclay was unable to continue because of wounds, and his senior lieutenant was killed. The British squadron fell into confusion, and as the Americans closed in, the senior surviving Royal Navy officer surrendered it. The United States now controlled Lake Erie.[42]

As a result of Perry's victory, Procter's communications were cut and enemy forces were free to land anywhere in his rear. Procter had instructions from Prevost that if a "retrograde movement" was unavoidable, it not "be resorted to until . . . the mode of carrying it into effect has been previously well weighed and considered and all necessary arrangements made."[43] Several days later, before returning to Montreal to deal with Hampton's threat against the lower province, Prevost again stressed to Procter the requirement for careful preparations, if he was "to relinquish the territory you have long ably defended"[44] and move his force east to the Center Division. In a letter that Procter did not receive until after his defeat in October, Prevost did approve of his decision to withdraw and "of your making a stand upon the Thames." In Prevost's mind, Procter's retreat was to be limited, deliberate, and conducted "so as to Afford the Enemy no decided Advantage over You."[45]

By mid-September, with supplies dwindling to dangerous levels, sickness rampant in his army, and Harrison approaching, Procter concluded that his situation was untenable. He decided to withdraw toward Burlington Heights, but preparations moved slowly. On 24 September, the unnecessary stores at Detroit were burned, and the garrison crossed the river to Sandwich in Upper Canada. Two days later, similar actions were taken at Amherstburg. The actual order to evacuate was given on 26 September, and the first elements of Procter's army departed the next morning, moving in easy marches and carrying much excess baggage. Meanwhile, Perry began landing Harrison's men at Amherstburg. Leaving garrisons at Detroit, Sandwich, and Fort Malden, Harrison then led 3,000 regulars and volunteers in pursuit of Procter, and on 1 October, the arrival of a mounted regiment of 500 riflemen provided him with the ability to overtake Procter, although the American general was cautious and remained somewhat reluctant to catch up with his opponent. Nonetheless, the failure of Procter's rear guard to destroy bridges behind them allowed the American advance elements to remain close. On 5 October, with the Americans very near, Procter decided to make a stand with 450 soldiers and 600 warriors at Moraviantown, near modern London, Ontario. The results were a disaster—Tecumseh was killed and only fifty men, including Procter, escaped the debacle. The retreat in good order envisaged by Prevost most certainly had not come to pass.[46]

When unsubstantiated reports circulated of Harrison's advance toward Burlington Bay, de Rottenburg withdrew several regiments from there to Kingston in anticipation of a general withdrawal. The blockade of Fort George ended in early October, and the troops on the Niagara Peninsula began to move to Burlington Bay, where Vincent, whose health had recovered, hoped he would meet Procter. When confirmation of the annihilation of Procter's army at Moraviantown was received, Vincent hastened the evacuation of the peninsula by a forced march. He also received discretionary authority to continue to Kingston if he decided the position at Burlington was untenable.[47]

At first, Prevost was not pleased with de Rottenburg's redistribution of his forces. In September, he had instructed de Rottenburg to maintain his position around Fort George and Queenston; he wrote him again on 12 October, after de Rottenburg had detached troops to Kingston, complaining of his subordinate having "dismembered the Center Division of so large a proportion of force which had been collected with so much difficulty."[48] As American intentions became clearer, Prevost saw the situation differently, as the precautionary measure de Rottenburg had taken by reinforcing Kingston in response to a perceived threat now enabled Prevost to form the corps of observation that was eventually employed against Wilkinson.[49]

The fate of Upper Canada appeared to be in the balance. After the loss of Detroit and the squadron on Lake Erie, the American occupation of Amherstburg and the Western District of Upper Canada was a serious setback. The Native confederacy now disintegrated, but wild rumors that Burlington Bay was Harrison's next objective proved unfounded as the American commander returned to Detroit. There he discharged his volunteers and then moved a large contingent of regulars to Buffalo using Perry's squadron. Fortunately for the British, the lateness of the season led to the postponement of American plans to retake Fort Mackinac. With the naval situation on Lake Ontario still unresolved, disaster loomed and de Rottenburg, the commander in Upper Canada, contemplated an evacuation of the Niagara Peninsula.[50]

Prevost saw the situation differently. A cogent assessment sent to Bathurst highlights the excellent intelligence he received on American plans and activity: Prevost claimed the Americans had failed "in their second plan of invasion of Upper Canada,"[51] because

Dearborn had ruined the spring offensive by disobeying orders and not commencing with an attack on Kingston, which allowed the British time to strengthen the defenses of this strategically important base, making any subsequent attempt to take it impracticable. Successive American strikes against York and Fort George had not yielded a strategic victory, and with the season growing late, the Americans had realized the error of launching simultaneous moves "of their Northern or Central army under [Major General James] Wilkinson, the North West Army under General Harrison and a considerable corps of observation under [Major-]General Hampton with the three flotillas on Lakes Ontario, Erie and Champlain."[52] In the formulation of strategy, Prevost argued, it was not "sufficient to conceive the idea of moving several armies in concert and combination[;] it is also necessary that the organization of these should in some degree correspond with principles upon which such a campaign was planned and is to be expected."[53] For the United States, the real results achieved in 1813 were merely a series of tactical victories that had little or no strategic importance; meanwhile, "His Majesty's forces continue[d] proudly to maintain their respective positions against the efforts of a greatly superior numerical force."[54]

The loss of an entire squadron was an embarrassment to Yeo and further strained his relationship with Prevost, but Yeo distanced himself from Barclay's defeat and eventually blamed him for the setback on Lake Erie. In his official report to Admiral Sir John Warren, Yeo stated that while he had instructed Barclay to cooperate with Procter, he could not fathom Barclay's "reasons for risking an action before his reinforcement of seamen arrived."[55] Yeo was even less complimentary after reading Barclay's report on the battle on Lake Erie in November and offered his opinion that Barclay had not been justified in seeking battle and should have awaited the reinforcements recently sent from Kingston. To Prevost, however, Yeo offered a different explanation, admitting that although the Lake Erie squadron was short of both men and guns, the British defeat was due to the high number of officer casualties suffered in the early stages of the battle.[56]

For his part, Prevost placed the blame squarely on Yeo. The "protracted contest on Lake Ontario for the naval ascendency" had led the commodore to detain "for this important object nearly the whole of the officers and seamen which were sent from England with himself, leaving Captain Barclay on Lake Erie to depend almost entirely on the exertions of soldiers"[57] provided by Procter. During his court-martial, which was held in England in September 1814, Barclay confirmed Prevost's complaints and testified that a single fifty-man draft had come not "from commodore Sir James Yeo, but from Sir George Prevost, through General Procter," and that he found "all applications to Sir James Yeo useless."[58] The court agreed that there was a "want of sufficient Number of able Seamen," despite the fact that Barclay "had repeatedly and earnestly requested"[59] them. The court not only cleared Barclay but praised him for his exertions in preparing his squadron for action and his command of it in battle. The court avoided direct mention of Yeo; however, his testimony given at the court-martial and Prevost's accusations led certain Admiralty officials to develop doubts about Prevost himself that would be further fueled in 1814.

Concluding that Procter exhibited negligence during his withdrawal from Detroit and in the dispositions he made before the battle of Moraviantown, Prevost ordered charges brought against him. In general terms, these charges claimed that Procter had unnecessarily delayed his withdrawal following Barclay's defeat on Lake Erie and, once the retreat began, had encumbered it by the quantity of commissary baggage that accompanied the army, which caused lengthy halts. Inadequate measures were taken to protect the ammunition and stores, which resulted in their capture by the enemy. Evidence was also produced demonstrating that he failed to destroy bridges to slow the enemy's pursuit and that his defeat at Moraviantown resulted from his poor use of the terrain and failure to lead the troops in battle. The court-martial sat between December 1814 and January 1815.[60] In examining the five charges against Procter, it criticized his judgment but was unwilling to condemn him as totally incompetent. The court recommended that Procter be reprimanded publicly and suspended from pay and rank for six months. As the reviewing authority, the Prince Regent confirmed the findings of all the charges, less one. He questioned how the court could find Procter guilty of one of the charges but "acquit him of all the facts [specifications] upon which the Charge is founded."[61] The Prince Regent upheld the public reprimand but dispensed with the suspension of pay and rank. As was customary, in September 1815, the Horse Guards issued a general order summarizing the findings of the court-martial and ordered that it be read "at the Head of every Regiment in His Majesty's Service."[62]

FACED by a revitalized U.S. Army and a growing naval threat on the inland waters that nearly overwhelmed the defenders of British North America, Prevost was correct in the analysis of American strategic planning that he submitted to Bathurst in September. From a military perspective, the loss of Lake Erie and the Western District of Upper Canada, while lamentable, did not jeopardize the vital position around Lake Ontario. Had the Americans been able to employ the resources and effort given to the Lake Erie squadron at Sackets Harbor instead in an attempt to capture control of Lake Ontario, it would undoubtedly have fallen, forcing Prevost to retire to Lower Canada. Logistics defeated Britain in the western theater as Prevost was unable to amass resources to the same extent as the enemy, and he could not rebalance the situation without seriously weakening his position in the center of the province. He thus had to accept the temporary loss of Lake Erie and Detroit so he could retain Lake Ontario, Kingston, and Montreal. Yeo faced a similar decision and kept his attention, and resources, on Lake Ontario. Both men had decided on similar courses of action, yet they were unable to admit so to one another. The question of which commander offered Barclay more assistance is less important than the matter of command. There was sufficient latitude in the commodore's instructions to permit him to operate independently of Prevost's plans, though he was dependent on Prevost for manpower. This distinction eventually led Prevost to question the command and control arrangements in the Canadas, while Yeo's decision to heap blame on Prevost for the loss of Lake Erie further soured his relations with his superior.

In his account to London about these events, Prevost used the opportunity to express his frustration over the lack of instructions from his superiors. "Since the commencement of the last campaign," Prevost had provided London with detailed reports and had "faithfully exposed the difficulties" of his situation, "including the inadequacy of the means afforded me by His Majesty's Government to the object—the preservation of the North American Provinces." Despite setbacks, Prevost had defended the Canadas "against the attacks of a foe whose war resources of every description are very considerable, when compared with those to myself." In 1813, the situation had changed dramatically, as improvements in the leadership and training of the American army and the unprecedented expansion of the U.S. inland naval force offered Prevost "difficulties of a new and imposing character," which, while not being insurmountable, were exacerbated by his not being "honoured with a single instruction from His Majesty's Government upon the mode of conducting the campaign since it opened to this late period."[63]

Prevost had every reason to complain. Aside from receiving the Prince Regent's "entire approbation"[64] for his decisions in the spring and early summer and notices of reinforcements or direction of specific matters, such as the exchange of prisoners of war, the government had not seen fit to amplify, modify, or expand on the instructions issued before the war, when expectations were very different. London would not respond to Prevost's appeal until the following summer, however, when the situation in Europe, not North America, changed. In 1813, Prevost's superiors were preoccupied with the dramatic fallout from Napoléon's disastrous campaign in Russia and the first significant successes that Britain had enjoyed in Europe after nearly twenty years of war, including Wellington's liberation of Spain and invasion of France. As commander of a secondary theater in what was viewed as a global conflict, Prevost was left on his own to deal with the muddled naval command arrangement, the logistical challenges of supporting land and naval forces over a huge region, and his enemy's improving capability.

Through the summer, the high hopes Prevost had for the Royal Navy ensuring British ascendancy on Lake Ontario and Lake Erie had gradually faded. Chauncey's regular appearances on Lake Ontario between July and September and Perry's emergence on Lake Erie made American dominance on these two lakes appear likely and threatened to "expose Upper Canada to devastation and insult."[65] As the naval balance shifted, Prevost's logistics were inhibited by poor waterborne communication with de Rottenburg on the Niagara Peninsula and Procter at Amherstburg. Despite the Americans' attack on York, their occupation of the Niagara area and the Western District, the loss of Lake Erie, the destruction of the Native alliance in the Northwest, and the U.S. offensive against Montreal, British North America remained intact. The situation improved in December when the American force withdrew from the Niagara Peninsula and the British were able not only to reoccupy Fort George but also to take Fort Niagara on the opposite bank. Cooperation between Prevost and Yeo, which had begun so well in May and June, deteriorated as the year progressed, and their relationship would be stretched to the breaking point in the following year.

7

"GIVE JONATHAN
A GOOD DRUBBING"

January to August

1814

Sir George Prevost maintained his defensive strategy into the midsummer of 1814, when he learned of major events in Europe that would have a major effect on the North American war. In April, Napoléon abdicated, ending a global conflict that had been waged almost without pause since 1793. About two weeks later, Earl Bathurst wrote Prevost outlining the consequences of these occurrences: "I take the earliest opportunity of acquainting you that His Majesty's Government have not failed to avail themselves of the present favorable state of affairs in Europe to order reinforcements, both of infantry and artillery, for the army under your command to proceed to Quebec as soon as they can be collected from the different quarters in which their services have hitherto been required."[1] Prevost's recent complaints to Bathurst about a lack of instructions may have prompted the secretary to write Prevost with immediacy of the coming changes.

Earlier in February 1814, at Bathurst's invitation, the Duke of Wellington, whose status as a theater commander made him an influential adviser to the British government, offered an assessment of how the North American conflict should be continued once the European war had ended—part of a debate in London regarding strategy following the defeat of France. Wellington believed that the defense of Canada "depends upon the navigation of the lakes," and he noted that "any offensive operation founded upon Canada must be preceded by the establishment of naval superiority on the lakes."[2] Even if that was achieved, however, Wellington doubted that Britain would be "able to do more than secure the points on those lakes at which the Americans would have access,"[3] as the northern theater was "very extensive, thinly peopled, and producing but little food in proportion of their extent."[4] Consequently, military operations by large forces "are impracticable, unless the party carrying them on has the uninterrupted use of a navigable river, or very extensive means of land transport, which such a country can rarely have."[5] These words from Britain's most successful general would prove prescient.[6]

While Bathurst pondered the future of the war effort in North America, it was becoming evident that Britain's only significant presence on the Continent—in the Pyrenees—was far from where Britain's interests in Europe truly lay; that is, in the Low Countries, where the war had begun two decades earlier.[7] Following the evacuation of the French from Amsterdam in November 1813, the Netherlands rose in revolt and a provisional government was formed. The Prince of Orange, who had lived in exile in England, returned to his country, followed by the first elements of an 8,500-man force commanded by Lieutenant General Sir Thomas Graham sent to protect British interests there.[8] When the European war ended in April 1814, British concerns in the Low Countries appeared secure. The government then decided that a portion of Wellington's Peninsular army, currently headquartered at Toulouse in southern France, along with troops from other garrisons, including a single battalion from the Low Countries, would be used to reinforce North America, while those Peninsular units that were not redeployed would be sent home.[9] This was good news for Prevost, but he was still forced to accept that his command, albeit heavily reinforced, would always be a secondary theater for Britain.[10]

This process of collecting reinforcements for North America commenced after Napoléon's abdication. On 14 April 1814, Colonel Henry Torrens, the military secretary to the Duke of York, wrote Wellington's quartermaster general, Lieutenant General Sir George Murray, that "the government have determined to give Jonathan [i.e., the Americans] a good drubbing, and orders have been sent to Lord Wellington to prepare a corps of 12,000 infantry and a small detachment of cavalry to be sent to America."[11] This contingent eventually included four companies of artillery, one regiment of cavalry, and fourteen battalions of infantry.

Having been given little direction over the last two years by London, Prevost was now told, in a secret letter, dated 3 June 1814, how these troops would be employed. The reinforcements would ensure that "the Canadas will not only be protected for the time against any attack which the enemy may have the means of making,"[12] but also allow Prevost "to commence offensive operations on the Enemy's frontier before the close of the [1814] Campaign [season]."[13] The wording used by Bathurst gave every hint that Britain was going to launch large-scale offensives against the United States to obtain a military victory, but this was not the case, as Britain was clearly thinking in defensive terms. "The object of your [Prevost's] operations will be; first, to give immediate protection [to Canada]," Bathurst wrote, and "secondly, to obtain if possible ultimate security to His Majesty's Possessions in America."[14] He then outlined the specific tasks to be completed to achieve these two goals:

> The entire destruction of Sackets harbour and the Naval Establishment on Lake Erie and Lake Champlain come under the first description.
>
> The maintenance of Fort Niagara and so much of the adjacent Territory as may be deemed necessary: and the occupation of Detroit and the Michigan Country come under the second.
>
> If our success shall enable us to terminate the war by the retention of the Fort of Niagara, and the restoration of Detroit and the whole of the Michigan Country to the Indians, the British Frontier will be materially improved. Should there be any advanced position on that part of our frontier that extends towards Lake Champlain, the occupation of which would materially tend to the security of the Province, you will if you deem it expedient expel the Enemy from it, and occupy it by detachments of the Troops under your command, always however taking care not to expose His Majesty's Forces to being cut off by too extended a line of advance.[15]

Prevost was responsible only for those parts of this plan pertaining to the Canadas, and the Royal Navy and Sherbrooke's Atlantic Command were assigned roles to support him. In April, Vice Admiral Sir Alexander Cochrane replaced Admiral John Warren as head of the North American Station. Cochrane was ordered to tighten the blockade of the American coast and to create a diversion "on the coasts of the United States of America in favour of the army employed in the defence of Upper and Lower Canada."[16] He received additional ships, and a reinforced brigade under Major General Robert Ross was sent to the Chesapeake;[17] the brigade's task was to strike against suitable targets on the mid-Atlantic coast.[18] In Halifax, Sir John Sherbrooke was to "occupy so much of the District of Maine, as shall ensure an uninterrupted [overland] communication between Halifax & Quebec."[19]

In formulating this strategy, London was taking on a more active role in the American war. Sherbrooke remained nominally under Prevost but also dealt directly with Bathurst, while the Admiralty was responsible for the seaborne operations off the American coast with Bathurst coordinating the whole and communicating directly with Prevost, Sherbrooke, Cochrane, and Ross. London was also supervising arrangements for the coming peace talks, which had been first considered in 1812, when an offer was made by Czar Alexander I—who saw the war as a threat to Russian trade and a distraction to his new ally, Britain—to mediate talks in St. Petersburg. Madison accepted the offer, but the delegation he sent to Russia learned that Britain was not interested in having a third party involved. In November 1813, Britain then formally proposed direct talks, which Madison agreed to, and arrangements commenced to begin negotiations sometime in 1814. The instructions for the British commissioners were controlled by London, and at no time was Prevost consulted on the possible terms to be presented to the United States. This occurred despite his major planning role in the 1814 operations, in combination with the offensives in the Chesapeake Bay and against Maine, that were intended to underpin the proposals put forward by the British commissioners to their American counterparts.

While Prevost had no role in operations outside the Canadas, he did influence the fate of Washington. The burning of the city's public buildings in August 1814 is often incorrectly attributed to having been done in retaliation for the destruction in 1813 of the Upper Canada parliament buildings at York. The actual impetus for this destruction was revenge for American raids against settlements on the Lake Erie shore of Upper Canada during early 1814. Following the destruction of communities along both sides of the Niagara frontier in late 1813, a temporary halt to these measures was put into effect in January 1814, only to be revoked by Prevost in May, following a devastating American raid on Dover in Upper Canada, followed by further acts of destruction at St. David's and Queenston in July 1814.[20]

Prevost reported these events to Vice Admiral Cochrane and suggested that, in return, Cochrane might wish to "assist in inflicting that measure of retaliation which shall deter the enemy from a repetition of similar outrages."[21] Cochrane agreed and eventually decided he would occupy Washington, which would deliver a great "Blow to the [American] Government,"[22] while offering good quarters and supplies for the army. Thus, with a retaliatory policy that was partially inspired by Prevost, the Royal Navy commenced raiding settlements in the Chesapeake Bay area , culminating in the occupation and burning of Washington in August 1814.[23]

The realization that Britain could now concentrate its strength against the United States worried the American government, which began to put more stress on the coming peace talks than on a military decision. During April 1814, two American officials, Albert Gallatin and James Bayard, who were in London awaiting confirmation of where these negotiations would take place, witnessed the embarkation of troops onto transports destined for North America. In June, they saw the arrival of the czar of Russia, the king of Prussia, and rulers and generals from several German states in London for victory celebrations on a scale that had not been witnessed since the 1740s, and this filled many Americans with gloom. Both men then learned that the venue for the negotiations, originally selected as Gothenburg in Sweden, had been changed to Ghent in the Netherlands and that the talks were scheduled to open in August 1814.[24]

With negotiations thus about to commence, the Americans attempted to secure a ceasefire in North America. In March 1814, Prevost had briefly toyed with an offer made by Secretary of State James Monroe to negotiate an armistice "to prevent a further effusion of blood."[25] Prevost found the prospect appealing, as it would "preserve the Canadas during the negotiations."[26] He solicited opinions on the offer from Yeo and Drummond, but both advised him to proceed cautiously as they had little faith in American assurances. Thinking of the Prevost-Dearborn ceasefire of 1812, the British commanders were suspicious of the enemy's intentions, fearing the armistice would allow the United States to reinforce its naval and military forces and "gain time for launching and equipping more ships."[27]

Prevost decided to proceed with talks, and in April 1814, he appointed his adjutant general, Colonel Edward Baynes, to negotiate with Colonel Ninian Pinkney at Champlain, New York. Prevost provided Baynes with detailed instructions for "the basis of an armistice,"[28] and the terms Prevost outlined heeded the advice from Yeo and Drummond. The terms were more comprehensive than those agreed to in the 1812 ceasefire and provided a mechanism for terminating the agreement, should that became necessary.

The first condition was that any cessation of hostilities would include land and sea forces in the Canadas, the other British provinces of North America, the United States, and the lakes of the northern theater. Second, any agreement would remain in effect until the talks in Europe were concluded. It was proposed that if a rupture occurred in the negotiations in Europe, "no act of hostility shall be committed on either side until at least 30 days shall have expired."[29] Prevost also sought guarantees that occupied posts or territories would not change hands until the details of the peace treaty were known, as well as restrictions on troop movements, reconnaissance activity, and the transfer of vessels between the lakes. The ceasefire would also be binding on Native warriors and would allow each side to restrict civilian interaction along the frontier.[30]

Baynes met with Pinkney at the beginning of May 1814. When Baynes presented Prevost's "guide-letter," he learned that Pinkney had not been granted any latitude and that he was not "at all acquainted with the views and designs of his government."[31] Baynes rejected a proposal that would allow any armistice to be annulled with twenty days' notice, regardless of the state of European negotiations. He explained that Prevost lacked authority to extend the terms to include the Atlantic coast of the United States. As nothing further could be achieved, the negotiations ended. In any event, Prevost had learned from London that he actually had no authority to participate in any talks at all, as all negotiations would be undertaken by the British government at a European location. As Prevost had not yet received Bathurst's letter of 3 June 1814 announcing the change in British strategy and the consequent influx of troops, the prospect of a ceasefire must have been appealing to Prevost, given his uncertainty regarding the strength of his forces for the coming campaign season.[32]

Prevost's decision to open talks was based partly on the condition of his command. With more than 15,000 troops in the Canadas, his army had more than doubled in size since the war began, placing him in a seemingly strong position. But many of his soldiers were sick or recovering from the campaigns of the previous year, and a shortage of gunners required the temporary employment of infantry in artillery companies. Four promised regiments had yet to arrive, but instead of waiting, Prevost shifted another regiment from New Brunswick to Lower Canada. Opposing him were 34,000 American regulars, most of whom were concentrated in the northern theater, including two strong divisions based in New York State, which threatened the Niagara Peninsula and Montreal. Only in the autumn of 1814 did the British land forces in *all* of British North America surpass the total strength of the U.S. Army. The numerical advantage enjoyed by the U.S. Army reinforced the premise that Britain was fighting a defensive war rather than seeking to conquer the United States.[33]

British plans for 1814 placed considerable emphasis on naval operations, including securing control of several lakes, and on conducting joint operations with the army. New construction at the dockyards meant the Great Lakes naval force would be expanded to nearly double its size in 1813. The growing strength and importance of the inland squadrons led to changes in the status of Yeo's command. As of May 1814, the entire naval force on the Great Lakes, along with its civilian establishments, was separated from the army and transferred to the Admiralty. Yeo's title was elevated from "Senior Officer on the Lakes" to "Commander-in-Chief of His Majesty's Ships and Vessels on the Lakes of Canada."[34] This officially ended any requirement for Prevost to support Yeo, as personnel and logistical support would now be provided directly by the Admiralty, making this the first occasion since the American War of Independence that the supervision of naval affairs on the inland waterways of North America was not managed by the army.[35]

The inland naval command now adopted Admiralty practices. Vessels were reclassified according to the standard naval rating system, and some were renamed to conform to Royal Navy practice.

Each ship received an official manning establishment, against which Yeo could make demands to fill shortfalls, though the details regarding arrangements for officering and manning rested with Yeo, meaning he could distribute personnel any way he wished. Royal Marines were deployed to replace the Canadian fencible troops currently serving on the vessels. Yeo was also invited to advise the Admiralty on "the reinforcements that may be required for completing their Complements [i.e., the ships in his command] as established, and for manning any other Vessels that may be likely to be brought forward for service on any of the Lakes: of the supplies of Stores of all descriptions that may be required."[36] To all intents and purposes, the Royal Navy had achieved the status of an independent service on the inland waters of North America.[37]

For Prevost, these changes were a mixed blessing similar to the transition of the Provincial Marine to Royal Navy control in 1813. He was freed from the responsibility of providing army personnel to bolster manpower, and his logistical responsibilities to the navy were now limited to ground transportation of personnel, ordnance, foodstuffs, and supplies. On the other hand, Prevost now had to contend with a naval commander who had greater independence because the Admiralty's instructions said nothing of Yeo having to support the commander in chief's plans. Prevost faced the prospect of having overall responsibility for the conduct of the war in the northern theater while control of naval operations lay outside his authority. Cooperation with Yeo had been poor during 1813, and there was no certainty in 1814 that a working relationship was salvageable. It proved impossible, and by the autumn, Prevost would complain to Bathurst that Yeo had lost all wish to collaborate and was operating under the notion "that the war is to be decided by the fleets, instead of by cooperation with the army."[38] This situation was not repeated in the Chesapeake, where in 1813 and 1814, Bathurst gave similar instructions to two different officers assigned to command the land forces in that theater—namely, Colonel Sir Thomas Sidney Beckwith and Major General Robert Ross—that they would be "under the command of the Naval Officer Commanding this Expedition."[39] Evidently the army could be placed under the navy, whereas the opposite was not deemed possible by Bathurst.

PREVOST acknowledged Bathurst's instructions on 12 July 1814. Once all the troops were in place, Prevost would implement his new orders, but to him the lengthy list of objectives must have appeared fanciful. Topping the list was the requirement to secure control of the lakes, destroy the enemy naval base at Sackets Harbor, and eliminate the American squadrons on Lakes Erie and Champlain. After Lake Erie was secured, Detroit was to be reoccupied and the Northwest retained for the Natives. Lastly, Prevost was to occupy an advanced position on American territory near the shore of Lake Champlain to prevent American incursions into Lower Canada. This ambitious plan was much greater than anything attempted by either side thus far in the war, including the large American offensives of late 1813. Achieving all of these objectives would require considerable planning and coordination and careful management of the logistical system. More important, it would necessitate Yeo's cooperation.[40]

In the event, Bathurst's orders arrived too late for all of the tasks to be achieved in 1814. The reestablishment of a presence on Lake Erie and the retaking of Detroit would have to wait until 1815, while current American naval supremacy on Lake Ontario ruled out an attack on Sackets Harbor for the time being. Major General James Kempt, who was to command the assault on that place, insisted that a combined operation of this scale and potential duration could not be undertaken until Lake Ontario was secure. Yeo would be unable to challenge American dominance of Lake Ontario until at least October when he would launch a new and powerful warship, which left insufficient time to conduct the attack. This left Prevost with the prospect of mounting only two of the objectives he had been assigned—the related objectives of destroying the enemy naval establishment on Lake Champlain and securing an advance position on the frontier that extended toward Lake Champlain. Prevost selected Plattsburgh, New York, as the ideal objective to improve the security of Lower Canada. This offensive would be his primary effort in 1814.[41]

In the spring and early summer of 1814, as officials in London completed the details for the new offensives in North America, President Madison's cabinet reviewed the events of the last year and began their own preparations for the coming year. The American campaign, poorly executed around Lake Ontario and against Montreal during 1813, had resulted in no appreciable success and ended with the complete devastation of the Niagara frontier by British

troops. The portion of western Upper Canada the Americans occupied offered them no strategic advantage, other than to partially
isolate the Northwest from British interference. The Royal Navy's
blockade of American coastal waters was seriously damaging the
republic's commerce, and its treasury was left with little money to
fund the war. Faced with sagging national morale, the cabinet was
divided over what strategy to employ in 1814. It was only in June
that they agreed to a three-pronged attack on the Canadas designed
to break up British posts on Lake Huron; disrupt communications
between the British and their Native allies in the Northwest; occupy
a portion of the Niagara Peninsula; and, with the help of Chauncey's
squadron, strike at Burlington Bay, York, or Kingston in order to
threaten Montreal. The emphasis of these operations lay in the west,
and the Niagara offensive came as an afterthought.[42]

Prevost had spent the winter months of 1813–14 making his own
preparations. Chief among his concerns were to determine American intentions and to find a means to reverse the situation on Lake
Erie and retake Detroit. Among his objectives were the retention of
Mackinac, the maintenance of the alliances with Native allies in
the west, and the recapture of Lake Erie. All of these goals were
linked to clearing the Americans from the western part of the province, but Prevost was also obliged to protect the interests of the
North West Company, which was struggling with American interference in its trading areas. When he formulated his plans for the
approaching campaign, Prevost was keenly aware of the important
contributions made by the North West Company toward the defense of British interests in the region, which valuable assistance he
still needed. However, in outlining his views to Drummond in January 1814, Prevost chose to downplay the interests of the company,
which, in his estimation, had to "be left out of the equation," in
light of other "advantages" that would result from "the preservation
of Mackinac."[43]

Foremost among these advantages was the safeguarding of the
Native alliance. As "the last link by which" warriors "still faithfully cling to our interest," Fort Mackinac was "the rallying point"
where warriors met to fight alongside their British allies. Without
this post, the Natives would "find themselves an abandoned people,
deserted by us" and forced "to seek the mercy from their bitter-
est foe." Prevost anticipated such an outcome would end British

influence with the Natives and irreparably damage any "prospect of [our] ever regaining their confidence." If British arms prevailed at Mackinac, Prevost was also confident that "the spirits of our auxiliaries," units raised from the local population, would be "revived" and would provide him with additional manpower needed for the recovery of other objectives.[44]

Although the expulsion of the British from the Detroit region ended Tecumseh's confederacy, relations with several aboriginal nations in the Mississippi Valley continued under Dickson's supervision and from the British base at Fort Mackinac. The assistance of Native allies—along with the resources of the North West Company and help from embodied, volunteer, and militia units raised from fur trappers, voyageurs, and traders residing in the Northwest—was necessary to retain the fort and other posts in the region. At the beginning of 1814, Prevost met with delegates from the Sioux, Menominee, and Winnebago nations who had made the long and arduous journey to Quebec to express their wish to continue relations with the British. Prevost immediately agreed to this request and promised help.[45] The only difficulty was in transporting reinforcements and supplies to them.[46]

Communication with the western posts and Native allies became difficult following the loss of the Lake Erie–Detroit River route that provided access to Lake Huron and the Northwest. As supplies ran low, the situation at Mackinac grew desperate, and by the end of 1813, the 100-man garrison, barely adequate to defend the place, was facing starvation. The established Ottawa River fur trade route offered a potential alternative, but it took almost sixty days to travel between Montreal and Mackinac and required thirty-five portages along the way.

Prevost expected the Americans would threaten British interests on the upper lakes by using the former British communication route along the Detroit River to transfer vessels and men from Lake Erie to Lake Huron. In January 1814, he asked Drummond, Yeo, and several other senior officers to comment on the practicability of destroying the American warships wintered at their base on Lake Erie. Drummond proposed an overland expedition using 1,700 regulars, marines, sailors, militia, and Natives to take Detroit and several outlying posts and to destroy the American flotilla at Put-in-Bay. Drummond would then send a portion of these men to reinforce

Mackinac. The assault force would be drawn from garrisons along the Niagara River, where Drummond was confident American forces were still weak following the recent devastation of that frontier by British troops. Prevost was impressed by this plan, and despite uncertainty about enemy dispositions and whether sufficient provisions could be obtained, he recognized that "in all great enterprises some risk must run and something [be] left to fortune" and approved it.[47] Unfortunately for Drummond, mild weather interfered with his scheme to conduct his movements by river and on the frozen lake; Prevost therefore canceled the operation, which, if successful, would have reopened communications with the Northwest.[48]

Unable to challenge the American squadron on Lake Erie, Prevost and Drummond considered other alternatives. The Ottawa River route had potential, but it was not efficient. Prevost decided instead to complete a shorter and less difficult route from York to Georgian Bay. A road from York to Lake Simcoe already existed, and surveys of the stretch from that lake to Georgian Bay revealed the need for several potentially expensive improvements, including a road. Prevost approved Drummond's recommendation to complete a twenty-mile-long road from Lake Simcoe to Nottawasaga Bay rather than a lengthier route to Penetanguishine Bay. The journey proved fatiguing and difficult; however, when this supply line was opened later in 1814, conditions in the northwest gradually improved.[49]

Aside from sending arms, ammunition, and presents to the Natives, 150 troops, and a large quantity of stores and supplies were transferred to Mackinac. Prevost also appointed Lieutenant Colonel Robert McDouall, a capable senior officer to take command at the fort and had Yeo provide a builder and several shipwrights to construct gunboats for use on Lake Huron. Later that year, Prevost ordered the establishment of a naval post at Penetanguishine Bay where a 44-gun frigate would be built. These improvements were undertaken to consolidate British control of the upper Great Lakes and to contribute to the eventual recovery of Detroit, Amherstburg, and Lake Erie in 1815.[50]

During the summer of 1814, the rejuvenated garrison at Fort Mackinac was joined by more than 300 warriors from several western tribes seeking to protect their homelands, and by fur traders who volunteered to serve. Together, they improved the defenses and, in August, successfully repulsed an American landing on the island.

Earlier in July a portion of the garrison had assisted with the capture of Fort Shelby (which the British renamed Fort McKay), at the confluence of the Mississippi and Wisconsin Rivers in the Illinois Territory, while the Winnebago, Sioux, and Sauk nations held the Mississippi for the British. These actions improved communication with Natives in the upper reaches of the Mississippi and allowed continued operation of the fur trade.[51]

As he monitored the situation in the Northwest, however, Prevost received evidence of a buildup of American troops near Buffalo. Drummond decided the large concentration indicated that he would be facing the main American offensive of 1814. As Prevost read these reports and began sending reinforcements to Drummond, he expressed concern whether it would be possible to provide enough supplies while the Americans controlled Lake Ontario. By the early summer, the British had 4,000 men, deployed between York and Fort Erie, known collectively as the Right Division of the Army of Upper Canada and commanded by Major General Phineas Riall. Reports indicated the Americans had amassed 4,500 men, ironically styled the Left Division of the Army of the United States, under Major General Jacob Brown. Riall proposed to leave garrisons at Forts George and Niagara but to concentrate the balance of his troops in a field force that would meet the Americans in the open. The flaw in this assessment was that Drummond and Riall believed they would be faced by poor quality troops, similar to those encountered during the previous winter. Their first encounter, however, which took place in July, revealed that Brown's troops were well trained and that the Right Division would require reinforcements. Prevost's fears regarding his ability to provide adequate support to Drummond quickly became reality.[52]

On 3 July 1814, Brown's division crossed the Niagara River into Upper Canada. Two days later, Riall was defeated at Chippawa and retired to the northern end of the peninsula, pursued by Brown. The American plan fell apart, however, when Brown learned that Chauncey was sick and unwilling to give command of his squadron to another officer, so it would remain in Sackets Harbor. After trying unsuccessfully to draw out the British from Fort George, Brown retired south. On 25 July, both armies met again at Lundy's Lane, and Brown gained a tactical victory. He was wounded in the battle, however, and the officer who assumed command decided to retire to Fort Erie. After a pause, Drummond advanced and laid siege to that place.[53]

As Prevost had predicted, moving stores and food to support the expanded forces on the Niagara Peninsula proved difficult. While Yeo waited for the completion of his new ship at Kingston, Chauncey dominated the lake, making it too risky for Prevost to use bateaux. He marched troops around Lake Ontario to the Niagara Peninsula, but he lacked the means to move large quantities of supplies by land as there were too few wagons and horses in the province to pull them. Some relief came with the arrival of a bateaux convoy from York, but this had little effect on the overall supply situation. Prevost continued to apply pressure on the Commissariat to push supplies from Kingston to the Niagara Peninsula, and craft laden with supplies at Kingston lay ready to move at the first opportunity the lake was open. Several of these bateaux carried ordnance that Drummond needed for the siege of Fort Erie. As the situation deteriorated in August, the weather worsened and Drummond continued appealing to Prevost for help even as he sent units he could not sustain back from Fort Erie.[54]

Prevost believed the only solution was to wrest control of the lake from Chauncey. The difficulty was that Yeo was unwilling to venture onto the water before his new ship was completed at Kingston. At a length of almost 200 feet and armed with 102 guns on three decks, the vessel would be the largest warship on the lakes when ready. Getting all the material to complete HMS *St. Lawrence*, as it was named, placed great strain on the upper St. Lawrence supply line, which slowed the delivery of needed equipment and delayed the launch date, from early summer to September. In the meantime, Yeo adamantly rejected Prevost's pleas to transport men and supplies to Drummond, citing the dangers of having his ships, overburdened with such cargo, on the lake while Chauncey's squadron was at large. Worse still, despite his earlier promises, Yeo still refused to sail when HMS *St. Lawrence* was finished at the beginning of October. As the final outfitting of ship was under way, Prevost urged the commodore to sail, but as Yeo considered his pleas, Prevost had part of an infantry unit destined for the Niagara Peninsula commence the march around the lake, while the remainder stood by at Kingston, ready to embark onto the ships. Yeo finally relented when he learned that Chauncey had returned to Sackets Harbor, and he reluctantly embarked half of the 90th Foot and a considerable quantity of stores, promising to return to Kingston with the sick and wounded from Fort George.[55]

Prevost complained bitterly to Bathurst about Yeo's reluctance to cooperate. In Prevost's opinion, the commodore's refusal to support the Right Division had endangered Drummond's forces and jeopardized Native support since there was insufficient quantity of food and gifts for them. The diversion of nearly all the transport to carry the ordnance for the *St. Lawrence* from Montreal to Kingston contributed to the postponement of the planned attack on Sackets Harbor until the following year. In October 1814, Prevost complained that by regarding the army's request for transport as "hampering the movements of the fleet and endangering its safety," Yeo had unfortunately ensured "that the war would be decided by fleets and not by cooperation with the army."[56]

Despite his complaints, Prevost appeared willing to resolve the impasse with Yeo without application to London. For now, his only recommendation was for the establishment of a transport service on the lakes independent of the navy. Within a few weeks, however, he would decide that Yeo's disregard of his instructions endangered the necessary unity of effort between the commander in chief of British North America and the navy and that an entirely new command structure was necessary to ensure British victory. This decision would come in the wake of the Plattsburgh campaign.[57]

8

PREPARING FOR THE PLATTSBURGH CAMPAIGN

Commence offensive operations on the Enemy's frontier.
—*Bathurst to Prevost, 3 June 1814*

Between late June and early August 1814, Prevost received reinforcements from Ireland, England, and other stations. These
additions included four complete brigade headquarters under Major
Generals Thomas Brisbane, James Kempt, Manley Power, and Frederick Robinson. Three of the brigades were assigned to the Montreal area, while Kempt's formation was immediately pushed forward to Kingston. On 17 August, Prevost reported to London that the
last of the reinforcement units had arrived. Most of the recent arrivals were placed in the Left Division, which also included units already stationed in Lower Canada.[1] This division was to form the
land component of the 1814 Plattsburgh campaign, and its brigades
were garrisoned south of Montreal, at Chambly, St. John's, and La
Prairie, close to where they would cross the frontier.[2]

By the end of August, Prevost's forces for the Plattsburgh campaign included the Left Division, with more than 10,000 troops distributed among the three infantry brigades, with fifteen field guns
and a seventeen-piece artillery train that included a rocket detachment and a contingent of Native warriors. The naval squadron destined for Lake Champlain, commanded by Captain Peter Fisher,
was based at Isle aux Noix on the Richelieu River; it comprised four
warships, one of which was still being completed, and several gunboats. As overall commander, Prevost was responsible for selecting
a divisional commander from among those general officers serving
in the Canadas and personnel for the headquarters staff. Lieutenant

General Gordon Drummond was unavailable as he was occupied with containing an American offensive on the Niagara Peninsula. The appointment might have gone to one of the recently arrived brigade commanders, but Prevost decided instead to select the most senior major general in the Canadas and assigned Major General Francis de Rottenburg, currently commanding the forces in Lower Canada. This was the first occasion during the war that a British force of this size had been assembled for a single operation in the northern theater.[3]

Historians' perceptions of Prevost's performance during the 1814 Plattsburgh campaign have been influenced by a persistent impression that the Left Division was made up exclusively of Wellington's "Invincibles," lately from the Peninsular army. The supposed defeat of elite troops from the finest army in the world in 1814, historians have argued, gave added significance to the American victory.[4] While the transfer of troops from Europe did leave Britain with "many of its best troops across the Atlantic in North America,"[5] not all of them came from Wellington's Peninsular army. Of the forty-four cavalry, artillery, and infantry units transferred to North America in 1814, twenty-one, or less than half, came from that force. The remaining twenty-three units were drawn from Germany, Italy, the East Coast Army in Spain, and from garrisons in Britain, Ireland, the West Indies, Gibraltar, South Africa, and the Mediterranean. The infantry component included sixteen Peninsular battalions, which represented less than one-quarter of Wellington's infantry strength, and of these battalions, only six were assigned to the Left Division. The soldiers under Prevost's command were sound and in some cases more experienced than those in Canada, but he did not command a red-coated juggernaut of elite troops as some veterans of the campaign and historians have claimed.[6]

Prevost was fortunate to have three brigade commanders whose experience was more extensive than most British general officers in North America. Major General Frederick Robinson, a veteran of the American War of Independence, had served on the Iberian Peninsula since 1812 and had commanded a brigade in several major actions during 1813, including the decisive victory over the French at Vitoria; the siege of St. Sebastian, where he was severely wounded; the passage of the Bidossa; and the Battle of the Nive, in which he was again gravely wounded. After recovering from his wounds,

Robinson briefly commanded a division before being selected for service in North America. Thomas Brisbane was also a Peninsular veteran who had commanded a brigade under Lieutenant General Thomas Picton, with whom Prevost had served in the West Indies. In 1813 and 1814, Brisbane had been involved in most of the major battles from Vitoria to Toulouse. Manley Power had commanded a brigade that had distinguished itself at Salamanca, Vitoria, Nivelle, and Orthes. Including James Kempt, who commanded the brigade deployed to Upper Canada, these four men were the most experienced general officers to serve in Canada during the War of 1812. What set them apart from the others was their service in Wellington's multidivision and multinational field army that was unique among the forces Britain fielded during the Napoleonic Wars. But they were now serving under Lieutenant General Sir George Prevost, an experienced commander whose service had been largely confined to the West Indies and North America. Prevost may have possessed greater skill in the conduct of amphibious operations, interservice cooperation, and logistical operations, but what made him different in the eyes of these Peninsular veterans was that he had not made his reputation under Wellington. To them Prevost was simply unknown.[7]

There were important differences in the experience and quality of the staffs employed by each commander. Brisbane, Power, and Robinson brought their own staffs with them, while the staff of the Left Division was drawn from officers serving in Canada. Major General Edward Baynes, appointed as the principal staff officer of that formation, had arrived in North America in 1807 and was currently adjutant general. Major General Sir Thomas Beckwith was a distinguished Peninsular veteran, who, after being invalided home, became quartermaster general of Canada in October 1813. He was appointed as the divisional quartermaster general and on campaign was responsible for movement, the quartering of the troops and intelligence. Lieutenant Colonel Philip Hughes, who came to Canada in 1812, was the commander and chief engineer of the Royal Engineers in Canada. The senior gunner was Brevet Major John Sinclair, who had arrived in Canada before the war. The commissary general for British North America, William Robinson—not to be confused with his brother, Major General Frederick Robinson—

would work with Beckwith in coordinating transport and logistical services.[8]

While the local officers were all experienced and well acquainted with the unique character of military operations in North America, they lacked familiarity with the workings of a field division. This was in sharp contrast to the recently arrived brigade commanders and their staffs. Certainly, each Peninsular commander and staff had their limitations, but their overall ability to plan and lead operations was superior to their North American counterparts. The short interval between the arrival of the new commanders and their staffs and the commencement of the Plattsburgh campaign left little opportunity for the newcomers to become familiar with Prevost, de Rottenburg, and the divisional staff.

There were other challenges. The logistical problems of campaigning in Spain and Portugal were very different from those in the Canadas. The limited land transportation resources had always posed problems for Prevost and his staff, and with the hurried creation of the Left Division, there was simply no time to create a transportation and wagon service to move provisions, stores, and ordnance. This significant shortfall would force the division to rely on whatever wagons and animals it could appropriate in the United States and would contribute to operational delays in the movement of guns and supplies.[9]

Throughout July and August 1814, Prevost oversaw the deployment of the Left Division south of Montreal, and made de Rottenburg responsible for the quartering of the troops. He assigned Robinson, Brisbane, and Power to command the 1st, 2nd, and 3rd Brigades, respectively, and allocated artillery to each unit, replacing militia gunners serving temporarily in the division with regulars from the Royal Artillery and assembling drivers and horses to move the guns.[10] Prevost caused an unfortunate, adverse reaction among the newly arrived officers by issuing a general order that chastised some of them for wearing dress that was "inconsistent with the rules of the service"[11] and by reminding commanding officers that in British North America uniform regulations were to be strictly observed. This order was the cause of much complaint by the recent arrivals despite the fact that, as commander in chief, Prevost had the authority to insist his officers appeared in proper uniform.[12]

A more important matter, as highlighted by Robinson and other officers, was that, unlike Wellington's standard practice in Europe, Prevost failed to issue a scheme of operations for the coming campaign.[13] At least one brigade commander understood the affair would be conducted under conditions different from the open warfare he had experienced in the Iberian Peninsula. To ready his men, Robinson conducted daily range practices, while the light companies drilled and also practiced skirmishing in the woods. In contrast, the divisional staff had to be urged into activity, which led an exasperated Robinson to comment, after observing the heads of the divisional staff departments in action, that "he had no idea such confusion existed in any part of the British Service."[14]

Unfortunately, an even worse situation existed concerning the naval squadron on Lake Champlain. Prevost placed great importance on the support of the Royal Navy, because, unlike the campaigns around Lake Ontario, he anticipated that the relatively short and direct land march from Lower Canada to Plattsburgh, despite the shortage of transport vehicles, would not require the navy to provide logistical support or transportation for the army. He believed cooperation between the services to be important since in North America, "military operations are unavoidably combined with naval cooperation and unconditionally dependent upon it,"[15] but he expected the Lake Champlain squadron would defeat its American counterpart and seize control of the lake. In other words, the successful attainment of the land and naval objectives, taking Plattsburgh and destroying the U.S. naval squadron, was necessary to achieve the strategic goal of the campaign, but the joint combination of these forces in securing tactical goals was not necessary.

As in 1813, Prevost and Yeo were intent on gaining supremacy on Lake Ontario. In response to reports that the Americans were building three frigates (two with forty-four guns, one with thirty-two guns) at Sackets Harbor, Yeo's decision to focus his efforts on one ship, the battleship HMS *St. Lawrence*, required the use of more materials, equipment, ordnance, and manpower than any previous shipbuilding project on inland waters. Yeo adamantly defended his decision to build this ship, even though Prevost worried that Yeo's "conviction has excited a struggle for the ascendency on the water that has drawn forth on both sides an array of vessels that could never have been anticipated in these inland waters."[16] Prevost believed that Yeo was being drawn into a false belief that a "trial of strength" would decide the outcome of the war, while "forgetting their [the navy's] necessary identity with the land force for the general prosperity of the common cause." [17] He feared the supplies needed to finish this ship were of such a scale as to absorb "nearly the whole of the summer transport," at the cost of other requirements.[18]

During 1814, Prevost, in accordance with the instructions he received from Bathurst, gave emphasis to the British naval presence on Lake Champlain. The British base on the lake had begun the war in a meager state. The Provincial Marine post, originally located at St. John's on the Richelieu River, was in decay, and the lone schooner stationed there was useless. During 1812, once Prevost learned of American plans to establish a naval force on the lake, he had selected Isle aux Noix, "a most important position" that "commands the navigation on the River Richelieu," as the new British naval base.[19] Prevost also ordered that improvements be made to the fortifications and that a small gunboat flotilla be assembled to protect the approaches to Montreal. These initiatives were consistent with his prewar assessment that the security of that city depended on maintaining "an impenetrable line on the South Shore . . . with a sufficient flotilla to command the Rivers St. Lawrence and Richelieu."[20] In 1813, Prevost had ordered several raids into American territory that brought the destruction of arsenals, barracks, blockhouses, and stores at Plattsburgh, Chazy, and other locations. Two American brigs were captured and brought into British service, providing the foundation of the Lake Champlain squadron and the establishment of British supremacy on the lake.[21]

Prevost had more direct influence on the development of the Lake Champlain squadron than did Yeo. During August 1813, the senior officer on the lake, Commander Daniel Pring, recommended that a 16-gun brig and heavy gunboats be constructed at Isle aux Noix.[22] Prevost opted for the construction of gunboats but not the brig, claiming its displacement would limit its use. Pring persisted and even offered to build two smaller sloops or schooners instead of one larger vessel. In October 1813, Prevost finally approved his request to build a brig, but construction was delayed until a naval yard was constructed on the Isle aux Noix. The 16-gun brig *Linnet* was finished in April 1814, one month ahead of its expected completion date.[23] The British now had three ships totaling forty guns and several gunboats on Lake Champlain.[24]

To match growing British strength, Master Commandant Thomas Macdonough, the American naval commander on Lake Champlain, was rebuilding his force after his setbacks of 1813 and requested permission to construct a new vessel. In turn, Pring filed a request to build an even larger warship, which Prevost immediately approved. Construction at Isle aux Noix reached its height in late May 1814, when work commenced on a 37-gun frigate that would become the largest warship on Lake Champlain.[25]

Another means of expanding the squadron available to Prevost was to make use of frigates-in-frame, which were essentially prefabricated ships. The frigate-in-frame project was developed in England as a method of easing the construction problem on the lakes. Prevost and Yeo rejected the plan as being impractical, since the transportation resources needed to move the sections up the St. Lawrence from Montreal to Kingston would sacrifice "more important objects."[26] Nonetheless, their concerns were in turn rejected by London, and they followed orders as best they could. The prefabricated frames of two 38-gun frigates and two 18-gun sloops arrived at Montreal in June and July 1814. Each of the vessels included all the items needed to complete them: fittings, rigging, and armament. Due to the cost of moving the sections farther inland, however, only one frigate, HMS *Psyche*, was ever completed at Kingston, while the remainder were left at Montreal. Yeo offered the frames left in Montreal to Pring and sent the additional shipwrights just arrived from Britain to assemble the four new vessels and the 900 naval personnel provided by the navy to man them to the naval base at Kingston. An inspection of two of the frames determined the frigates would draw too much water to navigate Lake Champlain safely. When an attempt to modify the vessels proved too difficult to complete, the project was dropped. Yeo took most of the fittings, rigging, and armament for the Lake Ontario squadron, offering the Lake Champlain commander the anchors and cables from the prefabricated sloops, but not those from the frigates. Yeo also took all the prefabricated ship's iron ballast as it was required for the squadron at Kingston.[27]

The most pressing problem at Isle aux Noix was not shortages of building materials, ordnance, or stores; it was a lack of seamen. By the fall of 1813, Pring had only thirty-eight sailors, and attempting to secure additional seamen from ships at Quebec, he found forty seamen, nine marines, and one boy, which still left the establishment seriously undermanned. Pring asked both Prevost and Yeo for assistance but received little.

Meanwhile, the Lake Ontario squadron steadily grew stronger. On 14 April 1814, two frigates, one with fifty-six guns and the other with forty, were launched at Kingston. Over the summer, the new 102-gun first-rate warship took form on the stocks. Together, these three ships required a complement of 1,400 seamen, and finding these crewmen was one of Yeo's priorities. Earlier, in March 1814, Yeo learned he was to receive 900 officers and men for the four frigates-in-frame. Then in May, Yeo suffered the loss of 220 seamen, who were captured in a disastrous encounter with the Americans at Sandy Creek. Prevost responded to the loss that threatened the British position on the lake by hastening "to Kingston the whole of the Officers, Seamen & Artificers who have just arrived from England,"[28] along with materials for the new first rate. The new detachment of seamen arrived at Kingston in June 1814 and was immediately distributed throughout the Lake Ontario squadron. Only a single officer from this group, Captain Peter Fisher, was sent to Isle aux Noix, where he took command of the station on Lake Champlain from Pring. With the new ship nearing completion at that place, the requirement for seamen was becoming more acute. Fisher continued his predecessor's appeals for 400 more men and additional supplies, but Yeo refused to provide them claiming, "I do not expect so many in the Country this year";[29] Yeo's claim, however, was less than honest as he had known since the spring that the Admiralty was sending him another 900 officers and men, while from Halifax Admiral Warren provided him with another 200 seamen.[30]

On 25 August 1814, while Prevost was completing the final preparations for the Plattsburgh campaign, the new flagship of the Lake Champlain squadron, HMS *Confiance*, named in honor of one of Yeo's previous commands, was launched. Once floated, the ordnance had to be fitted, quoins—wood wedges used to adjust the elevation and depression of the gun—fashioned for the guns, and the magazine completed, among other tasks.[31] John Hoffmeister, the acting naval storekeeper of the dockyard, optimistically believed that "as every species of store is now at hand," *Confiance* "will be ready to proceed up the river in ten days at the furthest."[32] At this critical juncture, Yeo suddenly replaced Fisher with Captain Robert Downie and ordered Fisher to return to Lake Ontario. Yeo later claimed the change was necessary because Fisher's demands for manpower verged on impertinence.[33] Downie, who arrived on 1 September, did not share Hoffmeister's optimism as to when *Confiance* would be ready. At the beginning of September, he reported that his flagship was "now nearly ready to proceed on service, but has not a lock to any gun or carronade. In a few days, she will be before the enemy and the want of locks may be seriously injurious in action."[34] Prevost was disturbed by this information and the reports of continued naval manpower shortages, as the news upset his own plans, though the lateness of the season did not permit much flexibility in the campaign schedule. In early September, Prevost ordered that Downie be given another 150 seamen from the transports at Quebec, followed by a further 200. A final draft of 250 men was dispatched on 9 September, only after the squadron had already departed for Plattsburgh.[35]

The final complement of the Lake Champlain squadron was 799 men. Of these, 442 men were distributed between the four warships and the remainder served on the gunboats. *Confiance* had the largest single crew of 270 men, a diverse collection of twenty officers, drafts from ten ships at Quebec, twenty-five men from transports, sixty-five Marines and ten soldiers. Many of the men were unskilled, since they were either impressed, taken from prison, or were recent volunteers. Others were "forced from their respective ships,"[36] as captains saw the opportunity to rid themselves of discipline problems. The majority of the ship's company embarked between 5 and 9 September 1814, just days before the naval battle at Plattsburgh Bay. Only two of the officers knew each other, and the crew had had little opportunity to train together before fighting commenced—including only two or three occasions to exercise the guns.[37]

IN spite of the difficulties in outfitting the naval squadron, the final preparations for the offensive coincided with some good news. After inspecting Robinson's brigade at Chambly at the end of August, Prevost moved to his headquarters at Odelltown, near the border with New York State. There he learned that the American Right Division, under the command of Major General George Izard, had withdrawn from Champlain and Chazy—which lay along the route he intended to take to Plattsburgh—in response to orders to move westward to join Major General Jacob Brown's Left Division currently besieged at Fort Erie.[38] Command at Plattsburgh devolved on Brigadier General Alexander Macomb, a regular army officer, who commanded 1,500 regulars, militia, and volunteers and a large number of convalescents. The departure of 4,300 well-trained regular troops under Izard meant that Prevost would now be facing considerably less opposition. With the departure of Izard, British allied Native warriors commenced raids against communities across the frontier.[39]

There is no evidence that Prevost was enthusiastic about the forthcoming offensive. Given the crucial situation on the Niagara Peninsula and the uncertain state of the naval balance on Lake Ontario, he was uneasy about sending a large force into the enemy's territory. The delay in completing the squadron at Isle aux Noix and in launching Yeo's new ship made it difficult both to convey desperately needed supplies and reinforcements to Drummond's army on the Niagara Peninsula and to support his own advance into New York. Prevost held the view that the cooperation of the squadrons on Lake Ontario and Lake Champlain, as the case might be, was absolutely essential to the success of the struggle on the peninsula and the advance on Plattsburgh, respectively. Without the aid and protection of the navy, he wrote in July, "nothing could be undertaken affording a reasonable hope of substantial advantage."[40] The government, he sensed, would be unmoved by his objections and the postponement until the following year of all of the tasks assigned to him by Bathurst in his letter of 3 June 1814. These suspicions would be proven correct when, following his return from Plattsburgh, Prevost read in a letter from Bathurst that if he did not "undertake offensive measures against the enemy," he would "very seriously disappoint the expectations of the Prince Regent and the country."[41]

Although he lacked effective naval support on Lake Champlain, Prevost ordered the Left Division forward into New York. He intended to confine his movement to the western shore of the lake, avoiding Vermont so as not to hinder the busy trade in cattle and provisions with the citizens of that state. As his line of communication lengthened, he planned to leave units to protect key points along the route. Prevost's objective was Plattsburgh, a commercial center twenty-five miles distant with a population of approximately 3,000. Once he had moved forward, Downie would protect his over-land supply line by securing command of the lake. Once Platts-burgh was taken and control of Lake Champlain achieved, Prevost intended, depending on the circumstances, either to remain in Platts-burgh or to return to Lower Canada. Aside from patrols and raids, Prevost had no intention of moving south of Plattsburgh.[42]

The Plattsburgh offensive began on 31 August 1814 with the advance of Brisbane's brigade across the border. That day, Prevost ordered de Rottenburg, the divisional commander, to move the re-mainder of the division forward on 1 September.[43] Once in Ameri-can territory, Prevost issued a proclamation to the "peaceable and unoffending inhabitants"[44] of New York State assuring them that "they have no cause for alarm from the invasion of their country for the safety of themselves or their families, or for the security of their property."[45] So long as they acted peaceably, the local populace would be permitted to continue with business as usual. Prevost also strove to limit the potential of difficulties with civilians by not allowing the Native warriors to accompany the expedition into any of the towns.

Mindful of the difficulties Drummond's Right Division faced on the Niagara Peninsula, the ongoing struggle for naval dominance of Lake Ontario, the uncertain state of affairs on the upper lakes, and the problems plaguing the Lake Champlain naval squadron, Sir George Prevost was about to enter enemy territory for a second time, as commander of the only offensive he could mount in 1814, despite the additional resources London had provided, from the lengthy list of objectives he had been ordered to secure.

9

A SINGLE STAIN

The Plattsburgh Campaign

On 1 September 1814, the day after Major General Thomas Brisbane's brigade crossed the frontier and occupied the town of Champlain, New York, Major General Manley Power moved his brigade into Burtonville, Lower Canada, where he made final preparations to advance into New York using a route to the east of that taken by Brisbane. On the following day, Major General Frederick Robinson's brigade moved "by many bad roads"[1] to Burtonville and, on 3 September, crossed the frontier, entering U.S. territory at Champlain later that day. It was left to the brigade commanders to select the routes they marched by, leaving de Rottenburg and his staff to play only a minor role in the advance. The difficulties of employing larger formations in North America became evident with the relatively slow movement of the heavier artillery pieces due to insufficient teams and wagons. Movement was also rendered difficult by the large number of troops moving on the few available routes. Robinson recorded that his brigade, which was in the rear, had to march "through many bad roads rendered much worse by the number of artillery and other carriages with the Second and Third Brigades."[2] It is possible that the slow pace may have also been deliberate so as to give Downie time to complete his naval preparations.[3]

Despite the difficulties, the advance was well conducted. On 4 September, Prevost halted the division at Chazy, a township with a population of 1,500, about nine miles north of Plattsburgh. From here the main road continued south, while another route led east to

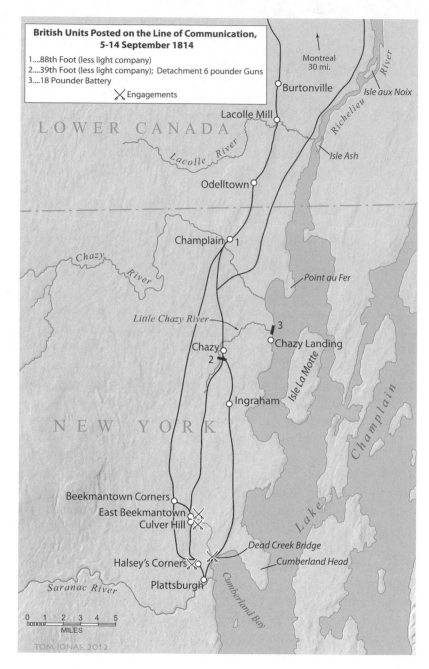

The Plattsburgh Campaign.

In September 1814, Prevost commanded a joint land-sea force that attempted to secure naval command of Lake Champlain and occupy Plattsburgh, New York. His aim was to eliminate the threat of American attacks against Montreal. The apparent failure to achieve these goals, and the loss of the naval squadron caused the Royal Navy to press for charges against Prevost, resulting in his recall in 1815 and plans for a court-martial.

the hamlet of Chazy Landing, a shipping outlet on the shore of Lake Champlain, just south of the area that would serve as a forward base for the naval squadron. Prevost ordered a reconnaissance party to examine routes leading to Plattsburgh, one of which was said to have been made impassable by the enemy. It was discovered that, although the bridge over the Little Chazy River (not to be confused with the Chazy River, which flowed southeast from Champlain into Lake Champlain) had been destroyed, the river was fordable. A western or higher road was elevated and dry, while the swampy road closer to the lake was deemed unsuitable for the artillery but passable for infantry. Trees that had been felled across the western route were of little consequence as they "could easily be removed."[4] The British gunboats, under the command of Commander Daniel Pring, had been ordered forward on 3 September to protect Prevost's left flank. They quickly established a powerful battery of three 18-pounder long guns at the mouth of the Little Chazy River to protect the supplies being deposited there for the Left Division. Prevost issued orders for the march to continue the next day.[5]

Because Prevost's line of communication back to Canada would lengthen the farther south he moved, he ordered one of the Peninsular battalions, the 39th Foot, and a detachment of light 6-pounder guns, to remain at Chazy. The 88th Foot was posted at Champlain for the same duty, but, in each case, the battalion light companies remained with the main army. Prevost had selected the most experienced units from Robinson's brigade for this duty to ensure that his line of communication was secure.[6]

From Chazy, the advance recommenced at daybreak on 5 September. Power's 3rd Brigade led off, taking the road to East Beekmantown, where Power established a camp, to the north of the town, that evening. The next day, the remaining two battalions and two detached light companies of Robinson's depleted formation, now termed a demi-brigade, marched to Ingraham, before turning west and onto a route that ran through a cedar swamp that Robinson described as "the worst I had ever seen."[7] Conditions were so difficult that the artillery was stuck for three hours.

On 6 September, the western column divided north of East Beekmantown, with Power's 3rd Brigade advancing south, while Brisbane continued on a parallel route farther to the west. Power's brigade soon had its first encounter with American troops, which had been sent by Macomb to slow the British advance. The lead elements of Power's brigade received a strong volley from 300 regulars, volunteers, and militia, supported by two guns, that were posted near the Ira Howe House, just north of East Beekmantown. Power "drove the enemy before him without the slightest trouble whatsoever" and then threw his light infantry into the fight as the Americans regrouped just to the south at Culver Hill.[8] Both sides suffered a few casualties, but the Americans had done little to slow the British advance.[9] A third skirmish occurred one and one-half miles north of Plattsburgh at Halsey's Corners, but, as in the previous two actions, the defenders were quickly dispersed. Power's column soon threatened to cut off the enemy north of Plattsburgh, and Macomb ordered his men to retire across the Saranac River, destroying the upper and lower bridges as they did. The two British columns then reunited and commenced their final march to the town. Intermittent sniping came from the defenders as they fell back in good order toward Plattsburgh, and several American gunboats beat a hasty retreat after their attempt to engage the British was met with artillery fire.[10]

The Left Division was now deployed in an arc to the north and west of Plattsburgh, along the western bank of the Saranac, a sinewy watercourse that twisted its way in a northeasterly direction from the Adirondack Mountains before emptying into Cumberland, or Plattsburgh, Bay on Lake Champlain. The village of Plattsburgh lay on both sides of the river, near its mouth. The bend in the river formed a peninsula that was occupied by the eastern part of the village and two bridges connected the peninsula with the western part of the village, now occupied by Prevost's troops. The river was more than seventy feet wide but could easily be forded by infantry at several points. The British left flank lay on the shore of Lake Champlain and the right near the westernmost bridge on the Saranac.[11]

So far, matters had gone well for Prevost. The opposition had been slight and no delays were encountered, while casualties had been just over 100 officers and men. His army now lay at the door to Plattsburgh, but it was in Prevost's execution of the next phase of the campaign that his critics, including Yeo, would find reason to complain. Already, some of Prevost's subordinate officers had begun to find fault with their commander in chief—Robinson was pleased neither with Prevost's conduct nor with that of his staff, later writing, "It appears to me that the army moved against Plattsburgh without any regularly digested plan."[17]

When Robinson, who had heard the skirmishing between Power and the Americans but was unable to provide support, arrived at Plattsburgh during the afternoon of 6 September 1814, he was approached by Major General Thomas Beckwith, the quartermaster general, whose department was responsible for encampment, the movement of the army, topographical information, and intelligence, to see if Robinson could mount an immediate attack on the American positions. Robinson promptly refused, as he had no information on the fords over the Saranac River, the ground beyond it, or the distance to the enemy. Incensed by Beckwith's failure to provide these details, Robinson curtly suggested that this information be gathered promptly. Robinson then proposed that the division be "posted in the best Position for investing the place."[13] Prevost arrived on the scene and, after listening to both officers, agreed that a detailed reconnaissance was necessary; however, as it was already late in the afternoon, the attack would be delayed until the next day.[14]

At 9:00 A.M. on 7 September, Prevost held a council at his headquarters. After passing on details gained from a reconnaissance of the American defences, he announced that the ground attack was postponed indefinitely because he had decided to wait "for the operation of the flotilla under Captain Downie."[15] In the meantime, the troops would "remain in their present positions until further notice."[16] He ordered that batteries be erected and that guns, ammunition, and stores be moved forward using whatever transport was available. The deficiency in transport delayed the arrival of two medium 12-pounders and two 8-inch mortars, both necessary for siege work, that Prevost had ordered taken from the garrison at Isle aux Noix. The result was that, by the time Prevost was ready to launch the attack on the 11th, the only siege ordnance in position were two experimental light brass 24-pounder guns that were unsuitable for the task ahead.[17]

The defenders of Plattsburgh were a mixed lot of regulars and state militia from New York and Vermont numbering 3,400. They were distributed between three forts and other fortified points on the east side of the Saranac. Almost 1,400 men were sick or unavailable for other reasons. The backbone of this army consisted of six regular army regiments numbering 1,800 men that were distributed in pairs between the three forts. Work on these fortifications had commenced earlier in the summer, after Izard dismissed a proposal by Major General James Wilkinson to erect a battery near the Canadian border that could close the narrows of the Richelieu River and deny entry of the British into the upper lake.[18] Instead, Izard assigned his senior engineer, Major Joseph Totten, a West Point graduate and professional with considerable experience in the northern theater, to build earthen redoubts between the Saranac and Plattsburgh Bay that would impede a British advance along the western shore of the lake. It was on this peninsula that Macomb centered his defense. Fort Moreau, the strongest of the positions, lay in the center of the American line, and it was armed with twelve guns of various calibers. To the west, near the high riverbank of the Saranac, was Fort Brown, while to the east, along the shore of Plattsburgh Bay, was Fort Scott.[19] The latter two forts had eight guns apiece, positioned with interlocking arcs of fire. A blockhouse, known as No. 1, was constructed in the center of the peninsula just north of Fort Moreau, while Blockhouse No. 2 was located on the northern end of the peninsula. A company of riflemen occupied the first blockhouse, and a detachment of artillery was in the second. A battery was also constructed east of the second blockhouse. During early September, Macomb had evacuated 720 sick men to a camp on Crab Island, located just outside of Plattsburgh Bay.[20]

Prevost prepared to lay siege to the American defenses. Sieges were deliberate operations that first isolated and then wore down a defended point, forcing its garrison to surrender, starve, or be taken by assault. A siege typically required a large number of heavy guns and considerable engineer stores, including shovels, picks, and axes. Personnel from the Royal Engineers and Royal Artillery were responsible for the establishment of the siege lines and other preparations prior to the assault. The British had more than enough troops to construct the siege lines, and each day a work party of 500 men drawn from the infantry battalions labored under the protection of another 1,000 men known as the covering party.

As strong as Prevost's force seemed, it had weaknesses in certain critical capabilities necessary for a siege—a shortage of ground transport was one; lack of engineers was another. With only nineteen officers of the Royal Engineers serving in all of British North America, few were available for the Left Division, and many of those

British and American
Positions around
Plattsburgh.

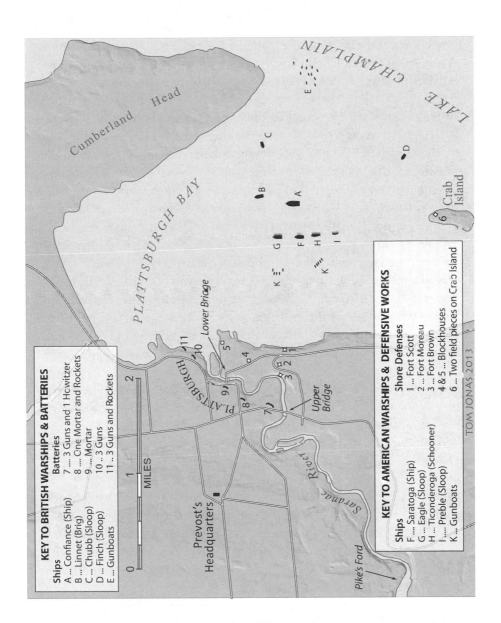

KEY TO BRITISH WARSHIPS & BATTERIES

Ships
A ... Confiance (Ship)
B ... Linnet (Brig)
C ... Chubb (Sloop)
D ... Finch (Sloop)
E ... Gunboats

Batteries
7 ... 3 Guns and 1 Howitzer
8 ... One Mortar and Rockets
9 ... Mortar
10 .. 3 Guns
11 ..3 Guns and Rockets

MILES

0   1   2

KEY TO AMERICAN WARSHIPS & DEFENSIVE WORKS

Ships
F ... Saratoga (Ship)
G ... Eagle (Sloop)
H ... Ticonderoga (Schooner)
I ... Preble (Sloop)
K ... Gunboats

Shore Defenses
1 ... Fort Scott
2 ... Fort Moreau
3 ... Fort Brown
4 & 5 ... Blockhouses
6 ... Two field pieces on Crab Island

TOM JONAS 2013

LAKE CHAMPLAIN

Cumberland Head

PLATTSBURGH BAY

Crab Island

PLATTSBURGH

Lower Bridge

Upper Bridge

Saranac River

Prevost's Headquarters

Pike's Ford

present lacked the requisite skill and experience for conducting a siege. Exasperated by the "neglect" on the part of Lieutenant Colonel Philip Hughes, which resulted in nothing being done "towards finishing the Batteries on the right,"[21] on the night of 8 September, Prevost dismissed his senior engineer and replaced him with Captain William Payne, who supervised the preparations for the remainder of the campaign. There were few engineer officers available to superintend the work. For example, a single engineer, Lieutenant Joshua Jebb, was assigned to supervise work on the entire left of the British lines. This work was dangerous as "sharp shooters on both sides were constantly engaged from day break until dark."[22]

The scale of this effort frustrated Robinson. He noted that the number of men assigned to the working party, covering party, "the pickets and the support amounted to more than the whole of the American force under General Macombe."[23] By now Prevost had 7,500 rank and file at Plattsburgh, with another 1,200 men guarding the line of communication.[24] Several officers believed that the matter could be settled quickly without waiting for the naval squadron. "Reports say," artillery Captain James Wood recorded in his diary, "that our troops should be permitted to follow up and carry the works at a dash, but timidity and indecision appear to prevail, where energy and vigor ought to exist."[25] If Prevost was aware of these sentiments, he did not let them affect his determination to await Downie.[26]

DESPITE the herculean efforts of the officers, ship's company, workmen, and contractors during the early days of September 1814, HMS Confiance, the flagship of the Lake Champlain squadron, was not yet completed. When Downie arrived at Isle aux Noix at the beginning of the month, he sent Captain Pring with Chub, Linnet, and Finch, accompanied by the gunboats, to rendezvous with the Left Division at Chazy Landing, while he remained at the naval base to complete Confiance. On 6 September, Prevost asked Downie to join him at Plattsburgh, to which the naval commander replied, on the "morning" of 7 September, that his flagship was in such "a state as to require at least a day or two to make her efficient before the enemy."[27] Good to his word, Downie left the dockyard on 8 September, and by "Warping, Sweeping, Towing and Sailing,"[28] he reached an anchorage at Point au Fer, near the mouth of the Chazy River, later that day. *Confiance* had departed "with the principle [*sic*] part of the Powder . . . put into a Boat and towed astern"[29] until the fore magazine could be completed. Downie asked Captain Clotworthy Upton, Royal Navy, in Quebec to forward the locks, the mechanism used to fire the naval ordnance, from two of his ships as quickly as possible as the *Confiance* had none.[30] The shortage of locks persisted, however, and desperate measures were taken to overcome this problem, including an unsuccessful attempt to modify locks from a carronade (a shorter-barreled gun introduced into the Royal Navy in 1779[31]). The only solution was to use matches to fire the guns As the frigate moved south, twenty-five carpenters and workmen, including Master Builder William Simons, labored feverishly, but there was insufficient time to finish the weather structure on the poop (the highest deck located at the stern) and top-gallant forecastle (the raised deck covering the bow area). A rail or ridge-rope was fabricated instead, which left the guns and their crews exposed.[32]

The ship's company of the *Confiance* had been assembled with such haste and at so late an hour that it made the confused personnel conditions on Lake Erie the previous autumn appear well organized by comparison. Training and gunnery practice were limited. With thirty-seven guns, *Confiance* possessed almost 50 percent of the firepower in the British Lake Champlain squadron; and one of its broadsides was nearly equivalent to what could be fired by the entire American squadron. Unfortunately for the British, shortages of men made it impossible to assign crews to the four 32-pounder carronades and two of the six 24-pounder carronades, and the improvised firing mechanisms proved defective.[33]

Yeo's replacement of Fisher with Downie the day after Prevost began his march for Plattsburgh led to predictable complications. Two rapid changes of command had occurred for reasons that were as obscure then as they are today. Downie arrived without any knowledge of the campaign plan nor time to familiarize himself with his command. By then, Prevost had begun his advance and Downie's decision to remain at Isle aux Noix to complete his flagship strained his relationship with Prevost somewhat. There was no opportunity for the two commanders to meet and discuss the finer points of the operation, and their communication was based on letters and messages passed through Prevost's aides, which was less than ideal. Once Downie arrived at the forward naval base near the mouth of the Chazy River, both officers exchanged several letters a day.

On 8 September, when Downie departed from Isle aux Noix, he received a letter from Prevost, written that day, stressing that it was "of the highest importance the Ship, Vessels and Gun Boats, under your Command should commence cooperation with the Division of the Army now occupying Plattsburgh."[34] Prevost advised Downie of his tasks for the first time and instructed him that "the first instance will be to destroy or capture the enemy's squadron . . . and afterwards cooperate with this Division of the Army."[35] If, by the time he got to Plattsburgh, the American squadron had moved farther south of its current position off Plattsburgh in Cumberland Bay, Downie was to present Prevost with options to engage the American squadron.

In his reply written that day, Downie did not comment on his orders but made it clear that his situation had not changed. "Yesterday I stated to you this ship is not ready—and she is not ready now—and until she is ready, it is my duty not to hazard the squadron before an enemy who will be superior in force."[36] That Prevost clearly got the message is evident from his letter to Downie written the next day, 9 September, that was delivered by his aide Major James Fulton: "In consequence of your communication of yesterday's date, I have postponed moving on the enemy's position . . . until your Squadron is in a state of preparation to cooperate with the Division of the Army."[37] Prevost then returned to the matter of the coming battle. "I need not dwell with you on the evils resulting to both services from delay, as I am well convinced you have done everything that was in your power to accelerate the armament and equipment of your Squadron, and I am also satisfied nothing will prevent its coming off Plattsburgh, the moment it is practicable."[38] Prevost closed his letter with intelligence obtained from deserters that the American squadron had too few men to crew its vessels. Interrogation of prisoners revealed that "after the arrival of the new Brig, they sent on shore for all [military] prisoners . . . to make up a crew for that vessel."[39] The brig was the *Eagle*, a 20-gun warship that had been launched on 11 August 1814, only nineteen days after its keel was laid. A week later, the finished vessel joined the three other warships under the command of Master Commandant Thomas

Macdonough.[40] The Lake Champlain squadron, now complete, was brought into Plattsburgh Bay on 1 September.[41]

Prevost received Downie's reply at midnight on 9 September, and he indicated he would attack in the morning. Downie, who had moved his squadron farther south and now lay off the Little Chazy River about fifteen miles north of Plattsburgh, reported the wind was favorable, giving him the "intention to weigh and proceed from this anchorage about Midnight in the expectation of rounding into the Bay of Plattsburgh about the dawn of day and commence an immediate attack upon the Enemy if they should be found in a position that will offer success. I rely on any assistance you can afford the squadron."[42] Still in need of men for his ships and gunboats, Downie reported that he had also applied for a company of the 39th Regiment, which was provided by the officer commanding at Chazy. Prevost was delighted with this information and immediately gave orders for the Left Division to prepare to attack on the morning of 10 September. The troops would be ready from "six o'clock this morning to storm the enemy's works at nearly the same moment as the naval action should commence in the Bay."[43] He arranged to receive confirmation of the squadron's departure from its current position off the Little Chazy River by detaching Captain William Watson, an officer of the Dorchester Provincial Light Dragoons, to Downie's anchorage, who would then ride to Prevost's headquarters with news of the naval movement.[44]

The wind then changed again, however, preventing Downie from sailing into position. Prevost's frustration was evident in his next letter to the naval commander: "I ascribe the disappointment I have experienced to the unfortunate change of wind and shall rejoice to learn that my reasonable expectations have been frustrated by no other means."[45] Major Foster Coore, another of his aides, was sent to deliver this letter to Downie. Coore caught up with the squadron three miles below Chazy Landing and presented it to Downie in his cabin on *Confiance*. Commander Daniel Pring was present during the interview. According to Pring, after reading Prevost's letter, Downie told Coore that "the Letter does not require an Answer, and I have nothing further to state to the Commander of the Forces than you can tell him."[46] Downie then stated "with some warmth": "I will not write him any more letters, this letter [meaning the letter of 10 September] does not deserve an Answer, but I will convince him the Naval Force will not be backward in their share of the Attack."[47] Coore had a similar recollection of the meeting and later wrote that once Downie had read Prevost's letter, he "said with some warmth, 'I am surprised Sir George should think it necessary to urge me upon this subject: he must feel assured, that I am as desirous of proceeding to active operations as he can be; but I am responsible for the Squadron I command, and no man shall make me lead it into action before I consider it in a fit condition.' "[48]

Coore then discussed the position of the enemy squadron, which he had "reconnoitred on my way to Chazy."[49] Despite Downie's estimate that the enemy's vessels were "collectively superior to his own," the captain appeared "full of confidence."[50] The plan of attack, which would be developed by Downie, was never discussed, and Coore "did not convey, nor was I ordered to convey" any instruction or opinion from Prevost as to how his attack should be made. Coore stated later that he had no recollection of Prevost having "an opinion as to the most eligible mode of engaging them [the Americans]."[51] Prevost's only wish was for the navy to act.

Coore returned to Prevost and reported that Downie would sail early on 11 September. The squadron's approach would be signaled by the scaling of the *Confiance*'s guns—that is, firing blank rounds— "in order they [the army] might know when their co-operation was wanted,"[52] meaning Prevost should commence his attack. According to Pring, Downie was dissatisfied with the tactical situation and the state of his command but weighed these shortfalls against what another delay might bring. "I would otherwise of course prefer fighting them on the Lake and would wait until our Force is in an efficient state," Downie stated, "but I fear they would if I waited take shelter up the Lake [i.e., move south], and not meet me on equal terms."[53] Downie believed these disadvantages could be reduced if the land attack coincided with that of the naval squadron: "When the Batteries are stormed and taken possession of by the British Land Forces which the Commander of the Land Forces had promised to do at the moment the naval action commences the Enemy will then at all events be obliged to quit their position whereby we shall obtain decided Advantage over them during their Confusion."[54]

It should be noted that Prevost never gave Downie a direct order to sail, and their correspondence, while terse, does not support the popular impression that Prevost goaded or forced Downie into action. The naval commander had good intelligence regarding his opponent and, despite its limitations, was confident in the capabil ity of his squadron. Following a careful assessment of the situation, the factors influencing both squadrons, and a weighing of the options, Downie had agreed to sail and engage the next morning on his own accord.

PREVOST had decided that the Left Division's attack on Plattsburgh would be executed in two parts. To the north, Brisbane was to "occupy the north bank of the Saranac and to cooperate by demonstration"[55] and cross the two bridges over the river. He was to press his attack "as far as may be practicable."[56] Robinson was to be responsible for delivering the main blow farther to the south. His brigade was reinforced with Power's four-battalion brigade, two squadrons of light dragoons, two 9-pounder guns, a Congreve Rocket section, and two or three wagons loaded with scaling ladders. Robinson was to cross the Saranac and "then to press forward until" he had "gained the ridge of high land on the south shore on which the enemy's field works are erected."[57] He would then "obtain possession of the Enemy's positions with as little delay as circumstances and the nature of the service will admit."[58] According to Edward Brenton, Prevost's civil secretary, Prevost issued these orders at de Rottenburg's headquarters at daybreak on 11 September and directed that they be passed immediately to the relevant officers. Captain Alexander Burke, the assistant adjutant general of the Left Division, personally delivered them to Brisbane, Robinson, and Power, and then also repeated the instructions from the previous day: to have their men eat and await the order to begin the attack.[59]

The deficiencies of the Left Division's artillery were once again evident in the number of guns that were allocated to support the attack. The majority of the pieces were the standard 6-pounder field gun that was more useful in an antipersonnel role than against fortified posts. The two 24-pounder guns were not much better. These were light, experimental pieces that had been cast during the Seven Years' War and sent to North America in 1777. They had remained in storage until 1814 when two were allotted to the Left Division and another two to the Right Division on the Niagara Peninsula. The 24-pounders were hybrid pieces meant to be employed as field artillery or in sieges, but they proved ineffective in both roles. The three 24-pounder carronades were naval guns with short barrels that not only reduced their weight but made for less accuracy at range.[60] Two 12-pounder guns, the heaviest field pieces within the division, could not be used in the attack as they did not arrive at Plattsburgh until the morning of 11 September. Two other pieces of ordnance designed to fire explosive shells—a 5.5-inch howitzer and an 8-inch mortar—were heavier weapons, but only the mortar was designed specifically for siege work. Finally, the rocket detachment operated a weapon that, when fired, flew so erratically that it did little more than harass the enemy if it did not amuse him.[61] During the night, as the gunners moved the siege pieces from the artillery park and into the prepared positions, the cost of having too few engineer officers to supervise the erection of the batteries became clear, as many of them were found to be unfinished or deficient in the "thickness of parapet, direction of embrasures, platforms and material."[62]

The guns of the Royal Artillery were distributed between Robinson's force and five batteries constructed along the left bank of the Saranac River. One of the three field artillery brigades, equipped with four 6-pounders and one 5.5-inch howitzer plus a detachment of rockets, was assigned to support Robinson's attack. Half of a brigade was guarding the line of communication at Chazy, and the other half of this brigade was held in reserve at Plattsburgh. Three 6-pounder guns and one 5.5-inch howitzers from the 3rd Brigade were placed in the southernmost of the three prepared battery positions, which, according to Robinson and Sinclair, was the "only one that could properly engage the enemy's works."[63] This battery, however, was "by no means completed," leaving it exposed to enemy fire.[64] The other two batteries were equipped with rockets and one 8-inch mortar.[65] Two batteries were erected near the mouth of the Saranac River. One had the two light brass 24-pounders with a detachment of rockets, and the other had the three 24-pounder carronades. All of the British batteries were placed within seven hundred yards of the enemy, within the effective range of the guns.[66]

An hour before dawn on 11 September, Robinson's force was ready in its camp to move and then waited for the order to advance. At 8:00 A.M., just after he heard the scaling of Downie's guns, which indicated his squadron was approaching Cumberland Bay, Robinson was summoned to Prevost's headquarters, located to the west of the town. There Prevost gave him the final orders for the attack stating, "It is now nine o'clock, march off at 10."[67] To meet this timing, Robinson had to march his brigade three miles south to a staging area at Pike's Ford; once he was across the Saranac, he would attack the American defensive line from the south. His reinforced brigade began moving at 9:30 A.M. using a route "to conceal the troops from the view of the enemy" that led to another road to Pike's Ford.[68] During the march, Robinson took the opportunity to stand on "rising ground to view the [naval] action."[69] Prevost had also moved from his headquarters to a position that permitted observation of Cumberland Bay and the peninsula.

The eight light companies were placed at the head of Robinson's brigade column, which moved under the guidance of officers from the divisional Quartermaster General's Department. After a mile, Robinson noticed the guides became "divided in opinion whether we were on the right road or not,"[70] which was a polite way of saying they were lost. Major Nathaniel Thorn, a member of Robinson's staff, "opined we were wrong and he would undertake to conduct us to Pike's Ford without any fear of further mistake."[71] An hour was then lost as the column moved to the correct route. It appeared the divisional staff were inadequately prepared for the march, whereas the staff of the brigades, who were experienced in the conduct of marches in Europe, had studied probable routes in some detail.[72]

Once Downie's flagship came into view, but before the squadron's guns opened up, Prevost directed Major John Sinclair, the senior gunner of the division, to commence fire, beginning with the battery farthest on the British left, following the first discharge by the British squadron. When he observed that Downie was facing an "incessant and galling fire," Prevost sent Sinclair to the northeasternmost batteries to "accelerate the immediate opening of the Batteries," and soon "the cannonade became General from all our Batteries and the Enemy defences."[73] The British fire effectively silenced one of the enemy blockhouses. Moving to the British right, however, Sinclair found the uncompleted southernmost battery was threatened by such "an Overpowering and in some degree plunging fire [coming from above rather than in a flat trajectory]" that it was unable to "keep up a brisk fire."[74] He instructed the battery commander to reduce his rate of fire—and thus the enemy's interest in his position—until Robinson advanced. Sinclair then ordered the gunners to take cover while he positioned a half battery of 6-pounder guns to their left rear to engage the Americans.[75]

Meanwhile, as Robinson's troops approached Pike's Ford, they could see that the banks were quite steep. Robinson then heard cheering, and, uncertain whether the source of this noise came from the north where Brisbane's brigade had commenced its attack or from Downie's squadron to the east, he sent Major William Cochrane, one of Prevost's aides who accompanied him, to determine what was going on. Returning to the matter at hand, Robinson found the river itself was some sixty to seventy feet across at the ford. He posted the light companies of the 3/27th and 88th Regiments to cover the other light companies as they closed up for a sudden rush across the river to the opposite bank. As the light companies crossed, they were met by fire from 400 American militiamen. Robinson sent the 3/27th in support. The enemy withdrew, and the light companies soon "reached the ground they were ordered to occupy."[76] The 76th Regiment followed "and formed in column about a mile on the opposite side of the ford";[77] meanwhile, the 58th formed up to their rear and two 6-pounder field pieces were positioned nearby. The British had taken only light casualties, and the troops were in good shape. Everything was ready for the attack, or so it seemed. Robinson had "hardly reached the front" to supervise the next stage of the attack when in the early afternoon Cochrane returned with an order from Prevost—who had witnessed the naval battle from his headquarters— that had been issued at noon.[78] It stated that since two of the British warships had struck their colors, Robinson and his men were to break off the action and return to Prevost's location.[79]

Captain Robert Downie had met with disaster. At around 8:00 A.M. that morning, the squadron hove to near Cumberland Head, and Downie then boarded a gig so he could more closely examine the American squadron in Plattsburgh Bay to determine his plan of attack. He decided to sail around Cumberland Head and direct his flotilla into the bay, where Macdonough had arranged his squadron in a line. The flagship, HMS *Confiance*, supported by the *Linnet* and the *Chub*, would attack two of the American warships, while a fourth warship, the *Finch*, and a flotilla of eleven gunboats were directed against the remaining two enemy ships. The Americans also had ten gunboats.[80] Unfortunately for Downie, the favorable wind that had allowed him to sail from Chazy Landing did not allow him to tack northward into the bay and take up the desired positions. The result was that when the battle opened at 9:00 A.M., the British were at a disadvantage and Downie's flagship faced "the concentrated fire of the Enemy's Squadron and Flotilla of Gun Boats."[81] Downie was killed near the outset of the action. The *Chub* was heavily damaged, and surrendered, while the *Finch* went adrift and ran aground on Crab Island near the middle of the channel. As the crew struggled to refloat their vessel, they had to deal with fire from a battery on the island, but after a brief exchange, the American gun was silenced.[82] The British gunboats contributed nothing to the action, as their commander, Lieutenant Mark Rayburn, ordered a withdrawal in the face of the combined fire from six American galleys and four gunboats. Both squadrons were heavily damaged, but with Downie dead, many casualties among *Confiance*'s crew, two vessels out of action, and the gunboats gone, Lieutenant James Walker, now commanding the ship, hauled down his colors, and twenty minutes later, Commander Pring, aboard the *Linnet*, did the same.[83]

Meanwhile, after reading Prevost's order for him to withdraw, Robinson passed the note to Power, "who was equally astonished" by its contents.[84] But Robinson obeyed and began pulling back his troops, except for the lead elements, which were closest to the American positions. The light companies of the brigade were awaiting permission to assault a nearby battery when the orders to withdraw arrived. This did not deter the commander of the light company of the 76th. Convinced he could take a gun from the enemy, he ordered his men forward. During the skirmish the American militia surrounded twenty-five to thirty of the men, and in the ensuing struggle, the company commander and eight or ten of his men were killed, with the remainder taken prisoner.[85]

Farther to the north, Brisbane's brigade had also commenced a feint but, on receiving Prevost's orders, quickly broke contact with the enemy and withdrew. The artillery continued to engage the enemy until 3:00 P.M. when it was ordered to cease fire. Once dusk approached, the gunners began the heavy and difficult work of withdrawing the guns from their positions, and by 10:00 P.M., they had all been pulled back. At no point did the Americans interfere.[86]

Once reassembled, the Left Division spent the night of 11 September near Plattsburgh. During the evening, Prevost had decided to withdraw back to Canada and ordered the movement to commence two hours before daybreak on 12 September. He then composed a report to Bathurst that explained his decision to withdraw:

> Scarcely had His Majesty's Troops forced passage across the Saranac and ascended the Height on which stand the enemy's works, when I had the Mortification to hear the Shout of Victory from the Enemy's Works in consequence of the British Flag being lowered on board the Confiance and Linnet. . . . This unlooked for event depriving me of the Co-operation of the Fleet without which the further Prosecution of the Service was become impracticable, I did not hesitate to arrest the course of the Troops advancing to the attack because the most complete success would have been unavailing, and the possession of the Enemy's Works offered no advantage to compensate for the loss we must have sustained in acquiring Possession of them.[87]

In making this difficult decision, Prevost had to weigh a number of factors. An assault on the American defenses might have been very costly. Robinson's reinforced brigade, representing a significant portion of the 7,500-strong Left Division present at Plattsburgh, would have had to advance across open ground against concentrated artillery fire from three redoubts occupied by 1,800 regulars and armed with twenty-eight guns of various calibers, the largest of which was a 42-pounder carronade. Significant casualties would have been caused by the "numerous and heavy artillery mounted"[88] in the forts, and the result may have been as bad as that suffered by British troops at New Orleans in January 1815. American preparations took some of the bite out of the Left Division, and against the 3,400 defenders, some of mixed quality, who occupied prepared positions with considerable artillery support, the division did not enjoy overwhelming strength. His campaign experience in the West Indies and more recently in the North American war, at Sackets Harbor, had taught Prevost the dangers of attacking prepared positions. He also knew that "without their [the naval squadrons'] aid, nothing can be undertaken affording a reasonable hope of substantial advantage."[89]

Deprived of water transport and having too few wagons, it was certain that the march could not afford to be impeded by the need to convey a large quantity of provisions and supplies, and that night

Prevost ordered the destruction of all surplus stores and munitions.[90] Fifteen men in the hospital, who could not travel due to the severity of their wounds, were left behind. Two hours before daybreak on 12 September, the Left Division began marching northward. A continual downpour created miserable conditions. The troops began crossing the frontier into Lower Canada on 14 September, and to the credit of the Royal Artillery gunners and drivers of the Left Division, "every piece of Ordnance of every description which had crossed that Province line was brought back," along with the "greater part of the Ammunition" and all of the artillery stores.[91] Ammunition stores that had been deposited in depots at Chazy were loaded onto bateaux and small ships on Lake Champlain and withdrawn. One of the ships carrying ordnance stores sank off Isle La Motte and was abandoned. The last elements of Power's brigade, which had remained at Champlain, New York, in case the division was pursued, finally left American territory on 25 September 1814.[92]

The conduct of the withdrawal was criticized by several participants and has since been debated by historians. Robinson was disgusted by the quantity of "guns, ammunition and commissariat stores" that were destroyed.[93] He was also shocked at the "precipitate and disgraceful manner" of the retreat, in which the division "retraced in three days, what had required six in the advance."[94] Robinson was angry with Prevost and his staff and seemed convinced that "nothing goes right but in the commissariat" (which was run by his brother).[95] For his part, historian Benson J. Lossing claims Prevost hastened the retreat after being duped into thinking that a large body of Vermont militia was attempting to cut the British off. The approach of 19,000 men was revealed in a letter that deliberately "fell" into British hands. No other source mentions this letter, although Prevost did report in one of his dispatches that "the Enemy's Militia was raising En Masse around me."[96] Neither Robinson nor Brisbane describe this incident in their papers, and had the letter existed or the information been acted on, Robinson and Brisbane certainly would have referred to it in their critiques of Prevost. The histories of the British regiments involved make no mention of this ruse either, and the lack of any further evidence suggests that the hoax probably did not occur. The only source Lossing provides to support his claim was an interview he had with a single individual many years after the events.

Nonetheless, Prevost did acknowledge that the American militia was a threat to his line of communication and may have been reminded of the fate suffered by Lieutenant General John Burgoyne in 1777. Burgoyne, after marching his army deep into enemy territory, was forced to surrender his entire command to the Americans. The present circumstances, however, were quite different as Prevost was only twenty-five miles from the frontier (with two battalions covering his line of communication), whereas Burgoyne had advanced nearly 150 miles into hostile territory and was forced to abandon his supply line to Canada. Prevost was also familiar with Vermont's opposition to the war and its lukewarm support of U.S. military operations, factors that contributed to his decision to confine his movement to the western shore of Lake Champlain in New York. As it was, at no time during the retreat to Lower Canada did the Americans harass the British columns.[97]

As for the march to Lower Canada being conducted in haste, the Left Division had to move roughly twenty-five miles from Plattsburgh to the border. This was conducted over three days, from 12 to 14 September, half the time it took to advance to Plattsburgh, which had required reconnaissance to determine the best routes and bridges and to locate obstacles and any enemy forces. The advance had also been conducted slowly to give the naval squadron time to catch up. At two points, Chazy and Champlain, the retreating division was met by the infantry battalions and artillery protecting the line of communication. The rain made the retreat to Lower Canada difficult, but it was not conducted at a breakneck pace.[98]

Historian George Stanley claims that the discipline of the troops disintegrated during the march, that desertion became rampant, and that the Left Division turned into "a mob of men devoid of discipline and spirit."[99] These claims are not supported by the division's official returns of 6 and 15 September, which Stanley apparently did not consult and which paint a very different picture. Not a single soldier deserted from Robinson's 1st Brigade; Brisbane lost 157 men to desertion, and Power's 3rd Brigade lost 75 men. These figures show that "Wellington's Invincibles," who had been divided between Robinson's and Power's brigades, did not turn into a mob, whereas units with long service in Canada, which were concentrated under Brisbane's command, made up 70 percent of all desertions. It must also be recalled that these desertions were not limited to the retreat; a portion of them occurred during the advance to Plattsburgh. If these desertions are added to the combat casualties sustained by the division—of 47 killed, 221 wounded, and 70 prisoners of war—then a total of 570 personnel were lost in the Plattsburgh campaign, far short of the 2,500 men Macomb claimed the British lost to all causes in his report to the secretary of war.[100] Rather than being a shambles, the Left Division emerged from the operation with its discipline intact, in good fighting order, and with losses of only 7 percent of its strength (the casualties suffered by the naval squadron and the loss of the squadron are quite another matter).[101] Prevost may have misemployed the division, but he had preserved it. He did not help his case, however, by informing Bathurst on 22 September that "desertion encreasing" within the Left Division was a reason for his withdrawal.[102]

Once he returned to Montreal, Prevost sent a second, private letter to Bathurst that elaborated on his decision to withdraw. He stated it was necessary due to the loss of naval support, rising desertion in the division, a potential threat from local militia, and the poor state of the roads, which so affected his line of communication that further delay would make a march back to Canada more difficult. Prevost had to choose, he said, "whether I should consider my own Fame by gratifying the Ardor of the Troops in persevering in the Attack, or consult the more substantial interests of my Country by withdrawing the Army which was yet uncrippled for the security of these Provinces."[103]

Given the course of the Plattsburgh campaign, Generals Robinson and Power both had every right to be critical of Prevost. Difficulties emerged from the moment planning commenced. Although Prevost had received sufficient infantry reinforcements to achieve his objective, shortfalls in trained staff and engineer personnel and important equipment, including artillery and transport, could not be rectified before the offensive began. Yeo's insolence and refusal to divert manpower and other resources from Lake Ontario to Isle aux Noix plagued the naval preparations, which were further hampered by two rapid changes in command of the squadron. The only positive development to this point was the departure of Izard's division for the Niagara frontier, which left the route to Plattsburgh open and the defenses manned by a mixed collection of regulars and militia.

Once the Left Division crossed the frontier, Prevost's supervision of the campaign was uninspired. His leadership could not overcome the shortfalls in the divisional staff, which proved incapable of coordinating the complexities of the advance, the construction of siege works, and the making of final preparations for the assault on Plattsburgh. His appointment of de Rottenburg as commander of the Left Division proved unsound; as a result, Prevost had to take direct command of that formation. Prevost's greatest transgression was in leaving the detailed coordination of the naval and land attacks to his aides, rather undertaking these arrangements personally with Downie. Had he instead chosen to ride the few short miles to where the naval squadron was moored, Prevost most certainly could have avoided the confusion that ensued on 11 September, and perhaps eliminated the acrimony that ensued afterward over the conduct of the campaign.

The commander in chief may have mishandled parts of his command, but at least he did not lead the Left Division to destruction. Nor was he responsible for the fate of the naval squadron, which he had supported in every way he could. He emerged from the campaign at the center of a great controversy that included not only the army's interests but also those of the navy and influential English merchants and civilians. When he reflected on these events nearly a year later, Frederick Robinson speculated on the possible outcome from any investigation the navy might insist on but decided that "they will make nothing of it, as Sir George could not be answerable for the failure of their plan of attack."[104] Events would demonstrate, however, that Robinson had it wrong and that the employment of the naval squadron during the campaign would cause a final falling out between Yeo and Prevost—and also cast a dark shadow on the commander in chief of British North America.[105]

**Lieutenant General Sir George Prevost
(1767–1816), Bart., ca. 1808–1816.**

Early nineteenth-century oil-on-canvas
portrait by Jean-Baptiste Roy-Audy (1778–ca.
1848), from the collection of the Museum of
Château Ramezay, Montréal; after an
original miniature by Robert Field (ca.
1769–1816) painted while Prevost was
lieutenant governor of Nova Scotia. (Courtesy McCord Museum, Montréal, M403)

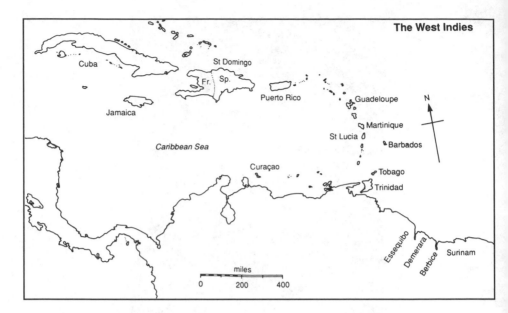

The West Indies.

This map depicts those colonies where Sir George Prevost served in a military capacity or as a colonial governor: St. Vincent (1794–96); St. Lucia (1798–1802); Dominica (1802 to June 1803, when he volunteered for service in St. Lucia; he returned to Dominica later that year and remained there until 1805); Nova Scotia, 1808–11 (with detached service in Martinique in 1809); and British North America, 1811–15. (From Christopher D. Hall, *British Strategy in the Napoleonic Wars*, 110)

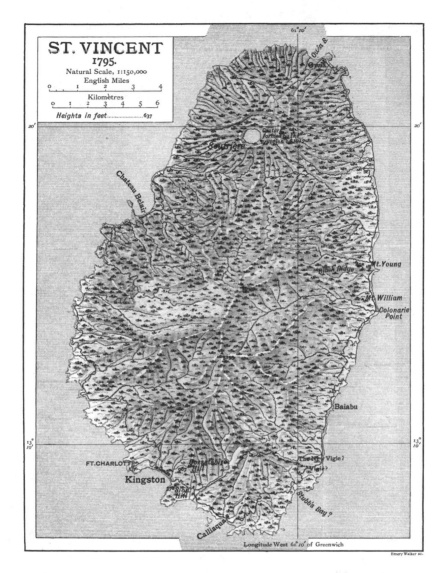

St. Vincent.

Prevost's baptism by fire in this former French island colony provided him with valuable lessons in leading soldiers of mixed quality, while campaigning under difficult conditions. (From *Maps and Plans Illustrating Fortescue's* History of the British Army, vol. 4, plate 17)

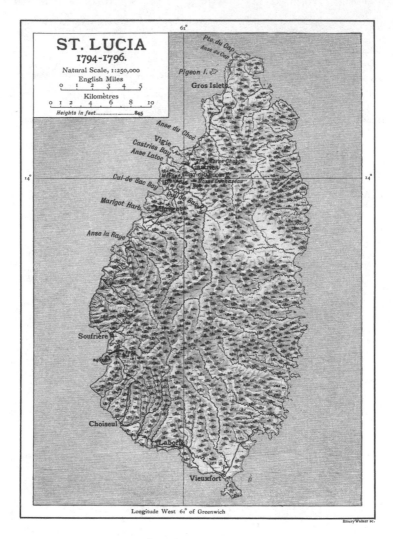

St. Lucia.

Prevost was appointed to command the garrison at St. Lucia in 1803, where he also received an introduction to colonial administration. He adopted a conciliatory policy toward the concerns of the island's French-speaking population, reforming the law courts and securing guarantees for the Catholic Church that won their hearts and brought his appointment as lieutenant governor of the colony in April 1801. After a brief spell in England during a short peace between England and France, Prevost returned to St. Lucia as second-in-command of an expedition that retook the island, which had been returned to France in 1802. (From *Maps and Plans Illustrating Fortescue's* History of the British Army, vol. 4, plate 15)

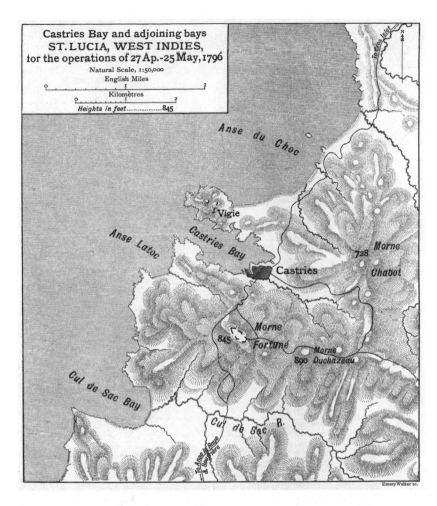

Castries region, St. Lucia.

(From *Maps and Plans Illustrating Fortescue's* History of the British
Army, vol. 4, plate 16)

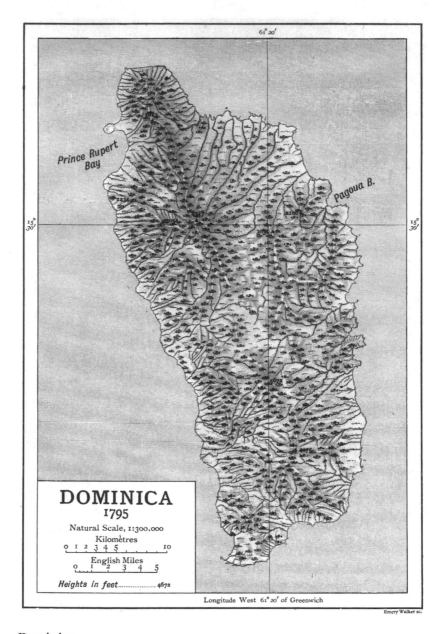

DOMINICA
1795

Natural Scale, 1:300,000

Kilomètres

0 1 2 3 4 5   10

English Miles

0   1   2   3   4   5

Heights in feet................4672

Longitude West 61° 20' of Greenwich

Emery Walker sc.

Dominica.

Beginning in 1802, Prevost commenced a successful term as governor
of Dominica. In 1805, his judicious deployment of forces defeated the
aims of a stronger opponent that enjoyed greater mobility and held the
initiative due to command of the sea. (From *Maps and Plans Illustrating Fortescue's* History of the British Army, vol. 4, plate 19)

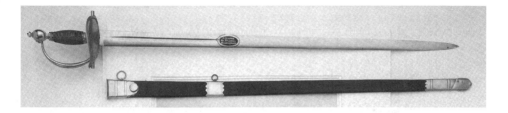

Presentation Sword to George Prevost from the People of St. Lucia.

This gold-hilted sword of the 1796 British heavy cavalry officer's pattern was presented to Prevost in 1802, following his term as governor of the island of St. Lucia. A short central fuller on both sides bears the inscription *Colonie de Ste Lucie Reconnoifsante* within a garter, while the 18 carat gold hilt is engraved *Les Colons de Ste Lucie Reconnoifsante au Brigadier General Prevost.* (Courtesy Sir Christopher Prevost)

The Lloyd's Patriotic Fund Presentation Sword of £100.

Presented to George Prevost for the Defense of Dominica, 1805. Between 1803 and 1809, the Lloyd's Patriotic Fund rewarded those officers who distinguished themselves with a piece of plate, a sword, or a sum of cash. A total of 164 swords were granted, 35 of which were of the prestigious £100 type. Only three of these went to army officers, including Prevost. The blade of Prevost's sword was engraved with the following: "From the Patriotic Fund at Lloyd's, to Brigadier General Geo. Prevost, Governor of Dominica, for the bravery, zeal and talent, manifested by him in the defence of that island in February 1805, when he was attacked by a French force of 4,000 men, as recorded in the London Gazette of the 7th May 1805." (Courtesy Sir Christopher Prevost)

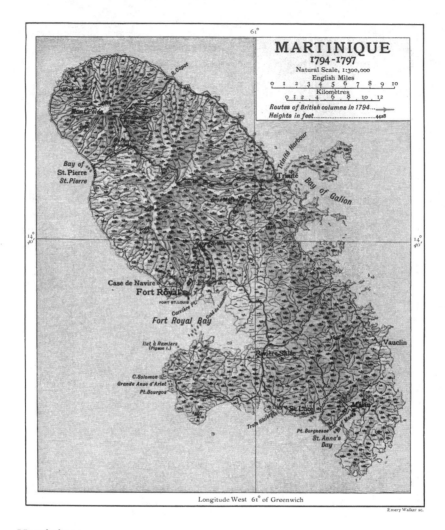

Martinique.

In 1809, Prevost left Nova Scotia to command the larger of two British divisions that reduced the French island of Martinique. (From John Fortescue, *A History of the British Army*, vol. 7 [Uckfield, UK: Naval and Military Press, 2004], n.p.)

Army Gold Medal.

Awarded to Lieutenant General Sir George Prevost for the Capture of Martinique. Prevost's conduct as commander of one of the two divisions that secured Martinique was acknowledged in 1809 with the award of the large version of the Army Gold Medal. Prevost received one of nine large medals—the type intended for general officers—that were awarded for the expedition. (Courtesy Sir Christopher Prevost)

Prevost Family Coat of Arms.

In 1818, the Prince Regent awarded the Prevost family with "supporters" for the family coat of arms, in acknowledgment of Prevost's many years of service. These were described as having on either side a grenadier of the 16th (or Bedfordshire) Regiment of Foot (of which Prevost had been colonel at the time of his death), each supporting a banner—one inscribed "West Indies," and the other, "Canada." Not visible is the motto *Servatum cineri* (Faith Kept with the Dead). (Courtesy College of Arms Grants, MS I 41, 215)

Prevost Family Crypt, St. Mary the Virgin, East Barnet, Hertfordshire.

The remains of Sir George Prevost, along with those of his parents and other family members, rest in this crypt in England. (Courtesy Sir Christopher Prevost)

SACRED TO THE MEMORY OF
LIEUTENANT GENERAL SIR GEORGE PREVOST BARONET,
OF BELMONT IN THIS COUNTY,
GOVERNOR GENERAL AND COMMANDER IN CHIEF OF THE BRITISH FORCES IN NORTH AMERICA,
IN WHICH COMMAND BY HIS WISE AND ENERGETIC MEASURES
AND WITH A VERY INFERIOR FORCE HE PRESERVED THE CANADAS TO THE BRITISH CROWN
FROM THE REPEATED INVASIONS OF A POWERFUL ENEMY
HIS CONSTITUTION AT LENGTH SUNK UNDER

(facing page, bottom) **Sir George Prevost Memorial, Winchester Cathedral.**

This memorial to Sir George Prevost was erected by his family in 1819. The inscription reads:

Sacred to the memory of
Lieutenant General Sir George Prevost
Baronet of Belmont in this county
governor general and commander in chief
of the British forces in North America
in which command by his wise and energetic measures
and with a very inferior force he preserved the Canadas
to the British Crown
from the repeated invasions of a powerful enemy
his constitution at length sunk under incessant mental
and bodily exertion
in discharging the duties of that arduous station
and have having returned to England he died
shortly afterwards in London
on the 5th of January 1816. Aged 48 years
thirty four of which had been devoted
to the service of his country
he was interred near the remains of his father
Major General Augustin Prevost
at East Barnet in Hertfordshire
his royal sovereign the prince regent
"to evince in an especial manner the sense he entertained
of his distinguished conduct and services
during a long period of constant and active employment
in stations of great trust both military and civil
was pleased to ordain as a lasting memorial of
his majesty's royal favour
that the names of the countries where
his courage and abilities had most signally displayed
the West Indies and Canada should be inscribed
on the banners of the supporters
granted to be borne by his family and descendents
in testimony of his private worth, his piety, integrity
and his benevolence
and all those tender domestic virtues which endeared him to
his family, his children, his friends and his dependents
as well as to prove his unfeigned love, gratitude and respect
Catherine Anne Prevost his afflicted widow
caused this monument to be erected anno domini 1819

(Courtesy Winchester Cathedral, Hampshire, England, and Ron Cassidy)

The Northern Theater of War.

From Donald E. Graves, *Where Right and Glory Lead: The Battle of Lundy's Lane, 1814* (Toronto: Robin Brass Studio, 1993), 12. (Courtesy Robin Brass Studio)

10

"RESPECTING MY CONDUCT AT PLATSBURGH . . ."

The Fate of Sir George Prevost

To historians, Prevost's decision to cancel the attack on Plattsburgh and withdraw to Canada announced the failure of the only British offensive in the northern theater during 1814. At first glance this seems a reasonable conclusion, since none of the stated objectives had been achieved. However, as Major General George Izard's division had been drawn away from Plattsburgh to the Niagara frontier, the forces left under Colonel Alexander Macomb were incapable of launching a counteroffensive into Lower Canada in September. Macdonough had won the naval battle, but his squadron was so badly damaged that it could not conduct further operations, giving the British time to recover from their defeat. Without any immediate threat, the frontier of Lower Canada remained secure. While peace negotiations continued at Ghent, the British Left Division that now guarded that boundary was a powerful deterrent to any American offensive. In October 1814, Macdonough began moving his squadron into winter station near the southern end of Lake Champlain to distance it from any potential threat from Lower Canada, and thus, despite the apparent failure of the Plattsburgh expedition, it was the Americans and not the British who felt threatened in this region.[1]

Despite the setback, British commanders showed a renewed interest in gaining control of Lake Champlain. In December 1814, Major General Thomas Brisbane, now commanding the Left Division, submitted a plan to Prevost that called for the employment of

7,000 troops to destroy the American squadron at its winter base at Whitehall, New York, at the southern end of the lake. More than a thousand sleighs would be used to move this force to its objective. Prevost readily supported the idea but cautioned Brisbane that "it remains to you to demonstrate its practicability with the means I place at your disposal, which cannot exceed 6,000 men."[2] Prevost also emphasized the need for detailed planning: "It is necessary I should ascertain that you are aware of the many difficulties you have to encounter & that the roads you are to use have been examined on the ground & not upon Maps alone. Have you a thorough knowledge of the country, in which the operation is to be executed? Do you propose moving by the East or West shore of Lake Champlain?"[3]

This insistence on careful planning was earned from hard experience and from watching many hastily mounted wartime operations encounter difficulties and achieve meager or no results. Given the size of the force Brisbane proposed to employ, Prevost also felt that more than a simple outline plan was necessary: "In order to enable you to mature your scheme for the destruction of the Enemy's Naval Force on Lake Champlain, I have taken this cursory view of it reserving to myself a more solicitous attention to so highly important a measure whenever the whole machinery is before me."[4] In the openness of the frontier, Brisbane could not hide his preparations, and when the Americans learned of the enterprise, they shifted troops to Whitehall. Prevost then informed Brisbane that, while planning could continue, execution of the scheme was suspended indefinitely.

After the campaign season had ended in the autumn of 1814, Prevost made preparations for the next year. He authorized the construction of three frigates and two heavy brigs at Isle aux Noix to be ready by May. Improvements were also made to expand the capacity of the bateau service on the line of communication between Montreal and Kingston, including the use of larger craft, the employment of more men, and the building of a canal between Montreal and Lachine, so as to avoid rapids. It was anticipated that for 1815, 850 boats would operate from eleven stations between Three Rivers and Niagara, requiring 4,250 men to crew them—more than three times the number employed in 1812.[5] The additional manpower required to operate the service would come from detaching a battalion of select embodied militia, a provincial unit, and possibly a regular regiment. Yeo ordered the construction of two more first-rates at Kingston, each of 2,158 tons and thus slightly smaller than the *St. Lawrence*, but with overall tonnage almost equal to the total built at the dockyard in 1814. Three gunboats and two large transports, one of 438 tons, were also to be laid down, and it was anticipated that twenty gunboats and fifty bateaux would be ready by spring, at which time Prevost hoped to mount another attack on Sackets Harbor.[6] Nothing came of these plans, however, since the war ended following ratification in February 1815 of the Treaty of Ghent, signed in December 1814.[7]

The final form of the army of the Canadas was reached during the autumn of 1814. Based on the experience of the recent campaign on the Niagara Peninsula, it was regrouped in October to allow it both to conduct sustained operations in the field and to protect the vital line of communication on the upper St. Lawrence. The Right and Center Divisions in Upper Canada were grouped into a *corps d'armée* under the immediate command of Lieutenant General Gordon Drummond. The Right Division, led by Major General Richard Stovin, was the primary field force, with one brigade on the Niagara Peninsula and another responsible for the area between Burlington Heights and York. It had 5,800 men. The 6,500-man Center Division had two brigades under Major General Frederick Robinson and was responsible for the line of communication between Kingston and Montreal. The large three-brigade Left Division with 9,300 troops was based near Montreal and commanded by de Rottenburg, who was later replaced by Brisbane. There were two groups that fell outside of this structure, the 1,900-strong garrison of Quebec under Major General George Glasgow and 336 men at Mackinac and St. Joseph's Islands under Lieutenant Colonel George Macdonell. From an initial strength of 9,777 in 1812, the regular forces in the Canadas had, by November 1814, reached a strength of 25,772 including all ranks.[8]

While Prevost prepared for the coming year, his reputation and leadership came under fire. Many officers in the Left Division disliked him, and he was a popular topic of their grumbling. Whether it was his efforts to enforce dress regulations, questions regarding his previous experience, or, more important, the apparent lack of any plan as the army had advanced on Plattsburgh, men such as

Major General Frederick Robinson and others voiced unhappiness with their commander. Wellington became somewhat irritated when he heard stories of Prevost's preoccupation with dress and the results of the Plattsburgh expedition. As he informed Bathurst, Prevost had "gone to war about trifles with the general officers I sent him, which are certainly the best of their rank in the army; and his subsequent failure and distresses will be aggravated by that circumstance."[9]

The severity of these verbal attacks increased once the results of the British summer offensives were more widely known. Washington had been temporarily occupied and many of its public buildings burned, but an attack on Baltimore was repulsed and the expedition leader, Major General Robert Ross, had been killed. A portion of Maine had been occupied by British troops, but that success did not offer much in the way of strategic advantages. The U.S. offensive on the Niagara Peninsula had been checked, and although the Americans had later withdrawn from Canada, Plattsburgh had the appearance of a dismal failure. Attention correspondingly focused on Prevost's leadership during the latter campaign.

The most vocal of Prevost's critics was Commodore Sir James Lucas Yeo, who had studied the correspondence between Prevost and Downie. Based on what he had learned, Yeo wrote a series of letters to the Admiralty complaining that Prevost had forced Downie into action despite repeated warnings that the squadron was not ready. A letter from Lieutenant James Robertson, the senior lieutenant on the *Confiance*, to Commander Daniel Pring contained several points that Yeo would go on to repeat:

> Previous to the action, it had been held out to the Ship's Company, that when it should commence, it was the intention of the Commander of the land forces, at the same time to storm the enemy's works.
>
> When the crew of the Confiance would no longer continue the action after the repeated attempts on the part of all the surviving officers to rally them, they stated that the want of cooperation on the part of the Army and our own Gun Boats keeping at a distance, the fire of the whole of the enemy's force being directed at the Confiance as their main reasons for not being able to continue it.

> . . . You are aware Sir, of the written orders issued by the
> Enemy two days previous to the Action, directing that their
> whole fire should be concentrated on the Confiance to en-
> sure her capture.[10]

When Pring forwarded this letter to Yeo, he added the following
passage:

> Captain Downie urged by Sir George to assist with the naval
> force under his command, in the intended operation against
> Plattsburgh, and relying on his promise that the works
> abreast of which the enemy fleet lay moored should be
> stormed at the same moment the naval attack should com-
> mence, determined to engage them under the difficulties
> adverted to in my letter of the 12th Inst—that time alone
> could not remedy the loss of which might frustrate the ob-
> ject of the Campaign.[11]

This summary of the reasons for the naval defeat at Plattsburgh
that Yeo presented to his superiors ignored two letters sent to him
by Commander Daniel Pring and Lieutenant James Robertson, both
dated 12 September 1814, and written while both officers were held
prisoner on board Macdonough's flagship, USS *Saratoga*. In his letter to the Admiralty, Yeo chose instead to refer to a second letter
Pring wrote on 17 September 1814, following his return to Isle aux
Noix, and another letter Robertson wrote, while he was still being
held prisoner, dated 15 September 1814.

Pring's first letter, which included "a statement of the different
Commanding Officers of Vessels relative to the circumstances attending their capture"[12] and returns of killed and wounded, offered
a different perspective than his second letter, written five days
later. Writing on 12 September, Pring did not attribute the naval
defeat to Prevost, for his role in Downie's decision to commit his
squadron to battle on 11 September, nor did he claim the outcome
to be the result of inaction on land by the commander in chief:

> In consequence of the earnest Solicitation of His Excellency
> Sir George Prevost, for the Co-operation of the Naval Force
> on this Lake, to attack that of the Enemy, who were placed
> for the support of their Works at Plattsburgh, which it was
> proposed be Stormed by the Troops at the same moment the

Naval Action should commence in the Bay. Every possible Exertion was used to accelerate the Armament of the New Ship [*Confiance*], that the Military movements might not be postponed at such an advance Season of the Year—longer than absolutely necessary."[13]

In his subsequent letter of 17 September 1814, Pring wrote that after "having performed the painful task of detailing to you the particulars of" the naval battle, it was his "Duty" to acquaint the commodore with "the disappointment which our Squadron experienced on that day in the want of the promised cooperation of the Land Forces to which I attribute the course of our failure"[14] (and which appear above). In his earlier letter of 12 September, however, Pring offered different reasons "for the misfortune which this day befell us": "*Confiance* was Sixteen days before, on the Stocks, with an unorganized Crew, comprised of several Drafts of Men; who had recently arrived from different ships at Quebec, many of whom only joined the day before, and were totally unknown to the Officers or to each other, with the want of Gun Locks as well as other necessary appointments."[15] Pring concluded that the combination of these factors resulted in the "decided advantage the Enemy possessed" in "this unequal contest."[16]

Like Pring, Robertson limited his letter of 12 September, to naval events and, in particular, to the "circumstances which led to the surrender of His Majesty's late Ship *Confiance*."[17] He says nothing about any understanding the crew might have had as to when the land attack would commence. Roberston did comment, as he did in his second letter, on the fire faced by his ship and recounted that "the concentrated fire of the whole of the Enemy's Squadron and Flotilla of Gun Boats had been . . . for some time directed against *Confiance*"; however, his assessment of the conduct of the officers and men was worded much like Pring's, whereby the men had "kept up the action" as much "as could be expected from men unacquainted with each other and with their Officers, and in a Ship which had been sixteen days before, on the stocks."[18] This passage, clearly a reference to the difficulties in manning the warship, did not appear in the letter Robertson wrote five days later to which Yeo referred in his letter to the Admiralty.[19]

Clearly, the first set of correspondence followed the typical pattern of reporting on the naval battle in anticipation of a future court-martial that would require the officers to account for their actions and the loss of their warships. Pring provided an accurate assessment of the state of *Confiance*, without attributing blame for its condition on anyone. The second set of letters, however, differ substantially and address more directly, as Pring noted, the timing and conduct of the land battle and Prevost's role in having Downie commit to a naval action. Conveniently, this second set of letters proved useful in deflecting any blame for the naval defeat from Yeo, while supporting allegations of Prevost's responsibility for the outcome.

Yeo sent a letter to the Admiralty, dated 24 September 1814, that included copies of Robertson's and Pring's second letters, dated 15 and 17 September, but not their letters written on the 12th. Yeo complained: "Captain Downie was urged and his ship hurried into Action before she was in a fit state to meet the Enemy."[20] Yeo continued that had "our troops taken their [the Americans'] Batteries first, it would have obliged the Enemy Squadron to quit the Bay and give ours a fair chance."[21] As he was unfamiliar with the local conditions and lacked a complete account of what transpired at Plattsburgh, including the positions of Macomb's artillery, Yeo could only have based these conclusions on the accounts by Pring and Robertson. Yeo had come into possession of the correspondence exchanged between Prevost and Downie;[22] on 29 September, he forwarded these letters to the Admiralty, repeating the allegation that "it appears very evident that Capt Downie was urged, even goaded on to his fate, by His Excelly [Prevost] who appears to have assumed the direction of the naval force."[23] Yeo added that had Prevost "adhered to the previous arrangement" and begun the land attack at "the same moment the naval action commenced":

> the Enemy's Squadron must have quitted their anchorage, particularly their Gun Boats that lay close under their Shore and whose heavy Metal and cool fire did more execution to our vessels than their Ship or Brig.
> Had his Excellency taken the Batteries even after this Action it must have led to the recapture of our Vessels, if

not those of the Enemy, as it is Notorious, and a fact, that the Enemy's vessels were so cut up and disabled as to be incapable of taking possession of our Ship and Brig.[24]

There were now three allegations regarding Prevost's conduct at Plattsburgh. First, he had ignored the deficiencies of Downie's flagship and pressed him into action. Second, he had failed to commence the land attack as previously arranged, in conjunction with the beginning of the naval action, which allowed the American shore batteries and gunboats to engage the British squadron. Third, despite the outcome of the naval battle, Prevost should have mounted an assault on Plattsburgh, as the American squadron was in no condition to oppose it, and success would have provided an opportunity to retake the captured British vessels.

Given Yeo's haste in reporting these accusations, he must either have rejected other accounts of the action or, more likely, been ignorant of them. Contrary to his claim that the Left Division was inactive, the brigades had already moved into position and started to engage the enemy as the naval battle raged. Earlier that morning, Prevost had ordered his artillery to fire into Plattsburgh. Major John Sinclair, commanding the Royal Artillery in the Left Division, reported:

> Betwixt 7 and 8 a.m. on the 11th September I received His Excellency's Orders to direct the Batteries to open fire (commencing on the left) so soon as the first Gun should be discharged by the British Ship or Brig at one of the Enemy's vessels, these orders I commanded at $\frac{1}{4}$ before 8 A.M. The British Fleet was then momentarily expected to round Cumberland Head, which it did shortly thereafter. . . . His Excellency dispatched me to the Left to accelerate the immediate opening of the Batteries, which was done, and soon the Cannonade became General from All our Batteries, and the Enemy's defences. On our Left the Batteries succeeded in silencing the Block House opposed to him and his Sea Batterie I have every reason to believe never fired (at least I could never perceive it from any situation in which I was placed) nor could I learn that it did.[25]

Major Sinclair, who was very qualified to judge such matters, noted that from his position, he "could not ascertain, whether it was possible for that [American] Battery to have annoyed our Fleet during the Action, or even if it was in Range of that of the Enemy—certainly no other of the Enemy's Works (that I ever discovered) could afford support or give an Annoyance to either of the Fleets by their Fire."[26] In his report, Macomb stated that at 8:00 A.M., the British "batteries opened up on us, and continued throwing bomb-shells, shrapnells, balls and Congreve rockets, until sun-set."[27] Macomb makes no mention of his guns supporting the fleet or engaging British vessels but does make the claim that Sinclair's guns were "silenced by the superiority of our fire."[28] This suggests Macomb concentrated his artillery against Prevost and not Downie. Testimony from the Plattsburgh naval court-martial does not specify whether the batteries in Plattsburgh fired on the British ships. When the artillery duel continued, Brisbane launched his fixing attack on the two bridges over the Saranac while Robinson crossed the Saranac, which would certainly have gained the attention of Macomb's gunners. Consequently, the evidence does not support Yeo's opinion that the British naval squadron would have had a better chance if the American guns had been silenced. Even though the enemy batteries were not stormed, the evidence indicates that Macomb's gunners were busily engaged with the British artillery, firing at Brisbane and Robinson, which would have left them unable to support the fleet or protect the American gunboats along the shore. The fact that Macdonough chose to hold his position in Plattsburgh Bay, while Downie lost the support of his own gunboats, cannot be held against Prevost—and it should not be.[29]

A potential answer to the question of whether or not the shore-based artillery influenced the naval action may be located in the records of the Plattsburgh naval court-martial. This lengthy document includes four large maps—probably prepared for use during the court-marital proceedings—each drawn to scale, depicting different stages of the naval battle. The first map, identified as "A Plan of the Situation of the British and United States Squadrons at the time the Confiance and Linnet Anchored," shows the location of every British and American shore battery, fortification, naval vessel, and gunboat. Of particular interest is a table accompanying the map giving the "Bearings from Confiance when engaged" to the shore positions and the other warships, including the distance between each.[30] Thus, Fort Scott, the work closest to Confiance, is shown as being two and one-eighth miles (3,740 yards) away from the British flagship. Put another way, a round fired from a 24-pounder gun at Fort Scott, elevated to 9 degrees, would travel approximately 2,200 yards before hitting the water, or 1,500 yards short of the British flagship. As the British batteries were located to the northwest of Fort Scott, it would have been impossible, according to this set of drawings, for any of the shore batteries to have influenced the naval battle. As for the American gunboats, the maps depict them as having opened their distance from Fort Scott from one-eighth of a mile at the opening of the action to about one and one-half miles (2,600 yards) by the time *Confiance* struck, which was beyond range of the closest American fort.[31]

When he submitted these allegations, Yeo was clearly trying to shift his own responsibility for the ill-founded preparations of the squadron onto Prevost. He avoided mentioning the marked difference between his allocation of resources to Lakes Ontario and Champlain. There was no discussion of his role in naval affairs on Lake Champlain, nor any mention of his repeated refusals to provide personnel, ordnance, equipment, and stores to Pring and Downie, who commanded on the lake. There was certainly no account of Prevost's efforts to obtain additional seamen for the squadron. Officials in Britain unfortunately failed to look into such matters— had they done so they might have been surprised by the significant difference of resources allocated to the two squadrons.

Adding to Prevost's unease was the credence officials in London gave to the views of his other critics. In his civil capacity, Prevost had adopted a conciliatory policy toward the French-speaking population of Lower Canada that "maintained his constitutional position without exceeding his authority or making a discernable fault in judgement."[32] This policy annoyed many of the English residents in the province, but, much as they tried between 1811 and 1813, the English merchants, members of the provincial government councils, and senior clergy of the Church of England could not find a nail on which to hang Prevost. His critics had thus been held in abeyance, searching for some blunder they could use to have him removed. Plattsburgh finally provided the needed ammunition.

A civilian who contributed to Prevost's misery was Alicia Cockburn, sister-in-law to Rear-Admiral George Cockburn, the naval second-in-command on the Atlantic coast, and wife of Lieutenant

Colonel Francis Cockburn of the Canadian Fencibles. Alicia spent most of the war in Montreal and Quebec and maintained a salon that was attended by many senior officers. She set herself to gathering all the political news and gossip she could and launched attacks on Prevost with her pen. She had long despised Prevost for his conciliatory policies toward the *Canadiens*, and wrote in October 1814 that "the recent disgraceful business of Plattsburgh has so completely irritated the feelings of the whole army, that it is in a state almost amounting to mutiny. The Governor [Prevost] who has hitherto made his own story good in England, & by a course of art & deception . . . contrived to blind the eyes of the Ministers at home, is now at his wits' end—too surely convinced that his infamous behaviour can no longer be concealed."[33]

Cockburn charged Prevost and his circle, including Adjutant General Edward Baynes and Civil Secretary Edward Brenton (whom she described as a "low, dirty fellow"[34]), with being the originators of "all the calamities which these provinces endure."[35] Alicia Cockburn did not just write letters; she also provided Lord Arthur Somerset, the aide-de-camp to the Duke of York, the commander in chief of the army, with documents, letters, and "a plan of the late operations at Plattsburgh"[36] for his inspection. Somerset's sudden appearance in Montreal in October 1814 caused Alicia Cockburn to speculate that he had been sent to investigate the allegations against Prevost. His receipt of the documents from her and his return to Britain later that year suggests Somerset may have been collecting information, although there is no evidence to explain his presence in Lower Canada.[37]

While military officers and society ladies gossiped about Prevost and the Plattsburgh expedition or recorded their thoughts in diaries, the "violence of the press in array against" Prevost, as one early historian of the War of 1812 wrote, "knew no bounds."[38] He was reproached publicly for "having on that memorable expedition, sacrificed the flotilla, and as far as in him lay, disgraced the army under his command."[39] Several letters denouncing him appeared in the *Montreal Herald* and were picked up by the *Morning Post* of London, whose editor added, "[We] perceive that Sir George Prevost is not entirely popular in Canada."[40] In October 1814, another London paper published an account that was among the first public reports about the Plattsburgh campaign:

> Private letters state, that to Major General Brisbane was chiefly entrusted with the attack on the enemy's defences; and so far as it went, the operation appears to have been conducted in a masterly manner, and adequately executed by the troops under his command. But at the very moment was all ready for an assault on Fort Moreau, by which, in all human probability, the place would have been carried in the space of *a few minutes*, an order from the Commander-in-Chief stayed the proceedings; and, while almost in their grasp, tore from the expectant victors the laurels which they had already earned, and plunged them into retreat.[41]

The article then continued with even more outlandish speculation:

> General Macomb, the American Commander at Fort Moreau, it seems, has stated to our Officers, that having no more than 1,400 effective men with him, he saw no use in defending the place, and was preparing to surrender, when the retreat commenced.- Sir George is severely censured in the private letters for this result. It was rumoured that General Robinson has been put under arrest, and that Generals Brisbane and Power have tendered their resignations to Sir G. Prevost. A general dissatisfaction prevailed against the latter, and had been openly manifested; Col. Williams of the 18th, is said to have declared his intention never to draw a sword under his command.[42]

The impact of these reports cannot be discounted, despite their being rife with errors. Brisbane and Power did not tender their resignations, of course, nor was Robinson under arrest. The 18th Foot did not serve in Canada during the war, and there is no evidence of Lieutenant Colonel William Williams, who actually commanded the 13th Foot, having made the pledge reported in the newspaper.[43]

Additional letters criticizing Prevost also appeared in the *Montreal Herald* under the pen names of *Veritas*, *Nerva*, and others.[44] In Nova Scotia, "A Free Speaker" writing in a Halifax paper questioned Prevost's loyalty because he was born in "republican" America and concluded that his conduct as commander in chief had been disastrous. Yet another correspondent, calling himself "Englishman," lambasted Prevost's "miserable mismanagement" of the Plattsburgh campaign and lamented that so many "valuable Officers & men have lost their lives in Canada . . . without effecting any one thing of consequence."[45]

Although Prevost received considerable attention from a host of writers in North American and British papers, he had written only two dispatches to London in September 1814. The first provided a general overview of the campaign, while the second sought "to more fully explain" his actions.[46] In this second dispatch, Prevost stated that he had no "reasons for discouraging the naval contest," as Downie had provided him "of his assurance not only of his readiness, but of his ability to co-operate with the Army."[47] Prevost explained that his rationale for retiring from Plattsburgh was for the reasons stated "in previous dispatches that no Offensive Operations could be carried on within the Enemy's Territory for the destruction of his Naval Establishments without Naval Support."[48] These explanations may have been self-serving, but they also offered sound justification for his actions.

Prevost's letter of 22 September was a "private communication" to Bathurst, and its content was not widely circulated.[49] The only other officer with whom Prevost shared some of its details was Lieutenant General Gordon Drummond, the commander of Upper Canada. In a letter to Drummond, which dealt principally with the military situation in Upper Canada, Prevost briefly explained that at Plattsburgh "the impracticability of carrying on any operations without sufficient Naval cooperation has caused me to turn the whole of my attention to Upper Canada."[50] Since he was not yet aware of them, neither of Prevost's dispatches addressed any of the charges Yeo was busy making against him.

For his part, Yeo appeared to offer strong evidence that Prevost had ignored Downie's warnings, and that he had misled Downie about his plan of attack. As a result, the idea took root that Prevost was responsible for the naval disaster, and these accusations seemed to have found further credence through repetition in anecdotes by officers who returned to Britain and by articles in British newspapers. These attacks created the popular image of a valorous Downie, his squadron doomed by a pathetic and timid Sir George Prevost:

History produces nothing superior to the valour and gallantry of the officers and crew of the *Confiance*; suffice it to say that she was literally fought to the water's edge. . . . The scientific brave Generals, Officers and soldiers of the Duke of Wellington's army, and the others who have before fought in our cause in the Canadas, did every thing which depended on them to support the noble efforts of their brothers on the water. . . . Some of the piquets of the [American] Fort were torn away, and a few minutes more would have given up the fortification with an immense train of artillery into our hands, and every American must have been made prisoner. It was thought necessary to check the ardor of the troops, and we must now instantly redouble our energies to obtain command of the Lake, or with humility await our future destiny.[51]

Gossip spread among those Peninsular officers who had returned to Britain instead of going to Canada and who wondered about the fates of their former comrades-in-arms. Among them was Lieutenant General Sir Thomas Picton, who had served with Brisbane and Robinson. Picton, writing to Brisbane about the operation at Plattsburgh, told of his having read "in some of the public Papers" that Major General Manley Power had "experienced dissatisfaction on the occasion" and observed how "it is much to be regretted than any thing of this kind should have happened."[52] The stories being circulated had an effect on influential senior Peninsular officers, who were unimpressed by Prevost's apparent command of their former subordinates, whose "exemplary manner . . . in all undertakings" was well known to them, while Prevost was not.[53]

The growing complaints against Prevost ultimately reached the ears of the government of Lord Liverpool. The prime minister was keen to avoid any scandal but was focused more on the important problems emerging at the Congress of Vienna, the conference of European powers that had opened in September 1814 to settle outstanding diplomatic and boundary problems resulting from the recent wars. Liverpool desired a swift conclusion to the war in America. Another complication was that Prevost and Yeo could no longer work together. The result was that, in October 1814, Bathurst, who had yet to see Yeo's letters regarding Prevost's conduct, sought Wellington's opinion. The response was short and to the point: "It is very obvious you must remove Sir George Prevost."[54] This was a damning recommendation against Prevost from the most highly respected and influential officer in the British service. Prevost had no powerful ally, and his only public defense came from Major Foster Coore, his aide, whose letter "deprecating" Commodore Yeo's "presumptions" on the state of Downie's squadron appeared in the *Montreal Gazette* in February 1815.[55] Unfortunately for Prevost, his family name no longer had the influence it had forty years earlier, and no patron came forward to rescue his reputation. To the government, the apparent loss of confidence in the governor general was much too serious to permit him to continue in office.[56]

By November 1814, the government concluded it had to replace Prevost because, as Liverpool explained to Wellington:

> The Navy in Canada have made serious charges against Sir George Prevost. They say that they never would have attacked the American fleet at anchor off Plattsburgh if he had not promised to attack the fort at the same time; that if he fulfilled his engagement, the misfortune to the fleet would not have occurred; and if even the fleet had been obliged to capitulate, it might have been retaken if the fort had been captured, as it was some hours before the Americans, in their crippled state, were able to take possession of the British ships.[57]

The prime minister admitted that his decision was based primarily on the charges made by Yeo: "There are not many letters yet arrived from the officers of the Army, but one which I have seen appears to corroborate, at least to a considerable extent the accusations of the Navy."[58] The letter Liverpool referred to may have been an account "Written by a Staff Officer from the Peninsula" or, more likely, a letter written by Major General Frederick Robinson on 22 September 1814, to Anthony Merry, former British minister to Washington, who was highly regarded in the Foreign Office. On the same day that it was decided to recall Prevost, Yeo's letter of 29 September 1814, including the enclosures, had been brought to the attention of Bathurst.[59] Thus it appears that Liverpool and his senior ministers of state decided to remove Prevost based on rumor, innuendo, and such evidence as was contained in "Sir James Yeo's opinion of the action of Sep 11," "a staff officer's opinion," and perhaps a letter from Robinson.[60] Sadly, Prevost's two dispatches seem to have made little impression on anyone.[61]

In November 1814, Bathurst had sent an update on American affairs, including confirmation of Prevost's recall, to Henry Goulburn, the Undersecretary of State for War and the Colonies and a member of the British commission at the Ghent negotiations. Goulburn's reply was decidedly supportive of the navy's perspective, despite some uneasiness about the evidence against Prevost:

> It will not be a very easy task to find a proper successor to Sir G. Prevost, nor will that officer who undertakes it have a pleasant situation. The differences which appear now to prevail between the officers of the naval and military service, when added to the system of thwarting and abusing the Governor which has long prevailed in Canada, must impede the exertions of that officer, however distinguished. I am glad Sir G. Prevost is recalled. The affair at Plattsburgh is to me still unaccountable, and I am, though perhaps unjustly, disposed to give weight to the charges brought forward by Sir J. Yeo.[62]

Wellington, however, now rendered a second opinion on Prevost. On this occasion, he was more forgiving, perhaps upon learning more about the Plattsburgh campaign, or as a result of an observation made by Colonel Henry Torrens, his former military secretary and now military secretary to the commander in chief at the Horse Guards. Torrens had written: "It is not fair . . . to prejudge Sir George Prevost's case before his own account is received."[63] Wellington's possible nomination as a potential successor to Prevost may also have influenced his thinking, given that he might soon be made responsible for British North America. Wellington wrote to Major General Sir George Murray, who was to deliver to Sir George the government's decision to recall him: "I admire all that has been done in America, as far as I understand it generally. Whether Sir George Prevost was right or wrong in his decision at Lake Champlain is more than I can tell; but of this I am very certain, he must have retired to Kingston [Montreal] after our fleet was beaten, and I am inclined to believe he was right."[64] Wellington added that Prevost "will justify his misfortunes, which . . . I am quite certain are not what the Americans have represented them to be."[65] The Duke may have been sincere in his sentiment, but he also could have been attempting to reinforce the reputations of his former generals and regiments who had been sent to North America and whose reputations now faced attack from the Royal Navy.

The government continued searching for a replacement for Prevost. Liverpool preferred Wellington and was "most anxious, under all circumstances, that he should accept command in America," as Wellington "would restore confidence to the army, place the military operations on a proper footing, and give us the best chance of peace."[66] Another candidate was Lord Niddry (Sir John Hope), a Peninsular veteran whom Wellington considered "the best you can choose to succeed Sir George Prevost";[67] however, Niddry's poor health eliminated his candidacy. Other officers who were considered included Sir John Sherbrooke in Nova Scotia and Lieutenant General Sir Rowland Hill, one of Wellington's most trusted subordinates during the Peninsular War. None of these officers was available or willing, however, to serve in North America, and Liverpool decided that Drummond, the commander of Upper Canada, would replace Prevost and issued orders to this effect early in the new year.[68]

Prevost, of course, sensed trouble was brewing. In December, he wrote Bathurst offering further evidence that would "account satisfactorily for my inability to shew Your Lordship who did not do their duty in the Naval Combat off Plattsburgh . . . as I had proposed in my private communications."[69] He also expressed his concern that Yeo would stifle an inquiry into the naval battle now that it was known the British squadron "was superior to that of the Enemy in every respect."[70] If Prevost was intent on saving his career, however, this letter lacked the punch it needed. In another communication to Bathurst, Prevost discussed his difficulties with Yeo from his perspective as commander in chief of British North America; Prevost proposed a change to the naval command structure that, if implemented, would distance him from direct dealings with Yeo. Prevost began by noting that the important role naval operations played in military campaigns should not "depend upon either for superintendence or final success upon the life and exertions of an officer personally commanding a squadron, whose situation might on some occasions give him a bias incompatible with the real good of the service."[71] Prevost advocated the appointment of a rear admiral who would command all naval forces on the Great Lakes and who would also have "superintendence over all [the commanders on each lake] and be instructed to cooperate with the commander of the forces."[72] Prevost foresaw a senior flag officer being selected for this post with Yeo being left to his squadron command on Lake Ontario, while other naval officers would be assigned to the other lakes. Nothing came of this suggestion.[73]

Prevost's complaint that the existing naval command arrangement undermined the unity of the war effort led him to conclude that the only solution was to centralize the direction of strategy in the Canadas at the highest level—meaning under his authority. By the late autumn of 1814, Prevost's complaints about Yeo appeared to be making some headway, as the Admiralty briefly questioned the veracity of Yeo's claims and challenged him about his conduct in North America. Admiralty officials read with great interest Prevost's account of his difficulties in obtaining Yeo's cooperation to resupply Drummond on the Niagara Peninsula. They also read with interest Prevost's complaints that Yeo was no longer interested in supporting the army as, using a now familiar argument, he had feared being goaded into a voyage that, like Barclay's on Lake Erie, could end in disaster on Lake Ontario. Officials at the Admiralty took notice of Prevost's complaints and noted discrepancies in the very few dispatches Yeo had sent them, along with the inadequacy of the details he provided on officers' postings to the lakes. The lack of clarity found in Yeo's reports was enough to cause Lord Melville, the First Lord of the Admiralty, to question whether the navy "was justified in pronouncing so decidedly on the cause of the failure"[74] at Plattsburgh without first hearing from Prevost or his staff. These questions came too late for Prevost, however, as he was unable to convince either the government or the Admiralty to change its views toward him.[75]

As with every decision regarding the level of commitment Britain would provide in defending its North American colonies between 1812 and 1815, the debate regarding Prevost's fate and his complaints about Yeo and about the command structure must be viewed in a similar context. As governor and commander in chief of this group of colonies, Prevost held authority over a large territory that, while incorporating several British interests, was an expensive economic and diplomatic backwater; moreover, it held memories of defeat from the American War of Independence. The outcome of the War of 1812 confirmed that Britain would retain possession of these colonies, but their future prospects were uncertain and overshadowed by more important imperial concerns elsewhere, such as in India, the West Indies, or Europe. Despite the fact that Prevost had achieved what was asked of him within the imperial administration, the simplest solution to the evident difficulties of his position was to recall him.[76]

PREVOST did continue as governor in chief and captain general of British North America until after the War of 1812 officially ended. Normally, his relief would have been a logical end to a successful governorship that would have concluded with honors. Rather than returning home to accolades and quiet retirement, however, Prevost found himself facing a court-martial.

On 2 March 1815, the day after Prevost learned that the Treaty of Ghent had been ratified by both governments and the war had officially ended, Major General Sir George Murray arrived at Quebec to "communicate to me [Prevost] a letter from Your Lordship addressed to him but of which I am the suspect."[77] Murray told Prevost that his commission had been revoked by the government and that he was to return to Britain to answer the charges that Yeo had made against him. Prevost's disappointment, especially with the method by which this news was delivered, was evident when he wrote Bathurst three days later:

> This is the first & only notice I have received from your Lordship respecting my conduct at Platsburgh, and I cannot but express the surprise excited by the nature, as well as the mode of this communication. Conscious of no fault I dread not the strictest investigation, but it appears adding unnecessary poignancy to the unexpected blow, that the mortification you have judged proper to inflict should be conveyed through a third person & this an officer so much my junior in the Service.
>
> Your Lordship states that the revocation of my commission as Governor General is not meant to mark His Royal Highness the Prince Regent's displeasure: unfortunately the

distinction will be very difficult for the world to discover, and I must confess that to my own feelings the circumstance is acutely painful. The consequence may probably be that I may remain some time from severity of climate, or other circumstances (as your Lordship observes) seeing myself deprived of every authority and every emolument after four years of the most arduous duties I have performed in the course of the five & thirty I have devoted to His Majesty's service, unless to avoid such an interval I should prefer passing through the United States like a fugitive.[78]

Despite his utter disappointment, Prevost continued to administer the affairs of government. He issued instructions that "proclaimed peace and a cessation of arms,"[79] disbanded the embodied militia, dealt with fiscal matters, and then, on 25 March 1815, prorogued the legislature of Lower Canada. As he prepared to depart, he must have found some consolation in the rumors that Commodore Sir James Yeo was also being recalled.[80]

The lack of clarity regarding the events that had transpired in North America during the war had actually given some in the Admiralty cause for concern. In December 1814, the first secretary of the Admiralty, John Croker, had written Yeo ordering him to return to Britain to answer complaints made against him by Prevost. He was also to clarify questions regarding his performance that had been raised during Captain Barclay's court-martial, the findings of which had indirectly blamed Yeo for the loss of the Lake Erie squadron. There were strong suspicions that Yeo had not kept the Admiralty properly informed of affairs in North America. Furthermore, the assurances of Rear Admiral Sir Robert Otway, who after bringing a convoy to Montreal had overseen the preparation of Downie's squadron, that the Lake Champlain squadron had been inspected and properly equipped were also suspect. Evidence from Commander Daniel Pring, Downie's second-in-command, had confirmed that *Confiance* was "deficient in gunlocks and other material, articles of stores";[81] it also established that Otway was to forward any information he had on the subject.[82] Prevost, however, remained the principal focus of the Admiralty's interest, and it took steps to ensure it could deal promptly with any defense Prevost might offer, as Yeo learned from Croker:

It appears indispensable that the Commander of His Majesty's Forces in Canada should be directed to return home for the purpose of his justification in regard to the charges against him contained in your letter and its enclosures on the subject of the late action on Lake Champlain. It is therefore highly desirable that measures should be taken in order to your being on the spot during any inquiry which may take place in consequence of your accusations. And I am to acquaint you in their Lordships concurring in the opinion expressed in the said letter as to the necessity of your being present in this country where an opportunity shall be afforded to Sir George Prevost of justifying his conduct in Canada.[83]

Commodore Sir Edward Owen was appointed to replace Yeo. Before Owen left Britain, he was told that there was a chance hostilities might continue and that he was to maintain diligence and ensure British North America, from Lake Huron to Lake Champlain, was adequately protected. Owen arrived at Kingston in mid-March 1815, and several days later Yeo commenced his journey home. Before leaving, he had staged an "elegant fete" that included fireworks, dancing, and a "sumptuous dinner," for ninety guests on board his flagship, HMS *St. Lawrence*.[84] During his journey, Yeo stopped briefly at Sackets Harbor, where he was entertained by Chauncey, and then continued to New York City and more meetings with U.S. naval officers—including the challenge of a duel from one American officer who claimed that Yeo had slighted him while he was in captivity; the affair came to nothing—before resuming his journey to England.[85]

Meanwhile, Prevost issued his final General Order, which contained an overview of the war and paid tribute to the officers and men who served under his command:

It has fallen to the lot of this army to struggle through an arduous and unequal contest, remote from succour and deprived of many advantages experienced in the more cultivated countries of Europe; yet His Excellency has witnessed with pride and admiration, the firmness, intrepidity and patient endurance of fatigue and privations, which have marked the character of the army of Canada. Under all these circumstances valor and discipline have prevailed, and although local circumstances and limited means have circumscribed the war, principally to a defensive system, it has, notwithstanding, been enobled by numerous brilliant exploits, which will adorn the pages of future history.– At Detroit, and at the River Raisin two entire armies with their commanding Generals were captured; and greatly superior armies were repulsed. The several battles of Queenstown, Stoney Creek, Chateauguay, Chrystler's, La Colle, Lundy's Lane, near the falls of Niagara, and the subsequent operations on that frontier, will ever immortalize the Heroes who were on those occasions afforded the opportunity of distinguishing themselves.– The capture of Michilimackinac, Ogdensburg, Oswego and Niagara by assault are trophies of the prowess of British Arms. The names of the respective officers who led his Majesty's Troops to these several achievements are already known to the world, and will be transmitted by the faithful historian with glory to a grateful posterity.

Reviewing past events, it is with exultation His Excellency reflects on the complete success which has crowned the valour, exertions and perseverance of this gallant army, by terminating each successive campaign in the defeat and discomfiture of all the enemy's plans, in which the utmost energies of the government of the U. States have been exhausted in vain efforts to accomplish his avowed object, the conquest of these provinces.[86]

Prevost's final act as commander in chief was to instruct Baynes to collect documentation on the Plattsburgh affair.

Prevost decided that, rather than wait several weeks for the navigation season to open and depart by ship from Quebec, he would proceed overland to New Brunswick and sail from Saint John. He left Quebec on 3 April 1815, just hours before Lieutenant General Gordon Drummond arrived to replace him, and Drummond regretted not "having a personal interview with His Excellency on account of the many subjects of a public nature."[87] Prevost's journey was arduous and often on foot along the route known as the "Portage."[88] Several members of his party, including Edward Brenton and his aides, Major Foster Coore and Major William Cochrane, noted that Prevost's "constitution had suffered a fatal injury," and his health "yielded to the excessive fatigues"[89] of the journey. Once he arrived in Saint John, Prevost boarded a frigate for England.[90]

Four days after Prevost left Quebec, the first public letters criticizing his governorship were published. The letters of *Veritas*, pen name for the Montreal merchant John Richardson, appeared in the *Montreal Herald* and were reprinted in the *Acadian Recorder*. Richardson's aim was to demonstrate that the "the merit of preserving them [the Canadas] from conquest belongs not to him [Prevost]."[91] In July 1815, the collected letters by Veritas were printed in a pamphlet. The *Montreal Herald* also published a feature titled "Interesting Particulars on the Late Distressing, Humiliating and Disastrous Affair at Plattsburgh."[92] This anonymous piece praised the actions of Downie and Robinson while criticizing Prevost.

Prevost's journey to England coincided with the outbreak of hostilities in Europe. In late February 1815, Napoléon escaped from Elba, the Mediterranean island he had been exiled to following his abdication, and by April had reestablished himself as emperor of France. British forces in the Netherlands were mobilized, Wellington was sent to command them, and a new coalition was formed against France. Prevost, meanwhile, arrived at Portsmouth on 11 May 1815, just as the Anglo-Allied and Prussian armies were concentrating in the Low Countries. Prevost's aspiration of promptly "satisfying himself to the command of His Majesty's Government"[93] was delayed momentarily, as his ship, the sixth-rate HMS *Cossack*, was placed in quarantine, a normal procedure for any vessel that had been in the Mediterranean, where it had previously served.[94] Near the end of May, Prevost was in London, where he anxiously wrote Bathurst from his hotel that he hoped that "it is the intention of Your Lordship to relieve me as early as practicable from the prejudgement and punishment I am labouring under, I now do myself the honor of addressing Your Lordship for the purpose of obtaining information respecting the nature of the investigation my conduct is to undergo."[95]

Within days, Prevost met with Bathurst to explain his conduct during the Plattsburgh expedition. According to historian J. Mackay Hitsman, the meeting must have concluded positively for Prevost, and his explanation was accepted by the government. Although no record of the meeting has survived, it is plausible, in the absence of any contrary evidence, including an official rebuke, which most certainly would have been made public, that Bathurst accepted Prevost's explanations.[96] Hitsman suggests that the Secretary of State for War and the Colonies may have heeded the more favorable assessment of Prevost's conduct Wellington had given Liverpool the previous December. Bathurst may also have desired to keep any potential quarrel between the navy and army quiet for fear of political repercussions or because North American affairs had now given way to the resumption of the war against Napoléon. For Prevost, the matter must have appeared concluded, and he left London for his country estate, known as Belmont, located at Bedhampton near Portsmouth. He had served there as lieutenant governor between 1805 and 1808.[97] As later events would show, however, Bathurst was not yet finished with Prevost.[98]

Yeo also arrived in England in May 1815 to find his reputation intact. He provided a written report to the First Lord of the Admiralty "on the late Naval Operations on the Lakes"[99] that outlined how a naval campaign might be carried out in a future North American war. During meetings at the Admiralty in June, Yeo was offered another squadron command and a commission as commodore, to suppress the slave trade in West Africa. Given the large-scale postwar reduction of the navy, Yeo was actually fortunate in obtaining this appointment; moreover, this offer appeared to be a repudiation of the questions that had been raised regarding his own conduct in North America.[100]

As he prepared his new command for sea, Yeo attended several meetings at the Admiralty that, ultimately, would result in charges being brought against Prevost.[101] Following a review of the draft charges and statements by Pring and other officers, Yeo was instructed to "prepare Charges arising out of the documents submitted to their Lordships . . . respecting Sir George Prevost."[102] These were then to be forwarded for approval to Charles Manners-Sutton, the judge advocate general, who was responsible for all court-martial processes in the army. Once the charges were approved, Yeo was to formally submit them to the Admiralty.[103]

The four charges were submitted to Manners-Sutton before the end of August 1815.[104] In his cover letter, Yeo wrote that he had "studiously confined them to his [Prevost's] conduct as it affected

His Majesty's Naval Service deeming it more proper to leave it to the Military Branch of His Majesty's Government to add any charge if it should be thought right respecting Sir George Prevost's retreat."[105] The charges Yeo submitted were as follows:

> For having on or about the 11th day of September, 1814 by holding out the expectation of cooperation of the Army under the command of Lieutenant General Sir George Prevost induced Captain Downie late of His Majesty's ship Confiance to attack the American naval squadron on Lake Champlain when it was highly imprudent to make such attack without the cooperation of the Land Forces and for not having afforded that cooperation.
>
> For not having stormed the American works on the shore at nearly the same time that the said Naval Action commenced as he had given Captain Downie reason to expect.
>
> For having disregarded the signal for cooperation which had been previously agreed upon and which was duly given by Captain Downie.
>
> For not having attacked the Enemy on shore either during the said naval action or after it was ended whereby His Majesty's Naval Squadron under the Command of Captain Downie might have been saved or recovered.[106]

In his reply, the judge advocate general restricted his comments to the technical aspects of the draft charges and wrote that "they are worded with sufficient precision to render them cognizable before a General Court Martial."[107]

Whatever impression Prevost had of his situation following his meeting with Bathurst in London, he was not aware of the role Bathurst had played in preparing charges against him. With the charges approved, Yeo formally submitted them to the Admiralty and, in a cover letter, wrote that he "deplored the necessity of this investigation more particularly being placed in the painful situation of a public accuser, but if I withheld my opinion I must have compromised the honor of our arms."[108]

Prevost first became aware of the strength of the forces arrayed against him in August 1815 when the findings of the Plattsburgh naval court-martial were published. A naval court-martial, requiring all the surviving officers to account for their actions, was automatic upon the loss or capture of a warship. Yeo served as one of the prime interrogators during the questioning of Commander Daniel Pring and the other surviving naval officers from the Lake Champlain battle, which was held at Portsmouth in August 1815.[109] The correspondence between Prevost and Downie, and the reports Pring and Robertson had submitted on 12 September 1814, but not their letters written later that month, were submitted as evidence. All the officers except for Lieutenant James McGie of the *Chubb*, who was accused of cowardice during the battle, and had deserted rather than face trial, were acquitted. The findings by the court strongly reflected Yeo's influence on it—the commodore attended the proceedings, questioned witnesses, and testified on the character of the senior officers of the Lake Champlain squadron, but he was asked nothing of the readiness of that squadron[110]—as the wording of the charges shared similarities to that used in the charges he had already submitted against Prevost:

> That the Capture of His Majesty's said late ship Confiance, the Brig Linnet and the Remainder of the said Squadron, by the said American Squadron, was principally caused by the British Squadron having been urged into Battle previous to its being in a proper state to meet its Enemy by a promised Cooperation of the Land Forces, which was not carried into Effect and by the very pressing Letters and communications of their Commander in Chief, whereby it appears he had on the 10th of September 1814, only, waited the naval Attack, to storm the Enemy's Works and the Signal, of the approach of the British Squadron on the following day, by scaling the Guns of the Confiance had been settled by the late Captain Downie and Major Coore . . . and which promised Cooperation was communicated to Other officers and Crews of the British Squadron before the Commencement of the Action.[111]

This was too much for Prevost, and he protested the publication of the findings to the Duke of York, the commander in chief of the army, complaining their public release was both premature and unjust. Prevost stated it was unfair of the court to reach these conclusions "as his conduct and that of the army under his command not being properly the subject of their inquiry."[112] Prevost was angered

by the failure of his accusers to address their accusations directly
against him and requested York's assistance in causing the charges
to be produced in legal form to provide him the opportunity of "vin-
dicating his character and conduct."[113] By now, Yeo's charges were
already in their final form, and the Judge Advocate General's Office
had commenced making arrangements for a court-martial, including the collection of names of witnesses in Britain, France, and
North America. Prevost became painfully aware of these preparations after a copy of the charges was sent by the Adjutant General's
Office to the Horse Guards and presented to him on 13 September
1815, more than a week since they had been filed.[114]

It is clear, however, that Prevost had anticipated that charges
would be brought against him. In March 1815, he had instructed
Baynes to collect evidence regarding the Plattsburgh expedition. Suspecting that Yeo had collected damaging evidence from American
officers while he was in the United States, Prevost's supporters at
Quebec obtained written testimony from the recently promoted
Major General Alexander Macomb and Captain Thomas Macdonough.[115] In particular, they sought to confirm whether the American squadron was within range of the British shore batteries and
thus if Prevost's artillery could have driven the American squadron
into the waiting British ships. Macdonough responded that this was
impossible, since his vessels lay "a mile and a half from the batteries
at Plattsburgh" well out of range of the guns.[114] Macomb also confirmed that "the squadron was moored beyond the effectual range
of the batteries."[116] He knew this "from a fruitless attempt made to
elevate our guns so as to bear on the British squadron" but no guns,
"however, were fired, all being convinced that the vessels were beyond their reach." Macomb also stated that fire from *Confiance* fell
"several hundred yards short of the shore when closely engaged
with our vessels."[118] As neither officer had any interest in either
destroying or preserving Prevost's reputation, their evidence would
have had a strong bearing on two of the four charges that had been
drafted by Yeo and approved by the judge advocate general.

After he had submitted these charges, Yeo sent a short list of
names to the judge advocate general to summon "as Witnesses on the
Trial of Lieutenant General Sir George Prevost."[119] The list named
nine persons: six naval officers, one midshipman, the master of the
Confiance, and one coxswain. Yeo also requested the Admiralty to

issue these individuals with "orders to hold themselves in constant readiness to attend the Court Martial."[120] In October 1815, the judge advocate general formally requested that the Admiralty provide not only these witnesses but two more, for the prosecution, several of whom were army officers. There was also the question whether one key witness would be available. As Yeo explained to the Admiralty: "The Judge Advocate General has informed me that Major-General Sir Frederick Robinson cannot be summoned by Him until the Warrant for the Court Martial is issued."[121] An added complication was that Robinson was not expected to leave Canada before the next navigation season opened, which would be sometime in May 1816.[122]

By late October 1815, a list of forty-one witnesses had been compiled that included six general officers (de Rottenburg, Robinson, Baynes, Brisbane, Power, and Beckwith), Commissary General Robinson, one rear-admiral (Otway), several former regimental commanders, aides and staff officers, and nine other naval officers, including Captain Fisher and Commander Pring, who had recently been promoted to post captain. Six of these officers—de Rottenburg, Robinson, Baynes, Brisbane, Pring, and Major Foster Coore—were to testify for both the defense and the prosecution; twenty-three others, including Power, Beckwith, Commissary General Robinson, Otway, Fisher, and four commanding officers, were identified as witnesses for the defense; and twelve were to appear for the prosecution alone. Among the latter group were one naval captain and four majors, while the remainder were junior officers of both services.[123] To everyone's surprise, Major General Robinson did manage to return to England. With only one other witness left in Canada, the Judge Advocate General's Office asked Prevost whether the "evidence of Sir Sidney Beckwith . . . was considered by His Lordship as being material, as to require his being summoned from Canada."[124] Given the delay this would create, Prevost agreed that Beckwith could be dropped from the final list of witnesses.[125]

The composition of the board was set as well. General John Cradock was appointed as president of the court. Cradock had served in the West Indies during the 1790s and later in Ireland, where he helped suppress the 1798 uprising and also met Wellington; he fought in Egypt in 1801 and two years later was appointed commander of the East India Company forces at Madras but was recalled in the aftermath of a rebellion in 1807. Cradock then led the army in Portugal from August 1808 until the more junior Wellington replaced him in April 1809. Cradock was an interesting choice as president as he never had the opportunity to clear his name following his dismissal from command at Madras, which might have made him sympathetic toward Prevost. The other board members included one other full general and fifteen lieutenant generals.[126] In December 1815, it was announced to all concerned, including Wellington, who was kept abreast of the pending trial, that the court-martial would sit on 15 January 1816 at the Royal Hospital in Chelsea.[127]

The charges preferred against Prevost became public when they were published in several journals, including the *Naval Chronicle*, under the heading "NAVY *versus* THE ARMY," which may have reflected the sentiment of how the Royal Navy viewed the matter. News of the coming trial was also reported in several American newspapers.[128]

Everything appeared ready for the board to sit when Prevost's health suddenly declined in December 1815. Tired from the many trips between his home near Southampton and London, Prevost had taken up residence in a family house in London to prepare for the court-martial and to have better access to medical care.[129] His health continued to worsen. At age forty-eight, he should still have been a vital man, but the cumulative effect of years of service in the West Indies, where he was twice wounded and suffered from illness; the pressures of wartime command in North America, the difficulties of the journey from Quebec to New Brunswick and the stress surrounding his recall and court-martial had slowly weakened him. He had developed dropsy, which caused internal swelling due to the accumulation of water, and his condition may also have been related to congestive heart failure, which is often associated with dropsy. Due to his poor health, the court-martial was postponed until 5 February 1816, but Prevost's condition continued to decline and he died on 5 January. Six days later, his body was interred alongside his father and other family members in the family crypt at St. Mary the Virgin Church in East Barnet, Hertfordshire.[130] The next day, the Judge Advocate General's Office announced that due to the death of Sir George Prevost, the court-martial was canceled.[131]

This abrupt decision was disputed by Prevost's brother, Colonel William Augustus Prevost, who wrote the Duke of York in protest and requested that it be allowed to continue. The matter was put to Charles Manners-Sutton, who advised the Duke that since Prevost was dead, a court-martial was out of the question. Whereas a court of inquiry, a military body created to report on any matter, including accusations against an officer, was the only other legal means of investigating the charges put forth by Yeo, in the estimation of Manners-Sutton, the "difficulties arising out of the form of the proceeding . . . in so singular a case, as an inquiry after the death of the Party are absolutely insurmountable." As courts of inquiry lacked the authority of courts martial—for example, oaths were not required to give testimony—the judge advocate general concluded that "no satisfaction can attend" it and that he thus "was strongly of the opinion that no proceeding can be adopted."[132] Any hope of holding an inquiry thereupon died. Undeterred, Yeo refused to accept the government's decision and endeavored to demonstrate the former commander in chief's guilt. Determined to acquit the navy, and thereby himself, of any complicity in the defeat on 11 September 1814, Yeo established his own inquiry, the findings of which were collected in a document titled "On the Court Martial held at Chelsea Hospital in February 1816 on the Conduct of Lieutenant General Sir George Prevost, Commander in Chief of His Majesty's Forces in Canada."[133] Although it presents itself as the proceedings of a court-martial, no such trial was held—no convening order was issued, no president or board members were appointed, and little new evidence was collected. The interrogators that are named were the same naval officers who fulfilled a similar role at the Plattsburgh naval court-martial of 18–21 August 1815, excerpts of which were included in this report. The thirteen military witnesses included Beckwith, Brisbane, de Rottenburg, Power, and Robinson, but only two of these officers were interviewed—the "testimony" of the remainder is nothing more than remarks on their character and an opinion of their potential evidence.

The report also includes Yeo's letters to the Admiralty recommending charges against Prevost; the correspondence Prevost and Pring exchanged in the days before the naval battle; and "a review of the American Navy and their modes of rating" from "The Letters of Veritas," written by Montreal merchant John Richardson, whose resentment of Prevost was matched only by his ignorance of naval affairs.[134] A fuller account of the campaign is provided in several unattributable narratives that serve to reinforce the impression of inadequate leadership and opportunities missed on the part of Prevost. For example, during the march to Plattsburgh, Prevost is described as having "traversed up and down the country (as Don Quixote as far as the *search* for adventures went through but not with the spirit to encounter them)." The account goes on to assert that on 6 September, the "10 to 12,000 men" of the Left Division that had arrived at Plattsburgh, "all of which were Veteran Troops," the "greater part" having "just arrived in America from the Peninsula," could have "easily have beaten the Americans" with "no other weapons but Broomsticks in their hands."[135]

The report ends abruptly, but not before condemning Prevost as guilty of three charges: for having forced Downie into a naval action, for ignoring Downie's signal to commence the land action, and for not having attacked the American land batteries. Not surprisingly, the use of evidence from the Plattsburgh naval court-martial achieved Yeo's goal of exonerating the navy of any wrongdoing during the Plattsburgh campaign. However, the purpose of the naval court martial held in 1815 had been to demonstrate whether the officers had discharged their duties to the fullest and not to make any determination on the conduct of Sir George Prevost. The remainder of the report, including the so-called evidence from the army officers, throws no new light on the affair. Inconsistencies in the text and errors with several officer's names suggest this document was produced in haste, and it may have been an initial draft.[136] Pressed for time, Yeo was undoubtedly dissatisfied by the results of the inquiry and, now preoccupied with his new command, was forced to abandon any hope of proving Prevost responsible for the defeat on Lake Champlain.

Meanwhile, given the circumstances, the Prince Regent, the head of state in the continued illness of George III, felt obliged to provide the Prevost family with an acknowledgment of Sir George's many years of dedicated service. An offer of a peerage was made to Prevost's son, George, who declined the honor because the family could not financially support a title. Unlike other family members, including his father, uncle James, and half brother Augustine, all of whom had amassed great fortunes from land holdings in North

America, Prevost had not secured any major source of extra income and had lived on his salary and the money he had inherited.[137] While he was in the West Indies, he had received presentation swords, silver plate, and some prize money in thanks for his service, but he never accumulated great wealth or titles, as had some other general and flag officers.[138] The Prince Regent therefore suggested the additional honor of granting "supporters" for the family coat of arms might be appropriate;[139] and this offer was accepted by Lady Catherine Prevost. The grant was published in the *London Gazette* in September 1816, with the following description: "On either side a grenadier of the 16th (or Bedfordshire) regiment of foot, each supporting a banner; that on the dexter side inscribed 'West Indies,' and that on the sinister, 'Canada;' and the said supporters, together with the motto *servatum cineri* [Faith Kept with the Dead], may also be borne by Sir George Prevost, Baronet, son of the said late Lieutenant General, and by his successors."[140] This was a rare distinction, and it is the oldest such award that has been made to a baronet in England.[141]

EPILOGUE

A Reexamination of
Sir George Prevost's
Leadership, 1811–1815

Lieutenant General Sir George Prevost was captain general and governor in chief of British North America for a period of forty-three months, from September 1811 to March 1815. In that time, he prepared his command for war and then successfully defended it between June 1812 and February 1815. The execution of any strategy is never perfect, and while setbacks occurred and mistakes were made by Prevost and others, the gloomy prewar prediction that the Canadas could not survive a war against the United States proved to be wrong. British military forces in Upper and Lower Canada repelled at least eight major invasions and countless raids, while the inland lakes witnessed the creation of the largest and most powerful naval forces of any North American colonial war. Despite British North America's disadvantages in population, agricultural production, and manufacturing relative to the United States, and given that its regular land and naval forces, ordnance, and most war-related stores had to come a distance of 3,200 miles, it is surprising that Canada survived at all, particularly as the odds were so great against it and keeping in mind that, for Britain, North America was always a secondary theater.

The historiography of the War of 1812 rarely attributes the success of the British war effort in the northern theater to Sir George Prevost. Instead, the credit had gone to subordinate commanders, such as Isaac Brock, Sir James Yeo, and a host of lieutenant colonels and more junior officers that commanded tactical actions.[1] Prevost was not in the thick of the fighting, nor should he have been, as his task was to lead the war effort in the Canadas—a point that is often forgotten. As a result, historians have effectively written him out of the narrative. Prevost—not Brock or Yeo or any other more junior officer, for that matter—held ultimate responsibility for winning or losing the war in North America. Prevost directed the operational and logistical activities of the Royal Navy, the army, the Commissariat, and other branches of the military and civil establishment toward a single goal: the successful defense of British territory in North America.

Prevost devoted much attention to naval forces. At the outbreak of the war, the Provincial Marine controlled all the lakes surrounding Upper Canada. This superiority was challenged on Lake Ontario during the fall of 1812, however, as the United States Navy began to assert itself on Lakes Ontario and Erie. To counter this threat, Prevost secured the help of the Royal Navy and incorporated these lakes into his defensive sphere, seeking to retain control of both but realizing that, with the limited resources and manpower available to him, the priority went to Lake Ontario. Commodore James Yeo too understood the strategic importance of that lake, and one would expect that, given their similar views, he would have encouraged a cordial working relationship with Prevost. While Yeo subordinated his activity with the plans of the commander in chief during the summer of 1813, he also exhibited a growing independence that was encouraged by the Admiralty when it changed the status of his command in 1814. Prevost's growing frustration with Yeo's failure to follow instructions was countered by the centralization of the British naval effort on Lake Ontario and the naval commander's growing suspicion of Prevost's competence, which Yeo believed was confirmed by the results of the Plattsburgh campaign. The consequence was Yeo's actively ending his cooperation with Prevost.[2]

The tragedy of this outcome is that in light of the vagueness of instructions from London, the two commanders could not resolve the difficulties between them and work together effectively toward a common goal. Their relationship is in sharp contrast to that between Wellington and Vice Admiral Sir George Berkeley, commander of the Royal Navy's Portuguese Station between 1809 and 1812. Berkeley, who is perhaps best remembered as commander of the North American squadron during the *Chesapeake-Leopard* crisis, directed all naval support to the Anglo-Portuguese army, and his remarkable willingness "to fully back his army colleagues" contributed to the defeat of the French on the Iberian Peninsula by 1813.[3] As Berkeley's biographer has observed, "His logistical preparations for the 1812 [Spanish] campaign provided Wellington with the forces and supplies to realize his operational vision."[4] What might have transpired had similar conditions been possible between Prevost and Yeo in British North America?[5]

Yeo was at once Prevost's greatest asset and his worst burden during the war. In a short period, naval forces could either completely unhinge an American campaign or, by their absence or ineffectiveness, hinder British operations. What neither officer could fully appreciate at the time was the lasting negative influence Yeo would have on Prevost's career and legacy. Yeo's immediate and forceful attempt to lay blame for the loss of Downie's squadron at Plattsburgh on Prevost proved so successful that the Admiralty agreed to charges against Prevost drafted by him and set preparations in motion for a court-martial. The government concurred and ordered Prevost home, but Yeo also had to return, for his presence was essential in prosecuting Prevost. It must be emphasized, however, that Prevost was recalled to respond to charges arising specifically from the Plattsburgh expedition and not for his general conduct of the wartime defense of Canada. Most historians unfortunately do not make this distinction and often conclude Plattsburgh was merely the last and most egregious in a series of major mistakes made by Prevost.

The pending court-martial was played out very much as a navy-versus-army event. It was, after all, the army, through Prevost, that dragged the Royal Navy onto the inland waters of Canada. Despite the great success achieved by that service on the high seas, its performance against the Americans on inland waters was disappointing. It suffered defeats on Lake Erie and Lake Champlain and had several indecisive and at times embarrassing encounters with the Americans on Lake Ontario. Prevost offered the navy both a convenient scapegoat and an exit strategy from Canada. The effect was so profound that afterward Wellington, as master general of the ordnance, centered the postwar plans for the defense of Canada on large fixed fortifications rather than naval power. In 1817, this decision was reinforced by the Rush-Bagot agreement and the limitations it placed on the number of warships each country could operate on the Great Lakes.

Since the court-martial never sat, the whispers, gossip, newspaper reports, letters, and charges against Prevost remained unanswered, and they have haunted his legacy to this day. Despite the evolution of approaches to the study and presentation of history, the tendency of far too many historians has been to reinforce and repeat conclusions, rather than reexamine the primary sources and with an openness to new views on Prevost. Compounding this is the limited interest many historians have in studying strategic matters; much more attraction, it seems, is spent in exploring the dramatic events surrounding tactical actions, or in writing the biographies of colorful individuals. Since the preponderance of historical writings offer only a narrow perspective of Prevost's direction of the British war effort, we are left with a view of his conduct of the Plattsburgh campaign that is best epitomized by an excerpt from the history of the 19th Light Dragoons, published in 1899:

> Sir George Prevost at once threw up the sponge. . . . In the many wars in which the British Army has fought, it would be hard to find a parallel instance in which British troops have been so mishandled. The cooperation of the fleet was unnecessary, as the enemy's squadron could not have maintained its position with the whole of Plattsburgh in British hands. Nine thousand of Wellington's veterans, who had defeated Napoléon's choicest troops again and again, were made to retreat from an inferior race that could not have withstood them for an hour, with the loss of less than 40 killed since they crossed the frontier. . . . In their anger at the fiasco, an immense number of men deserted during the retreat, causing a greater loss than a successful prosecution of the enterprise could possibly have entailed.[6]

Another popular perspective is that "Prevost, worn out by the weary months of anxiety, would take no risks."[7] If this were indeed the case, why would the British government have appointed him to Canada in 1811 and tolerated his continued employment until the conclusion of hostilities? There were many other general officers that could have been found to replace him. The reason for his appointment is that, as we have seen, Prevost had a good record of success both as a military commander and as a colonial administrator.

Prevost fell into disgrace because of the accusations made by the navy. As the war appeared to be nearing an end in late 1814, the government could afford to recall him to respond to the navy's charges. There was public interest in the forthcoming court-martial, yet nothing of the sort was associated with the signing of the Convention of Cintra six years before, which led to a public inquiry that might easily have ended Wellington's career. The War of 1812 never brought such public embarrassment as no British armies were lost, no territory permanently surrendered, and the overall power of the Royal Navy undiminished, despite the loss of two small inland squadrons. The war itself was soon overshadowed by developments in Europe that ended on the field of Waterloo. As with the Seven Years' War and the American War of Independence, Britain's interests in North America, had of necessity to give way to its interests in Europe.

Prevost was a capable wartime leader. He strove to achieve the best possible results given the limited resources and restricted courses of action available to him. He ensured his actions worked toward, and not against, larger strategic considerations, choosing not to be swept up by the euphoria surrounding tactical successes that might have served to expand the scale of the conflict to the ultimate detriment of the defense of the Canadas. He was flexible and modified his strategy to suit conditions; yet he never let enthusiasm for fame or glory compromise his goals. Although his discretion as a commander in chief in specific tactical matters, such as accompanying the raid on Sackets Harbor, is open to debate, he achieved the mission he was given: to preserve British North America against invasion. Despite the criticisms made of him, that success is indisputable.

It is hoped that this examination of the conduct of Sir George Prevost during the War of 1812 will restore him as a central figure in the history of that conflict. Far from home, with irregular communication, and responsible for the defense of a massive and complex theater, he commanded a mix of regular soldiers, sailors, locally raised forces, and indigenous peoples with prudence and economy that completely thwarted his opponent's plans. Prevost has no great field victory to his credit, such as Wellington at Talavera, Salamanca, Vitoria, or Waterloo, but he preserved the independence of British North America, ensuring it was maintained militarily and thus allowing diplomats to preserve its continued existence by political means.

Appendix A

Correspondence respecting British Strategy in North America

During his appointment as governor in chief and captain general of British North America, Prevost shared a lengthy correspondence with his superior, who until May 1812, was Lord Liverpool, and thereafter Lord Bathurst, the Secretary of State for War and the Colonies. Prevost wrote his first official dispatch, No. 1, to Liverpool on 23 September 1811, and his last to Bathurst, No. 242, was dated 1 April 1815. Liverpool's first dispatch to Prevost was dated 31 December 1811, and Bathurst's last important piece of correspondence, dated 3 June 1814, was the order instructing Prevost to undertake offensive actions against the United States. Prevost and Bathurst also exchanged considerable private correspondence on various matters apart from their numbered dispatches.

The majority of Prevost's dispatches reported on military, naval, and political developments leading up to the American declaration of war and thereafter provided details regarding the military situation, reports of actions, and intelligence on American intentions and capabilities. Few of the letters Prevost received offered strategic or operational direction. Indeed, Prevost would complain in 1813 of the lack of direction sent to him by London.

Of all the correspondence exchanged between Prevost and Bathurst, two pieces stand out. The first, a report Prevost submitted to the government on 18 May 1812, offered an assessment of the defenses of British North America and his plan for defending those colonies. The second, a letter Bathurst sent on 3 June 1814, instructed

Prevost to undertake a series of limited offensives against the United States, designed to secure the frontier of British North America prior to the commencement of peace talks in Europe. The text of both letters is reproduced in full below.

This second document has enjoyed a sensational history. The "secret" heading of the letter caused one historian to claim that when this plan drawn up in London to attack the United States failed, the records of the Plattsburgh campaign were purposely allowed to fall into obscurity as "the British kept it confidential for over a century." Describing it in the introduction of *The Final Invasion: Plattsburgh, the War of 1812's Most Decisive Victory* as "one of the best kept secrets in military and diplomatic history," author David Fitz-Enz claims that the original document went missing sometime after 1922 and that he obtained "a rare copy" of the order from a descendant of Sir George Prevost.[1] A more careful examination of archival holdings in Britain and Canada would have revealed this is not true. A copy of this "secret order" was obtained from the Prevost family in the first decade of the twentieth century and has been available to researchers in the Colonial Office documents (CO 42, Secretary of State, In Letters, Canada) at the National Archives at Kew since 1910 (then the Public Record Office). Copies can also be found at the Library and Archives Canada (CO 42/146 or CO 43/23) in Ottawa and in the Special Collections of the Massey Library at the Royal Military College of Canada in Kingston, Ontario. In addition, the full text of the document was printed in 1965 in J. Mackay Hitsman's *The Incredible War of 1812* (reissued in a revised edition by Robin Brass Studio in 1999). In fact, the existence and contents of this document are well known; historians have used it for decades. Fitz-Enz's interpretation is simply erroneous.

LIEUTENANT GENERAL SIR GEORGE PREVOST TO THE
EARL OF LIVERPOOL, SECRETARY OF STATE FOR WAR AND
THE COLONIES, 18 MAY 1812

Quebec, 18th May 1812

My Lord,

In obedience to the Commands signified to me in your Lordship's dispatch No. 7 of the 13th February, I now have the honor to report upon the Military position of His Majesty's North American Provinces, and the means of defending them.

UPPER CANADA

Commencing with Upper Canada, as the most contiguous to the Territory of the United States and frontier to it along its whole extent, which renders it, in the event of War, more liable to immediate attack.

Fort St. Joseph. Fort St. Joseph, distant about 1,500 miles from Quebec, consists of Lines of Strong Pickets enclosing a Block House. It stands on the Island St. Joseph within the detour communicating the head of Lake Huron with Lake Superior: It can only be considered as a Post of Assemblage for friendly Indians, and in some degree a protection for the North West Fur Trade: The Garrison at St. Joseph's consists of a small Detachment from the Royal Artillery, and one Company of Veterans.[2]

Fort Amherstburg. Fort Amherstburg, situated on the River Detroit at the head of Lake Erie, is of importance from it's being the Dock Yard and Marine Arsenal for the Upper Lakes: It is also a place of reunion for the Indians inhabiting that part of the Country, who assemble there in considerable numbers to receive Presents: The Fort has been represented to me as a temporary Field Work in ruinous State; it is now undergoing repair to render it tenable: The Garrison at Amherstburg consists of a Subaltern's Detachment of Artillery, and about 120 men of the 41st Regiment—the whole commanded by Lieutenant-Colonel St. George[3] an Inspecting Field Officer: The Militia in its Vicinity amounts to about 500 men.

Fort George. Fort George is a temporary Work at the head of Lake Ontario, now repairing to render it tenable, but in its most improved State, it cannot make much resistance against an Enemy in considerable force: The Garrison at Fort George consists of a Captain's Command of Artillery, and about 400 men of the 41st Regiment, the who commanded by Colonel Procter:[4] the Militia Force in the Neighbourhood of Fort George, does not exceed 2,000 Nominal men.

Fort Erie, Chippawa and Fort George form the chain of Communication between Lake Erie and Lake Ontario.

Fort Erie. At Fort Erie, there is a Captain's Command[5] from the 41st Regiment, and at Chippawa a subaltern's.[6] The American

Posts directly opposite to this Line are Fort Niagara, Fort Schlosser, Black Rock, and Buffalo Creek: In the event of Hostilities, it would be highly advantageous to gain possession of Fort Niagara[7] to secure the Navigation of the River Niagara.

York. York is situated on the North Shore of Lake Ontario, has a good Harbour, and is the position in Upper Canada best adapted for the deposit of Military Stores, whenever it is converted into a Post of defence, and also for a Dock Yard and Marine Arsenal for this Lake. Its retired situation from the American frontier, makes it a position particularly desirable for those purposes: The project of fortifying and strengthening this Post has been submitted for consideration: York is the Head Quarters of Upper Canada, its Garrison consists of three Companies of the 41st Regiment: The Militia in its vicinity is computed at 1,500 men.

Kingston. Kingston is situated at the head of the Boat Navigation of the St. Lawrence, contiguous to a very flourishing Settlement on the American frontier, and is exposed to sudden attack, which, if successful, would cut off communication between the Upper and Lower Province, and deprive us of our Naval resources: The Garrison of Kingston consists of Four Companies of the 10th Royal Veteran Battalion, under the Command of Major Macpherson:[8] The Militia in the Neighborhood is about 1,500 men.

The Americans have Posts in the vicinity of Kingston, not only opposite, but both above & below with good Harbours, which are open to the resources of a very populous Country: In the event of Hostilities it will be indispensably necessary for the preservation of a Communication between the Lower and the Upper Province, to establish some strong Post for the Regulars and Militia, to secure the Navigation of the St. Lawrence above the Rapids to Lake Ontario: The total number of Militia in Upper Canada is calculated at 11,000 men, of which it might not be prudent to Arm more than 4,000.

LOWER CANADA

Montreal. Montreal is the principal commercial city in the Canadas, and in the event of War, would become the first object of Attack: It is situated on an extension Island, and does not possess any means of defence: Its security depends upon our being able to maintain an impenetrable line on the South Shore, extending from

La Prairie to Chambly, with a sufficient Flotilla to command the Rivers St. Lawrence and the Richelieu.

The Garrison of Montreal at present, consists of a Brigade[9] of Light Artillery, and the 49th Regiment: The Militia in its neighborhood, and easily collected, would exceed 12,000 men, ill armed and without discipline, and 600 embodied,[10] now assembled for training at La Prairie.

St. John's. St. John's is considered a frontier Post: there ends the Navigation from Lake Champlain: It is occupied by a Company of Royal Veterans[11] and one of the 49th Regiment: The Field Works formerly erected for the defence of this Post, are now in ruins, and could not be resumed to much advantage, as they are commanded by ground contiguous, and the Post can be turned by following the New Roads leading from the United States to Montreal.

Chambly. Chambly is unimportant, but as a Post of Support to St. John's, and a place of assemblage for the Militia and a Depot for their Arms and Ammunition: It is occupied by 300 Voltigeurs, and a Detachment of Artillery having two Field Guns.

William Henry.[12] William Henry is 13 leagues from Chambly, and is situated at the junction of the Richelieu & St. Lawrence: It is unquestionably a position which deserves being made tenable against a sudden or irregular attack: From thence down the St. Lawrence are many excellent positions for arresting the progress of an Enemy marching on either Shore upon Quebec, particularly if he is not in possession of the Navigation of the River: The Garrison at William Henry consists of one Field Officer[13] and four Companies of the 100th Regiment.

Quebec. Quebec is the only permanent Fortress in the Canadas: It is the Key to the whole and must be maintained: To the final defence of this position, every other Military operation ought to become subservient, and the retreat of the Troops upon Quebec must be the primary consideration: The means of resistance afforded by the Fortifications in their present imperfect State, are not such as could justify a hope of its being able to withstand a vigorous and well conducted siege: It requires Bomb proof Casmates[14] for the Troops, as the Town is completely commanded from the South Shore at Point Levi, a position which it has frequently been recommended to occupy in force: The Casmates ought to be erected on Cape Diamond, a position that points itself out for a Citadel. It is advisable that the whole circumference of the summit of this Hill should be occupied, being the only elevation within the Walls not commanded by the height of Land on the plains of Abraham: Such a Work would essentially defend the extension Line of Fortification, sloping from Cape Diamond to the Artillery Barrack which is old and imperfect, is commanded from the high land opposite, and is besides seen in reverse and open to an enfilade fire from positions on the bank of the St. Charles River.

The Garrison of Quebec at present consists of about 2,500 Rank and File: The Militia of Lower Canada amounts to 60,000 men, a mere posse, ill arm'd, and without discipline, where of 2,000 are embodied for training.

In framing a general out line of Cooperation for defence with the Forces in Upper Canada, commensurate with our deficiency in strength, I have considered the preservation of Quebec as the first object, and to which all others must be subordinate: Defective as Quebec is, it is the only Post that can be considered as tenable for a moment, the preservation of it being of the utmost consequence to the Canadas, as the door of entry for that Force The King's Government might find it expedient to send for the recovery of both, or either of these Provinces, altho' the pressure of the moment in the present extended range of Warfare might not allow the sending of that force which would defend both, therefore considering Quebec in this view, its importance can at once be appreciated.

If the Americans are determined to attack Canada, it would be in vain the General should flatter himself with the hopes of making an effectual defence of the open Country, unless powerfully assisted from Home: All predatory or ill concerted attacks undertaken presumptuously and without sufficient means, can be resisted and repulsed: Still this must be done with caution, that the resources, for a future exertion, the defence of Quebec, may be unexhausted.

NEW BRUNSWICK & NOVA SCOTIA

The Province of New Brunswick and the peninsula of Nova Scotia present so many vulnerable points to an invading Army, that it is difficult to establish any precise Plan for the defence of either, and consequently much must depend upon Contingencies in the event of Invasion: Their security very materially depends upon the Navy, and the vigilance of our Cruizers in the Bay of Fundy.

In the event of Hostilities with America, it would be an advisable measure to take possession of Moose Island, in the Bay of Passamaquoddy, improperly occupied by a small American Garrison, where we should derive great advantage from the cooperation of our Navy, and should remove the scene of Warfare to the American frontier.

Fredericton. The defence of Fredericton is out of the question, and the course of the River St. John must be defended at the discretion of the Officer Commanding that Garrison, according to the description and number of the assailing Army: The Garrison at Fredericton at present consists of a small Detachment of Artillery, and six companies of the 104th Regiment.[15]

St. John. The Town of St. John is totally indefensible on the land side, it would therefore be requisite to make provision for the removal of the Ordnance and Stores from thence: Two or three small Vessels of War stationed in the River St. John (part of whose Crews might Man Gun Boats) would very much conduce to its security, and in case of a hasty retreat might bring away the Ordnance and Stores:

St. John is at present Garrisoned by two Companies of the 104th Regiment, and a proportion of the Artillery: The Militia of New Brunswick amount to about 4,000 men, much scattered, and but few of them have been trained to the use of Arms.

Halifax. In the event of an Enemy approaching Halifax by Land, Nature has done much for its protection: At the Isthmus near Cumberland, the Militia supported by a proportion of the regular Troops, may make a very protracted defence, were its Flanks secured by the Navy: No point can be fixed upon for the defence of the Basin of Minas, as the entrance of that Bay is too wide to admit of being fortified: If the Enemy escapes the squadron stationed in the Bay of Fundy, he may have his choice of Ground for debarkation, but must look to the destruction of his Flotilla, and no further support by water. Margaret's Bay on the Eastern Coast of Nova Scotia, offers a spacious and safe Harbour, and should any Enemy meditate the capture of Halifax, that point would probably attract his attention: The attempt however would be very hazardous, and he must not calculate either on a Retreat, or Succour, which it is presumed would be prevented by the Squadron from Halifax: The approach from this Bay is through a Country easily defended, and

unfavourable for the Transport of Ordnance or Stores of any kind:
The Sea defences of the Harbour of Halifax offer much to rely on,
but the Land defences are so imperfect as to be undeserving of
notice: The Garrison of Halifax at present consists of about 1,500
men, including three Companies of Artillery; The Militia of Nova
Scotia amounts to upwards of 11,000 men: about 6,000 of whom
have been furnished with Arms and accoutrements, and from the
assistance and instruction afforded them by the Inspecting Field
Officers in that District, they have made as much progress in training and discipline, as could be expected from a Class of People, who
are so much scattered.

CAPE BRETON AND PRINCE EDWARD ISLAND

The Island of Cape Breton & Prince Edward Island, dependencies
of the British North American Provinces, are Garrisoned by small
Detachments of Troops stationed at the principal Town in each, but
their Works of defence are so insignificant, as to be unworthy of
Observation: Nor does their Militia amount to any considerable
number deserving to be noticed.

NEWFOUNDLAND

The Island of Newfoundland, also a dependency of this Command, is principally defended by the Navy upon that Station during
the Summer: The Chief Town and Military depot, St. John's, is
Garrisoned by the Nova Scotia Fencible Regiment,[16] and a company
of Artillery.

BERMUDA

Of the Bermudas, their strength and resources against an attack,
I cannot as yet presume to report upon, to your Lordship, as they
have but recently been made a part of this Command.
I have the honor to be My Lord,
Your Lordship's Most Obedient and most humble Servant

George Prevost
Quebec, 1st June 1812

P.S. The following alterations have taken place since the foregoing
Report was prepared—five companies of the Royal Newfoundland
Fencibles[17] have proceeded from Quebec, and are now on their Route
to York in Upper Canada, for the Marine Service[.]

Four hundred Recruits belonging to the Glengary[18] Levy are assembled at Three Rivers in Lower Canada, to be formed into a Regiment, trained and disciplined.

The detachment of the Royal Newfoundland Fencibles from Quebec, has been replaced by an equal number of the 100th Regiment from Three Rivers.

EARL BATHURST, SECRETARY OF STATE FOR WAR AND THE COLONIES TO LIEUTENANT GENERAL SIR GEORGE PREVOST, 3 JUNE 1814

In the summer of 1814, Lord Bathurst, the Secretary of State for War and the Colonies, provided new instructions to Prevost and confirmation of the reinforcements he was to receive. The objectives listed in the letter to be achieved in 1814 were ambitious, given the lateness of the season in which the orders were sent and the time in which Prevost had to mount the required operations. The offensives staged from the Canadas as outlined in this document were limited and were to be coordinated with diversionary actions around Chesapeake Bay.

The New Orleans expedition was not part of this plan. Proposals to attack that city were first proposed in November 1812, but it was not until August 1814 that plans were put in motion and instructions issued for an expedition in early September.

Secret
Downing Street
3rd June 1814

Sir,

I have already communicated to you in my dispatch of the 14th of April the intention of His Majesty's Government to avail themselves of the favourable state of Affairs in Europe, in order to reinforce the Army under your command. I have now to acquaint you with the arrangements which have been made in consequence, and to point out to you the views with which His Majesty's Government have made so considerable an augmentation of the Army in Canada.

[R. & F.: 768] The 4th Battalion of the Royal Scots of the strength stated in the margin sailed from Spithead on the 9th ulto. [ultimo, or last month] direct for Quebec, and was joined at Cork by the 97th Regiment destined to relieve the Nova Scotia Fencibles at Newfoundland, which latter will immediately proceed to Quebec

[R. & F.: 6th 980; 82nd 837] The 6th and 82nd Regiments of the strength as per margin sailed from Bordeaux on the 15th ulto. direct for Quebec. Orders have also been given for embarking at the same port, twelve of the most effective Regiments[19] of the Army under the Duke of Wellington[20] together with three Companies of Artillery[21] on the same service.

This force, which (when joined by the detachments about to proceed from this Country[22]) will not fall short of ten thousand infantry, will proceed in three divisions to Quebec. The first of these divisions will be embarked immediately, the second a week after the first and the third as soon as the means of Transport are collected. This last division however will arrive at Quebec long before the close of the year.

Six other regiments[23] have also been detached from the Gironde and the Mediterranean, four of which are destined to be employed in a direct operation against the Enemy's Coast, and the other two intended as a reinforcement to Nova Scotia and New Brunswick; available (if circumstances appear to you to render it necessary) for the defence of Canada, or for the offensive operations on the Frontier, to which your attention will be particularly directed. It is also in contemplation at a later period of the year to make a more serious attack on some part of the Coasts of the United States; and with this view a considerable force will be collected at Cork without delay. These operations will not fail to effect a powerful diversion in your favour.[24]

[R. & F.: 3,127] The result of this arrangement, as far as you are immediately concerned, will be to place at your disposal the Royals, The Nova Scotia Fencibles, the 6th & 82nd Regiments amounting to three thousand one hundred and twenty seven men; and to afford you the course of the year a further reinforcement of ten thousand British troops [10,000].

When this force shall have been placed under your command, His Majesty's Government conceive that the Canadas will not only be protected for the time against any attack which the enemy may have the means of making, but it will enable you to commence offensive operations on the Enemy's Frontier before the close of this Campaign. At the same time it is by no means the intention of His Majesty's Government to encourage such forward movements into the Interior of the American Territory as might commit the safety of the Force placed under your command. The object of your operations will be; first, to give immediate protection; secondly, to obtain if possible ultimate security to His Majesty's Possessions in America.

The entire destruction of Sackets harbour[25] and the Naval Establishment on Lake Erie and Lake Champlain come under the first description.

The maintenance of Fort Niagara and so much of the adjacent Territory as may be deemed necessary: and the occupation of Detroit and the Michigan Country come under the second.

If our success shall enable us to terminate the war by the retention of the Fort of Niagara, and the restoration of Detroit and the whole of the Michigan Country to the Indians, the British Frontier will be materially improved. Should there be any advanced position on that part of our frontier that extends towards Lake Champlain, the occupation of which would materially tend to the security of the Province, you will if you deem it expedient expel the Enemy from it, and occupy it by detachments of the Troops under your command, always however taking care not to expose His Majesty's Forces to being cut off by too extended a line of advance.

If you should not consider it necessary to call to your assistance the two Regiments which are to proceed in the first instance to Halifax, Sir J. Sherbroke[26] will receive instructions to occupy so much of the District of Maine[27] as will secure an uninterrupted intercourse between Halifax and Quebec.

In contemplation of the increased force which by this arrangement you will be under the necessity of maintaining in the Province directions have been given for shipping immediately for Quebec, provisions for ten thousand men for six months.

The Frigate which conveys this letter has on board one hundred thousand pounds in Specie for the use of the Army under your command. An equal sum will also be embarked on board the Ship of War which may be appointed to convoy to Quebec the fleet which is expected to sail from the Country on the 10th or at the latest 15th instant.

I have the honour etc.,
BATHURST

APPENDIX B

The Land and Naval Forces at
Plattsburgh, 11 September 1814

LAND FORCES

British

Lieutenant General Sir George Prevost, commanding the expedition[1]

Left Division Order of Battle
Commanding: Major General Francis de Rottenburg
Adjutant General: Major General Edward Baynes
Quartermaster General: Major General Sir Sidney Beckwith
Chief Engineer: Lieutenant Colonel Phillip Hughes
Commissary General: William Robinson
Artillery: Major John S. Sinclair, RA
Three field brigades each with five 6-pounder guns and a 5.5-inch howitzer.[2]

- Sinclair's Company (Captain John Sinclair, RA)
- Wallace's Company (Captain Peter Wallace, RA)
- Maxwell's Company (Captain S Maxwell, RA)
- Detachment Captain James Addam's Company
- Provincial Royal Artillery Drivers[3]
- Train of Artillery

    - 2×24-pounder brass guns
    - 8-inch brass howitzer
    - 3×24-pounder naval carronades on field carriages

- ○ Later augmented by 2×12-pounder iron guns and two 8-inch mortars from Isle aux Noix
- ○ Congreve Rocket Detachment

Main Attack Force (Robinson in overall command)
1st, or *Demi, Brigade*: Major General Frederick P. Robinson
  Assistant Quartermaster General: Major Nathaniel Thorn

- **3/27th Foot**[4]
- **76th Foot**

3rd Brigade, Major General Manley Power

- **3rd Foot**
- **5th Foot**
- 1/27th Foot
- 58th Foot
- Light Company, 39th Foot
- Light Company, 88th Foot
- Two squadrons, 19th Light Dragoons
- 2×6-pounder guns
- Congreve Rocket Detachment

Secondary Attack (Brisbane)
2nd Brigade, Major General Thomas Brisbane

- 2/8th Foot
- 13th Foot
- 49th Foot (two-thirds of the unit)
- De Meuron's Regiment (one-half of the regiment)[5]
- Voltigeurs Canadiens
- Chasseurs Canadiens[6]

The **1/39th Foot** and **1/88th Foot** (Robinson's brigade), less their light companies, were left on lines of communication.
One division (half of a field brigade) of artillery was also left at Chazy.

American

Commanding: Brigadier General Alexander Macomb[7]
Acting Adjutant General: Lieutenant William R. Duncan
Fort Moreau: Colonel Melancton Smith, 29th Infantry

- 6th Regiment of Infantry
- 29th Regiment of Infantry

Redoubt No. 1 (Fort Brown): Lieutenant Colonel Hickens Stores

- 30th Regiment of Infantry (detachment)
- 31st Regiment of Infantry (detachment)

Redoubt No. 2 (Fort Scott): Major Thomas Vinson

- 33rd Regiment of Infantry
- 34th Regiment of Infantry

Blockhouse (near Platt's, south of the lower bridge): Captain John Smyth, 1st Rifle Regiment

- Detachment, company 1st Rifle Regiment
- 4th Regiment of Infantry (convalescents)

Blockhouse (on the point where the river enters Lake Champlain): Lieutenant Abram Fowler

- Detachments of artillery

Light troops under Lieutenant Colonel Daniel Appling and Captain John Sproull
Corps of Rocketeers, Mr. Paris, Captain of Artificers
500 men on Crab Island under Dr. James Mann
Major General Benjamin Mooers, New York state militia

- 3rd Division: New York state militia, Clinton, Essex, and Franklin Counties

Vermont militia: General Samuel P. Strong

NAVAL FORCES

British[8]

Captain Robert Downie, RN
Flagship, HMS *Confiance*

Name or type	Total guns	Carronades	Long guns	Ship's company
Confiance	37	4×32; 6×24	27×24[9]	270
Linnet	16	—	16×24	99
Chubb	11	8×18	3×6	41
Finch	11	6×18; 1 Columbiad[10]	4×6	32
2 Gunboats[11]	4	1×32 each	1×24 each	82
1 Gunboat[12]	2	1×24	1×18	41
1 Gunboat[13]	2	1×18	1×18	35
3 Gunboats[14]	3	—	1×18 each	99
4 Gunboats[15]	4	1×32 each	—	100
Totals	90	33	57	799

American[16]

Master Commandant Thomas Macdonough, USN
Flagship, USS *Saratoga*

Name or type	Total guns	Carronades	Long guns	Ship's company
Saratoga	26	6×42; 12×32	8×24	250
Eagle	20	12×32	8×18	152
Ticonderoga	17	3×32	4×18; 10×12	115
Preble	9	—	9×9	45
6 Galleys[17]	12	1×18 each	1×24 each	100
4 Gunboats[18]	4	—	1×12 each	210
Totals	88	45	49	862

Appendix C

The Pring and Robertson
Letters to Yeo

The charges that Commodore Sir James Yeo submitted against Sir George Prevost were based on a report sent to him on 17 September 1814 by the senior surviving officer of the naval battle of Plattsburgh: Commander Daniel Pring, captain of HMS *Linnet*. Pring included another account, drafted on 15 September, by Lieutenant James Robertson, the first lieutenant on HMS *Confiance*. On 29 September 1814, when Yeo forwarded these letters and the correspondence exchanged between Prevost and Downie given him by Pring, he did not include two other letters written by Pring and Robertson dated 12 September 1814, the day after the naval battle at Plattsburgh while both of these officers were prisoners of war. A discussion of these letters appears in chapter 10.

The text of the four letters is reproduced below. They have been transcribed from the originals available in the National Archives, at Kew, England, Admiralty 1/2737: 201–203; transcriptions can also be found in William Wood, ed., *Select British Documents of the Canadian War of 1812*, vol. 3, pt. 1 (Toronto: Champlain Society, 1928): 368–77 and 383–87. The spelling is at it appears in the original documents.

From Pring at Plattsburg, to Yeo at Kingston

United States Ship Saratoga
Copy Plattsburg Bay, Lake Champlain
12th September 1814.

Sir,

The painful task of making you acquainted with the circumstances attending the capture of His Majesty's Squadron yesterday, by that of the American under Commodore McDonough, it grieves me to state, becomes my duty to perform, from the ever to be lamented loss of that worthy and gallant Officer Captain Downie who unfortunately fell early in the Action.

In consequence of the earnest Solicitation of His Excellency Sir George Prevost, for the Co-operation of the Naval Force on this Lake, to attack that of the Enemy, who were placed for the support of their Works at Plattsburg, which it was proposed should be Stormed by the Troops at the same moment the Naval Action should commence in the Bay, Every possible Exertion was used to accelerate the Armament of the New Ship, that the Military movements might not be postponed at such an advanced Season of the Year—longer than was absolutely necessary.

On the 3d Inst I was directed to proceed in Command of the Flotilla of Gun Boats to protect the left Flank of our Army advancing towards Plattsburg and on the following day, after taking possession and paroling the Militia of Isle la Motte, I caused a Battery of 3 Long 18 Pounder Guns to be constructed for the support of our position abreast of little Chazy where the supplies for the Army were ordered to be landed.

The Fleet came up on the 8th Instant but for want of Stores for the Equipment of the Guns could not move forward until the 11th—At daylight we weighed and at 7 were in full view of the Enemy's Fleet, consisting of a Ship, Brig, Schooner and one Sloop, moored in line, abreast of their encampment, with a Division of 5 Gun Boats on Each Flank;—at 7.40 after the Officers Commanding Vessels and the Flotilla had received their final instructions, as to the plan of attack; we made sail in order of Battle, Capt Downie had determined on laying his Ship athwart hawse of the Enemy's, directing Lieut McGhee of the Chub to support me in the Linnet, in engaging the Brig to the right, and Lieut Hicks of the Finch with the Flotilla of Gun Boats, to attack the Schooner & Sloop on the left of the Enemy's line.

At 8 the Enemy's Gun Boats and smaller Vessels commenced a heavy and galling fire on our Line, at 8.10 the Confiance having two Anchors shot away from her Larboard Bow, And the wind baffling was obliged to anchor (though not in the situation proposed) within two Cables length of her Adversary. The Linnet and Chub soon afterwards took their allotted Stations, something short of that distance, when the Crews on both sides cheered and commenced a spirited and close Action, a Short time however deprived me of the valuable services of Lieutenant McGhee who, from having his Cables, Bowsprit and Main Boom shot away drifted within the Enemy's line and was obliged to surrender. From the light airs and the smoothness of the water, the Fire on each side proved very destructive from the commencement of the Engagement, and with the Exception of the Brig, that of the Enemy, appeared united against the Confiance.

After two hours severe Conflict with our opponent; she cut her cable, run down, and took Shelter between the Ship and Schooner which enabled us to direct our fire against the Division of the Enemy's Gun Boats, and Ship, which had so long annoyed us, during our close Engagement with the Brig, without any return on our part: At this time, the fire of the Enemy's Ship slackened considerably, having several of her Guns dismounted—when she cut her Cable, and winded her Larboard Broadside to bear on the Confiance who, in vain endeavoured to effect the same Operation, at 10.30 I was much distressed to observe the Confiance had struck her Colours—The whole attention of the Enemy's Force then became directed towards the Linnet, the shattered and disable[d] state of the Masts sails, rigging and Yards, precluded the most distant hope of being able to effect an Escape by cutting the Cable, the result of doing so, must in a few minutes have been her drifting alongside the Enemy's Vessels, Close under our Lee—but in the hope that the Flotilla of Gun Boats who had abandoned the object assigned them would perceive our wants and come to our assistance, which would afford a reasonable prospect of being towed clear, I determined to resist the then destructive Cannonading of the whole of the Enemy's Fleet, and at the same time dispatched Lieutenant W. Drew to ascertain the state of the Confiance.

At 10.45 I was apprized of the irreparable loss she had sustained by the Death of her brave Commander (whose merits it would be presumption in me to Extol) as well as the great Slaughter which had taken place on board, and observing from the Manoeuvres of the Flotilla, that I could enjoy no further expectation of relief; the situation of my gallant Comrades, who had so nobly fought, and even now fast falling by my side, demanded the surrender of His Majesty's Brig entrusted to my Command, to prevent a useless waste of valuable lives, and, at the request of the surviving Officers & Men, I gave the painful orders for the Colours to be Struck.

Lieutenant Hicks of the Finch had the Mortification to strike on a reef of Rocks, to the Eastward of Crab Island, about the Middle of the Engagement; which prevented his rendering that assistance to the Squadron that might from an Officer of such ability have been expected.

The misfortune which this day befell us by Capture, will, Sir I trust Apologize for the lengthy detail, which in Justice to the Sufferers, I have deemed it necessary to give of the particulars which led to it; And when it is taken into consideration that the Confiance was Sixteen days before, on the Stocks, with an unorganized Crew, comprized of several Drafts of Men; who had recently arrived from different ships at Quebec, many of whom only joined the day before, and were totally unknown either to the Officers or to each other, with the want of Gun Locks as well as other necessary appointments, not to be procured in this Country; I trust you will feel satisfied of the decided advantage the Enemy possessed, Exclusive of their great superiority in point of force, a comparative Statement of which I have the honor to annex.—It now becomes the most pleasing part of my present duty, to notice to you, the determined skill and bravery of the Officers and men in this unequal Contest, but it grieves me to State, that the loss sustained in Maintaining it, has been so great; that of the Enemy, I understand amounts to something more than the same number.—

The fine style in which Captain Downie conducted the Squadron into Action admidst a tremendous fire, without returning a Shot, until secured, reflects the greatest credit to his Memory, for his Judgment and coolness as also on Lieuts McGhee & Hicks so strictly attending to his Example and instructions, their own accounts of the Capture of their respective Vessels, as well as that of Lieutenant Robertson, who succeeded to the Command of the Confiance, will, I feel assured, do ample Justice to the Merits of the Officers and Men serving under their immediate Command, but I cannot omit noticing the individual Conduct of Lieutenants Robertson,

Creswick and Hornby, and Mr Bryden Master, for their particular Exertion in Endeavouring to bring the Confiance's Starboard side to bear on the Enemy, after most of their guns were dismounted on the other.

It is impossible for me to Express to you, my Admiration of the Officers and Crew serving under my personal Orders, their coolness and steadiness, the effect of which was proved by their irresistible fire, directed towards the Brig opposed to us, claims my warmest acknowledgements, but more particularly for preserving the same, so long after the whole strength of the Enemy had been directed against the Linnet alone, my 1st Lieutenant Mr William Drew, whose merits I have before had the honor to report to you, behaved on this occasion in the most exemplary manner. By the death of Mr Paul, Acting 2nd Lieutenant the Service has been deprived of a most Valuable and brave Officer, he fell early in the Action, Great Credit is due to Mr Giles, Purser, for Volunteering his Services on deck, to Mr. Mitchell, surgeon for the Skill he evinced in performing some amputations required at the moment as well as his great attention to the Wounded during the Action, at the close of which the Water was nearly a foot above the lower Deck, from the number of shot which struck her, between Wind and Water.—I have to regret the loss of the Boatswain Mr. Jackson, who was killed a few minutes before the Action terminated.

The assistance I received from Mr Muckle the Gunner and also from Mr Clarke, Master's Mate, Messrs Fouke and Sinclair, Midshipmen, the latter of whom was wounded on the head and Mr Guy my Clerk, will, I hope, recommend them, as well as the whole of my gallant little Crew, to Your Notice.

I have much Satisfaction in making you acquainted with the humane treatment the wounded have received from Commodore McDono[u]gh. They were immediately removed to his own Hospital on Crab Island, and were furnished with every requisite. His generous and polite attention also to myself, the Officers and Men, will ever hereafter be gratefully remembered.

Enclosed I beg leave to transmit you the statement of the different Commanding Officers of Vessels relative to the circumstances attending their capture, also the Return of killed & Wounded, an[d] I have honor to be

&c

(Signed) Dan. Pring
Captain
late of H.M. Sloop Linnet

ENCLOSURE, ROBERTSON TO PRING

Copy   United States Ship of War
                                        Saratoga, off Plattsburg
                                        12th September 1814.

Sir,

In compliance with your Commands that I should relate the circumstances which led to the surrender of His Majesty's late Ship Confiance, I have the honour to acquaint you that, in leading into the Action, the small bower Anchor was shot from the bows, and when the spare Anchor was let go, the Cable was shot away—the best bower was then let go, the spring on which suffered the same fate—About 15 minutes after we commenced the Action, our gallant Commander, Captain Downie, was mortally wounded, and only lived to be carried below. The Action was kept up with Great Spirit a considerable time afterwards, and until the Enemy's Ship was Silenced and he found it necessary by means of his Springs to bring his other broadside to bear on us. The Enemy's Brig at the same time finding her situation too warm, cut her cable, and anchored again in a position so as to enable her to do us much injury.

Our loss, at this time, amounted to a great number in Killed and Wounded, and on the side opposed to the Enemy we had nine long Guns two Carronades and the pivot Gun disabled; on the other side, three long Guns and two Carronades.

It then became absolutely necessary to shift our broadside, and a Spring was accordingly got on the Cable for the purpose, and our broadside was nearly got to bear on the Enemy again, when the Ship's Company declared they would stand no longer to their Quarters, nor could the Officers with their utmost exertions rally them.

The concentrated fire of the whole of the Enemy's Squadron and Flotilla of Gun Boats had been then, for some time directed against the Confiance, and the Ship's Company had until now kept up the Action with as much Spirit as could be expected from men unacquainted with each other and with their Officers, and in a Ship which had been sixteen days before, on the Stocks. I had previous to this ordered a Boat to inform you of the fate of Captain Downie, but I found that both our boats were shot from the Stern—Our Gun Boats were, at this time, at a distance from the Action, and when I ordered the Signal to be made for them to engage Closer, the Signal book, in consequence of the Captain's Death, had been mislaid.

The Ship was making Water very fast. The Rigging, Spars and hull completely Shattered; upwards of forty men killed, and the wind from that Quarter as not to admit of the smallest prospect of escaping, had the ship been in a condition. It was my own opinion and that of the Officers, that keeping up the colours any longer would be a Wanton and useless waste of human blood, I was therefore under the most distressing circumstances that an Officer could be placed in compelled to order the colours to be struck.

It would be presumption in me to attempt saying anything of the merits of my late brave and meritorious Captain—they are too well known to require any Commendation of mine as well as those of Captain Anderson of the Marines who likewise fell performing the duty of a Gallant Officer; as did Mr Gunn, Midshipman, a very promising Young Officer.

It now becomes my duty to advert to the surviving Officers whose conduct on the occasion merits a better fate, and the warm-est Approbation of their Country, for their unceasing exertions dur-ing so destructive a fire; it would be an injustice to them were they not mentioned individually. Lieutenant Charles Creswick and Act-ing Lieutenant Hornsby set the best example; Mr Bryden, the Mas-ter Carri[e]d the ship into Action in the most gallant style: Lieuten-ant Childs of the Marines, and Fitzpatrick of the 39th Regiment distinguished themselves in encouraging their men—Messrs Sim-monds and Lee, Midshipman, were particularly zealous, the former had passed his examination for a Lieutenant, and is in my opinion very deserving of promotion; the latter was wounded in two places. Messrs Dowie, Whitesides and Kooystra, young Midshipmen, con-ducted themselves uncommonly well. It would be injustice to pass over the humanity and attention paid by Mr William Martin, Acting Surgeon, and Mr C. C. Todd, assistant, to the numerous Wounded and at a time when the water was above the Gun room deck. The Warrant Officers conducted themselves to my satisfaction in their different Departments, I have not been able to ascertain the exact number of Killed and wounded—Thirty eight bodies were sent on shore for interment, besides those thrown overboard during the Action.

I have the honour to be

&ca &ca

> (Signed) James Robertson
> Late 1st Lieut: Confiance

ROBERTSON TO PRING, 15 SEPTEMBER 1814

> U.S. Saratoga off Plattsburg,
> 15 Sept 1814

Sir

I have the honour of inclosing for the information of the Commander in Chief, a return of the Killed and Wounded on board the Confiance in the late Action, which from circumstances you are acquainted with, could not be produced before.

I beg leave to add further particulars which led to the surrender of the Confiance, not adverted to in my Letter of the 12th instant, in consequence of the limited time I had for transmitting it.

Previous to the Action it had been held out to the Ships Company that when it should commence it was the intention of the Commander of the Land Forces, at the same time to storm the Enemy's Works.

When the Crew of the Confiance would no longer continue the Action at the reiterated attempts on the part of all the Surviving Officers to rally them, they stated the want of co-operation on the part of the Army, and our Gun Boats keeping at a distance, the fire of the whole of the Enemy's Force being directed at the Confiance, as the reasons of their not being able to continue it.

The numerous wounded below were frequently moved from place to place to prevent their being drowned, though the utmost exertions were made by Mr Cox, the Carpenter; who during the Action drove in sixteen large Shot plugs under the water line.

Having to contend with such distressing circumstances, I joined in the opinion with the remaining Officers that while making no longer resistance it would be the height of inhumanity any longer to expose the lives of the unfortunate wounded.

A Considerable time from the surrender of the Confiance until the Enemy were in a Condition to take possession of her, during which time the greatest exertions were made in pumping and baling at the different Hatchways, for the preservation of the wounded.

Mr W. Martin and his assistant Mr A. Todd all the time being unremitting in their attention to the unfortunate Sufferers: the latter was wounded by a Splinter, and a woman attending him was killed by the side of the Surgeon.

You are aware, Sir, of the written orders issued by the Enemy two days previous to the Action, directing that their whole fire should be concentrated on the Confiance to ensure her Capture.
I have the Honour to be

> Jas Robertson
> late Senior Lieut
> H.M.S. Confiance

FROM PRING AT ISLE AUX NOIX TO YEO AT KINGSTON

> Isle aux Noix
> 17th September 1814

Sir.

Having performed the painful task of detailing to you the particulars of the Action of the 11th—I now feel it my duty to make you acquainted with the disappointment which our Squadron Experienced on that day, in the want of the promised co-operation of the Land Forces, to which I attribute the cause of our failure.

Captain Downie urged by Sir George Prevost to assist with the Naval Force under his Command in the intended operations against Plattsburg, and relying on his promise that the works abreast of which the Enemy's Fleet lay moored, should be stormed at the same moment the Naval Action should commence, determined to engage them under the difficulties adverted to in my Letter of the 12th Inst, that time alone could remedy, the loss of which might frustrate the object of the Campaign.

The Enemy's Gun Boats, who were moored under protection of their Batteries, it was confidently expected would be driven from such an advantageous position, and with the full persuasion that the possession of their works, would give our Squadron a decided advantage over theirs (placed for the purpose of aiding their Military Force) Captain Downie acceded to the plan of attack: unfortunately however it was not carried into execution on the shore, which enabled the Enemy's Flotilla to inflict the deliberate and destructive fire which obliged the Confiance to strike, and was also in my opinion the reason of our efforts on the occasion not being crowned with success.

It may not be improper to remark that had the Enemy's works been stormed even after the Action had terminated our Squadron might have been preserved from falling into their hands by running under cover of the Batteries, as the Enemy's force was for some considerable time unequal to take possession of us.

I have the Honour to be

Daniel Pring
Commander of H.M.
late Sloop Linnet.

APPENDIX D

The Court-Martial of Major General Henry Procter

In his *A Wampum Denied: Procter's War of 1812*, historian Sandy Antal criticized Prevost for his decision to charge Procter and claimed he delayed and manipulated the proceedings. Procter, Antal believes, thus became a scapegoat for Prevost's mistakes. This is not the case. Procter learned in May 1814 of the charges against him, and the delay in holding the trial until December was not due to connivance on the part of Prevost; rather, it resulted from the demands of the war as several key witnesses were held as prisoners of war or were not available until the end of 1814.[1]

Antal asserts the composition of the court-martial board was weighted against Procter and that its findings were unjust. The appointment of Major General Francis de Rottenburg as president, he argues, created a conflict of interest since, as the commander of Upper Canada during the autumn of 1813, he was "an accessory to the events."[2] De Rottenburg's seniority in rank made him the most suitable officer and, technically, the only choice available in North America for the presidency. The other sixteen members of the board included four major generals, six colonels, and six lieutenant colonels. Antal claims that the majority of the members were recent arrivals to the Canadas, making them unfamiliar with local conditions. Of the seventeen officers who served on the board, four had arrived in British North America in the summer of 1814, six others had been in Canada since 1813, and the remaining seven arrived in British North America before the war began. The board members were experienced officers who had seen considerable active service in the Canadas and overseas. Lieutenant Colonel Joseph Morrison commanded the victorious army at the battle of Crysler's Farm in 1813 and also fought at Lundy's Lane in 1814. Lieutenant Colonel Charles de Salaberry commanded the forces at the Battle the Châteauguay in 1813. Colonel John Murray was at Fort Niagara during the 1813 assault and at Plattsburgh in 1814. Finally, Lieutenant Colonel John Harvey planned the night attack that resulted in the battle of Stoney Creek and functioned as the chief of staff to Lieutenant General Gordon Drummond during the Niagara campaign of 1814. Six of these officers were experienced battalion commanders, and the others represented a cross-section of arms, including the artillery and cavalry, with service going back to the end of the previous century.[3] To suggest, as Antal has, that these officers were Prevost's lackeys stretches credulity; and, as historian Stuart Sutherland notes in his own response to Antal's claims, Procter "received a fair hearing from an intelligent and experienced group of officers very much his peers," who "rendered a fair verdict."[4]

A total of thirty-four witnesses appeared before the court, leaving a transcript 430 folio pages in length.

Each of the charges against Proctor was divided into two parts: the first part was the charge itself; and the second part comprised the specification, the detail on which the charge was based. A finding of guilt or innocence of the charge generally meant the same finding for the specification. The testimony in Procter's court-martial addressed five charges, and the results were as follows:

Procter was cleared of both parts of the first charge: that he "did not immediately after the loss of the fleet was known by him make the military arrangements best calculated from promptly effecting" a retreat.[5]

He was found guilty of the first part of the second charge, whereby he had not taken proper "measures for conducting the retreat." He was acquitted of the specification of the second charge, which claimed Procter had "encumbered the Division with large quantities of useless baggage, having unnecessarily halted the troops for whole days and having omitted to destroy the Bridges over which the enemy would be obliged to pass."[6]

Procter was found guilty of the third charge, in that the court agreed he failed to take "measures for affording security to the boats, Waggons and Carts laden with the ammunition, Stores and provisions required for the troops on their retreat"[7] but was cleared of the specification of the charge, which accused him of abandoning his carts, wagons, and stores to the enemy on the day of the battle.

Procter was also found guilty of the fourth charge—that he had "formed it [his division] in a situation highly unfavorable for receiving the attack." He was cleared of the specifications of this charge for "conduct manifesting great professional incapacity."[8]

Finally, Procter was found guilty of the fifth charge—failing to "make the military dispositions best adapted to meet or to resist the said attack"—but not of the specification: displaying further "professional incapacity" by not encouraging his troops or rallying the Natives under his command. The court's recommendations to the Prince Regent and his ruling are given at pages 141 and 142.[9]

Antal maintains that Procter's trial was the only occasion during the war where the British used failure as a measure of guilt. He wonders why Brock, Sheaffe, or even Yeo were not treated in a similar fashion. There was no reason to charge Brock posthumously, especially in the wake of the British victory at Queenston Heights. Sheaffe, the victor of Queenston Heights, was hotly criticized for abandoning York in 1813, and while charges were not laid against him, his active career effectively ended after his abandonment of the provincial capital. In 1815, Yeo was recalled to face an inquiry into his management of the Great Lakes command that was never convened. Prevost returned to England to face charges submitted by the Royal Navy for his actions in the Plattsburgh expedition. To say that Procter was the only officer to face formal proceedings based on performance during the War of 1812 is therefore not correct, and indeed, there are other examples of general officers being tried for their actions in other theaters.[10]

APPENDIX E

*Composition of the Court-Martial
Board and Witnesses for the
Trial of Lieutenant
General Sir George Prevost*

Sir George Prevost's court-martial was scheduled for 15 January 1816 at the Royal Hospital, Chelsea; however, as Prevost's health declined, the proceedings were rescheduled for 5 February 1816. The board never sat, as Prevost died in January 1816. The names of the seventeen members of the court-martial board and of the forty-one witnesses for the prosecution and defense follow.

MEMBERS OF THE BOARD[1]

1. General Sir John Cradock, president
2. General Sir Charles Asgill
3. Lieutenant General The Honourable Edward Finch
4. Lieutenant General Isaac Gascoyne
5. Lieutenant General Duncan Campbell
6. Lieutenant General William Cartwright
7. Lieutenant General Lord Lyndock (Thomas Graham)
8. Lieutenant General Sir Brent Spencer
9. Lieutenant General Sir Ronald Craufurd Ferguson
10. Lieutenant General Sir Henry Warde
11. Lieutenant General Christopher Chowne
12. Lieutenant General Sir William Henry Clinton
13. Lieutenant General Sir William Houston
14. Lieutenant General Sir William Lumley
15. Lieutenant General Henry Tucker Montresor

16. Lieutenant General Sir H. J. Campbell
17. Lieutenant General Sir George Bingham

Witnesses[2]

Appearing for the prosecution and the defense:

1. Major General Francis de Rottenburg
2. Major General Frederick Robinson
3. Major General Edward Baynes
4. Major General Thomas Brisbane
5. Captain Daniel Pring, Royal Navy (RN)
6. Major Foster Coore, aide de camp (ADC) to Prevost

Appearing for the defense:

1. Major General Manley Power
2. Major General Sidney Beckwith
3. Commissary General William Robinson
4. Lieutenant Colonel Sir William Williams, 13th Foot
5. Lieutenant Colonel William Wauchope, 26th Foot
6. Lieutenant Colonel Jonathan Yates, 49th Foot
7. Major Nathaniel Thorn, 3rd Foot
8. Captain Hardes Robert Saunderson, 39th Foot
9. Captain Friedrich Karl Ludwig Kirchberger, de Watteville's Regiment
10. Major James Fulton, Canadian Fencibles
11. Major William Cochrane, 103rd Foot
12. Captain Noah Freer, New Brunswick Fencibles
13. Captain Edward Davies, New Brunswick Fencibles
14. Major Thomas Powell, Glengarry Light Infantry Fencibles
15. Lieutenant Colonel the Hon. Gerald de Courcy, 70th Foot
16. Major John Sinclair, Royal Artillery (RA)
17. Lieutenant James Love, RA
18. Lieutenant Henry Cubitt, RA
19. Rear Admiral Robert Otway, RN
20. Lieutenant Matthew Fitzpatrick, 39th Foot
21. Captain Peter Fisher, RN
22. Lieutenant Jonathan McGhie, RA
23. W. Gillis, late purser *Linnet*

Appearing for the prosecution alone:

1. Ensign J. Fennell, ADC to Brisbane
2. Major T. Campbell, brigade major to Brisbane
3. Captain James Robertson, RN
4. Lieutenant W. Hornby, RN
5. Mr. Brydon, RN
6. Lieutenant C. Bell, RN
7. Lieutenant William Hicks, RN
8. W. Robertson, HMS *Inconstant*
9. Major Henry Balneavis, ADC to Power
10. Major Thomas Turner, ADC to Power
11. Major Robert Anwyl, 4th Foot
12. Captain Robert Nickle, 88th Foot

APPENDIX F

On the Court Martial held at
Chelsea Hospital in February 1816
of the Conduct of Lieutenant General
Sir George Prevost, Commander in Chief
of His Majesty's Forces in Canada

As related in chapter 10, the recent discovery of the document titled "On the Court Martial held at Chelsea Hospital in February 1816 on the Conduct of Lieutenant General Sir George Prevost, Commander in Chief of His Majesty's Forces in Canada" reveals the determination with which Sir James Yeo sought to clear the Royal Navy and himself of any wrongdoing in the naval preparations for the Plattsburgh Campaign and the naval action fought on Lake Champlain. This 107-page handwritten "transcript" of an "inquiry" that Yeo prepared in early 1816 was located in the records of the Treasury Solicitor at the National Archives (TS 11, vol. 365), in London, England, where it was filed with another document titled "Case Against Captain Pring and other officer in command of the squadron engaged in Lake Champlain, Canada on 11 Sept. 1814; proceedings at general court martial aboard HM ship Gladiator in Portsmouth Harbour." The provenance of this document remains a mystery, and the reason the Treasury Solicitor, an office that the Secretary of State for War and the Colonies sometimes called on for advice, came to possess it is unknown. Equally puzzling is Yeo's objective in producing it and what, if anything, he intended to do with the results had the inquiry been completed to his satisfaction.

I am indebted to Mr. Roy Carter for providing a copy of this document from The National Archives, and for sharing his analysis of it.

Nonetheless, this document provides insights into the character and motivations of Commodore Yeo, while also offering insight into the potentially messy interservice problems that may have arisen had Prevost's court-martial sat. Perhaps, in making its decision to forgo an inquiry following Prevost's death, the government wisely avoided a public scandal.

The original document is in two parts: the first is a list of seven charges against Prevost, which had been edited in blue pencil, suggesting they were in draft form. The testimony, found in part 2, also included findings on three of the charges.

What follows are the charges as listed in part 1, and excerpts from the second part. The original document is badly faded and heavily edited, making it difficult to transcribe. Those passages that proved difficult to transcribe are shown in italic type, or in square brackets.

PART 1: THE CHARGES

Charges to be produced against Lieutenant General Sir George Prevost as character relative to his defective co-operation with the British Squadron on Lake Champlain under the order of the late Captain Downie on the 11th September 1814

1ST

For having on or about the 11th September, 1814 *by holding out to Captain George Downie late of HMS Confiance and then commanding HM Naval Squadron on Lake Champlain the expectation of a co-operation from the forces on shore then under the command of Sir George Prevost induced the said Captain Downie of His Majesty's Ship Confiance to attack the American Flotilla when it was at anchor in the Bay of Plattsburgh when the Squadron was without such co-operation and not having afforded the co-operation* in the Bay of Plattsburgh whilst the said ships were not in a fit state for such service.

2ND

For having induced Captain Downie to carry His Majesty's Squadron into action with an Enemy of a Superior Force and in a situation highly disadvantageous to the British, under the assurance of a promised co-operation and assistance from the Army on shore, which co-operation and assistance were unafforded.

3RD

For not having attacked the land batteries of (under)which the American Flotilla was anchored *at or about the time the naval action commenced in* [text illegible] he had promised to do and thereby withholding that co-operation on Lake Champlain. An operation so necessary for the success of the Naval enterprise.

4TH

For having disregarded the signals previously agreed upon that were made by Captain Downie going in to Action for that expectation what the said Sir George Prevost had before given this [?] Captain Downie [?]

Promised co-operation and for allowing the Army to reason to expect, commenced cooking at the very moment when the good of the service required that the land forces should have attacked the Enemy's Works and there have obliged the Enemy's Squadron to quit their advantageous position and afforded the British Navy a more equal chance of victory.

5TH

For having continued to view, with an unaccountable apathy the whole of the Naval Engagement without making the least exertion or effort to support the British Squadron and denied the attention of the Enemy.

[6TH CROSSED OUT REPLACED BY 4TH]

For not having stormed the Enemy's Batteries after the Naval Action was over, which would have enabled the British Squadron to seek protection under their [?]*was it preferable for the English vessels to be under the batteries* the Enemy at that time being so [text illegible] crippled as to be unable to take possession of our vessels for a considerable time after they surrendered.

7TH

For retreating from a very inferior Force of the Enemy and then leaving the British Squadron to their fate.

James Lucas Yeo

Late Commodore and Commander in Chief

On the Lakes in Canada

PART 2: TESTIMONY AND PARTIAL FINDINGS

This part is divided into the following sections:

- Statement on the part of the party preparing the charges;
- Copies of letters between several naval officers and officials, including Sir James Yeo, John Croker, Daniel Pring, James Robertson, and Sir George Prevost dated between September 1814 and September 1815;
- A list of the four charges Yeo submitted against Prevost in September 1815;
- Copies of letters between Sir George Prevost and George Downie during September 1814;
- A lengthy narrative commenting on earlier operations on Lake Champlain and the conduct of the Plattsburgh campaign that is highly critical of Prevost;
- An extract from *The Letters of Veritas* giving a description of the American navy and its method of rating its warships;
- A commentary on naval aspects of the Plattsburgh campaign, including references to Daniel Pring, James Robertson, Sir George Prevost, and other officers;
- Findings by the court on the first three charges;
- Statements by James Robertson, Robert Brydon (master of the *Confiance*), and other personnel who served on the vessels of the naval squadron; interspersed throughout is cross-examination of the witnesses by Yeo and other senior naval officers;
- The document concludes with the evidence of the military officers.

What follows are extracts from several of these sections.

ON THE COURT MARTIAL HELD AT CHELSEA HOSPITAL
IN FEBRUARY 1816 OF THE CONDUCT OF LIEUTENANT
GENERAL SIR GEORGE PREVOST COMMANDER IN CHIEF
OF HIS MAJESTY'S FORCES IN CANADA

Statement on the part of the party preparing the Charges

The Jealousies that have at all times existed between the Naval and Military Services of this country and which perhaps have occasionally increased since the Campaigns in the Peninsular render it particularly desirable that the greatest delicacy should be observed on the Introduction to a Court Martial of any matter in which the two services are engaged. But in the present instance the observance of this caution is particularly necessary in assuming as the enquiry is set on foot at the instance of one of the Services (the Naval) against the other (the Military)and there never perhaps was any Individual good understanding between the party (Sir James Lucas Yeo)whom the Admiralty have here put forward as the promoter of the present Court Martial and the party (Sir George Prevost) against whom the measure has been taken, the principal object in the commencement of the proceedings will be to show that it does not arise from any personal pique. That it is not a measure suggested by Sir James Lucas Yeo. That the prosecution does not commence so much from any observation or letter of his own as from letters and communications which he had received from others, and which it was his duty as the principal Naval Officer on the Canada Station to forward it to the Naval Department in this Country and such indeed is the real origins of the present Court Martial.

The first official communications that reached this Country of the unfortunate affair at Plattsburg was in the following letter of Sir James Lucas Yeo written in his official character to Mr. Croker. Enclosed in this letter he forwards from others viz: two from each of the principal officers who commanded the squadron at Lake Champlain and who were the best competent to speak of the misfortunes of that day. Sir James Lucas Yeo would have been guilty of a notorious dereliction of his duty if he had not forwarded copies of these letters in the Shape in which he received them and it was upon these letters that the present proceedings were grounded. Copies of these letters follow.

[Following the list of four charges is an interesting passage commenting on Prevost's actions prior to Plattsburgh:]

Sir George Prevost having traversed up and down the country (as a Quixote as far as the search for adventures went though not with the spirit to encounter them) came before Plattsburg on the 6th September 1814 when General Power drove in the Enemy through the town of Plattsburg to their Works which were situated on the opposite side of the Saranac, a River which runs out of the Lake Champlain[,] and Sir George Prevost occupied the Town with an Army of from 10 to 12,000 Men all of which were Veteran Troops and the greater part of them were just arrived in America from the Peninsula of Spain and Portugal where they had been gaining Laurels under Lord Wellington. If General Gower [Power?] had also conducted the subsequent part of the Campaign all would have been well and the present Court Martial would not have been held. From the Information that can be obtained the force of the Americans were at the time they were thus driven across the Saranac not more than from 800 to 1000 Men and of these very few of them were regular troops. The works to which they were driven were merely Field works and has been emphatically observed by one of the Generals (who witnessed the disgrace and who may perhaps be called upon to state his opinion in the course of this investigation). If the British army had only been allowed to follow up the success of General Power with no other weapons but Broomsticks in their hands they would have beaten the Americans and of these works.

[The narrative continues with an account of operations on Lake Champlain during 1813 "that terminated most favourably for the English" since "Sir George Prevost had no share in the Affair";[1] it is followed by an account of the Plattsburgh campaign, which includes this denunciation of Prevost:]

It has been said that his [Prevost's] General Order and Official Letters were often compared with a view to deceive

at a distance; and his Plattsburgh Letter furnishes direct
proof of this accusation being correct. It is dated there the
11th September 1814 as if written on the Spot immediately
after the Naval Battle and before the degrading retreat commenced, whereas it is well known that the letter did not go
from Canada until it was carried by Mr Secretary Brenton[2]
who sailed from [?] on the 9th October consequently it was
written in Montreal long after the date it bears. In proof of
this read the following paragraph of that Letter "As the
Troops concentrated and approached the line of separation
between this province" (is Plattsburgh then in Canada?)
"and the United States the American Army etc" what a sad
slip of the Pen in memory in here![3] But if for Plattsburgh
11th September there be substituted Montreal 21st September or any subsequent day then the blunder will be explained. It is true that such was the celerity of his personal
retreat that on the 13th he issued an order dated at Odell
Town; but I strongly suspect that on the 11th after the action he was not in a state to write Letters anywhere. Another proof of its having been written at Montreal, and not
at Plattsburgh is that in the first General Order afterwards
the Gun Boats were in a manner commended for affecting
[sic] their retreat in safety probably from the sympathetic
felling [sic] of the moment. However, in the revision of the
Order they are left out but mentioned in this false Letter
dated Letter as flying, because upon a reflection, their not
having done their duty might lead people aside from the
consideration that he had not done his own.

[The findings presented on three of the charges are outlined as presented in their entirety:]

After these several defences had been made, and the
evidence was heard, which proceedings occupied the
greater part of a Week, the Court came to the following
determination.

"The Court having maturely weighed the evidence, is of
opinion that the capture of His Majesty's said Ship Confiance, and the remainder of the Squadron by the said American Squadron was principally caused by the British Squadron
having been urged into Battle previous to its being in a

proper state to meet its Enemy, by the promised Co-operation of the Land Forces not being carried into effect, and by the pressing letter of their Commander in Chief, whereby it appears that he had on the 10th day of September 1814, only waited for the naval attack to storm the Enemy's works, the signal for the approach on the following day having been made by scaling the guns as settled between Captain Downie and Major Coore, which promised co-operation was communicated to the other Officers and Crew of the British Squadron before the Commencement of the Action. The Court is further of opinion that the attack would have been attended with more effect if a part of the Gun Boats had not withdrawn from the Action, and other of the Vessels had not been prevented by baffling winds from getting into the station assigned them. That Captain Pring of the Linnet and Lieutenant Robertson who succeeded to the command of the Confiance, after the lamented fall of Captain Downie, whose conduct was marked by the greatest valour, and Lieutenant Christopher Bell, commander of the [gunboat] Murray, and Mr Robertson Commander of the [gunboat] Beresford, who appeared to take their trials at this Court Martial and conducted themselves with great zeal, bravery, and ability, during the Action. That Lieutenant Hicks, Commander of the Finch, also conducted himself in the Action with becoming bravery. That the other surviving officers and ship's crews except Mr McGhie of the Chubb, who has not appeared to take his trial, also conducted themselves with bravery, and that Captain Pring Lieutenant Robertson, Lieutenant Christopher Bell, Lieutenant Hicks and Mr James Robertson and the rest of the surviving officers, and ship's Companies except Mr McGhie ought to be most honourably acquitted, and they are hereby most honourably acquitted accordingly".

The Judgement of the Court as above copied must completely clear the Characters of the naval men employed upon the Lake Champlain. And it remains next to be enquired whether that co-operation which was promised was afforded, and in the event of its not having been afforded it must be shown by Sir George Prevost that he was prevented by some unforeseen accident from not having attacked (as promised) the Batteries on shore the Moment the Naval Action commenced.

Every one of the Military Officers who will be examined upon the present Occasion will prove that no attack was made on the Batteries on shore. One of them (Brisbane) will, it is conceived, prove that he was anxiously waiting for the expected arrival of the Fleet, that when he did see them, he expressed the utmost astonishment that there were no corresponding operations on shore.

This has been stated by Sir Charles Brisbane[4] during his stay in America, where he was speaking in confidence to some of his Military friends upon the proceedings of 11th September 1814. The Gentleman who is professionally employed in this Business[5] saw Sir Charles in Paris and interrogated him upon the subject. But he replied that in as much as he might be called upon to state what he knew of the circumstances at a Court Martial he had rather declined answering any Questions till then. It was evident however, from his manner that he had no very favourable opinion of Sir George Prevost's movements of that day, and it would be quite safe to interrogate him at the Court Martial upon any of the points detailed in this statement, and which may be supposed to come within his knowledge. While we are speaking upon this subject it may be said at once that there is not any person whose name appears in this Statement as a Witness who may not be asked any questions which occurs to the Court. The Conduct of Sir George Prevost was so extra-ordinary that it was at this time observed upon by everyone, and it is only on account of that high sense of honour. Fortunately so prevalent amongst Persons of both the services that there is a reserve about each, the moment he fancies that the character of his Comrade might become the subject of a judicial investigation.

After the Battle took place and the British sailors were Prisoners with the Americans, it was a matter of surprise to the Americans how they could have been Victors of the day. Before the Action commenced they were entirely in despair. They were blockaded by Sea and beleaguered by Land, and had not a place to escape as the Commander of the

American Squadron and the Principal Officer of the Field Works were only considering of the best terms of Capitulation. But when they found that the Batteries were not attacked they directed the fire of their Batteries on the shipping, and thus caused the destruction of the Fleet. All the Naval Men [British] were taken Prisoner and they can one and all prove, (though there may be some doubt whether it is admissible as evidence) the deplorable state in which the Americans conceived themselves to be. The very circumstance of the Americans being so weakened by our Attack on the Lake as not to be able to take possession of the Vessels which they had captured till so long after the Battle, plainly proves what must have been the Result of a co-operation.

The only attempt which was made at a Co-operation was made as follows. The Saranac was fordable only at a pass about two miles distance from the Head Quarters. This ford had been reconnoitred a few days before by the Orders of Sir George Prevost. On the day of the Action instead of having his Army or Part of it at the very ford in order to cross it so as to carry the Batteries, the moment the Vessels began their Operations, which might well have been done by following the same line of signals which had been agreed upon between Downie and Sir George Prevost. No part of the Army moved from Head Quarters until the Guns were scaled. They had then to march a Couple of miles to the Ford and then from the Ford to the Batteries and then if the accident hereafter mentioned had not taken place the Army could not well have been at the Batteries in proper time. But instead (as he ought to have done according to the opinion of the Military Men)sending the same person who had before reconnoitred the Ford with the detachment that attempted The Ford on the 11th September, he sent a person totally unknown to the place, and who could only find his way by the description of another. The consequence of this was that this person lost his way and did not cross the Ford until after all the ships had struck.

But another Charge of the Case still remains.

Even after the Fleet had been captured it was quite in the power of the Army to have stormed and taken the

Batteries. . . . We have seen before that the condition of the American Fleet was such that it could not take possession of the English Squadron till some hours after they had struck. Not presuming that the American Works had been stormed and taken by the party that had lost its way, the British Ships would then have been (as they could not move from their situation) under the Fire of the Batteries, which by now becoming British would have covered them from the attacks of the Americans, and the disabled Fleet of the Americans might have become the plunder of the British.

That the force of the British was fully competent to the accomplishment of this even without the cooperation of the Naval Squadron any officer that will be examined will fully prove.

It will remain therefore, for Sir George to say why he did not continue such an attack, or rather why when Captain Nichol was making his approach to the Works he was recalled by Sir George Prevost. It has been said that Sir George Prevost excuses himself by saying that as the rainy season was approaching he was afraid in the event of his being beaten that he would have lost the whole of his Artillery and heavy Luggage. In making this excuse he goes, it is presumed, rather too far, for unless he knew (and he knew the contrary) that Captain Downie was ready to co-operate the moment Sir George came to Plattsburgh. Why did he go there at all? He must have known that the rainy season was about to commence, even then why therefore did he run such a risk as to attempt such a scheme when he had so short a time before him. The very reason therefore which he gives for not making the attack on the works after the Capture of the British Squadron is the reason why he should never have attempted Plattsburgh at all. But the persons who were acquainted with the ground and with Military matters laugh at such an excuse. The Army alone was strong enough to have driven the Enemy from their Works with "Broomsticks" and such an Enemy could not therefore have much retarded the progress of the Artillery. But to go farther in our story, and we have the true cause of Sir George Prevost's recalling the Detachment that had been sent across the Ford.

[The "evidence" of army officers, only two of whom (Major General Power and a captain from the 27th Foot) were interviewed, is given in its entirety:]

The Evidence of General Brisbane

General Brisbane will prove that the Army was to begin its Co-operation the moment the Confiance scaled her guns. That being anxious to make a movement the first moment that he observed the Fleet he (not choosing to trust to his Aide de Camp went himself and sat down behind a bush where he could discern the first Vessel) that upon observing over a point of land forming the Plattsburgh Bay the Masts of the Vessel, he hastened to get his Troops ready but had orders for [?] instead of preparing for engaging the Enemy.

The Evidence of Major General de Rottenburg

He has not yet been examined on the part of this prosecution. He is an old officer, almost effete. He may be termed as it were, one of the old fashioned sort of Soldiers, who always deliberated sufficiently before they attempted anything, and never thought of a Coup de main. It is most probable that he will be called by Sir George Prevost in which event and he may be made use of by us in proving the hand writing of Sir George Prevost if necessary to any document that may be produced. He was constantly with Sir George Prevost at headquarters, and will therefore, be able to prove what passed there, As circumstances may turn up to make it necessary to examine him. It may be as well to say therefore that he is not so devoted to Sir George Prevost as to torture his Conscience into an acquiescence with anything that may be approved of by Sir George.

The Evidence of Major General Sir Manley Power

That he received orders from Sir George Prevost on the 10th September 1814, to attack the Enemy who were stationed at the town of Plattsburgh.

That he had under his Command from 10 to 12,000 Veteran Troops. That he made the Attack accordingly and drove with considerable ease without any loss whatever the Americans across the Bridge into their Works on the other side of the Saranac. That the Americans having destroyed the Bridge, and the River not being fordable at that place, he could not push his success any further on that day. That the River was then reconnoitred, and a Ford was discovered about 2 miles or $2^{1}/_{2}$ miles down the River. That Sir George Prevost told him that he should attempt the next day the destruction of the Work, and that he should obtain the co-operation of the British Naval force on the Lake. That Sir George Prevost informed him the next day (the 11th)that he had agreed with Captain Downie to attack the Forts by land at the same time. The Naval Flotilla attacked the American Fleet which was lying under the cover of their own Batteries. That Sir George also told him that the Army was to storm the Works at the same moment the Fleet came into action. That the scaling of the Guns of the Fleet which was to be the signal for the preparation of the Army, took place in ample time for a sufficient number of Troops to have proceeded from Headquarters to the Ford to the Enemy's Works. That if he had been Commander in Chief I should not have trusted to the Troops on reaching the Ford from headquarters after the signal was given, but I should have stationed the Troops at the Ford ready to proceed at a moment's notice. The Troops then could have got up to the Ford in proper time. The English Troops were well covered by the Woods at the Ford, and could be put out of the danger of the American Sharp Shooters. That no attack of the Batteries on the land took place. That I am of opinion that for the purpose of carrying the Batteries alone the naval power was not wanted, the British force being quite sufficient for that purpose. That the only use of employing the naval force was to prevent the American fleet from escaping to the other side of the Lake, and that I am thoroughly of opinion that if the attack had been made as agreed upon, the American Flotilla as well as the Works must with the Americans themselves have fallen into the hands of the English.

The Evidence of Major Coore

This witness may be made use of in proving the transactions that took place, and the orders that were given at the Headquarters but it is thought not safe to examine him upon any points of consequence that may be obtained from other witnesses. This Gentleman was the Military Secretary of Sir George Prevost, and it may therefore be unfair to press him too much upon the different points connected with this unfortunate affair at Platsburgh, even if he were disposed to be candid upon them. But a reference to the letter has been before copied from him to Sir James Lucas Yeo shows which way his feelings preponderate upon this Occasion.

It must however be observed that he and Captain Pring were the only witnesses present when the Co-operation was finally agreed on, but in this event of the testimony of Coore and Pring conflicting, the balances of truth will be easily discovered by the production of Sir George Prevost's own letters. There is therefore, nothing to apprehend from this cause.

NOTES

NOTE TO THE READER

1. An Act of Congress of 11 January 1812 created ten new regiments having its eighteen companies arranged in two battalions; however, in June 1812 a new organization reduced the establishment of a regiment to ten companies. René Chartrand and Donald E. Graves, "The United States Army of the War of 1812: A Handbook" (unpublished ms., n.d.).

2. A full, or post, captain commanded a ship of the sixth rate or above, whereas sloops were generally commanded by officers with the rank of commander. The pay of post captains, most warrant officers, and those members of the ship's company holding specific appointments also varied, depending on the rating of the ship they served on. The pay of commanders and lieutenants was fixed, the only exception being that the latter received a higher rate of pay if serving on a flagship. Surgeons were paid according to their seniority. See "1807 Scale of Sea Pay," in N. A. M. Rodger, *The Command of the Ocean: A Naval History of Britain, 1649–1815* (London: Allen Lane, 2005), 626–27.

INTRODUCTION

1. Pronunciation of the Prevost family name varies from the French acute-accented é ("Pray-voh") to an Anglicized "Pree-voh" or "Preh-vost" with the "ost" being pronounced as in "lost." According to the current baronet, Sir Christopher Prevost, the French style was never used and the family name is pronounced as "Prayer-voh." Sir Christopher Prevost, e-mail to author, 6 April 2010.

2. *Quebec Mercury*, 16 September 1811, 293–94.

3. This figure represents the majority of the more than 48,163 enlisted personnel that were distributed between the Canadas, the Atlantic Provinces, and on American territory by 1815. See J. Mackay Hitsman, *The*

Incredible War of 1812: A Military History, updated by Donald E. Graves (Toronto: Robin Brass Studio, 1999), 295.

4. Wesley Turner, *British Generals in the War of 1812: High Command in the Canadas* (Montreal: McGill-Queen's University Press, 1999), 24.

5. Ibid.

6. See Veritas [John Richardson, pseud.], *The Letters of Veritas, Re-Published from the Montreal Herald; Containing a Succinct Narrative of the Military Administration of Sir George Prevost during His Command in the Canadas* (Montreal: W. Gray, July 1815); Philalethes [George Macdonell, pseud.], "The Late War in Canada," *United Services Magazine* (June 1848, pt. 2): 271–83; [Henry Procter], "Indian Warfare," in *The Lucubrations of Humphrey Ravelin, Esq.* (London: W. and G. B. Whitaker, 1823), 319–59.

7. Veritas, *Letters of Veritas,* 22.

8. Ibid., 17.

9. Ibid.

10. [Henry Procter], "Campaigns in the Canadas," *Quarterly Review* 27 (1822): 405–49.

11. Ibid., 414.

12. Ibid., 449.

13. The name *Philalethes* was used by several ancient writers and in Masonic circles.

14. Winston Johnston, *The Glengarry Light Infantry, 1812–1816* (Charlottetown, P.E.I.: n.p., 1998), 242, 243, 244; Philalethes, "The Late War in Canada," *United Services Magazine* (March 1848, pt. 1): 425–41; Philalethes, "Late War in Canada," June 1848, 271–83. For an account of Macdonell's career, see George Raudzens, "'Red George' Macdonell, Military Saviour of Upper Canada?" *Ontario History* 62, no. 4 (1970): 199–212.

15. Philalethes, "Late War in Canada," March 1848, 430, 431, 435.

16. J. W. Norie, *The Naval Gazetteer, Biographer, and Chronologist; Containing a History of the Late Wars* (London: J. W. Norie & Co., 1827), 70, 71, 403.

17. Ibid., 71.

18. Brock's popular appeal is so strong that the months leading up to the bicentenary of the War of 1812 witnessed the publication of two new biographies: Jonathon Riley, *A Matter of Honour: The Life, Campaigns and Generalship of Sir Isaac Brock* (Montreal: Robin Brass Studio, 2011); and Wesley Turner, *The Astonishing General: The Life and Legacy of Isaac Brock* (Toronto: Dundurn, 2011). In addition, in 2012 the provincial government of Ontario enacted legislation proclaiming October 13 as "Major General Sir Isaac Brock Day." A Canadian company has even produced a collectible Brock "action figure" as part of the "Canadian Legends Series." The accompanying literature describes Brock as a "Canadian hero," who "helped keep this country together . . . during the War of 1812." Sonia Nafekh, *The Story of Isaac Brock* (Kirkland, Qc.: Nafekh Technologies Inc., 2006), 1, 10. Unlike their American counterparts, who have written extensively on their national military and naval leadership, British and

Canadian historians have not produced any major biographical studies of senior British naval and army leaders of the War of 1812, other than Brock.

19. Hitsman introduced his research regarding Prevost in J. Mackay Hitsman, "Sir George Prevost's Conduct of the Canadian War of 1812," *Canadian Historical Association Report* (1962): 34–43.

20. J. C. A. Stagg, *The War of 1812: Conflict for a Continent* (Cambridge: Cambridge University Press, 2012), 158; Hitsman, *Incredible War of 1812*, 30–32, 153, 253–56; Harry L. Coles, *The War of 1812* (Chicago: University of Chicago Press, 1965), 256; Donald R. Hickey, *The War of 1812: A Forgotten Conflict* (Urbana: University of Illinois Press, 1990), 190, 195; Donald R. Hickey, *Don't Give Up the Ship! Myths of the War of 1812* (Toronto: Robin Brass Studio, 2006), 140–42; Jeremy Black, *The War of 1812 in the Age of Napoleon* (Norman: University of Oklahoma Press, 2009), 61, 96.

1. THE MAKING OF A GENERAL, 1767–1808

1. Augustin lived from 1723 to 1786. His brother Jacques, or James Prevost (1725–78), was appointed colonel on the formation of the 60th. James gained an unsavory reputation due to his arrogance and mismanagement of public funds and also used his influence at court, through his friendship with the Duke of Cumberland, to obtain appointments for his brothers, including a battalion command for Augustin. The youngest Prevost, Jean Marc, or Marcus (1736–81), was wounded at Ticonderoga in July 1758; in 1781, he succumbed to illness in Jamaica. Jean Marc had two sons, Augustus James Frederick and John Bartow Prevost, who also joined the 60th Foot. Both were adopted by the American Aaron Burr (the third vice president of the United States), who had married Jean Marc's widow, Theodosia, and they became prominent American citizens. Augustin's older brother, Jean Louis (1718–48), also pursued a career in the British army and is believed to have died in India. In 1744, Augustin had, from another relationship, one son, whom he named after himself, who served in the 60th. The illegitimate Augustine (1744–1821) had four sons, three of whom joined the British army, including one who served with the 60th. Through marriage Augustine became connected with Sir William Johnson, George Croghan, and Joseph Brant. Lewis Butler, *The Annals of the King's Royal Rifle Corps*, vol. 1: *The Royal Americans* (London: Smith, Elder & Co., 1913), 3, 17, 19, 288, 323, 324, 345; Sir Christopher Prevost, e-mail to author, 14 February 2008; Alexander V. Campbell, *The Royal American Regiment: An Atlantic Microcosm, 1755–1772* (Norman: University of Oklahoma Press, 2010), 43, 206; Robert Scott Davis, Jr., "Prevosts of the Royal Americans," in Richard L. Blanco, ed., *The American Revolution: An Encyclopaedia*, vol. 2: *M–Z* (New York: Garland, 1993), 1319.

2. The colonial origin of the 60th Foot and its connection with the Crown are the reasons it was given the title the Royal Americans. Butler, *King's Royal Rifle Corps*, 1:6, 17, 18; Campbell, *Royal American Regiment*, 40, 41.

3. During 1759, Major Augustin Prevost commanded the 2/60th in Wolfe's army. On 21 July, while leading a raid above Quebec, Augustin was

"dangerously wounded in the head," and the resulting scar earned him the nickname "Old Bullethead" from the men. Butler, *King's Royal Rifle Corps*, 1:77.

4. E. B. Brenton, *Some Account of the Public Life of Lieutenant General Sir George Prevost: Particularly of His Services in the Canadas* (London: T. Egerton, 1823), 4–5; C. P. Stacey, *Quebec, 1759: The Siege and the Battle* (Toronto: Robin Brass Studio, 2002), 212; Butler, *King's Royal Rifle Corps*, 1:77, 293; Stephen Conway, "To Subdue America: British Army Officers and the Conduct of the Revolutionary War," *William and Mary Quarterly*, 3rd ser., vol. 43, no. 3 (1986): 402; Carole Watterson Troxler, "Refuge, Resistance and Reward: The Southern Loyalist's Claim on East Florida," *Journal of Southern History* 44, no. 4 (1989): 572; Campbell, *Royal American Regiment*, 106, 205.

5. In 1769, Grand (1716–1793) returned to the Netherlands, where he and his brother later arranged financial loans to support the rebels during the American War of Independence. "Grand, Isaac-Jean-Georges-Jonas," The Papers of Benjamin Franklin, http://franklinpapers.org/franklin/framed Names.jsp?ssn=001-20-0201.

6. Nanette Grand was born in 1742 and died in 1809. James Prevost lived near where George was born, and the infant George was baptized at a church in Hackensack, New Jersey. See H. C. G. Matthew and Brian Harrison, eds., *Oxford Dictionary of National Biography* (Oxford: Oxford University Press, 2004), 45:278; Sir Christopher Prevost, e-mail to author, 14 February 2008.

7. T. A. Bowyer-Bower, "A Pioneer of Military Education: The Royal Military Academy Chelsea, 1801–1821," *British Journal of Educational Studies* 2, no. 2 (1954): 122.

8. Among Lochée's works are *An Essay on Military Education* (London, 1776) and *Essay on Castrametation* (London, 1778). Théophile Konrad Pfeffel (1736–1809) opened the academy in 1773 and employed some of the most advanced pedagogical principles of the time. Information from Sir Christopher Prevost, 18 February 2008; Bowyer-Bower, "Pioneer of Military Education," 122.

9. Between 1766 and 1811, the official price for an ensigncy in a line infantry regiment was between £400 and £900 for a foot guards regiment; a captaincy, £1,500; and for the rank of lieutenant colonel, £3,500. Before 1795, there was minimum time in which an officer had to stay at one rank before purchasing the next. Thereafter, no officer could be promoted captain until he had served two years as a subaltern, and a period of six years' service was required for a majority. These restrictions were sometimes waived as vacancies became available due to wartime demands. Anthony Bruce, "The System of Purchase and Sale of Commissions in the British Army" (PhD diss., University of Manchester, August 1973), 106; Adjutant General, *General Regulations and Orders for the Army* (London: W. Clowes, 1811), 32; J. A. Houlding, *Fit for Service: The Training of the British Army, 1715–1795* (Oxford: Clarendon Press, 1981), 100, 101; Robert Burnham and Ron McGuigan, *The British Army against Napoleon: Facts, Lists and Trivia, 1805–1815* (Barnsley, UK: Frontline Books, 2010), 150, 152.

10. George's half brother, Augustine (1744–1821), was born in Geneva and was raised by his aunt Jeanne Gabrielle Prevost. The identity of his mother is unknown. Augustine was sent to a military school in England at an early age and in 1761 was commissioned into the 60th Foot. In 1782, he was evacuated from Charleston to New York. When his regiment returned to Britain at the end of the American War of Independence, Augustine stayed in America and lived a quiet life at his home called "Hush Hush," at Greenville, New York, where he died on 17 January 1821. In 1765, Augustine married Susannah Croghan (1750–1790), the daughter of George Croghan, who was Sir William Johnson's deputy Indian agent for the western Natives. Augustine became a close friend of Joseph Brant, who had married Croghan's Native daughter. Augustine had four sons that lived beyond childhood: James served with the 60th Foot, while Henry joined the 7th Foot and in 1811 died of wounds received while serving in the Iberian Peninsula. A third son, William Augustus, or John Augustine, also joined the army and served in Iberia with the 67th Foot and was lost at sea in 1822. Lastly, George William Augustin retired from the British army as a major and took over administration of the Croghan estate in New York State. Rev. Evelyn Bartow, "The Prevost Family in America," *New York Genealogical and Biographical Record* 13, no. 1 (1862): 27, 28; Butler, *King's Royal Rifle Corps*, 1:348; John A. Hall, *A History of the Peninsular War* (London: Greenhill Books, 1998), 8:478; author's interview with Sir Christopher Prevost, 14 February 2008; "The Journal of Augustine Prevost: 1774," The Loyalist Collection, Harriet Irving Library, University of New Brunswick, http://www.lib.unb.ca/collections/loyalist/sccOnc.php?id=704&string.

11. "Sir George Prevost," q.v., *Dictionary of Canadian Biography Online*, http://www.biographi.ca/009004-119.01-e.php?BioId=36742. The assertion made in this biographical entry that Prevost advanced at an accelerated rate has been repeated in published works; see Stuart Sutherland, *His Majesty's Gentlemen: A Directory of British Regular Army Officers in the War of 1812* (Toronto: ISER Publications, 2001), 5, 6, 304.

12. John Phipps was present at Gibraltar during the Great Siege of 1779–1783 and remained there afterward. In 1793, he became a major general. Catherine Phipps's brother, George William, also joined the Royal Engineers and became a lieutenant general in 1837. Sutherland, *His Majesty's Gentlemen*, 304; Sir Christopher Prevost, e-mail to author, 18 February 2008; T. W. J. Connolly, *Roll of Officers of the Corps of Engineers from 1660 to 1898* (Chatham: W. & J. Mackay and Company, 1898), 7, 11; Butler, *King's Royal Rifle Corps*, 1 228; Nesbit Willougby Wallace, *A Regimental Chronicle and List of Officers of the 60th or the King's Royal Rifle Corps* (London: Harrison, 1879), 108.

13. Michael Duffy, *Soldiers, Sugar, and Seapower: The British Expeditions to the West Indies and the War against Revolutionary France* (Oxford: Clarendon Press, 1987), 5, 8; Rory Muir, *Britain and the Defeat of Napoleon, 1807–1815* (New Haven, Conn., and London: Yale University Press, 1996), 1, 2.

14. During the French Revolutionary and Napoleonic Wars, the first four battalions of the 60th served in the West Indies, while four newly

raised battalions were employed elsewhere. In 1813, the restriction on where the regiment could serve outside of Britain was finally removed, although in practice the 5th Battalion, raised in 1797, had been in Ireland in 1798 and, from 1808, in the Iberian Peninsula. The 6th through 8th Battalions saw service in the West Indies, Gibraltar, and Canada. Gibbes Rigaud, *Celer et Audax: A Sketch of the Services of the Fifth Battalion, 60th Regiment (Rifles)* (Oxford: H. Pickard Hall, 1879), 1, 2.

15. John Fortescue, *A History of the British Army* (London: Macmillan, 1899–1930), vol. 4 (pt. 1): 135.

16. Duffy, *Soldiers, Sugar, and Seapower*, 142; Butler, *King's Royal Rifles Corps*, 1:xxii, 229, 234; Sutherland, *His Majesty's Gentlemen*, 304; Christopher D. Hall, *British Strategy in the Napoleonic Wars, 1803–1815* (Manchester: Manchester University Press, 1999), 77; Wallace, *Regimental Chronicle of the 60th*, 286.

17. Butler, *King's Royal Rifle Corps*, 1:249; Fortescue, *History of the British Army*, 4 (pt. 1): 135, 441.

18. Duffy, *Soldiers, Sugar, and Seapower*, 145, 146; Butler, *King's Royal Rifle Corps*, 1:249; Fortescue, *History of the British Army*, 4 (pt. 1): 441.

19. Thomas Southey, *Chronological History of the West Indies* (London: Longman, Rees, Orne and Green, 1827), 3:87.

20. Duffy, *Soldiers, Sugar, and Seapower*, 145; Charles Sheppard, *Historical Account of St. Vincent* (London: W. Nichol, 1831), 107, 108, 109.

21. Caseshot, or canister, was an antipersonnel round consisting of a canister filled with balls used against close-range targets. Once fired, the canister would disintegrate and the balls would continue forward forming an expanding cone. In this particular action, Prevost chose to rely on the effect caseshot produced rather than the musket fire of his infantry, which was a reasonable response to the tactical situation. See David McConnell, *British Smooth-Bore Artillery: A Technological Study* (Ottawa: Parks Canada, 1988), 319.

22. Fortescue, *History of the British Army*, 4 (pt. 1): 443; Southey, *Chronological History of the West Indies*, 3:82–87; Butler, *King's Royal Rifle Corps*, 1:250, 251, 252; Sheppard, *Historical Account of St. Vincent*, 110; Brenton, *Some Account of the Public Life*, 6.

23. Southey, *Chronological History of the West Indies*, 3:114.

24. Fortescue, *History of the British Army*, 4 (pt. 1): 449.

25. Ibid., 252.

26. Sheppard, *Historical Account of St. Vincent*, 144; Fortescue, *History of the British Army*, 4 (pt. 1): 449; Southey, *Chronological History of the West Indies*, 3:114.

27. Butler, *King's Royal Rifle Corps*, 1:253; Brenton, *Some Account of the Public Life*, 6; Duffy, *Soldiers, Sugar, and Seapower*, 153, 154.

28. Sutherland, *His Majesty's Gentlemen*, 6, 7, 304; Wallace, *Regimental Chronicle of the 60th*, 65.

29. Sir Christopher Prevost, e-mail to author, 18 February 2008. One of Prevost's nephews by his half brother Augustine, George William Augustin of the 60th, served on his staff as brigade major during 1800. George William Augustin Prevost appears on the Army List as serving with the

3/60th in 1779, but in 1783 the battalion disbanded and his name disappears from the list. His rank at this time is uncertain.

30. David P. Henige, *Colonial Governors from the Fifteenth Century to the Present* (Madison: University of Wisconsin Press, 1970), 168; Hall, *British Strategy in the Napoleonic Wars*, 109; Portland to Prevost, 29 April 1801, in Brenton, *Some Account of the Public Life*, appendix 3, 14.

31. In recognition of his service, the colonists presented Prevost with a gold-hilted 1796 pattern heavy cavalry officer's sword. Glendining's, *Orders, Decorations, Medals and Militaria for the Campaigns 1793–1840* (London: Glendining and Co., 1991), 20; Portland to Prevost, 29 April 1801, in Brenton, *Some Account of the Public Life*, appendix 3, 14; Trigge to Brownrigg, n.d., in Brenton, *Some Account of the Public Life*, appendix 5, 17–18.

32. Fortescue, *History of the British Army*, 5:182; Grinfield to His Royal Highness, Commander in Chief, 23 June 1803, TNA, WO 1/118: 180.

33. Fortescue, *History of the British Army*, 5:183; William Laird Clowes, *The Royal Navy: A History from the Earliest Times to 1900* (London: Chatham Publishing, 1997), 5:55, 56; Frederick Myatt, *Peninsular General: Sir Thomas Picton, 1758–1815* (London: David & Charles, 1980), 47, 48.

34. Grinfield to His Royal Highness, Commander in Chief, 23 June 1803, TNA, WO 1/118: 169, 171, 172.

35. Among the casualties was Lieutenant Colonel Edward Pakenham of the 64th, who received a round in the neck. Pakenham later led British forces in the assault on New Orleans in 1815.

36. Grinfield to His Royal Highness, Commander in Chief, 23 June 1803, TNA, WO 1/118: 173, 174, 175, 178.

37. Six of the ships were of the line, meaning they had at least two decks and were capable of fighting in the line of battle against similarly sized ships. Clowes, *Royal Navy*, 5:92, 93; A. B. Ellis, *History of the First West India Regiment* (London: Chapman and Hall Limited, 1885), 104.

38. Clowes, *Royal Navy*, 5:92, 93; J. Holland Rose, "British West India Commerce as a Factor in the Napoleonic Wars," *Cambridge Historical Journal* 3, no 1 (1929): 37; Mark Adkin, *Trafalgar Companion: The Complete Guide to History's Most Famous Sea Battle and the Life of Lord Nelson* (London: Aarum Press, 2005), 50.

39. The climate of the West Indies caused significant casualties among European troops. Period accounts refer to fevers, diseases of the lungs, and dropsy. Malarial parasites, which transferred these diseases from person to person, were not identified as the cause until the end of the nineteenth century. Sickness rates were particularly high during the "sickly season," between July and October of each year, when the trade winds died, which allowed disease to spread even further. See Captain M. A. Tulloch, "On the Sickness and Mortality among the Troops in the West Indies, Part 1," *Journal of the Statistical Society of London* 1, no. 3 (1838): 129, 132.

40. "Annals of the British Army," *United Service Journal* (1831, pt. 2): 282n; Fortescue, *History of the British Army*, 5:245, 246; Brian Dyde, *The Empty Sleeve: The Story of the West India Regiments of the British Army*

(St. John's, Antigua: Hansib Caribbean, 1997), 76; "A Letter from Lieut. Gen. Sir William Myers," dated 1 March 1805, in *Jackson's Oxford Journal*, 2715 (11 May 1805). Sources vary on the names of the fortresses on the island. For example, the fortress at Rupert's Bay is referred to as Fort Prince Rupert. Clowes, *Royal Navy*, 5:182; Adkin, *Trafalgar Companion*, 25, 49, 50.

41. Prevost to Myers, 1 March 1805, in Southey, *Chronological History of the West Indies*, 3:312.

42. Ibid.

43. One source claims Prevost sent the captain of one of the forts to meet the commodore. This version is not described in any other documentation related to the operation. See Ellis, *First West India Regiment*, 105.

44. Prevost to Myers, 1 March 1805, in Southey, *Chronological History of the West Indies*, 3:312.

45. Fortescue, *History of the British Army*, 5:246, 247.

46. Prevost to Myers, 1 March 1805, in Southey, *Chronological History of the West Indies*, 3:313.

47. Ibid., 312, 313. Fortescue, *History of the British Army*, 5:247; "Journal of the Occurrences at Dominica," *Royal Military Chronicle*, vol. 4 (London: J. Davies, May 1812): 204, 205. According to Prevost's official report, the other officer to accompany Prevost was a local militia officer named Hopley, who was serving as deputy quartermaster general. Prevost's family was well treated during their captivity (although a French soldier had eaten one of his daughter's guinea pigs) because Legrange had been a prisoner of Prevost's at St. Lucia and reciprocated the kind treatment he had received. Prevost to Myers, 1 March 1805, in Southey, *Chronological History of the West Indies*, 3:313.

48. Fortescue, *History of the British Army*, 5:248; Dyde, *Empty Sleeve*, 77; Ellis, *First West India Regiment*, 113; "Occurrences at Dominica," 207, 208.

49. Prevost to Myers, 1 March 1805, in Southey, *Chronological History of the West Indies*, 3:313, 315; Fortescue, *History of the British Army*, 5:248; Dyde, *Empty Sleeve*, 77; Adkin, *Trafalgar Companion*, 50; Rose, "British West India Commerce," 38, 39.

50. "Occurrences at Dominica," 211, 212; Adkin, *Trafalgar Companion*, 49, 50, 51.

51. Beginning in 1803, a committee of the Lloyd's Patriotic Fund granted money to wounded service members and gave annuities to the dependents of those killed. They also rewarded those who distinguished themselves with "successful exertions of value or merit," in the form of a piece of plate, a sword, or a sum of cash. Three types of sword were awarded: one of £100 value would be given to commanders and naval captains; the £50 sword was given to naval lieutenants and Royal Marine captains; and a £30 sword was awarded to midshipmen, master's mates, and marine lieutenants. Awards were not restricted to the navy, and seven swords were presented to army officers. A total of 164 swords were granted between 1803 and 1809, 35 of which were of the £100 type—only 3 of which went to army officers, including Prevost. The sword came in a mahogany

case with brass escutcheon engraved with Prevost's name and was accompanied by a blue and gold bullion sword knot and a sword belt. Inside the lid of the case was a label that explained the classical iconography of the hilt. Each recipient also received a letter with an engraving of Britannia and a lion surrounded by naval trophies above an address to the recipient detailing the action concerned. These were hand written by boys from Christ's Hospital, London. Lloyd's Patriotic Fund, http://www.lloydsswords.com/background.php; Glendining's, *Orders, Decorations, Medals and Militaria*, 20. Prevost's sword is currently held by a private collector in Europe.

52. Prevost to Myers, 1 March 1805, in Southey, *Chronological History of the West Indies*, 3:314; Brenton, *Some Account of the Public Life*, appendix 16, 10; Dyde, *Empty Sleeve*, 76; "Occurrences at Dominica," 214; "Baronet," in *Burke's Peerage and Gentry*, http://www.burkes-peerage.net/articles/peerage/page66-baronet.aspx (accessed 14 October 2009); Sir Christopher Prevost, e-mail to author, 14 February 2009.

53. The post of governor of Portsmouth originated in the thirteenth century, and the title varied between governor and lieutenant governor depending on the prestige of the incumbent. The governorship was abolished in 1834, after which the post was recognized as the garrison commander until 1968, when it was eliminated. The commander in chief of Portsmouth, also known as the port admiral, was an Admiralty appointment responsible for manning, victualing, courts-martial, and ensuring the readiness of the fleet and the defense of the coastal area, while the dockyard was managed by a commissioner who was appointed by the Navy Board. Admiral Sir George Montagu was the commander in chief of Portsmouth between 1803 and 1809. Brian Lavery, *Nelson's Navy: The Ships, Men and Organization, 1793–1815* (Annapolis: U.S. Naval Institute, 1986), 21, 221, 226, 234, 254; Roger Knight, "The Dockyards in England at the Time of the American War of Independence" (PhD diss., University of London, 1972), 26, 72, 76; Charles Dupin, *A Tour through the Naval and Military Establishments of Great Britain: In the Years 1816–1820* (London: Sir Richard Phillips and Company, 1822), 115, 116; David Wilson, "Government Dockyard Workers in Portsmouth, 1793–1815" (PhD diss., University of Warwick, 1975), 10; and "Portsmouth, Saturday March 28," *Hampshire Telegraph and Sussex Chronicle*, 30 March 1807.

54. Burnham and McGuigan, *British Army against Napoleon*, 235, 236.

55. Wallace, *Regimental Chronicle of the 60th*, 67, 165, 168; Butler, *King's Royal Rifle Corps*, vol. 2: *The Green Jacket* (London: John Murray, 1923): xix.

56. At least two sources present the relationship between Prevost and de Salaberry as having soured due to a disagreement over regimental recruitment. Between July 1806 and March 1807, when Prevost was lieutenant governor of Portsmouth, de Salaberry was in England, at the request of the Duke of Kent—who was a friend of the family—to recruit soldiers for the 5/60th and the 1st Foot. What followed is unclear, but one historian has claimed that Prevost "created difficulties" for de Salaberry, while another considers that the latter's "success" in obtaining 120 men "antagonized"

Prevost, since de Salaberry was "hiring good men away from him." As no source is identified in either account, the reasons for Prevost's strong reaction to the recruitment of men for the 5/60th, the battalion for which he was colonel commandant, remain unclear. If this was what happened, whatever may have transpired between the two men would have been nothing more than a regimental spat, although one could speculate that Prevost may have been concerned by the unusual tasking of a regimental officer, albeit by a member of the Royal Family, but one whose active military career had ended. Unfortunately, no documentation has been located that could shed light on this curious event. See Michel Guitard, "Charles-Michel d'Irumberry de Salaberry," q.v., *Canadian Dictionary of Biography Online*; and J. Patrick Wohler, *Charles de Salaberry: Soldier of the Empire, Defender of Quebec* (Toronto: Dundurn, 1984), 44.

57. James perished in 1811 from wounds received in battle. Wallace, *Regimental Chronicle of the 60th*, 67, 165, 168; Butler, *King's Royal Rifle Corps*, 2:36, 37.

58. Muir, *Britain and the Defeat of Napoleon*, 22–25; Fortescue, *History of the British Army*, 6:64, 64n2; *Caledonian Mercury*, 20 September 1806.

59. Wentworth to Castlereagh, 3 January 1808, Public Archives of Nova Scotia (hereafter cited as PANS), CO 217 A 140: 17; Castlereagh to Wentworth, 24 January 1808, PANS, CO 217 A 140: 43; Castlereagh to Prevost, 24 January 1808, PANS, CO 217 A 140: 221; Kevin Lynch, "The Recruitment of the British Army, 1807–1815" (PhD diss., University of Leeds, 2001), 105; "Portsmouth, Saturday May 2," *Hampshire Telegraph and Sussex Chronicle*, 4 May 1807; "Portsmouth, Saturday May 18," *Hampshire Telegraph and Sussex Chronicle*, 18 May 1807; "Portsmouth, Saturday 23 January," *Hampshire Telegraph and Sussex Chronicle*, 25 January 1808.

60. Roger Norman Buckley, ed., *The Napoleonic War Journal of Captain Thomas Henry Browne, 1807–1816* (London: Army Records Society, 1987), 66.

61. Donald T. Trenholm, "The Military Defence of Nova Scotia during the French and American Wars (1789–1815)" (Master's thesis, Mount Allison University, 1939), 79, 83; W. S. McNutt, *The Atlantic Provinces: The Emergence of a Colonial Society* (Toronto: McClelland and Stewart, 1965), 131, 133; Brenton, *Some Account of the Public Life*, 11; *London Gazette*, 18 January 1808; J. Mackay Hitsman, *Safeguarding Canada, 1763–1871* (Toronto: University of Toronto Press, 1968), 74; and Buckley, *Journal of Captain Thomas Browne*, 66, 69, 70.

62. "Portsmouth, Saturday 30 January," *Hampshire Telegraph and Sussex Chronicle*, 1 February 1808.

63. Donald E. Graves, *Fix Bayonets! A Royal Welch Fusilier at War, 1796–1815* (Toronto: Robin Brass Studio, 2006), 110.

2. NOVA SCOTIA, MARTINIQUE, AND QUEBEC, 1808–1811

1. A. D. L. Cary and Stouppe McCance, *Regimental Records of the Royal Welch Fusiliers (Late the 23rd Foot)*, vol. 1: *1689–1815* (London: Foster, Groom & Company, 1929), 218; John Percy Groves, *Historical Records*

of the Royal Regiment of Fusiliers (London: F. P. Guerin, 1903), 87, 88; Graves, *Fix Bayonets!*, 110, 111; Richard Cannon, *Historical Record of the Eighth or The King's Regiment* (London: Parker, Furnivall and Parker, 1844), 84; Buckley, *Journal of Captain Thomas Browne*, 66, 69, 70; "Dispute with America," *Aberdeen Journal*, 2 March 1808; Hitsman, *Safeguarding Canada*, 74; *Caledonian Mercury*, 18 February 1808; Castlereagh to Craig, Royal Military College of Canada [RMC], Colonial Office [CO] 42 vol. 136: 22 (hereafter "vol." is replaced by "/").

2. J. C. A. Stagg, *Mr. Madison's War* (Princeton, N.J.: Princeton University Press, 1983), 16, 17, 20, 22.

3. McNutt, *Atlantic Provinces*, 133.

4. The appointment of Prevost to Halifax began the practice of having the post of lieutenant governor of Nova Scotia serve as a stepping-stone for the governorship of British North America until 1830. Four officers followed this route: Prevost, John Sherbrooke (1816–18), the Earl of Dalhousie (1820–28), and James Kempt (1829–30). Henige, *Colonial Governors*, 105, 155.

5. Wentworth to Castlereagh, 3 January 1808, PANS CO 217 A 140: 17; Castlereagh to Wentworth, 24 January 1808, PANS, CO 217 A 140: 43; Castlereagh to Prevost, 24 January 1808, PANS, CO 217 A 140: 221.

6. Castlereagh to Prevost, 13 February 1808, in "Secret Reports of John Howe, I," *American Historical Review* 17, no. 1 (1911): 72, 73.

7. Ibid.

8. Ibid.

9. Hitsman, *Safeguarding Canada*, 74; Castlereagh to Prevost, 24 January 1808, PANS, CO 217 A 140: 221.

10. Wentworth to Castlereagh, 26 April 1808, PANS, CO 271 A 140: 207.

11. Castlereagh to Prevost, 13 February 1808, PANS, CO 217 A 140: 227; J. McNutt, *Atlantic Provinces*, 147; "Secret Reports of John Howe, I," 73; Beamish Murdoch, *The History of Nova Scotia or Acadie*, vol. 3 (Halifax: James Barnes, 1867), 278.

12. On the Iberian Peninsula during 1811, Pakenham commanded the Fusilier Brigade of the 4th Division, which included both battalions of his regiment the 7th Foot and the 1/23rd Foot. Two of Prevost's nephews were serving in Iberia at this time. Henry Prevost, who was in the 7th Foot, died on 30 May 1811 as a result of wounds received in action at Albuera. James Prevost also served with the 60th Foot and was an aide de camp for Pakenham when he was wounded at Aldea de Ponte; he died on 20 October 1811. Pakenham replaced Major General Robert Ross, who was killed at Baltimore, as the commander of the New Orleans expedition. Pakenham arrived in Louisiana in late 1814, and he was killed during the Battle of New Orleans in January 1815.

13. Prevost to Castlereagh, 28 May 1808, PANS, CO 218 A 140: 257, 262, 265.

14. See Prevost to Castlereagh, 28 May 1808 and enclosures, PANS, CO 218 A 140: 254; Chartrand and Graves, "United States Army of the War of 1812," 48.

15. Prevost to Bathurst, 18 May 1812, RMC, CO 42/146: n.p.

16. Prevost to Bathurst, 18 May 1812, RMC, CO 42/146: 292.

17. Ibid.

18. Julian Gwyn, *Frigates and Foremasts: The North American Squadron in Nova Scotia Waters, 1745–1815* (Vancouver: UBC Press, 2003), 124.

19. The National Archives, Kew, England [hereafter cited as TNA], Berkeley to Poole, 19 December 1807, Admiralty [hereafter cited as Adm] 1, vol. 497: 493.

20. Gwyn, *Frigates and Foremasts*, 134.

21. Ibid., 124, 125, 126, 134.

22. Hoghton had served with Wellington in India. After 1810, he served at Cádiz before taking command of a brigade in the 2nd Division. Hoghton was killed leading the Fusilier Brigade at Albuera in 1811.

23. Other units, such as the Nova Scotia Regiment of Fencible Infantry along with the 98th Regiment, divided their time between Nova Scotia and New Brunswick. Hall, *History of the Peninsular War*, 8:285–86; Groves, *Historical Records of the 7th or Royal Regiment of Fusiliers*, 99; Cary and McCance, *Royal Welch Fusiliers*, 1:233; Cannon, *Historical Record of the Eighth*, 84; W. Austin Squires, *The 104th Regiment of Foot (The New Brunswick Regiment), 1803–1817* (Fredericton, N.B.: Unipress, 1962), 86; Hitsman, *Safeguarding Canada*, 74.

24. Prevost to Castlereagh, 28 May 1808, quoted in Trenholm, "Military Defence of Nova Scotia," 86.

25. Hitsman, *Safeguarding Canada*, 73.

26. W. B. Armit, "Halifax 1749–1906: Soldiers Who Founded and Garrisoned a Famous City" (photocopy, ca. 1958), various regimental entries; Buckley, *Journal of Captain Thomas Browne*, 293–94; Prevost to Castlereagh, 28 May 1808, PANS, CO 218, A 141: 64; Trenholm, "Military Defence of Nova Scotia," 84, 85, 86, 88, 89; Joseph Plimsoll Edwards, *The Militia of Nova Scotia, 1749–1867* (Londonderry, N.S.: n.p., 1913), 17, 18.

27. Prevost to Castlereagh, 28 May 1808, PANS, CO 218 A 141: 64; Nicolls to Prevost, 25 May 1808, quoted in Trenholm, "Military Defence of Nova Scotia," 88, 89.

28. Prevost to Castlereagh, 28 May 1808, PANS, CO 218 A 181: 65; Ivan J. Saunders, *A History of Martello Towers in the Defence of North America, 1796–1871* (Ottawa: Parks Canada, 1976), 26.

29. Wentworth to Skerrett, 8 October 1807, quoted in Trenholm, "Military Defence of Nova Scotia," 80.

30. Monk to Prevost, 23 April 1808, quoted in Trenholm, "Military Defence of Nova Scotia," 86–87.

31. Trenholm, "Military Defence of Nova Scotia," 87.

32. "Secret Reports of John Howe, I," 72.

33. Prevost to Cooke, 27 April 1808, quoted in ibid., 73.

34. "Secret Reports of John Howe, I," 73; "Queries and Instructions for Howe," 30 November 1808, in "Secret Reports of John Howe, II," *American Historical Review* 17, no. 2 (1912): 334–38.

35. "Secret Reports of John Howe, II," 350.

36. Ibid., 354.

37. Ibid.

38. Howe to Prevost or Croke, 7 January 1809, in ibid.

39. Ibid.

40. Ibid.

41. Ibid., 351.

42. Ibid.

43. Ibid.; "Secret Reports of John Howe, I," 73; "Queries and Instructions for Howe," 30 November 1808, in "Secret Reports of John Howe, II," 334–38.

44. Ibid., 350.

45. Nancy Isenburg, *Fallen Founder: The Life of Aaron Burr* (New York: Penguin Books, 2007), 371, 372, 383; Murdoch, *History of Nova Scotia*, 283, 296, 297; Prevost to Castlereagh, 17 June 1808, PANS, CO 217 A 141: 69; Prevost to E. Cooke, 18 June 1808, PANS, CO 217 A 141: 70; Matthew L. Davis, *The Private Journal of Aaron Burr* (New York: Harper and Brothers, 1838), 1:21. Prevost's letter to Burr is dated 20 June 1808.

46. Muir, *Britain and the Defeat of Napoleon*, 18; Michael Duffy, "The French Revolution and British Attitudes to the West Indies Colonies," in David Barry Gaspar and David Patrick Geggus, eds., *A Turbulent Time: The French Revolution and the Great Caribbean* (Bloomington: Indiana University Press, 1997), 85, 86, 87; Fortescue, *History of the British Army*, 7:11, 12; Hall, *British Strategy in the Napoleonic Wars*, 185; Buckley, *Journal of Captain Thomas Browne*, 85.

47. Prevost to Castlereagh, 24 August 1808, quoted in Trenholm, "Military Defence of Nova Scotia," 90, 91.

48. Fortescue, *History of the British Army*, 7:12n2; Butler, *King's Royal Rifle Corps*, 2:270; Dyde, *Empty Sleeve*, 84; W. Wheater, *Historical Records of the Seventh or Royal Regiment of Fusiliers* (Leeds, 1875), 88; Lt. Col. M. E. S. Laws, "The Royal Artillery at Martinique, 1809," *Journal of the Royal Artillery* 77, no. 1 (1950): 70; Buckley, *Journal of Captain Thomas Browne*, 88.

49. "South America, West Indies & c," *Aberdeen Journal*, 14 December 1808.

50. "West India Expedition," *Aberdeen Journal*, 25 January 1809; "Secret Reports of John Howe, II," 349; Wheater, *Historical Records of the Seventh*, 88; Clowes, *Royal Navy*, 5:283; Gwyn, *Frigates and Foremasts*, 126; Thomas Haliburton, *An Historical and Statistical Account of Nova Scotia* (Halifax: Joseph Howe, 1829), 1:318.

51. Hoghton's first brigade included the 1/7th Foot, 23rd Foot, and five companies of the 1st West India Regiment. As the 1st Brigade included two fusilier regiments, it is sometimes referred to as the "Fusilier Brigade." Colville commanded the second brigade, which included the 1/8th Foot, 13th Foot, and four companies of the 1st West India Regiment. Finally, the 3rd Brigade, under Nicholson, had the flank companies of the 25th Foot; the 3rd and 4th Battalions of Prevost's old regiment, the 60th; the 4th West India Regiment; and a Light Infantry Battalion made up of the light companies drawn from all regiments. A company of artillery Prevost had brought from Halifax was also placed under his command. Fortescue, *History of the British army*, 7:12n2; Laws, "Royal Artillery at Martinique," 78, 79.

52. Fortescue, *History of the British Army*, 7:12, 12n2, 13; Laws, "Royal Artillery at Martinique," 73, 88; Butler, *King's Royal Rifle Corps*, 2:270; Dyde, *Empty Sleeve*, 84; Wheater, *Historical Records of the Seventh*, 88; Wallace, *Regimental Chronicle of the 60th*, 297.

53. Regimental Museum, The Royal Welch Fusiliers, Caernarfon, Wales, *Diary of Drummer Richard Bentinck, 23rd Foot*, 2; Fortescue, *History of the British Army*, 7:12.

54. Joyeuse had been defeated by Lord Howe at the Glorious First of June (Third Battle of Ushant) in 1794. Clowes, *Royal Navy*, 5 283; Regimental Museum, *Diary of Drummer Bentinck*, 2.

55. Beckwith's plan was similar to that used by Lieutenant General Sir Charles Grey, who commanded an assault on the French-held island in February and March 1794. In that operation, the 7,000-man force was organized into three divisions: the first division landed at the Bay of Galion, north of where Prevost would land in 1809; the second landed north of Fort Royal; and the third made its landing near the location where Maitland would land in 1809. After the garrison surrendered, the British reinstated a Royalist government. In 1802, Martinique was returned to France, in accordance with the terms of the Treaty of Amiens. See Fortescue, *History of the British Army*, 4 (pt. 1): 354–61.

56. Dyde, *Empty Sleeve*, 74, 85; Clowes, *Royal Navy*, 5 281, 282; Graves, *Fix Bayonets!*, 122; Laws, "Royal Artillery at Martinique," 73.

57. Wheater, *Historical Records of the Seventh*, 88; Dyde, *Empty Sleeve*, 85; Regimental Museum, *Diary of Drummer Bentinck*, 4; Lewis, "Royal Artillery at Martinique," 75.

58. Wheater, *Historical Records of the Seventh*, 88; Laws, "Royal Artillery at Martinique," 75.

59. Laws, "Royal Artillery at Martinique,"75; Regimental Museum, *Diary of Drummer Bentinck*, 5.

60. Regimental Museum, *Diary of Drummer Bentinck*, 6.

61. Wheater, *Historical Records of the Seventh*, 89; Regimental Museum, *Diary of Drummer Bentinck*, 5, 6; Dyde, *Empty Sleeve*, 85; Laws, "Royal Artillery at Martinique," 75.

62. Dyde, *Empty Sleeve*, 86; Laws, "Royal Artillery at Martinique," 75; Regimental Museum, *Diary of Drummer Bentinck*, 6.

63. Ibid.

64. Laws, "Royal Artillery at Martinique," 76.

65. Ibid., 78, 80; Fortescue, *History of the British Army*, 7:17.

66. The garrison was originally to have been shipped as prisoners of war to Quiberon Bay, France, where they would be exchanged for an equal number of British prisoners. Napoléon's refusal to release any British prisoners led to the French captives being sent to camps in England instead. Fortescue, *History of the British Army*, 7:16.

67. Dyde, *Empty Sleeve*, 86; Wheater, *Historical Records of the Seventh*, 90; Laws, "Royal Artillery at Martinique," 80; Cannon, *Historical Record of the Eighth*, 81, 82; Fortescue, *History of the British Army*, 7:17.

68. Prevost's conduct at Martinique was acknowledged with the award of the Army Gold Medal. This award was introduced in 1810 for officers

above the rank of major. There were two versions: the large medal was awarded to general officers, while field officers received the small medal. Prevost received one of nine large medals that were awarded for the expedition. *Army Officers Awards of the Napoleonic Period* (London: Savannah Paperback Classics, 2002), 28, 29, 30; Glendining's, *Orders, Decorations, Medals and Militaria*, 20.

69. Sir Charles Oman, *Wellington's Army, 1809–1814* (Oxford: Clarendon Press, 1903), 163–65.

70. Fortescue, *History of the British Army*, 7:28; Muir, *Britain and the Defeat of Napoleon*, 54, 104.

71. *Nova Scotia Gazette*, 18 April 1809.

72. Ibid.

73. Diary of Anne Elinor Prevost, LAC, MG 24, A9, 37.

74. Ibid., 39.

75. *Nova Scotia Gazette*, 2 May 1809.

76. Inspection Return, 1/23rd Foot, TNA, WO 27/94, 27 June 1809.

77. For example, in his 1809 report for the attack on heights overlooking French-held Fort Bourbon in Martinique, Prevost praised four officers whose conduct enabled him "to retain this valuable position without artillery, within three hundred yards of the enemy's entrenched camp covered with guns." Cary and McCance, *Royal Welch Fusiliers*, 1:223.

78. Ibid.

79. Ibid., 36, 54.

80. *Nova Scotia Gazette*, 22 May 1809.

81. Diary of Anne Elinor Prevost, 28, 29; Regimental Museum, *Diary of Drummer Bentinck*, 11; Hall, *British Strategy in the Napoleonic Wars*, 186; Andrew Neffleship, *That Astonishing Infantry! A History of the 7th Foot (Royal Fusiliers) in the Peninsular War, 1809–1814* (N.p., 1998), 25; Graves, *Fix Bayonets!*, 128, 129, 135.

82. Colonel Nick Lipscombe, *The Peninsular War Atlas* (London: Osprey Publishing, 2010), 160; Dundas to Liverpool, 12 July 1818, British Library Add Ms 38,245 f 131–32.

83. Stagg, *Mr. Madison's War*, 76–78; Hitsman, *Incredible War of 1812*, 22, 23.

84. Prevost to Liverpool, 29 May 1811, quoted in Trenholm, "Military Defence of Nova Scotia," 93.

85. Jean-Pierre Wallat, "Sir James Craig," q.v., *Dictionary of Canadian Biography Online*, http://www.biographi.ca/EN/ShowBio.asp?BioId=36468&query=craig; Haliburton, *Historical and Statistical Account of Nova Scotia*, 1:318; Murdoch, *History of Nova Scotia*, 298, 312.

86. Craig to Downing St [draft], January 1811, RMC, CO 42/142: 97; Craig to Liverpool, No. 34, 27 February 1812, RMC, CO 42/143: 106.

87. Castlereagh to Wentworth, No. 10 [draft], 24 January 1808, TNA, CO 218/140: 43; Liverpool to Craig, 31 May 1811, TNA, CO 43/22: 336.

88. Castlereagh to Prevost, No. 2 [draft], 24 January 1808, TNA CO 218/140: 219. This document also outlined the succession of military command within Nova Scotia and New Brunswick should Prevost have to assume the governorship of British North America.

89. Liverpool to Craig, 31 May 1811, TNA, CO 43/22: 336.

90. Ibid.; Liverpool to Prevost, No. 11 [draft], 31 May 1811, TNA, CO 218/146: 83; Prevost to Liverpool, 28 July 1811, TNA, CO 218/146: 85; Alexander Croke to Liverpool, 30 August 1811, TNA, CO 218/146: 108; Henige, *Colonial Governors*, 105, 155.

91. Prevost received several letters congratulating him on his new appointment. The residents of Halifax expressed their "gratitude for the many real benefits which this province has derived from" his "short administration of the government." They also stated their belief that Prevost's "appointment to the supreme command of British North America" represented "an earnest of the blessing which His Majesty's subjects, on the western side of the Atlantic, are to enjoy under the government of the august personage. . . . At this critical period, when the prejudices and misguided councils of a neighbouring nation render it not improbable that we may be called upon to defend the invaluable privileges of Englishmen, it must be a source of satisfaction to every loyal subject, that His Royal Highness, in the name of our venerable sovereign, has entrusted the defence of these colonies to an officer, who has so frequently proved himself worthy of commanding British colonies." Address from the Inhabitants of Halifax, in Brenton, *Some Account of the Public Life*, 4, Appendix No. 19, 6, 47.

92. "Diary of Ann Elinor Prevost," LAC, MG 24 A9, 52.

93. Ibid., 54.

94. Prevost was accompanied by W. H. Robinson, the new commissary general of North America, who was aboard the sloop *Rattler. Quebec Mercury*, 16 September 1811, 293, 294.

3. PLANNING THE DEFENSE OF BRITISH NORTH AMERICA, SEPTEMBER 1811–JUNE 1812

1. Craig to Gore, 6 December 1807, RMC, CO 42/136: 209.

2. The rank of captain general originated in the fourteenth century and later became associated with the designation of a commander in chief of a deployed army. The rank fell into disuse when George II made the first appointment to field marshal in 1736; thereafter the title was honorific. The term "commander in chief" will be the rank used throughout this work.

3. Newfoundland was not included in British North America and was under separate administration. In 1811, Bermuda became part of British North America as it could not be accommodated within the West Indian Command. See Sutherland, *His Majesty's Gentlemen*, 25, 26. Prevost to Liverpool, No. 1, 23 September 1812, RMC, CO 42/143: 170; Prevost to Liverpool, No. 2, 24 September 1812, RMC, CO 42/143: 172.

4. A 1794 reorganization and expansion of the secretaries of state led to the creation of a secretary for war. In 1801, responsibility for the colonies was transferred from the Home Office to the Secretary of State for War, who then became known as the Secretary of State for War and the Colonies. The secretary of state was head of the Colonial Office. Provision was made originally for one undersecretary, while in 1806, an undersecre-

tary for war was first appointed. A staff of ten clerks supported the secretary and undersecretaries in their duties. J. C. Sainty, *Colonial Office Officials* (London: Institute of Historical Research, 1970), 1, 2, 8, 9.

5. Bathurst to Prevost, 21 October 1811, TNA, CO 43/23: 184–86. The coordination task conducted by the Secretary of State for War and the Colonies proved daunting, as he had to liaise with a great many officials outside of his authority and some who held cabinet posts equal to his. Bathurst held this post until 1827. Muir, *Britain and the Defeat of Napoleon*, 10, 11, 197; Richard Glover, *Peninsular Preparation: The Reform of the British Army, 1795–1809* (Cambridge: Cambridge University Press, 1963), 28, 39, 49; Sutherland, *His Majesty's Gentlemen*, 25.

6. S. G. P. Ward, *Wellington's Headquarters: A Study of the Administrative Problems in the Peninsula, 1809–1814* (Oxford: Oxford University Press, 1957), 6–15.

7. Glover, *Peninsular Preparation*, 256; Ward, *Wellington's Headquarters*, 73, 77, 78; Glenn A. Steppler, "A Duty Troublesome beyond Measure: Logistical Considerations in the Canadian War of 1812" (Master's thesis, McGill University, 1974), 18, 19, 30–33, 270.

8. Gerald S. Graham, *Sea Power and British North America, 1783–1820* (London and Cambridge, Mass.: Harvard University Press, 1941), 4, 5, 179, 210, 216; P. J. Marshall, ed., *The Oxford History of the British Empire*, vol. 2: *The Eighteenth Century* (Oxford: Oxford University Press, 2001), 387.

9. Sutherland, *His Majesty's Gentlemen*, 26, 27; Ward, *Wellington's Headquarters*, 10, 11; L. Homfrey Irving, *Officers of the British Forces in Canada during the War of 1812* (Welland, Ont.: Welland Tribune Print, 1908), 1, 2, 4–6, 14–18; Secretary of War, *Collection of Orders, Regulations and Instructions for the Army; on Matters of Finance and Points of Discipline* (London: T. Egerton, 1807), 340; *General Orders and Regulations, 1811* (London: W. Clowes, 1811), 27, 28.

10. Prevost to Thomas Barclay, 4 January 1812, in George Lockhart Rives, ed., *Selections from the Correspondence of Thomas Barclay* (New York: Harper and Brothers, 1894), 302.

11. Ibid.

12. Although Prevost's rank allowed him two aides in peacetime, he could, and did, authorize additional aides for himself during the war. McDouall was also present at Sackets Harbor and carried dispatches to England in 1813, along with colors captured at Ogdensburg. Prevost to Liverpool, 14 June 1813, RMC, CO 42/150: 22; Sutherland, *His Majesty's Gentlemen*, 27, 33n14; Prevost to Brock, 31 August 1812, in E. A. Cruikshank, ed., *Documentary History of the Campaigns upon the Niagara Frontier in 1812 to 1814* (Welland, Ont., 1896–1908; hereafter cited as Cruikshank, *DH*), 3:228; Brock to Prevost, 4 September 1812, in Cruikshank, *DH* 3:236; Vincent to Baynes, 4 June 1813, LAC, RG 8 C vol. 3172: 19; Vincent to Prevost, 18 June 1813, LAC, RG 8 C vol. 3172.

13. Mark Romans, "Professionalism and the Development of Military Intelligence in Wellington's Army, 1809–1814" (PhD diss., University of Southampton, 2005), 1, 3.

14. Bathurst to Prevost, 22 October 1811, TNA, CO 43/23: 66.

15. The complete instructions are in ibid., 1–68. An excerpt of these instructions appears in Hitsman, *Incredible War of 1812*, 41; and Robert S. Allen, *His Majesty's Indian Allies: British Indian Policy in the Defence of Canada, 1774–1815* (Toronto: Dundurn, 1993), 119.

16. Hall, *British Strategy in the Napoleonic Wars*, 190.

17. The letter is quoted in ibid., 192; Muir, *Britain and the Defeat of Napoleon*, 141, 193, 194, 196; and David French, *The British Way of War: 1688–2000* (London: Unwin Hyman, 1990), 118.

18. Sir Charles Oman, *A History of the Peninsular War* (Oxford: Clarendon Press, 1903), 4:647, and 5:599; Hall, *British Strategy in the Napoleonic Wars*, 193, 252n23; Richard Glover, *Britain at Bay: Defence against Bonaparte, 1803–1814* (London: George Allen and Unwin, 1973), 146; Hitsman, *Incredible War of 1812*, 295.

19. Hall, *British Strategy in the Napoleonic Wars*, 196.

20. Hitsman, *Incredible War of 1812*, 295.

21. Before the outbreak of the War of 1812, it was common practice during the winter months, normally between November and February, for packet vessels carrying mail to North America to follow the trade winds of the "southern route" and sail for Bermuda. From there, the packets would sail north to New York, where they would winter before continuing their journey. During the summer months, the packets would bypass New York and continue to Halifax. The return journey was easier since the prevailing westerlies of the northern route made for a shorter journey home. The closing of the port of New York in 1812 forced the packets to sail to Halifax whatever the season. During the war, American frigates and privateers were responsible for intercepting eighteen packet vessels and their mails (which were often thrown over the side to avoid capture, although the Americans did retrieve at least one) each year. The overall loss rate to the total number of sailings is unknown as these statistics have not yet been compiled. The figures presented here do not include dispatches and army mail carried by vessels of the Royal Navy. Howard Robinson, *Carrying British Mails Overseas* (London: George Allen and Unwin, 1964), 94, 95, 99, 100, 103, 314.

22. Prevost to Liverpool, 17 May 1812, RMC, CO 42/146: 282; Prevost to Liverpool, 28 October 1811, RMC, CO 42/143: 191, Hitsman, *Incredible War of 1812*, 31.

23. Prevost to Liverpool, 20 April 1812, RMC, CO 42/146: 214, 220; Prevost to Brock, 30 April 1812, Cruikshank, *DH* 3:59, 60; Chartrand and Graves, "United States Army of the War of 1812," 36, 37; Robert S. Quimby, *U.S. Army in the War of 1812: An Operational and Command Study* (Lansing: Michigan State University Press, 1998), 1:2, 3, 18.

24. Johnston, *Glengarry Light Infantry*, 6, 7, 28, 31; Michelle Guitard, *The Militia of the Battle of the Châteauguay: A Social History* (Ottawa: Parks Canada, 1983), 11; Liverpool to Prevost, 20 April 1812, RMC, CO 42/146, 52; René Chartrand, Brian Leigh Dunnigan, and Dirk Gringhuis, "10th Royal Veteran Battalion, Fort Mackinac, 1812," *Military Historian* 23 (1972): 47.

25. Maxwell Sutherland, "The Civil Administration of Sir George Prevost, 1811–1815: A Study in Conciliation" (Master's thesis, Queen's University, 1959), 4, 5, 43.

26. Prevost to Ryland, 7 November 1811, in R. Christie, *A History of the Late Province of Lower Canada* (Quebec: T. Cary and Company, 1855), 282.

27. During this time, Herman Ryland, Prevost's civil secretary, "seemed incapable of taking" hints of policies advocated by Prevost and remained "oblivious to Prevost's intentions" while expressing his own views fully, resulting in his being ousted from his position in June 1812. See Sutherland, "Civil Administration of Sir George Prevost," 54, 56; and James H. Lambert, "Ryland, Herman Witsius," q.v., *Dictionary of Canadian Biography Online*, http://www.biographi.ca/009004-119.01-e.php?&id _nbr=3645&interval=20&&PHPSESSID=dbo413tnaovte41jpmnn4eck56.

28. Prevost to Bathurst, 2 July 1812, quoted in Sutherland, "Civil Administration of Sir George Prevost," 57.

29. Ibid.

30. Prevost to Ryland, 7 November 1811, quoted in Robert Christie, *The Military and Naval Operations in the Canadas, during the Late War with the United States . . .* (Quebec: n.p., 1818), 281; Sutherland, "Civil Administration of Sir George Prevost," 53, 56, 57, 59, 61.

31. Hitsman, *Incredible War of 1812*, 38; Guitard, *Militia of the Battle of the Châteauguay*, 11. The amendments to the militia act were terminated in 1816.

32. Hitsman, *Incredible War of 1812*, 25.

33. In 1658, the first such court was organized in Jamaica. There was also a vice admiralty court in Halifax. George Stuart, comp., *Reports of Cases Argued and Determined in the Courts of King's Bench and in the Provincial Court of Appeals of Lower Canada with a few of the more important Cases of the Court of Vice Admiralty* (Quebec: Neilson & Cowan, 1834), 38, 39; James Stewart, *Report of Cases Argued and Determined in the Court of Vice-Admiralty at Halifax, Nova Scotia* (London: J. Butterworth and Son, 1814), 401–406; Faye Margaret Kert, *Prize and Prejudice: Privateering and Naval Prize in Atlantic Canada in the War of 1812* (St. John's, Nfld.: International Maritime Economic History Association, 1997), 48, 49.

34. Sawyer commanded at Halifax between 1810 and August 1812. Admiral John Borlase Warren succeeded him, and in 1814, Vice Admiral Alexander Cochrane replaced Warren (Cochrane had been appointed to the post in November 1813, but command could not be transferred until his arrival at Bermuda the following year).

35. Richard A. Preston, ed. *Kingston before the War of 1812* (Toronto: Champlain Society, 1959), 272; Robert Malcomson, *Lords of the Lake: The Naval War on Lake Ontario, 1812–1814* (Toronto: Robin Brass Studio, 1998), 29; Sutherland, *His Majesty's Gentlemen*, 170; Irving, *Officers of the British Forces in Canada*, 8n28; Robert Malcomson, *Warships of the Great Lakes, 1754–1834* (Annapolis: Naval Institute Press, 2001), 39, 41, 42.

36. Report on the Provincial Marine, 7 December 1811, in William S. Dudley, *The Naval War of 1812: A Documentary History* (Washington, D.C.: Naval Historical Center, 1985), 1:268–71.

37. Prevost to Liverpool, 14 April 1812, RMC, CO 42/146: 197.

38. Ibid.

39. Captain Alexander Grant had joined the Royal Navy in 1755 and in 1812 was replaced by George Hall. Malcomson, *Warships of the Great Lakes*, 85.

40. The vessels launched in 1812 were the 8-gun schooner *Prince Regent* and the 13-gun schooner *Lady Prevost*. Named after Catherine Prevost, the *Lady Prevost* was captured by the Americans in September 1813. Thereafter, it saw service on Lake Erie and Lake Huron before being sold off as a commercial carrier in 1815. A 23-gun schooner that was launched in April 1813 at Kingston was to have been named *Sir George Prevost*; however, Prevost did not approve and the vessel was renamed *Wolfe*. Malcomson, *Lords of the Lake*, 98.

41. Ibid., 120.

42. The British used several types of vessel to transport supplies and move personnel between Upper and Lower Canada. While bateaux, Durham boats, and Schenectady boats varied in dimension, performance, and capacity, the Commissariat or the Quartermaster General's Department of the army did not distinguish between each type of vessel in its records, which means that the term "bateau" applied to any riverboat, whether it was a Durham boat, Schenectady boat, or bateau that was used to move supplies. "Bateau" will be used throughout to describe any watercraft used on the line of communication. John R. Grodzinski, "The Vigilant Superintendence of the Whole District: The War of 1812 on the Upper St Lawrence" (Master's thesis, Royal Military College of Canada, 2002), 13–15.

43. Between 1807 and 1812, some 350 men operated 50 bateaux between Montreal to Kingston. By 1812, this had risen to 165 boats worked by 1,300 men.

44. John P. Heisler, *The Canals of Canada* (Ottawa: National Historic Sites, 1973), 19, 20, 24; Robert Legget, *Ottawa River Canals and the Defence of British North America* (Toronto: University of Toronto Press, 1982), 29, 30; Prevost to Drummond, 29 November 1814, LAC, RG 8 C vol. 1222: 244.

45. General Order Quebec, 24 April 1812, LAC, RG 8 C vol. 1168: 129–30; Prevost to Brock, 24 December 1811, Cruikshank, *DH* 3:27. See Steppler, "Duty Troublesome beyond Measure," 35, 128–31.

46. "List of Indian Warriors as They Stood in 1812 at the Time War was Declared," reproduced in Allen, *His Majesty's Indian Allies*, 219, 220 (the original document is in the Ontario Archives, Toronto, Strachan Papers, MS 35); Hitsman, *Incredible War of 1812*, 100, 302, 303.

47. Carl Benn, *The Iroquois in the War of 1812* (Toronto: University of Toronto Press, 1998), 32, 33; Carl F. Klinck and James J. Talman with Additional Notes by Carl Benn, *The Journal of Major John Norton, 1816* (Toronto: Champlain Society, 2011), ciii, civ, cv.

48. In an effort to preserve the Native alliance in the aftermath of the American War of Independence, Britain retained seven outposts that were now within the borders of the United States. British officials believed that holding the three westernmost outposts at Mackinac, Detroit, and Miami would also serve to check American expansion into the Northwest and realize hopes for the establishment of a Native territory in the region. The transfer of these posts to the United States in 1796 ended this phase of Anglo-Native relations and necessitated the rebuilding of the alliance. Allen, *His Majesty's Indian Allies*, 55, 56, 88.

49. Ibid., 112, 113, 115.

50. Benn, *Iroquois in the War of 1812*, 62.

51. The lands of the Hudson's Bay Company lay northwest of the North West Company's territory, and their traders and bateau operators were of less assistance.

52. Prevost to Liverpool, No. 44, 16 May 1812, RMC, CO 42/146: 255.

53. Gray to Prevost, 13 January 1812, *Michigan Pioneer and Historical Record* 15 (1909): 70; Reginald Horsman, "British Indian Policy in the Northwest, 1807–1812," *Mississippi Valley Historical Review* 45, no. 1 (1958): 52, 61, 62; Lothier to Gray, n.d., "Memoranda from the Agents of the North West Company for the Information of Captain Gray," *Michigan Pioneer and Historical Record* 15 (1909): 69, 70; No. 2 Confidential Communication Transmitted by Mr. Robert Dickson, 18 June 1812, in Wood, *Select British Documents*, 1:424.

54. Chartrand and Graves, "United States Army of the War of 1812," 36, 37; Robert S. Quimby, *U.S. Army in the War of 1812*, 1:2, 3; Stagg, *Mr. Madison's War*, 146, 162, 164.

55. Quimby, *U.S. Army in the War of 1812*, 1:18.

56. Chartrand and Graves, "United States Army of the War of 1812," 36, 37, 41, 42, 43; Quimby, *U.S. Army in the War of 1812*, 1:2, 3, 55; Alec R. Calpin, *The War of 1812 in the Old Northwest* (Toronto: Ryerson Press, 1958), 23, 29.

57. Robert Malcomson, *Historical Dictionary of the War of 1812* (Latham, Md.: Scarecrow Press, 2006), 577; Malcomson, *Warships of the Great Lakes*, 55, 85.

58. Liverpool to Prevost, 13 February 1812, TNA, CO 43/23: 90–91.

59. Prevost to Liverpool, 18 May 1812, RMC, CO 42/146: 197.

60. Ibid.

61. Ibid., 198.

62. Ibid.

63. Ibid.

64. Ibid., 196.

65. Prevost to Liverpool, 18 May 1812, RMC, CO 42/146: 198, 199.

66. Ibid., 201. Prevost may have borrowed this idea from Craig, who wrote much the same thing to Lieutenant Governor Gore in December 1807: "It would be in vain for us to flatter ourselves with the hope of making any effectual defence of the open country, unless powerfully assisted from home." Craig to Gore, 6 December 1807, RMC, CO 42/136: 209.

67. Prevost to Liverpool, 18 May 1812, RMC, CO 42/146: 199.
68. Ibid., 200.
69. Prevost to Liverpool, 18 May 1812, CO 42/146: n.p.
70. Liverpool to Prevost [draft], 15 May 1812, RMC, CO 42/146: 170.
71. Craig was instructed that the preservation of Quebec was his principal object as it would be impossible to defend both Canadas. See Craig to Gore, 6 December 1807, RMC, CO 42/136: 154.
72. Liverpool to Prevost [draft], 15 May 1812, RMC, CO 42/146: 171.
73. Extract from a letter from Prevost to Brock, 31 March 1812, RMC, CO 42/146: 122.
74. Baynes to Brock, 21 May 1812, Cruikshank, DH 1:64. Baynes quoted British reports written in April in this letter.
75. Prevost to Brock, 24 December 1811, Ferdinand Brock Tupper, ed., The Life and Correspondence of Major General Sir Isaac Brock (London: Simpkin, Marshall & Company, 1845), 153.
76. Extract from a letter from Prevost to Brock, 31 March 1812, RMC, CO 42/146: 122.
77. Prevost to Brock, 27 May 1812, Cruikshank, DH 1:65.
78. Prevost to Brock, 31 March 1812, RMC, CO 42/146: 183. The same wording was used in a letter to Sherbrooke; see Prevost to Liverpool, 3 April 1812, RMC, CO 42/146: 181.
79. Prevost to Brock, 31 March 1812, RMC, CO 43/146: 183.
80. Bathurst to Prevost, 4 July 1812, TNA, CO 43/23: 126.

4. DECLARATION OF WAR AND
MILITARY OPERATIONS IN 1812

1. Hickey, Don't Give Up the Ship!, 41.
2. The British government did not respond with its own declaration of war and chose to proceed on the hope that repeal of the Orders in Council would reverse the American decision. When it became clear that a state of war would continue, the Orders in Council were reinstated in October 1812. From the American perspective, this reaffirmation of the British position regarding trade was tantamount to a declaration of war against the United States. For a discussion of this topic, see Hickey, Don't Give Up the Ship!, 43–44.
3. Prevost to Liverpool, 29 June 1812, RMC, CO 42/147: 5.
4. Bathurst to Prevost (No. 5) [draft], 10 August 1812, RMC, CO 42/147: 32.
5. Harrowby to Bathurst, 17 September 1812, in Report on the Manuscripts of Earl Bathurst (London: His Majesty's Stationery Office, 1923), 214.
6. Turner, British Generals, 82.
7. A. M. J. Hyatt, "The Defence of Upper Canada in 1812" (Master's thesis, Carleton University, 1961), 12; Turner, British Generals, 82.
8. Hyatt, "Defence of Upper Canada," 39, 40.
9. This island and its fort are sometimes referred to as Michilimackinac. In 1715, the French established Fort Michilimackinac on the northern tip of the Lower Michigan Peninsula, now the location of modern Mackinaw City. In 1761, France relinquished control of the fort to Britain. During the

American War of Independence, the British feared this location was too exposed to attack and relocated the post to Mackinac Island, where a new fort was completed by 1781. In 1796, the island was transferred to the United States and became the northernmost outpost of the United States. The distinction between the two names may have been just as lost on people at the time as it has been to historians today. Brian Leigh Dunnigan, *King's Men at Mackinac: The British Garrisons, 1780–1796* (Mackinac, Mich.: Mackinac State Historic Parks, 1973), 7, 8; Brian Leigh Dunnigan, *The British Army at Mackinac, 1812–1815* (Mackinac, Mich.: Mackinac State Historic Parks, 1992), 5.

10. Gore to Craig, 5 January 1808, RMC, CO 42/136: 238.

11. Brock to Gordon, 6 September 1807, in Tupper, *Life and Correspondence of Brock*, 65.

12. Brock presented most of these ideas in a letter to Prevost dated 2 December 1811, LAC, RG 8 C vol. 3171: 171–81.

13. Baynes to Brock, 8 July 1812, Cruikshank, *DH* 3:114.

14. Castlereagh to the Lords Commissioners of the Admiralty, 9 May 1812, quoted in Brian Arthur, *How Britain Won the War of 1812: The Royal Navy's Blockades of the United States, 1812–1815* (Woodbridge: Boydell Press, 2011), 28.

15. Ibid., 29, 68, 72, 73.

16. Prevost to Liverpool, No. 57, 15 July 1812, RMC, CO 42/147: 39; Prevost to Brock, 7 July 1812, Cruikshank, *DH* 3:113, 114; Brock to Prevost, 3 July 1812, LAC, RG 8 C vol. 3172: 115; Baynes to Brock, 4 July 1812, Cruikshank, *DH* 3:100; Baynes to Brock, 8 July 1812, Cruikshank, *DH* 3:114, 115.

17. The fort was named after the local community, and it was later referred to as Fort Malden. The original name of Fort Amherstburg will be used here.

18. Secretary of War Eustis to Hull, 24 June 1812, in E. A. Cruikshank, ed., *Documents Relating to the Invasion of Canada and the Surrender of Detroit, 1812* (Ottawa: Government Printing Bureau, 1912), 37.

19. Brock to Prevost, 3 July 1812, in Cruikshank, *DH* 3:94; Baynes to Brock, 8 July 1812, Cruikshank, *DH* 3:115; Prevost to Liverpool, 30 July 1812, in Cruikshank, *Documents Relating to the Invasion of Canada*, 109, 110; Prevost to Brock, 31 July 1812, in Cruikshank, *Documents Relating to the Invasion of Canada*, 114; Prevost to Brock, 12 August 1812, Cruikshank, *DH* 3:167; Prevost to Liverpool, 15 July 1812, RMC, CO 42/118: 39; Hyatt, "Defence of Upper Canada," 77; Monthly Returns for 25 May 1812, TNA, WO 17/1516.

20. The number of regulars varies between forty-five, forty-six, or forty-seven men depending on the source. One sergeant and two gunners of the Royal Artillery accompanied the expedition. Dunnigan, *British Army at Mackinac*, 11, provides a figure of forty-six, four of whom were officers. His figures are derived from an inspection report dated 25 June 1812; forty-seven are reported in Barry Gough, *Fighting Sail on Lake Huron and Georgian Bay The War of 1812 and Its Aftermath* (Annapolis: Naval Institute Press, 2002), 22. Malcomson, *Historical Dictionary of the War of 1812*, 337,

gives a figure of forty-six. Among the Native contingent were members of the Ottawa, Chippewa, Sioux, Menominee, and Winnebago peoples. Dunnigan, *British Army at Mackinac*, 11.

21. Roberts to Baynes, 17 July 1812, in Cruikshank, *Documents Relating to the Invasion of Canada*, 65; Prevost to Brock, 12 August 1812, in Cruikshank, *DH* 3:168, 169; Hyatt, "Defence of Upper Canada," 70, 71; Gough, *Fighting Sail*, 22, 23; John Abbott, Graeme S. Mount, and Michael J. Mulloy, *The Story of Fort St. Joseph* (Toronto: Dundurn, 2000), 97, 98.

22. Prevost to Brock, 2 August 1812, in Tupper, *Life and Correspondence of Brock*, 232.

23. Brock to his brothers, 3 September 1812, in Tupper, *Life and Correspondence of Brock*, 297.

24. Prevost to Brock, 27 July 1812, in Wood, *Select British Documents*, 1:382.

25. Prevost to Liverpool, 15 July 1812, RMC, CO 42/147: 35. This passage was omitted from the dispatch reproduced in Cruikshank's documentary history of the war. See Prevost to Liverpool, 15 July 1812, in Cruikshank, *DH* 3:128–30.

26. Brock to Prevost, 20 July 1812, LAC, RG 8 C vol. 3173: 203; Prevost to Brock, 27 July 1812, in Wood, *Select British Documents*, 1:381; Robert H. Patterson, *Pontius Pilate's Bodyguard: A History of the First or the Royal Regiment of Foot*, vol. 1 (Edinburgh: Royal Scots History Committee, 2000), 111.

27. Steppler, "Duty Troublesome beyond Measure," 70, 71, 75, 77, 79; Graham, *Sea Power and British North America*, 199; P. J. Marshall, "British North America, 1760–1815," in Marshall, *Oxford History of the British Empire*, 2:386, 387; W. Freeman Galpin, "The American Grain Trade to the Spanish Peninsula, 1810–1814," *American Historical Review* 28 (1923): 24, 25, 26, 28. Almost 2 million barrels of grain were sent to Portugal and Spain before this trade was terminated in late 1813.

28. Prevost to Brock, 12 August 1812, in Cruikshank, *DH* 3:169.

29. Tupper, *Life and Correspondence of Brock*, 223; Baynes to Roberts, 25 June 1812, LAC, RG 8 C vol. 3231: 121.

30. Brock to Prevost, 17 August 1812, in Cruikshank, *Documents Relating to the Invasion of Canada*, 158; Sandy Antal, *A Wampum Denied: Procter's War of 1812* (Ottawa: Carleton University Press, 1997), 35, 36, 80, 94; Gillum Ferguson, *Illinois in the War of 1812* (Urbana: University of Illinois, 2012), 56, 61.

31. Prevost to Bathurst, 5 October 1812, RMC, CO 42/147: 265; Prevost to Bathurst, 9 December 1812, RMC, CO 42/147: 238. Prevost's correspondence following the American capitulation at Detroit says nothing of this matter, including his dispatch to Bathurst, which announced the victory at Detroit. He did make this the subject of a lengthy report to Bathurst in October 1812. Prevost to Bathurst, 26 August 1812, in Cruikshank, *Documents Relating to the Invasion of Canada*, 181–84; Prevost to Brock, 14 September 1812, in Tupper, *Life and Correspondence of Brock*, 291, 292; Antal, *Wampum Denied*, 105, 106.

32. Prevost to Dearborn, 2 August 1812, RMC, CO 42/147: 123; Prevost to Brock, 2 August 1812, in Tupper, *Life and Correspondence of Brock*, 231,

232, Baynes to Brock, 13 August 1812, in Cruikshank, *DH* 3:172; Dearborn to Hall, 8 August 1812, in Cruikshank, *DH* 3:169; Dearborn to Prevost, 26 August 1812, in Cruikshank, *DH* 3:215; Sheaffe to Prevost, 22 August 1812, in Wood, *Select British Documents*, 1:580, 581.

33. Secretary of War to Dearborn, 15 August 1812, in Cruikshank, *DH* 3:181.

34. Brock to Prevost, 13 September 1812, in Cruikshank, *DH* 3:258.

35. Wood, *Select British Documents*, 1:32; Brock to Prevost, 13 September 1812, LAC, RG 8 C vol. 3172: 81; Brock to Prevost, 18 September 1812, LAC, RG 8 C vol. 3172: 90.

36. Parish to Hamilton, 21 June 1812, in Dudley, *Naval War of 1812*, 1:276; Prevost to Bathurst, 17 August 1812, RMC, CO 42/147: 177; Malcomson, *Lords of the Lake*, 35, 47, 48, 329, 330; David Curtis Skaggs and Gerard T. Altoff, *A Signal Victory: The Lake Erie Campaign, 1812–1813* (Annapolis: Naval Institute Press, 1997), 37, 38.

37. Brock to Prevost, 7 September 1812, in Cruikshank, *DH* 3:243; Prevost to Brock, 14 September 1812, LAC, RG 8 C vol. 3172: 64; Robert Malcomson, *A Very Brilliant Affair: The Battle of Queenston Heights, 1812* (Toronto: Robin Brass Studio, 2003), 272–74.

38. The original letter has been lost but is referred to in Brock to Prevost, 18 September 1812, in Wood, *Select British Documents*, 1:592.

39. Brock to Prevost, 18 September 1812, in Wood, *Select British Documents*, 1:593, 594.

40. Brock to Prevost, 7 September 1812, LAC, RG 8 C vol. 3172: 64; General Brock to Savery Brock, 18 September 1812, in Cruikshank, *DH* 3:278.

41. Prevost to Brock, 14 September 1812, in Tupper, *Life and Correspondence of Brock*, 309.

42. Van Rensselaer to Dearborn, 27 September 1812, in Cruikshank, *DH* 3:298, Van Rensselaer to Dearborn, 8 October 1812, in Cruikshank, *DH* 4:42.

43. Both Malcomson and Riley note that Brock "probably" sent riders out for reinforcements. See Malcomson, *Very Brilliant Affair*, 143, 145, 147–50; and Riley, *Matter of Honour*, 280.

44. Van Rensselaer to Dearborn, 27 September 1812, in Cruikshank, *DH* 3:298; Van Rensselaer to Dearborn, 8 October 1812, in Cruikshank, *DH* 4:42. For a discussion of Van Rensselaer's role in the battle, see Malcomson, *Very Brilliant Affair*, 209–12. For an examination of the role played by Sheaffe and Native forces in the battle, see Benn, *Iroquois in the War of 1812*, 96, 97, 98.

45. Allan S. Everest, *The War of 1812 in the Champlain Valley* (Syracuse, N.Y.: Syracuse University Press, 1981), 90, 91, 92; Quimby, *U.S. Army in the War of 1812*, 1:81, 82.

46. Chauncey to Hamilton, 13 November 1812, in Dudley, *Naval War of 1812*, 1:346.

47. Chauncey to Hamilton, 17 November 1812, in Dudley, *Naval War of 1812*, 1:328.

48. Malcomson, *Lords of the Lake*, 31, 33, 34, 328, table 3; Prevost to Bathurst, 17 October 1812, RMC, CO 42/147: 273.

49. Gray to Prevost, 3 December 1812, LAC RG 8 I vol. 3243: 135.

50. Ibid. For an account of the Provincial Marine raid on Sackets Harbor, see Richard A. Preston, "The First Battle of Sackets Harbor," *Historic Kingston*, no. 11 (1961–62): 3–7.

51. Ibid.; Gray to Prevost, 11 December 1812, LAC, RG 8 C vol. 3172: 243.

52. Ibid.

53. Gray to Prevost, 3 December 1812, LAC, RG 8 C vol. 3242: 135.

54. Ibid.

55. Prevost to Gray, 19 December 1812, LAC, RG 8 C vol. 3243: 197.

56. Ibid.

57. Prevost to Bathurst, 26 October 1812, RMC, CO 42/148: 2.

58. Prevost to Gray, 19 December 1812, LAC, RG 8 C vol. 3243: 197.

59. Prevost to Warren, 18 December 1812, enclosed with Warren to Croker, 21 February 1813, TNA, Adm 1/503: 163; Warren to Croker, 21 February 1813, TNA, Adm 1/503: 163, 170. Warren stipulated that the men and stores be sent as early in the season as possible, suggesting this would occur in May 1813.

60. Malcomson, *Lords of the Lake*, 31, 33, 34; Prevost to Bathurst, No. 16, 5 November 1812, RMC, CO 42/148: 5–17; Chauncey to Hamilton, 13 November 1812, in Dudley, *Naval War of 1812*, 2:344–46.

61. Following the Napoleonic Wars, Douglas turned his attention toward improving naval gunnery and is best known for his influential text *Treatise of Naval Gunnery*, which went through five editions between 1820 and 1861. See "Sir Howard Douglas," q.v., *Oxford Dictionary of National Biography*, doi:10.1093/ref:odnb/7888; *Oxford DNB* online entries cited in the notes also may be found in the print edition).

62. Douglas to Bathurst, 20 December 1812, in Cruikshank, *DH* 4:332, 333.

63. Ibid.

64. Commodore was not a rank in the Royal Navy but a post identifying the senior captain in command of a detached squadron or important shore post. This post was a temporary appointment that allowed the Admiralty to reach as far down the list of captains they chose without that individual suffering a loss of seniority or ruffling the feathers of more senior flag rank appointees. The appointment of commodore had the further distinction of being commodore "with a captain" and "with a pendant," which by 1805 became commodore first class and second class, respectively. A commodore first class commanded a squadron or station and for the purposes of pay and uniform was a temporary rear admiral. The commodore with pendant commanded a detached squadron or a division of the fleet. Yeo arrived in Canada as a commodore with a pendant and was elevated to commodore first class in early 1814. See N. A. M. Rodger, "Commissioned Officers Careers in the Royal Navy, 1690–1815," in N. A. M. Rodger, ed., *Essays in Naval History, from Medieval to Modern* (Farnham, UK: Ashgate, 2009), pt. 15: 4–5; Michael Lewis, *A Social History of the Navy, 1793–1815* (London: Chatham Publishing, 1960), 187; N. A. M. Rodger, *The*

Wooden World: An Anatomy of the Georgian Navy (London: Fontana Press, 1988), 17; Rodger, *Command of the Ocean*, 119, 325, 326.

65. Stuart Reid, *Wellington's Officers*, vol. 1 (Leigh-on-Sea: Partizan Press, 2008), 211–12; "Sir Howard Douglas," *Oxford DNB*.

5. OPERATIONS AROUND LAKE ONTARIO INTENSIFY

1. Prevost to Bathurst, 21 April 1813, RMC, CO 42/151: 194.

2. On 15 March 1813, Prevost inspected the six companies of the 104th Foot at Quebec. Lieutenant John Le Couteur later recorded that the commander in chief "paid us the highest compliments." In May, two other companies followed by sea and the last two companies, stationed on Prince Edward Island and Cape Breton, remained there until 1814 when they joined the regiment at Kingston. Bathurst to Prevost, 9 December 1812, RMC, CO 42/147: 239; Prevost to Bathurst, 16 January 1813, RMC, CO 42/150: 19; Squires, *The 104th Regiment of Foot*, 113, 136, 137; Inspection Report 104th Foot, 11 June 1813, TNA, WO 27/108; Donald E. Graves, ed., *Merry Hearts Make Light Days: The War of 1812 Journal of Lieutenant John Le Couteur, 104th Foot* (Ottawa: Carleton University Press, 1993), 102, 107n25, 107n26.

3. Prevost to Bathurst, 8 February 1813, RMC, CO 42/150: 59; Sheaffe to Prevost, 13 March 1813, Cruikshank *DH* 5:111; Prevost to Bathurst, 21 April 1813, RMC, CO 42/150: 194; Hitsman, *Incredible War of 1812*, 117. The terms of service and capabilities of the sedentary and embodied militias are presented in William Gray, *Soldiers of the King: The Upper Canadian Militia, 1812–1815* (Toronto: Stoddart, 1995), 32, 179, 180, 187–194.

4. "Instructions for Robt Dickson Esqr Appointed Agent for the Indians of the Nations to the Westward of Lake Huron," 14 January 1813, in *Michigan Pioneer and Historical Record* 15 (1889): 220.

5. Ibid., 220, 221.

6. Galpin, *War of 1812 in the Northwest*, 195, 195; Ferguson, *Illinois in the War of 1812*, 73.

7. Prevost to Bathurst, 6 February 1813, RMC, CO 42/150: 56.

8. The termination of the move of the naval base was not announced in any specific order, but through a series of letters to various commanders. See Robert Malcomson, *Capital in Flames: The American Attack on York, 1813* (Montreal: Robin Brass Studio, 2008), 116, 117, 428n48. Bruyeres enjoyed Prevost's confidence and emphasized the advantages of concentrating the naval establishment at Kingston. Bruyeres to Prevost, 19 January 1813, LAC, RG 8C vol. 387: 10; Prevost to Bathurst, 15 January 1813, RMC, CO 42/150: 2; Prevost to Bathurst, 21 April 1813, RMC, CO 42/150: 194; and General Order, 1 March 1813; District General Order No. 1, 3 March 1813; District General Order No. 2, 3 March 1813; District General Order No. 3, 3 March 1813, in Cruikshank, *DH* 5:84–86.

9. Prevost to Bathurst, 27 February 1813, RMC, CO 42/150: 122.

10. Notes on the Conduct of Major General R. H. Sheaffe and Major General Vincent, n.d., in Cruikshank, *DH* 5:35. The author of this document, Lieutenant Colonel Cecil Bisshopp, the commander of Fort Erie, complained that in November 1812 Sheaffe had willingly left the fort weak and

was willing to surrender it to the Americans despite having reinforcements at hand.

11. Prevost to Bathurst, 19 March 1813, RMC, CO 42/150: 146.

12. Prevost to Sheaffe, 8 November 1812, LAC, RG 8C vol. 677: 173; Malcomson, *Capital in Flames*, 39; Turner, *British Generals*, 87.

13. Prevost to Bathurst, 16 January 1813, RMC, CO 42/150: 18.

14. Hitsman, *Incredible War of 1812*, 132.

15. W. S. Buell, "Red George: One of the Macdonells," *Canadian Historical Review* 4 (1923): 152.

16. Prevost to Macdonell, 22 February 1813, in Philalethes, " Late War in Canada," March 1848, 436, 437.

17. General Orders, Montreal, 25 February 1813, in Cruikshank, *DH* 3:70.

18. This name was used by several ancient writers and in Masonic circles. Johnston, *Glengarry Light Infantry*, 242, 243, 244; Philalethes, "Late War in Canada," March 1848, 425–41; Philalethes, "Late War in Canada," June 1848, 271–83.

19. Philalethes, "Late War in Canada," June 1848, 274, 275.

20. Macdonell to Earl Gray, 8 April 1850, quoted in Carol M. Whitfield, "Macdonell (McDonald), George Richard John," q.v., *Dictionary of Canadian Biography Online*, http://www.biographi.ca/009004-119.01-e.php?&id _nbr=4559&interval=20&&PHPSESSID=j7p6npeiov6eipuap8p55v1br2.

21. Philalethes, "Late War in Canada," March 1848, 437.

22. Ibid., 426, 431, 435; Philalethes, "Late War in Canada," June 1848, 271, 274, 283. Macdonell was not wholly critical of Prevost and was critical of the limited resources he was given during the war and shocked by the treatment he received afterward.

23. Bruyeres to Prevost, 12 January 1813, LAC, RG 8C vol. 387: 5–8; Grodzinski, *Superintendence of the Entire District*, 118, 122–24.

24. Warren to Prevost, 7 June 1813, LAC, RG 8C vol. 3172: 43–46. I am indebted to Dr. Gary M. Gibson for providing details of the friendship between Warren and Yeo.

25. Douglas to Bathurst, 20 December 1812, in Cruikshank, *DH* 4:332, 333; D. Murray Young, "Douglas, Sir Howard," q.v., *Dictionary of Canadian Biography Online*, http://www.biographi.ca/009004-119.01-e.php?&id _nbr=4402; *Naval Chronicle* 15 (1806): 223, in Dudley, *Naval War of 1812*, 1:595; Lords Commissioners of the Admiralty to Yeo, 13 March 1813, in Dudley, *Naval War of 1812*, 1:436; Croker to Yeo, 19 March 1813, in Dudley, *Naval War of 1812*, 1:436, 437; Prevost to Bathurst, 8 February 1813, RMC, CO 42/150: 68.

26. In early 1806, Yeo had also been one of more than 100 naval captains in the procession at Vice Admiral Lord Nelson's funeral in London.

27. As in all cases where a ship was lost, Yeo sat before an Admiralty court-martial; he was acquitted of any blame for the incident. J. K. Laughton, "Sir James Lucas Yeo," q.v., *Oxford Dictionary of National Biography*, doi:10.1093/ref:odnb/30217; Malcomson, *Lords of the Lake*, 116, 119; Christopher D. Hall, *Wellington's Navy: Sea Power and the Peninsular War, 1807–1814* (London: Chatham Publishing, 2004), 24. For an account of

Yeo's capture of the American brig *Vixen,* see *Narrative of the Capture of the United States Brig* Vixen *by the British Frigate Southampton and the Subsequent Loss of Both Vessels* (New York, 1813).

28. Croker to Yeo, 19 March 1813, in Dudley, *Naval War of 1812,* 1:436–37; Bathurst to Prevost, 12 March 1813, LAC, RG 8 C vol. 3172: 123.

29. Prevost to Bathurst, 18 May 1813, RMC, CO 42/150: 225.

30. Captain Gray to Prevost, 12 March 1813, in Cruikshank, *DH* 5:107–11; Prevost to Bathurst, 21 November 1812, RMC, CO 42/148: 43.

31. Prevost to Bathurst, 18 May 1813, RMC, CO 42/150: 225.

32. Lords Commissioners to Yeo, 19 March 1813, in Dudley, *Naval War of 1812,* 2:435, 436.

33. Ibid., 436.

34. Croker to Yeo, 19 March 1813, in Dudley, *Naval War of 1812,* 2:436.

35. Admiralty to Yeo, 23 March 1813, TNA ADM 2/1376: 823; Lords Commissioners to Yeo, 19 March 1813, in Dudley, *Naval War of 1812,* 2:436; Gwyn, *Frigates and Foremasts,* 138.

36. Lords Commissioners to Yeo, 19 March 1813, in Dudley, *Naval War of 1812,* 2:436.

37. In contrast to British practice, the American secretary of the navy appointed a commodore to command both Lakes Ontario and Erie, with separate commanders on Lake Champlain and the Upper Great Lakes as required. Each of these commanders reported directly to the secretary of the navy. Lakes Ontario and Erie were the most important initially, with a lieutenant being assigned to Lake Champlain, but as the magnitude of the naval war increased, the rank of the commander on Lake Champlain was advanced to captain. See related correspondence in Dudley, *Naval War of 1812,* 1:296, 319.

38. Ibid., 2.435–36; Lavery, *Nelson's Navy,* 245, 251.

39. Yeo to Croker, 26 May 1813, in Cruikshank, *DH* 5:244.

40. Chauncey to Jones, 18 March 1813, in Dudley, *Naval War of 1812,* 2:431, 432.

41. Prevost to Brock, 31 July 1811, in Cruikshank, *DH* 3:154; Carl Benn, *Historic Fort York, 1793–1993* (Toronto: Natural Heritage, 1993), 49, 50; Malcomson, *Capital in Flames,* 95.

42. Benn, *Historic Fort York,* 51, 53, 54, 56, 63; C. P. Stacey, *The Battle of Little York* (Toronto: Toronto Historical Board, 1977), 21; Malcomson, *Capital in Flames,* 72; Malcomson, *Warships of the Great Lakes,* 45, 100; Chauncey to Jones, 18 March 1813, in Dudley, *Naval War of 1812,* 2:431.

43. Prevost to Bathurst, 26 May 1813, LAC, RG 8 C vol. 1221: 106.

44. Prevost to Bathurst, 24 June 1813, RMC, CO 42/151: 41; General Order, 6 June 1813, in Cruikshank, *DH* 6:5; Prevost to Bathurst, 24 June 1813, RMC, CO 42/151: 41; "An Account of the Capture of York," in Cruikshank, *DH* 5:176; Malcomson, *Capital in Flames,* 278, 441n8.

45. Chauncey to the Secretary of the Navy, 21 January 1813, in Dudley, *Naval War of 1812,* 2:418.

46. Chauncey to Jones, 18 March 1813, in Dudley, *Naval War of 1812,* 2:431.

47. Dearborn to Armstrong, 28 April 1813, in Dudley, *Naval War of 1812*, 2:451, 452. See Malcomson, *Capital in Flames*, 349, 355; and Distribution of Forces in Canada, May 1813, LAC, RG 8 C vol. 1707, 61.

48. The abandonment of the peninsula by the British and fears that the withdrawal would continue to Kingston, leaving the Grand River reserve exposed to American attack, caused the Iroquois warriors to leave Vincent's army for their homes. Appeals by Indian Department officials for them to return to the field were ignored. Benn, *Iroquois in the War of 1812*, 109.

49. Freer to Sheaffe, 23 March 1813, LAC, RG 8 C vol. 3232: 28; Prevost to Bathurst, 1 June 1813, RMC, CO 42/150: 175.

50. Prevost to Bathurst, 1 June 1813, RMC, CO 42/150: 175.

51. Ibid.; Malcomson, *Lords of the Lake*, 129.

52. Donald E. Graves, *The Attack on Sackets Harbor, 29 May 1813: The British/Canadian Side* (Ottawa: Directorate of History, ca. 1991). For an overview of Yeo's career, see Malcomson, *Lords of the Lake*, 115–19, 130; Graves, *Attack on Sackets Harbor*.

53. Graves, *Attack on Sackets Harbor*; Malcomson, *Lords of the Lake*, 130.

54. Baynes to Prevost, 30 May 1813, in Cruikshank, *DH* 5:276; Brenton to Freer, 30 May 1813, in Cruikshank, *DH* 5:279; Patrick Wilder, " 'We Will Not Conquer Canada This Year': The Battle of Sacket's Harbor" (unpublished manuscript in the author's possession), chap. 5, pp. 10, 12, 13.

55. David Ellison, "David Wingfield and Sacketts Harbour," *Dalhousie Review 52* (1972): 409.

56. Brenton to Freer, 30 May 1813, in Cruikshank, *DH* 5:280.

57. Brenton, *Some Account of the Public Life*, 82.

58. David Wingfield, "Four Years on the Lakes in Canada in 1813, 1814, 1815 and 1816; by a Naval Officer under the Command of the late Sir James Lucas Yeo," LAC, MG 24, F 18: 7.

59. Brenton, *Some Account of the Public Life*, 85.

60. Ibid., 82, 83, 85.

61. Patrick A. Wilder, *The Battle of Sackets Harbour, 1813* (Baltimore: Nautical and Aviation Publishing Company, 1994), 72, 82; Graves, *Attack on Sackets Harbor*.

62. Wilder, "We Will Not Conquer Canada," chap. 3, pp. 10, 14, 18; chap. 4, pp. 18, 19, 20.

63. Prevost to Bathurst, 1 June 1813, RMC, CO 42/150: 175; Graves, *Attack on Sackets Harbor*.

64. Graves, *Attack on Sackets Harbor*.

65. Baynes to Prevost, 30 May 1813, in Cruikshank, *DH* 5:277, 278; Graves, *Attack on Sackets Harbor*.

66. Prevost to Bathurst, 1 June 1813, RMC, CO 42/150: 175.

67. Prevost to Bathurst, 1 June 1813, RMC, CO 42/150: 281; Baynes to Prevost, 30 May 1813, in Cruikshank, *DH* 5:277, 278; Brenton to Freer, 30 May 1813, LAC, RG 8 C vol. 1707: 236; Graves, *Attack on Sackets Harbor*; Wilder, *Battle of Sackets Harbour*, 72, 108.

68. Wilder, *Battle of Sackets Harbour*, 110; Brenton to Freer, 30 May 1813, LAC, RG 8 C vol. 1707: 236.

69. Graves, *Merry Hearts Make Light Days*, 116; Dearborn to Armstrong, 8 June 1813, in Cruikshank, *DH* 6:55; Chauncey to Secretary of the Navy Jones, 11 June 1813, in Dudley, *Naval War of 1812*, 2:493.

70. Chauncey to Secretary of the Navy Jones, 2 June 1813, in Dudley, *Naval War of 1812*, 2:477, 478.

71. Ibid.

72. For an overview of these firsthand accounts, see Wilder, *Battle of Sackets Harbour;* and Graves, *Attack on Sackets Harbor.*

73. Graves, *Merry Hearts Make Light Days*, 116.

74. Ibid., 117.

75. Ibid.

76. Yeo to Croker, 31 May 1813, NA, Adm 1/2736: 82.

77. Richardson Memoir, in Robert Malcomson, ed., *Sailors of 1812: Memoirs and Letters of Naval Officers on Lake Ontario* (Youngstown, N.Y.: Old Fort Niagara Association, 1997), 29.

78. Wingfield, "Four Years on the Lakes," LAC, MG 24, F 18: 10.

79. Ibid.

80. Wesley Turner, *The War of 1812: The War Both Sides Won* (Toronto: Dundurn, 1990), 66.

81. Turner, *British Generals*, 37, 38.

82. J. Mackay Hitsman, "Alarum on Lake Ontario, Winter 1812–13," in Morris Zaslow, ed., *The Defended Border: Upper Canada and the War of 1812* (Toronto: Macmillan of Canada, 1964), 55.

83. Dudley, *Naval War of 1812*, 2:467; Wilder, *Battle of Sackets Harbour*, 118, 120, 121.

84. Fortescue, *History of the British Army*, 9:321.

85. George F. G. Stanley, *The War of 1812: Land Operations* (Ottawa: Macmillan of Canada, 1983), 239.

86. Ibid.

87. Graves, *Attack on Sackets Harbor.*

88. Ibid.

89. Ibid.

90. Lavery, *Nelson's Navy*, 310, 313, 316. The map at p. 311 illustrates the location of major operations around the globe between 1793 and 1815. Hugh Boscowen, *The Capture of Louisbourg, 1758* (Norman: University of Oklahoma Press, 2011), 316, 317, 319; Paul M. Kennedy, *The Rise and Fall of British Naval Mastery* (Malabar, Fla.: Robert E. Krieger Publishing Company, 1982), 138; Hall, *Wellington's Navy*, 1, 30, 232; Nick Lipsombe, *The Peninsular War Atlas* (London: Osprey Publishing, 2010), 64, 96.

91. British casualties at Queenston Heights totaled about 105 soldiers and five warriors. The losses at Stoney Creek included 23 killed, 135 wounded, and 55 missing, for a total of 213. At Châteauguay the British lost 22 men: two killed, 16 wounded, and four prisoners of war; 179 casualties were suffered at Crysler's Farm, including 22 dead, 148 wounded, and nine missing. Total losses at York, including militia, volunteers, dockyard workers, Provincial Marines, and regular troops, were 475; 166 of them were regulars. "General Return of Killed Wounded and Missing in an Action with the Enemy Near the Head of Lake Ontario, 6 June 1813," LAC,

RG 8 C vol. 3172: 35; Malcomson, *Very Brilliant Affair*, 196; Donald E. Graves, *Field of Glory: The Battle of Crysler's Farm, 1813* (Toronto: Robin Brass Studio, 1999), 109.

92. Dearborn responded to the loss of Brigadier Generals John Chandler and William Winder by ordering Major General Morgan Lewis to take command of the troops at Forty Mile Creek, while Brigadier General John Parker Boyd and Brigadier General Robert Swartout were to take command of the brigades. Elliot, *Strange Fatality*, 159.

93. The outcome at Stoney Creek restored the confidence of the Grand River Iroquois, and a number of warriors rejoined the Center Division. They were joined by a reinforcement arranged by agents of the Indian Department from the Seven Nations around Montreal that arrived in the Niagara region around the same time. The arrival of these two groups, which on 24 June 1813 would play a key role at the Battle of Beaver Dams, increased the strength of Vincent's Native contingent to nearly 800 tribesmen. Benn, *Iroquois in the War of 1812*, 109, 114.

94. Summary from Malcomson, *Lords of the Lake*, 148–51.

6. THE CANADAS SURVIVE REPEATED INVASION

1. Both officers had been promoted to the rank of major general in June 1813.

2. Prevost retained responsibility for the civil administration and military command of Upper Canada until 19 September 1813, when he announced that de Rottenburg "will unite in his person the civil and military command in Upper Canada, upon my [Prevost's] withdrawing back from the Province." Prevost to Yeo, 19 September 1813, in Cruikshank, *DH* 7:149; Hezekiah Niles, ed., *The Weekly Register*, vol. 5: *September 1813 to March 1814* (Baltimore: Franklin Press, n.d.), 204; General Order, Kingston, 19 June 1813, in Cruikshank, *DH* 6:97; Prevost to Bathurst, 24 June 1813, RMC, CO 42/151: 57; Turner, *British Generals*, 99, 100.

3. Synopsis from Malcomson, *Historical Dictionary of the War of 1812*, 482; Prevost to Bathurst, 24 June 1813, RMC, CO 42/151: 41.

4. In *British Generals of the War of 1812*, Turner presents the argument that de Rottenburg was poorly treated; see chap. 5, p. 108. See also Graves, *Field of Glory*, 285.

5. Duke of York to Prevost, 10 August 1813, LAC, RG 8 C vol. 3172: 386, 387.

6. Freer to de Rottenburg, 18 October 1813, LAC, RG 8 C vol. 1221: 188.

7. Prevost to the Duke of York, 23 June 1813, LAC, RG 8 C vol. 1220; Hitsman, *Incredible War of 1812*, 334n40.

8. Prevost to Bathurst, 24 June 1813, RMC, CO 42/151: 42; de Rottenburg to Procter, 1 July 1813, LAC, RG 8 C vol. 3173: 218. De Rottenburg claimed the North West Company had forty canoes that could move a thousand men plus equipment. Even if this were the case, the journey would have been difficult and dangerous to such a large body of men.

9. In late June, many of these Natives won the greatest aboriginal victory of the war, over the Americans at Beaver Dams. This was the largest

engagement of the war by Iroquois and other indigenous peoples without the participation of white troops. See Benn, *Iroquois in the War of 1812*, 115–20.

10. Turner, *British Generals*, 39.

11. Vincent to Baynes, 14 June 1813, LAC RG 8 I vol. 3172: 91; de Rottenburg to Prevost, 7 July 1813, LAC RG 8 I vol. 3172: 201; James E. Elliott, *Strange Fatality: The Battle of Stoney Creek, 1813* (Montreal: Robin Brass Studio, 2009), 181.

12. Prevost to Bathurst, 8 August 1813, RMC, CO 42/151: 133.

13. Malcomson, *Capital in Flames*, 309, 310; Prevost to Bathurst, 8 August 1813, RMC CO 42/151: 133; General Order, Kingston, 3 August 1813, in Cruikshank, *DH* 6:307.

14. General Order, 23 August 1813, in Cruikshank, *DH* 7:52.

15. Jones to Chauncey, 27 January 1813, in Dudley, *Naval War of 1812*, 2:419–20; Chauncey to Hamilton, 1 January 1813, in Dudley, *Naval War of 1812*, 2:406–407; Chauncey to Jones, 16 February 1813, in Dudley, *Naval War of 1812*, 2:426; Jones to Chauncey, 26 June 1813, in Dudley, *Naval War of 1812*, 2:508; Chauncey to Perry, in Dudley, *Naval War of 1812*, 2:530; Thomas Malcomson and Robert Malcomson, *The Battle for Lake Erie* (St. Catharines, Ont.: Vanwell Publishing Ltd., 1990), 30, 34, 39.

16. Yeo to Prevost, 22 August 1813, LAC, RG 8 C vol. 3244: 96; State of the Troops, 22 August 1813, in Cruikshank, *DH* 7:51; Prevost to Bathurst, 25 August 1813, RMC, CO 42/151: 158; Malcomson, *Lords of the Lake*, 184; Brian Leigh Dunnigan, *Forts within a Fort: Niagara's Redoubts* (Youngstown, N.Y.: Old Fort Niagara Association, 1989), 44.

17. Turner, *British Generals*, 39, 41; Benn, *Iroquois in the War of 1812*, 124; *Quebec Mercury*, 7 September 1812, in Cruikshank, *DH* 7:59.

18. Prevost to Bathurst, 1 August 1813, RMC, CO 42/151: 125.

19. Ibid.

20. Ibid.

21. Prevost to Bathurst, 15 September 1813, RMC, CO 42/151: 146.

22. Prevost to Bathurst, 25 August 1813, RMC, CO 42/151: 158.

23. Yeo to Prevost, 15 September 1813, LAC, RG 8 C vol. 3244: 164.

24. Prevost to Yeo, 19 September 1813, in Cruikshank, *DH* 7:148, 149; Yeo to Prevost, 15 September 1813, LAC, RG 8 C vol. 3244: 164.

25. Among the losses was one of the two prize gigs Yeo had brought with him from England. The boat, which was being transported to Kingston on the *Confiance*, a captured American schooner, was hacked in two and thrown over the side. Malcomson, *Lords of the Lake*, 209.

26. Prevost to Torrens, 30 October 1812, LAC, RG 8 C vol. 1221: 216, 217; Prevost to Yeo, 12 October 1813, LAC, RG 8 C vol. 1221: 182; Malcomson, *Lords of the Lake*, 209; Yeo to Prevost, 7 October 1812, in Dudley, *Naval War of 1812*, 2:588; Prevost to Yeo, 19 September 1813, in Cruikshank, *DH* 7:149.

27. Yeo to Prevost, 17 October 1813, LAC, RG 8 C vol. 731: 47; Prevost to Yeo, 21 October 1813, LAC, RG 8 C, vol. 1221: 205; Darroch to Prevost, 8 October 1813, in Cruikshank, *DH* 7:213; Pearson to Baynes, 12 October 1813, in Wood, *Select British Documents*, 2:435.

28. Prevost to Bathurst, 8 October 1813, RMC, CO 42/151: 199.

29. De Salaberry, prompted in part by Lieutenant Colonel George Macdonell, complained to Baynes and Prince Edward, the Duke of Kent, that
Prevost's general order on the engagement had given him insufficient recognition for his actions during the battle. A second general order was issued in early November that corrected this oversight. In January 1814,
Prevost nominated de Salaberry and eight other officers for the Army Gold
Medal to acknowledge their role in the campaign. Prevost also requested
that colors be awarded to the five battalions of select embodied militia. See
Prevost to Bathurst, 30 October 1813, in Wood, *Select British Documents*,
2:392–94; de Salaberry to Baynes, 1 November 1813, in ibid., 396, 398; General Order Montreal, 4 November 1813, in ibid, 399; Duke of Kent to de
Salaberry, 15 March 1814, in ibid., 415–16; Freer to de Salaberry, 19 April
1814, in ibid., 416; and General Order, 27 October 1813, in Cruikshank, *DH*
8:100, 101.

30. The presence of Wilkinson's army on the St. Lawrence disrupted
the delivery of much-needed provisions for the forces in Upper Canada,
and in November 1813, de Rottenburg, facing pressure from the Commissariat, imposed martial law. The proclamation was restricted to two districts on the upper river, and it limited the Commissariat to collecting
forage and provisions for Prescott. The House of Assembly censured de
Rottenburg for his imposition of martial law as he had not secured the
concurrence of its members. In January 1814, his successor, Lieutenant
General Gordon Drummond, revoked the proclamation. Drummond too
misunderstood his authority in these matters. Upon taking command of
the province, Drummond had assumed, until Prevost corrected him, that
his authority alone as the commander of Upper Canada allowed him to
impose martial law. Prevost fully appreciated the resentment marital law
could create and the disaffection that might result. His preference was to
reduce the negative effects of martial law by issuing degrees specifying
the types of produce to be collected within a limited geographical area.
From a legal perspective, Prevost's commission as governor general allowed
him unilaterally to declare martial law; however, the provincial commanders could only do so in their capacity as administrators of the government
and required the agreement of the provincial parliament. The House of
Assembly in Upper Canada was generally loath to support declarations of
martial law, thus making the passage of bills extremely difficult. A Proclamation, 22 November 1813, in Cruikshank, *DH* 8:226; A Proclamation, 25
January 1814, in Cruikshank, *DH* 8:226; Drummond to Prevost, 14 March
1814, LAC, RG 8 C vol. 3174: 200, 201; Prevost to Drummond, 20 April 1814,
LAC, RG 8 C vol. 3527: 103–105.

31. Swift to Armstrong, 17 July 1836, in Benson J. Lossing, *The Pictorial Field-Book of the War of 1812* (New York: Harper and Brothers Publishers, 1896), 655n.

32. Prevost to de Rottenburg, 12 October 1813, LAC, RG 8 C vol. 1221:
179; Prevost to Yeo, 12 October 1812, LAC, RG 8 C, vol. 1221: 182; Yeo to
Croker, 14 October 1813, in Cruikshank, *DH* 7:221; Prevost to Yeo, 21 November 1813, LAC, RG 8 C vol. 1221: 218; Malcomson, *Lords of the Lake*,

219; Mulcaster to Yoo, 2 November 1813, in Cruikshank, *DH* 8:123, 124; Prevost to Bathurst, 15 November 1813, RMC, CO 42/152: 11; Prevost to Bathurst, 8 October 1813, RMC, CO 42/151: 199.

33. Graves, *Field of Glory*, 294, 296, 297.

34. Antal, *Wampum Denied*, 152, 372, 373; Hitsman, *Incredible War of 1812*, 342n43.

35. Steppler, "Duty Troublesome beyond Measure," 133.

36. Barclay to Prevost, 6 July 1813, TNA, Adm 1/2737: 4.

37. In contrast, the American squadron had 585 men by September 1813, one-third of whom had come from the army and militia or were inexperienced landsmen. Procter to Prevost, 26 August 1813, in Dudley, *Naval War of 1812*, 2:550; Malcomson, *Warships of the Great Lakes*, 95; Malcomson, *Lords of the Lake*, 335, 336; Skaggs and Altoff, *Signal Victory*, 83.

38. Prevost to Barclay, 21 July 1813, in Dudley, *Naval War of 1812*, 2:545.

39. Prevost to Bathurst, 22 September 1813, RMC, CO 42/151: 177. Continued shortages of seamen led Yeo in December 1813 to send Lieutenant John Scott, RN, to Halifax to make a direct appeal to Griffith. Scott was successful in securing a draft of 210 officers and men. The party moved to Kingston overland between January and March 1814, and upon arriving at Kingston they joined Yeo's squadron. See Malcomson, *Lords of the Lake*, 233, 239, 240.

40. Skaggs and Altoff, *Signal Victory*, 40, 45, 70, 71, 61, 110; Malcomson, *Warships of the Great Lakes*, tables on pp. 45, 55, 85, 88.

41. Skaggs and Altoff, *Signal Victory*, 84, 85; Antal, *Wampum Denied*, 261; Hitsman, *Incredible War of 1812*, 167, 168.

42. Barclay to Yeo, 12 September 1813, in Dudley, *Naval War of 1812*, 2:555, 556; Hitsman, *Incredible War of 1812*, 171, 172.

43. Baynes to Procter, 18 September 1813, in Logan Esary, *Messages and Letters of William Henry Harrison* (Indianapolis: Indiana Historical Commission, 1922), 2:583.

44. Prevost to Procter, 23 September 1813, in Wood, *Select British Documents*, 2:284.

45. Prevost to Procter, 6 October 1813, in Wood, *Select British Documents*, 2:286.

46. Quimby, *U.S. Army in the War of 1812*, 1:272.

47. De Rottenburg to Prevost, 30 September 1813, LAC, RG 8C vol. 3158: 123; de Rottenburg to Prevost, 3 October 1813, LAC, RG 8C vol. 3173: 137; Vincent to de Rottenburg, 9 October 1813, LAC, RG 8C vol. 3173: 184; Vincent to de Rottenburg, 14 October 1813, LAC, RG 8C vol. 3173: 235.

48. Prevost to de Rottenburg, 12 October 1813, LAC, RG 8C vol. 1221: 179, 180.

49. Darroch to Prevost, 7 October 1813, LAC, RG 8C vol. 3173: 151.

50. De Rottenburg to Prevost, 17 September 1813, LAC, RG 8C vol. 3173: 78.

51. Prevost to Bathurst, 22 September 1813, RMC, CO 42/151: 177.

52. Ibid.

53. Ibid.

54. Ibid.; de Rottenburg to Prevost, 28 September 1813, LAC, RG 8 C vol. 3173: 119.

55. Yeo to Warren, 10 October 1813, in Cruikshank, *DH* 7:219.

56. Yeo to Prevost, 15 November 1813, RMC, CO 42/152: 54.

57. Prevost to Bathurst, 22 September 1813, RMC, CO 42/151: 177.

58. Narrative of the Proceedings during the Command of Captain Barclay, in Wood, *Select British Documents*, 2:303.

59. Lake Erie Court-Martial Papers, in Wood, *Select British Documents*, 2:318.

60. The court-martial of Major General Henry Procter is examined in appendix D.

61. General Order, Horse Guards, No. 376, 9 September 1815, TNA, WO 71/239: 3.

62. The summary was four pages in length. Ibid., 1–4.

63. Prevost to Bathurst, 15 September 1813, RMC, CO 42/150: 168.

64. Bathurst to Prevost, 10 August 1813, RMC, CO 42/151: 145.

65. Prevost to Bathurst, 21 April 1813, RMC, CO 42/150: 194.

7. "GIVE JONATHAN A GOOD DRUBBING"

1. Bathurst to Prevost, 24 April 1814, RMC, CO 42/156.

2. Wellington to Earl Bathurst, 22 Feb 1814, in John Gurwood, ed., *The Dispatches of Field Marshal The Duke of Wellington* (London: J. Murray, 1838), 11:525–26.

3. Ibid., 526.

4. Ibid.

5. Ibid.

6. Ibid., 525, 526.

7. Hall, *British Strategy in the Napoleonic Wars*, 94, 95; Muir, *Britain and the Defeat of Napoleon*, 306, 307.

8. Between 1811 and 1813, Graham had served on the Iberian Peninsula as Wellington's second-in-command until poor health caused him to return to England. Once recovered, he was given command of the army in the Low Countries. Following an unsuccessful attempt on the French-held fortress of Bergen op Zoom, much of Graham's force was redeployed to other areas, including the Canadas. Following Napoléon's first abdication, Graham returned home to great acclaim, but he never held another field command. Andrew Bamford, "The British Army in the Low Countries, 1813–1814," The Napoleon Series, http://www.napoleon-series.org/military/battles/c_lowcountries1814.html.

9. In the spring of 1814, the army in the Netherlands was to have been withdrawn and sent to North America. However, the need to maintain security in the Netherlands terminated this plan and only five battalions were withdrawn, including the 4/1st Regiment, which was sent to the Canadas. The remaining units formed the nucleus of the army that fought at Waterloo. Ibid.

10. Hall, *British Strategy in the Napoleonic Wars*, 201, 203; Muir, *Britain and the Defeat of Napoleon*, 332. For a brief account of the operations

of this force, see Quartermaster General's Department, *British Minor Expeditions, 1746 to 1814* (London. Her Majesty's Stationery Office, 1884), 80–88.

11. Colonel Torrens to Major General Sir G. Murray, 14 April 1814, in Second Duke of Wellington, ed., *Supplementary Dispatches, Correspondence and Memoranda of Field Marshal The Duke of Wellington* (London: Walter Schoberl, 1862; hereafter cited as Wellington, *SD*), 9:58.

12. Bathurst to Prevost, 3 June 1814, RMC, CO 43/23: 153.

13. Ibid.

14. Colonel Torrens to Major General Sir G. Murray, 14 April 1814, in Wellington, *SD* 9:58; Bathurst to Prevost, 3 June 1814, RMC, CO 43/23: 153.

15. Bathurst to Prevost, 3 June 1814, RMC, CO 43/23: 153.

16. Bathurst to Barnes, 20 May 1814, in Michael J. Crawford, *The Naval War of 1812: A Documentary History*, vol. 3 (Washington, D.C.. Naval Historical Center, 2002), 72.

17. Major General Edward Barnes, who was serving in Iberia, originally received command of the brigade until Wellington replaced him with Ross.

18. Some historians have presented this change in British strategy as marking the beginning of a second attempt to quash American independence. With the "failure" of this plan, it was then said that the British attempted to cover up these events by hiding the documentation. This is not true as the correspondence has been available in the National Archives in London since 1910, with copies in the Library and Archives of Canada and the Special Collections of the Royal Military College of Canada since 1965. The perspective of a second war of independence has recently been disputed by new American voices. For a discussion of this topic, see Hickey, *Don't Give Up the Ship!*, 46–47.

19. A fourth offensive, designed to further damage American commerce in the Gulf of Mexico, was not included in this scheme and was authorized later in the year. Bathurst to Barnes, 20 May 1814, in Crawford, *Naval War of 1812*, vol. 3: 72; Bathurst to Ross, n.d. [ca. May 1814], TNA, WO 6/2: 1.

20. Prevost to Drummond, 1 June 1814, in Cruikshank, *DH* 2:401, 402; Drummond to Prevost, 27 May 1814, in Crawford, *Naval War of 1812*, 3:489; Wilkinson to Prevost, 28 January 1814, enclosed in Prevost to Bathurst, 10 February 1814, RMC, CO 42/156: 139.

21. Prevost to Cochrane, 2 June 1814, in Cruikshank, *DH* 2:402.

22. Cockburn to Cochrane, 17 July 1814, in Crawford, *Naval War of 1812*, 3:137, 138.

23. Croker to Cochrane, 19 May 1814, in Crawford, *Naval War of 1812*, 3:72; Cochrane to Cockburn, 1 July 1814, in Crawford, *Naval War of 1812*, 3:130; Cockburn to Cochrane, 27 August 1814, in Crawford, *Naval War of 1812*, 3:222.

24. While Ghent is today a city in Belgium, it was not so following the end of the Napoleonic Wars. Beginning in 1815, and until it gained its independence in 1830, Belgium was part of the United Kingdom of the Netherlands. Fred L. Engleman, *The Peace of Christmas Eve* (London: Rupert

Hart-Davis, 1962), 94, 95; Patrick C. T. White, *A Nation on Trial: America and the War of 1812* (New York: John Wiley & Sons, 1965), 135, 145; Robin Reilly, *The British at the Gates: The New Orleans Campaign in the War of 1812* (Toronto: Robin Brass Studio, 2002), 133, 134.

25. Prevost to Bathurst, 27 March 1814, RMC, CO 42/156: 199, 200.

26. Ibid.

27. Yeo to Prevost, 13 April 1814, LAC, RG 8 C vol. 3174: 30–33; Drummond to Prevost, 2 April 1814, LAC, RG 8 C vol. 3174: 1; Prevost to Bathurst, 17 May 1814, RMC, CO 42/157: 360–67.

28. Prevost to Baynes, 29 April 1814, LAC, RG 8 C vol. 3174: 68.

29. Ibid.

30. Monroe to Pinkney, 11 April 1814, LAC, RG 8 C vol. 3174: 79; Prevost to Baynes, 29 April 1814, LAC, RG 8 C vol. 3174: 88–92.

31. Baynes to Prevost, 1 May 1814, LAC, RG 8 C vol. 3174: 92.

32. Baynes to Pinkney, 1 May 1814, LAC, RG 8 C vol. 3174: 87.

33. Baynes to Prevost, 3 May 1814, LAC, RG 8 C vol. 3174: 83; Prevost to Bathurst, 14 January 1814, RMC, CO 42/156: 95; Stagg, *Mr. Madison's War*, 385–86.

34. Croker to Yeo, 29 January 1814, in Crawford, *Naval War of 1812*, 3:390; Malcomson, *Lords of the Lake*, 242.

35. The elevation of Yeo's command also advanced him to a commodore first class, which allowed him to employ a post captain to command his flagship. He was also entitled to the pay and uniform of a rear admiral. N. A. M. Rodger, "Commissioned Officers' Careers in the Royal Navy, 1690–1815," in Rodger, *Essays in Naval History*, pt. 15: 5.

36. Croker to Yeo, 29 January 1814, in Crawford, *Naval War of 1812*, 3:388.

37. Ibid.

38. Malcomson, *Lords of the Lake*, 264; Prevost to Bathurst, 18 October 1814, RMC, CO 42/157: 316.

39. See Bathurst to Beckwith, 20 March 1813, in Dudley, *Naval War of 1812*, 2:325; and Crawford, *Naval War of 1812*, 3:73.

40. Prevost to Bathurst, 12 July 1814, RMC, CO 42/156: 33.

41. Kempt to Prevost, 18 September 1814, in Brenton, *Some Account of the Public Life*, appendix 28, 77; Bathurst to Prevost, 3 June 1814, TNA, CO 43/23; Prevost to Bathurst, 5 August 1814, RMC, CO 42/ 157: 136.

42. Quimby, *U.S. Army in the War of 1812*, 2:498, 501, 502; Benn, *Iroquois in the War of 1812*, 154, 175.

43. Prevost to Drummond, 8 January 1814, in Crawford, *Naval War of 1812*, 3:379.

44. Ibid.

45. The Sioux were represented by Wabasha and Little Crow, the Menominee by Tomah, and the Winnebago by Lassammic. Ernest Cruikshank, "Robert Dickson, The Indian Trader," in *Collections of the State Historical Society of Wisconsin*, vol. 12, ed. Reuben Thwaites (Madison: Democrat Publishing Company, 1892), 151; Ferguson; *Illinois in the War of 1812*, 102, 103, 110, 111.

46. The Michigan Fencibles had been raised in 1813, and three other units—the Mississippi Volunteers, Dease's Mississippi Volunteers, and the Green Bay Militia—were formed in 1814. Dunnigan, *British Army at Mackinac*, 14, 45; Cruikshank, "Robert Dickson," 151, 152.

47. Prevost to Drummond, 29 January 1814, LAC, RG 8 C vol. 1222: 32, 33.

48. Drummond to Prevost, 21 January 1814, LAC, RG 8 C vol. 3235: 32. This detailed report incorporated details on routes, force composition, logistical support, and transportation, including the use of sleighs. Drummond to Prevost, 3 February 1814, LAC, RG 8 C vol. 3174: 90; Military Secretary to Drummond, 4 February 1814, LAC, RG 8 C vol. 3527: 38.

49. Drummond to Prevost, 23 January 1814, in Cruikshank *DH* 9:143; Drummond to Prevost, 28 January 1814, LAC, RG 8 C vol. 3174: 67; Steppler, "Duty Troublesome beyond Measure," 133, 134.

50. McDouall had arrived in Lower Canada in 1810. His previous service included the expedition to Egypt in 1801, the Copenhagen expedition of 1807, and the capture of Martinique in 1809. Between September 1812 and September 1813, McDouall was an aide de camp to Prevost, and he was commanding officer of the 1st Battalion Militia Light Infantry when Prevost ordered him to the northwest. As for the naval construction at Penetanguishine Bay, work on the frigate had just commenced when news arrived announcing the end of the war. The stores and guns for the vessels were in York and were to have been dragged north to Lake Simcoe and then onward to the naval base at Penetanguishine. Sutherland, *His Majesty's Gentlemen*, 241; Malcomson, *Warships of the Great Lakes*, 138.

51. Prevost to Drummond, 8 January 1814, in Crawford, *Naval War of 1812*, 3:379, 380; Prevost to Bathurst, 8 February 1814, RMC, CO 42/156: 105; Prevost to Drummond, 13 November 1814, LAC, RG 8 C vol. 686: 170; Drummond to Prevost, 24 November 1814, in Cruikshank, *DH* 9:315; Dunnigan, *British Army at Mackinac*, 16, 17, 19, 20; Ferguson, *Illinois in the War of 1812*, 172, 185.

52. Prevost to Drummond, 5 January 1814, LAC, RG 8 C vol. 1222: 15.

53. Donald E. Graves, *Where Right and Glory Lead: The Battle of Lundy's Lane, 1814* (Toronto: Robin Brass Studio, 1997), 211, 213, 215.

54. Steppler, "Duty Troublesome beyond Measure," 181, 183, 186.

55. Drummond to Prevost, 19 September 1814, LAC, RG 8 C vol. 685: 225, 226; Malcomson, *Warships of the Great Lakes*, 115; Prevost to Bathurst, 11 October 1814, RMC, CO 42/115: 303.

56. Prevost to Bathurst, 18 October 1814, RMC, CO 42/157: 315.

57. Benn, *Iroquois in the War of 1812*, 167.

8. PREPARING FOR THE PLATTSBURGH CAMPAIGN

1. The land forces stationed in the Canadas were divided into three "divisions," which were geographical commands rather than tactical formations. In 1814, the Right Division stretched from the Niagara region to York, the Center Division extended from Kingston to the border with Lower Canada, and the Left Division was based around Montreal. During

the Plattsburgh campaign the Left Division operated as a field formation in the classic sense.

2. Duke of York to Wellington, 14 April 1814, in Wellington, *SD* 9:82–84; State of Divisions Formed in Compliance with Instructions from Earl Bathurst, dated 18 May, in Wellington, *SD* 9:119; Reilly, *British at the Gates*, 146; Prevost to Bathurst, 5 August 1814, in Wood, *Select British Documents*, 3 (pt. 1): 346; General Order, Montreal, 7 August 1814, in Wood, *Select British Documents*, 3 (pt. 1): 346, 347; Brenton, *Some Account of the Public Life*, 132.

3. The American campaign against Montreal during 1813 included 10,000 men, but they were divided between two separate armies.

4. See Stanley, *War of 1812*, 349, 350. Popular writers have also emphasized this point, such as David G. Fitz-Enz, *The Final Invasion: Plattsburgh, the War of 1812's Most Decisive Battle* (New York: Cooper Square Press, 2001).

5. Hall, *British Strategy in the Napoleonic Wars*, 204.

6. Donald E. Graves, "The Redcoats Are Coming: British Troop Movements to North America in 1814," *Journal of the War of 1812* 6, no. 3 (2001): 2, 3.

7. Oman, *Wellington's Army*, 362, 365, 366, 369, 372; "Sir Manley Power," *Oxford Dictionary of National Biography*, doi:10.1093/ref:odnb /22668; John R. Grodzinski, "Much to Be Desired: The Campaign Experience of British General Officers of the War of 1812," The Napoleon Series, http://www.napoleon-series.org/military/Warof1812/2007/Issue7/c_British Generals.html.

8. Commissary General Robinson to Prevost, 12 February 1814, LAC, RG 8 C 2682: 40–42; Sutherland, *His Majesty's Gentlemen*, 199, 333, 409, 410; L. Irving, *Officers of the British Forces in Canada*, 2, 4n1, 7n3, 16n2.

9. Toby Redgrave, "Wellington's Logistical Arrangements in the Peninsular War, 1809–1814" (PhD diss., King's College, University of London, 1979), 4–15.

10. The selection of which brigade each officer would lead was determined by seniority. As Brisbane, Power, and Robinson each held the same seniority for the ranks of major general and colonel, the decision came down to their seniority in the rank of lieutenant colonel. See Sutherland, *His Majesty's Gentlemen*, 75, 203, 317.

11. General Order, 23 August 1814, in William Kingsford, *History of Canada*, vol. 8 (London: Keegan, Paul, Trench, Tubner & Co., 1895), 532n.

12. The dress of British army officers has often lacked uniformity and on occasion has received additional latitude from such commanders in chief as Wellington. Lieutenant William Gratton's observations regarding Wellington's relaxed views on dress have been presented in several War of 1812 studies to highlight the reaction to Prevost's General Order. While this passage from edited version of Gratton's memoir offers insight into the conditions of dress, it refers to Gratton's experiences in November 1810 and has nothing to do with Prevost or the situation in 1814. See William Gratton, *Adventures with the Connaught Rangers, 1809–1814*, ed. Charles Oman (London: Edward Arnold, 1902), 50. An example of how this quote

has been used appears in Hitsman, *Incredible War of 1812*, 254; and Jon Latimer, *1812: War with America* (London: Belknap Press, 2007), 352. Gratton's original two-volume memoir contrasts the appearance of the battle-hardened Peninsular veterans that arrived in Montreal during 1814 with the better-dressed soldiers from England, but it says nothing of Prevost's General Order regarding dress. William Gratton, *Adventures of the Connaught Rangers* (London: Henry Colburn, 1847), 2:275, 276; General Order, 7 August 1814, in Wood, *Select British Documents*, 3 (pt. 1): 346, 347; General Order, 24 August 1814, in Wood, *Select British Documents*, 3 (pt. 1): 349.

13. RMC, Papers of Major General F. P. Robinson, 22 August 1815, 261.

14. Ibid., 240, 241.

15. Prevost to Bathurst, 18 October 1814, RMC, CO 42/157: 316.

16. Ibid.

17. Ibid.

18. Ibid. The Americans commenced building two 74-gun first-rates at Sackets Harbor in early 1815. Neither ship was completed. Paul H. Silverstone, *The Sailing Navy, 1775–1854* (Annapolis: Naval Institute Press, 2001), 66.

19. Prevost to Bathurst, 22 September 1812, RMC, CO 42/147: 195.

20. Moore to Hamilton, 29 August 1812, in Dudley, *Naval War of 1812*, 1:296; Prevost to Liverpool, 18 May 1812, RMC, CO 42/146.

21. Taylor to Stovin, 3 June 1813, in Dudley, *Naval War of 1812*, 2:489; Thomas Hooper, *The Royal Navy Station at Ile-aux-Noix* (Ottawa: Parks Canada, 1967), 54.

22. One author has suggested that Yeo caused Pring's transfer to rid himself of an officer he disliked. See Hooper, *Royal Navy Station at Ile-aux-Noix*, 55.

23. The original name of this vessel was *Niagara*. The name was changed to conform to Royal Navy nomenclature following the elevation of Yeo's command. Malcomson, *Lords of the Lake*, 264.

24. General Order, Kingston, 19 July 1813, LAC, RG 8C vol. 1170: 314; Pring to Prevost, 7 October 1813, LAC, RG 8C vol. 731: 4; Freer to Pring, 19 October 1813, LAC, RG 8C vol. 1221: 200; Pring to Freer, 18 February 1814, LAC, RG 8C vol. 732: 37.

25. Macdonough to Jones, 23 November 1813, in Dudley, *Naval War of 1812*, 2:604; Report of a Board of Officers on the Subject of Conveying the Frames of Two Frigates and Two Brigs to Kingston, 6 April 1814, TNA, WO 57/15; Jones to Macdonough, 22 February 1814, in Crawford, *Naval War of 1812*, 3:396; Macdonough to Jones, 7 March 1814, in Crawford, *Naval War of 1812*, 3:397; Hooper, *Royal Navy Station at Ile-aux-Noix*, 57.

26. Prevost to Bathurst, 9 May 1814, RMC, CO 42/156: 312.

27. Simons to Freer, 23 May 1814, LAC, RG 8C vol. 732: 174; Hooper, *Royal Navy Station at Ile-aux-Noix*, 57, 59; Sheaffe to Prevost, 5 August 1813, LAC, RG 8C vol. 679: 348; Yeo to Fisher, 29 July 1814, TNA, Adm 1/2737: 189.

28. Prevost to Yeo, 11 June 1814, in Crawford, *Naval War of 1812*, 3:521, 522.

29. Yeo to Fisher, 29 July 1814, TNA, Adm 1/2737: 189.

30. Statement of the Number and Force of His Majesty's Squadron on Lake Ontario, TNA, Adm 1/2737: 35; Dimensions of His Majesty's New Ship, TNA, Adm 1/2737: 226; Croker to Yeo, 22 February 1814, TNA, Adm 2/1379: 217; Malcomson, *Lords of the Lake*, 282.

31. Lake Champlain Court-Martial, TNA, Adm 1/5450: 20.

32. Admiralty Lake Service III, LAC, RG 8 C vol. 6: 9.

33. Yeo's action sparked the so-called Yeo-Fisher Controversy, in which Fisher complained of unfair treatment; however, when Yeo was recalled in 1815, the matter proved to be of little consequence. Unfortunately, the documentation on this incident is sparse and the full story may never be known. See Malcomson, *Historical Dictionary of the War of 1812*, 618–19.

34. Downie to Capt Upton, 1 September 1814, TNA, Adm 1/2262: n.p. The carronade was introduced in the 1770s, as a short gun with a relatively large bore. It was adopted by the navy, where the tight confines of a ship and the relatively short ranges of engagements did not require the longer standard piece. Carronades also found their way into field service. Lavery, *Nelson's Navy*, 82, 83.

35. Hitsman, *Incredible War of 1812*, 251; Upton to Croker, 3 September 1814, TNA, Adm 1/2263: 324; Hooper, *Royal Navy Station at Ile-aux-Noix*, 67.

36. Plattsburgh Court-Martial, 18–25 August 1815, in Wood, *Select British Documents*, 3 (pt. 1): 411.

37. Malcomson, *Warships of the Great Lakes*, 122, table 40; William James, *Naval Occurrences of the Late War between Great Britain and the United States* (London: T. Egerton, 1817), 405, 406; Plattsburgh Court-Martial, 18–25 August 1815, in Wood, *Select British Documents*, 3 (pt. 1): 411.

38. The British and American armies serving in the northern theater applied the term "division" differently. In the former, it was used to denote a geographical territory, such as the area between the Niagara River and York, under the command of a general officer; in the latter, a "division" was a fixed organization of artillery, cavalry, and infantry units for field operations anywhere within a theater. The designation of a division came from its position relative to another one. In 1814, there were two divisions based in New York: the Left Division at Buffalo and the Right Division at Plattsburgh. The British first employed divisions of this type in the northern theater in 1814, when the British Right Division on the Niagara Peninsula and the Left Division at Montreal were transformed from geographical command areas to field formations.

39. Quimby, *U.S. Army in the War of 1812*, 2:607, 608.

40. Prevost to Bathurst, 12 July 1812, RMC, CO 42/157: 35.

41. Bathurst to Prevost, 22 August 1814, quoted in Everest, *War of 1812 in the Champlain Valley*, 157.

42. Everest, *War of 1812 in the Champlain Valley*, 166.

43. Written orders were issued for the advance by Baynes. For an example, see Baynes to Brisbane, 1 September 1814, Clements Library, Brisbane Papers.

44. Proclamation by Lieutenant General Sir George Prevost, 1 September 1814, Clements Library, Brisbane Papers.

45. Ibid.

9. A SINGLE STAIN

1. RMC, Papers of Major General F. P. Robinson, 22 August 1815, 244.

2. Ibid.; Brenton, *Some Account of the Public Life*, 141, 142; Quimby, *U.S. Army in the War of 1812*, 2:607, 608; Sinclair to Baynes, 20 March 1815, RMC, CO 42/161: 154, 155.

3. The historiography of the Plattsburgh expedition is riddled with problems. Historians generally have made use of the same five sources: two reports written by Prevost; an account by Major Sinclair, the British artillery commander at Plattsburgh; published excerpts from a journal kept by Major General Frederick Robinson, who commanded a brigade; and the report by the American commander, Brigadier General Macomb. The historian is faced with problems in each of these documents; therefore, they will be examined in detail. The Robinson journal and the report by Macomb will be explored first, along with the secondary literature. Observations on the reports by Prevost and Sinclair will be provided later.

Few historians have consulted Robinson's original diary and have relied on excerpts that were published in 1916. Robinson wrote his journal entries dealing with North America in August 1815. His grandson, Major General Charles W. Robinson, heavily edited the excerpts he used in an article he prepared for the *United Services Magazine*. For example, Sir Frederick Robinson was extremely critical of Prevost, and Charles Robinson combined two passages from the journal to read as one. In so doing, he "revised Sir Frederick's severe censure of Prevost to make it appear as a valid defence of his conduct." The article also omits important details on the British march to Plattsburgh, the investment of the village, Prevost's actions, the land battle, and the march back to Canada. Along with the hand-written entries, the journals include copies of letters, reports, and orders issued during the Plattsburgh campaign. As such, they are a rich source of information resting in near obscurity in the Special Collections of Massey Library at the Royal Military College of Canada. To date, they have not been used by any historians in preparing their accounts of the expedition.

There are also inconsistencies in American Brigadier General Alexander Macomb's report, written four days after the battle. Ideally, the report should be viewed as a credible account from the American perspective; however, it cannot be taken as such. Macomb believed Prevost's ultimate objective was farther south at Crown Point or Ticonderoga, perhaps expecting a repeat of Lieutenant General John Burgoyne's Saratoga campaign of 1777. Macomb did not appear to understand the diversionary role assigned to Major General Brisbane's brigade and attributed the withdrawal of the main force led by Robinson to its having "suffered severely in killed, wounded and prisoners." One gets the impression that Macomb never fully appreciated British intentions and movements. Since Macomb never felt the full weight of Prevost's Left Division, he made assumptions as to what happened and embellished his own role to enhance his reputation. To be fair, Macomb was probably unaware that Prevost ordered the main attack halted before it began. Macomb also elevated the significance of his victory by inflating the strength of the British Left Division to fourteen thousand men, far more than the actual number present that day. The problems within Macomb's account were perceptively addressed by historian J. Mackay Hitsman, who concluded that Macomb never fully understood the British plan and chose to conclude "the British failure to make any serious attack into a military victory for his own men."

The secondary literature also has many problems. Canadian historian George F. G. Stanley readily accepted the established narrative that Prevost's army fell apart as it returned to Canada: "[It was] not the same army that had entered [the United States] three weeks before. It was no longer an army, but a mob of men devoid of discipline and spirit, and reduced in numbers as individuals deserted in disgust." Stanley then wrote that the officers and men "cast aside the discipline instilled by the great Duke [Wellington] and to drop out of the trudging column to escape from a commander [Prevost] they had no respect for and from an army that had been defeated by an enemy made up, for the most part, of despised militia." The claims made by Stanley are examined in the text. See Prevost to Bathurst, 11 September 1814, in Wood, *Select British Documents*, 3 (pt. 1): 350–53; Prevost to Bathurst, 22 September 1814, in Wood, *Select British Documents*, 3 (pt. 1): 363–66; Sinclair to Baynes, 20 March 1815, RMC, CO 42/161: 154–59; Major General C. W. Robinson, "The Expedition to Plattsburgh, Upon Lake Champlain, Canada, 1814," *Royal United Services Institution* 61, no. 443 (August 1916): 499–522; H. A. Fay, *Collection of Official Accounts, in detail, of all the Battles Fought by Sea and Land, between the Navy and Army of the United States and the Navy and Army of Great Britain, during the Years 1812, 13, 14, & 15* (New York: E. Conrad, 1817), 241–46; see also Wood, *Select British Documents*, 3 (pt. 1): 360; Richard A. Preston, "The Journals of General Sir F. P. Robinson, GCB," *Canadian Historical Review*, no. 4 (December 1956): 352; Hitsman, *Incredible War of 1812*, 262; Stanley, *War of 1812*, 349, 350.

4. Letter dated 5 September 1814, RMC, Papers of Major General F. P. Robinson, 22 August 1815, 245.

5. Ibid.; Pring to Yeo, 12 September 1814, in Wood, *Select British Documents*, 3 (pt. 1): 368. See also Nell Jane Barnett Sullivan and David Kendall Martin, *A History of the Town of Chazy, Clinton County, New York* (Burlington, Vt.: George Little Press, 1970), 99.

6. Before the march continued, the brigades were inspected to ensure they carried sufficient ammunition. General Order, Chazy, 4 September 1814, Clements Library, Brisbane Papers.

7. RMC, Papers of Major General F. P. Robinson, 22 August 1815, 245, 246.

8. Ibid.; Quimby, *U.S. Army in the War of 1812*, 2:610, 611.

9. Among the casualties was Lieutenant Colonel James Wellington (sometimes spelled "Willington") of the 3rd Buffs, whose death became

part of the local mythology as he was wrongfully believed to be a relative of the Duke of Wellington. James Wellington had served in the army since 1794, and aside for being on half-pay between 1797 and 1803, he had seen much service. Everest, *War of 1812 in the Champlain Valley*, 173; Sutherland, *His Majesty's Gentlemen*, 374.

10. Quimby, *U.S. Army in the War of 1812*, 2:610, 611.

11. This description comes from study of period maps of Plattsburgh.

12. Major General C. W. Robinson, "The Expedition to Plattsburg, Upon Lake Champlain, Canada, 1814," *Journal of the Royal United Service Institution* 61 (August 1916): 512.

13. RMC, Papers of Major General F. P. Robinson, 22 August 1815, 247, 248.

14. Ibid. The Left Division had suffered about 100 casualties as it occupied western Plattsburgh.

15. Ibid., 249.

16. Ibid.

17. Sinclair to Baynes, 20 March 1815, RMC, CO 42/161: 155.

18. Wilkinson to Macdonough, 5 April 1814, in Crawford, *Naval War of 1812*, 3 (pt. 1): 426.

19. Two of the forts were named after American generals serving on the Niagara Peninsula, while Fort Moreau was named after a general who had been exiled by Napoléon.

20. David Curtis Skaggs, *Thomas Macdonough: Master and Commander in the Early U.S. Navy* (Annapolis: U.S. Naval Institute, 2003), 111, 112; Quimby, *U.S. Army in the War of 1812*, 2:608; "Return of the Forces, 28 August 1814," in Keith A. Herkalo, *The Battles at Plattsburgh: September 11, 1814* (Plattsburgh, N.Y.: n.p., 2007), 121; Everest, *War of 1812 in the Champlain Valley*, 165.

21. Captain J. H. Wood, "Extracts from the Diary of Captain, afterwards Colonel J. H. Wood, R.A.: Plattsburgh, 1814," *Women's Canadian Historical Society of Toronto* 5 (1905): 11.

22. RMC, Papers of Major General F. P. Robinson, 22 August 1815, 250, 253; Everest, *War of 1812 in the Champlain Valley*, 165.

23. RMC, Papers of Major General F. P. Robinson, 22 August 1815, 253.

24. The strength of the British Left Division before Plattsburgh also has been a matter of debate among historians. Macomb claimed he faced 14,000 men, of which 2,500 were lost—a major exaggeration of the 577 shown by official records. American and Canadian historians have provided differing figures for the starting strength of Prevost's division. In the United States, Robert Quimby estimates it as 10,351; John K. Mahon, at just under 12,000; and Harry L. Coles, 15,000. A recent study by American writer David Fitz-Enz states there were "at least 12,000 if not more." Canadians Hitsman, Turner, and Stanley use the same figure as Quimby: 10,351, which is based on returns dated 6 and 15 September 1814 and appended to a letter sent by Prevost to Bathurst on 1 April 1815 that is in CO 42, a record group that was not used by American historians. The 6 September 1814 return shows that Prevost had 10,420 officers, sergeants, drummers, and rank and file from the infantry, cavalry, and Royal Artillery drivers in

the division. However, this figure is not the total personnel available at Plattsburgh, as those sick and "on command" (that is, away on other duties) must be deducted. Two battalions were on the line of communication, although their light companies were at Plattsburgh. One-third of a battalion and one-half of another from Brisbane's brigade were also absent. With these deductions, the British Left Division totals 7,468 or more than half of Macomb's claim. See Quimby, *U.S. Army in the War of 1812*, 2:611; John K. Mahon, *The War of 1812* (Gainesville: University Press of Florida, 1972), 318; Coles, *War of 1812*, 167; Fay, *Collection of Official Accounts*, 241; Fitz-Enz, *Final Invasion*, 247n13; Hitsman, *Incredible War of 1812*, 254; Turner, *British Generals*, 47; Stanley, *War of 1812*, 344; and Prevost to Bathurst, 1 April 1815, RMC, CO 42/161: 161, 163.

25. Wood, "Extracts from the Diary," 11.

26. RMC, Papers of Major-General F.P. Robinson, 22 August 1815, 250; Weekly State of the Left Division, 8 September 1814, attached to Prevost to Bathurst, 2 April 1815, RMC, CO 42/161.

27. Downie to Prevost, 7 September 1814, TNA, Adm 1/2737: 198.

28. Plattsburgh Court-Martial, in Wood, *Select British Documents*, 3 (pt. 1): 471.

29. Ibid., 421.

30. A gun lock is a larger version of the flintlock mechanism used to ignite the charge in pistols and muskets. Attached to the breach of the great guns of a warship, the lock afforded a faster and more reliable means of firing the gun than the traditional methods of linstock (a three-foot-long staff that held a lighted match, which when touched to the vent, fired the gun) or priming powder. Adrian B. Caruana, *The History of English Sea Ordnance, 1523–1875*, vol. 2: *The Age of System: 1715–1815* (Ashley Lodge, UK: Jean Boudriot Publications, 1997), 389, 397, 398.

31. The introduction of the carronade by the Royal Navy came during the middle years of the American War of Independence, at a period when Britain faced an ordnance crisis; the technical advantages and logistical savings the carronade afforded both are bedeviled by myth. See Roger Morriss, *The Foundations of British Maritime Ascendency: Resources, Logistics and the State, 1755–1815* (Cambridge: Cambridge University Press, 2011), 206–14; and in particular, Caruana, *History of English Sea Ordnance*, 2:161–214, for a detailed examination of the carronade in British service.

32. Malcomson, *Warships of the Great Lakes*, 131; Downie to Prevost, 7 September 1814, TNA, Adm 1/2737: 198; Plattsburgh Court-Martial, in Wood, *Select British Documents*, 3 (pt. 1): 421; James, *Naval Occurrences of the Late War*, 414; Downie to Upton, 1 September 1814, TNA, Adm 1/2737: 200.

33. Lake Champlain Court-Martial, TNA, Adm 1/5450: 106, 113; Everest, *War of 1812 in the Champlain Valley*, 180.

34. Prevost to Downie, 8 September 1814, TNA, Adm 1/2737: 196.

35. Ibid.

36. Downie to Prevost, 8 September 1814, TNA, Adm 1/2737: 199.

37. Prevost to Downie, 9 September 1814, TNA, Adm 1/2737: 197.

38. Ibid.

39. Ibid.

40. Historians generally refer to Macdonough as "Commodore," despite his never having attained that rank. Macdonough, who had been in the U.S. Navy since 1800, remained a substantive lieutenant throughout the War of 1812. He received the local rank of master commandant in July 1813. After the Battle of Plattsburgh, Macdonough was promoted to captain. Everest, *War of 1812 in the Champlain Valley*, 64; Malcomson, *Historical Dictionary of the War of 1812*, 303.

41. Macdonough to Jones, 12 August 1814, in Crawford, *Naval War of 1812*, 3:540; Macdonough to Jones, 27 August 1814, in Crawford, *Naval War of 1812*, 3:541.

42. Downie to Prevost, 9 September 1814, TNA, Adm 1/2737: 199.

43. Prevost to Downie, 10 September 1814, TNA, Adm 1/2737: 198.

44. Ibid.

45. Ibid.

46. Plattsburgh Court-Martial, in Wood, *Select British Documents*, 3 (pt. 1): 442.

47. Ibid.

48. Coore to Downie, Letter Published in the *Montreal Gazette*, 26 February 1815, in Wood, *Select British Documents*, 3 (pt. 2): 394, 395.

49. Ibid., 396.

50. Ibid.

51. Ibid.

52. Statement by Downie, Plattsburgh Court-Martial, in Wood, *Select British Documents*, 3 (pt. 1): 463.

53. Statement by Downie, quoted in Hitsman, *Incredible War of 1812*, 258.

54. Ibid.

55. Baynes to Robinson, 10 September 1814, RMC, Papers of Major General F. P. Robinson.

56. Ibid.

57. Ibid.

58. RMC, Papers of Major General F. P. Robinson, 22 August 1815, 253, 254, 256; Baynes to Robinson, 10 September 1814, RMC, Papers of Major General F. P. Robinson.

59. Brenton, *Some Account of the Life*, 148.

60. The shorter barrel resulted in a gun that was upwards of a quarter of the weight of a similar caliber long gun. The reduced accuracy was partly compensated for by improved boring of the barrel that improved the flight of the projectile. The lighter weight was desirable on naval vessels while the smaller barrel also allowed a reduction in the size of the gun crew. Carronades were also employed in various capacities ashore. Morriss, *British Maritime Ascendancy*, 206–208.

61. Sinclair to Baynes, 20 March 1815, RMC, CO 42/161: 154, 155; British Positions around Plattsburgh, 1814, LAC, General Francis de Rottenburg Papers, MG 24, A 78: n.p.; Donald E. Graves, "'The Finest Army Ever to Campaign on American Soil?' The Organization, Strength, Composition

and Losses of British Land Forces during the Plattsburgh Campaign, September 1814" (unpublished paper in author's possession).

62. Wood, "Extracts from the Diary," 12.

63. RMC, Papers of Major General F. P. Robinson, 252.

64. Sinclair to Baynes, 20 March 1815, RMC, CO 42/161: 156.

65. Although Sinclair noted that the arrival of the two 12-pounder iron guns from Isle aux Noix on the 11th came too late for them to be sited, he remained silent on the status of the two 8-inch mortars that arrived on the same date. It has been assumed in this study that these mortars also arrived too late to be deployed. Sinclair to Baynes, 20 March 1815, RMC, CO 42/161: 155.

66. Robinson's list of ordnance in his journal, which was prepared sometime after the battle, differs in number and types of ordnance from what Sinclair reported. As the latter was the senior gunner in the Left Division, with responsibility for the siting and employment of the guns, his figures will be considered as accurate. Sinclair to Baynes, 20 March 1815, RMC, CO 42/161: 154, 155; British Positions around Plattsburgh, 1814, LAC, General Francis de Rottenburg Papers, MG 24, A 78: n.p.; RMC, Papers of Major General F. P. Robinson, 252.

67. RMC, Papers of Major General F. P. Robinson, 22 August 1815, 255.

68. Ibid.

69. Ibid., 253, 255.

70. Ibid., 257.

71. Ibid.

72. Ibid., 257, 258.

73. Sinclair to Baynes, 20 March 1815, RMC, CO 42/161:154, 155.

74. Ibid., 156.

75. Ibid.; Brenton, *Some Account of the Public Life*, 148.

76. RMC, Papers of Major General F. P. Robinson, 22 August 1815, 258.

77. Ibid. Sir George Prevost was the colonel of the 76th Regiment during 1813 and 1814. See F. A. Hayden, *Historical Record of the 76th "Hindoostan" Regiment* (Lichfield, UK: A. C. Lomax, 1908), 148.

78. RMC, Papers of Major General F. P. Robinson, 22 August 1815, 258.

79. Ibid.

80. See the eyewitness description of Downie's plan in Pring to Yeo, 12 September 1812, in Crawford, *Naval War of 1812*, 3:610.

81. Robertson to Yeo, 12 September 1814, in Crawford, *Naval War of 1812*, 3:613.

82. Pring to Yeo, 12 September 1814, in Crawford, *Naval War of 1812*, 3:610, 611.

83. Robertson to Yeo, 12 September 1814, in Crawford, *Naval War of 1812*, 3:613.

84. RMC, Papers of Major General F. P. Robinson, 22 August 1815, 259, 260.

85. Hayden, *Historical Record of the 76th Regiment*, 105. Robinson gives this figure as twenty-five, Hayden, as thirty-one.

86. The company commander was Captain John Purchase, or, as he is sometimes named, "Perchase." For example, see the "Weekly Parade State

of the Left Division, 15 September 1814," RMC, CO 42/161: 162, where the name is spelled "Purchase"; and Fitz-Enz, *Final Invasion*, 169. Purchase may have been trying to stop the Americans from firing, as one source indicates he was "waving a white waistcote at the end of his sword." Hayden, *Historical Record of the 76th Regiment*, 105; RMC, Papers of Major General F. P. Robinson, 22 August 1815, 259, 260; Lynch to Robinson, 30 September 1814, Papers of Major General F. P. Robinson, 9, 10; Sinclair to Baynes, 20 March 1812, RMC, CO 42/161:157.

87. Prevost to Bathurst, 11 September 1814, in Wood, *Select British Documents*, 3 (pt. 1): 352.

88. Sinclair to Baynes, 20 March 1812, RMC, CO 42/161: 157.

89. Prevost to Bathurst, 5 August 1814, RMC, CO 42/157: 116.

90. Commissary General Robinson submitted a detailed summary of the provisions that were lost or destroyed between 6 and 15 September 1814. The total lost and destroyed included forty barrels of flour, 397 quintals of biscuit (a large proportion of which had been exposed to the weather rendering it useless), twenty-two barrels of beef, six barrels of port, almost five puncheons (a puncheon held 318 liters) of rum and 3 1/2 bushels of oats. "Account of Provisions Lost and Destroyed on the Expedition to Plattsburgh between the 6th and 15th September 1814," RMC, CO 42/161: 151.

91. Sinclair to Baynes, 20 March 1812, RMC, CO 42/161: 157, 158. Most of the 12-pounder round shot and "a small quantity of shot and shells" could not be retrieved due to a lack of transport and was destroyed. Several wagons carrying shot broke down during the march, leaving no alternative but to destroy their loads. Fifty shells were also thrown into Lake Champlain at Chazy Landing.

92. Power lost another 460 men on this frontier duty. Everest, *War of 1812 in the Champlain Valley*, 190; RMC, Papers of Major General F. P. Robinson, 22 August 1815, 259, 260. Power's brigade remained at Champlain until 25 September. During 11 September, all the ammunition for the carronades was destroyed. Sinclair to Greene, 11 September 1814, RMC, Papers of Major General F. P. Robinson; Thomas Brisbane, *The Reminiscences of Major General Sir Thomas Makedougall Brisbane* (Edinburgh: Thomas Constable, 1860), 29. During the retreat, Brisbane's men came across a gun that had been captured by American forces during Burgoyne's Saratoga Campaign of 1777 and dumped it into a ditch. RMC, Papers of Major General F. P. Robinson, 261; Lossing, *Pictorial Field-Book of the War of 1812*, 875n3; Brenton, *Some Account of the Public Life*, 169.

93. Robinson to Mr. Merry, 22 September 1814, in *Report on the Manuscripts of Earl Bathurst* (London: His Majesty's Stationery Office, 1923), 292.

94. Ibid.

95. Ibid.

96. Lossing, *Pictorial Field-Book of the War of 1812*, 875n3; Prevost to Bathurst, 22 September 1814, in Wood, *Select British Documents*, 3 (pt. 1): 365.

97. Prevost to Bathurst, 5 August 1814, in Wood, *Select British Documents*, 3 (pt. 1): 346.

98. Prevost to Bathurst, 22 September 1814, in Wood, *Select British Documents*, 3 (pt. 1): 365.

99. Stanley, *War of 1812*, 349–50.

100. Macomb to Secretary of War, 15 September 1814, in Wood, *Select British Documents*, 3 (pt. 1): 360. One historian states Macomb lost 115 soldiers killed and 130 wounded on 11 September. In his report, Macomb reported a total of 123 casualties from all causes. Both sets of figures are for regular troops only. There is no record of casualties suffered during the three encounters on 6 September, or those personnel lost elsewhere during the campaign, to skirmishing and other reasons. See Herkalo, *Battles of Plattsburgh*, 182.

101. To the losses must be added the 129 officers, seamen, and marines who were killed or wounded during the naval battle and the remaining members of the squadron who were taken prisoner. Return of Killed and Wounded on Board His Majesty's Late Squadron in Action with the Enemy's Squadron on Lake Champlain, in Wood, *Select British Documents*, 3 (pt. 1): 376.

102. Prevost to Bathurst, 22 September 1814, in Wood, *Select British Documents*, 3 (pt. 1): 365; Prevost to Bathurst, 1 April 1815, RMC, CO 42/161: 161, 163. The figures were arrived at by comparing the returns. Brenton, *Some Account of the Public Life*, 169.

103. Prevost to Bathurst, 22 September 1814, in Wood, *Select British Documents*, 3 (pt. 1): 365.

104. RMC, Papers of Major General F. P. Robinson, 22 August 1815, 263, 264.

105. Ibid.

10. "RESPECTING MY CONDUCT AT PLATSBURGH . . ."

1. Macdonough to Jones, 15 October 1814, in Crawford, *Naval War of 1812*, 3:642, 643.

2. Prevost to Brisbane, 24 December 1814, in Crawford, *Naval War of 1812*, 3:682.

3. Ibid.

4. Ibid.

5. Proposed Arrangements for 1815, LAC, RG 8 C vol. 1223: 40; General Order Quebec, 24 April 1812, LAC, RG 8 C vol. 1168: 129, 130.

6. Malcomson, *Lords of the Lake*, 136, 314, 317.

7. Prevost to Brisbane, 12 January 1815, in Crawford, *Naval War of 1812*, 3:684; Monroe to Macomb, 12 January 1815, in Crawford, *Naval War of 1812*, 3:684; Yeo to Prevost, 6 January 1815, in Crawford, *Naval War of 1812*, 3:683. The British goal was to divert American forces from Lake Ontario, which in 1815 would again have been the cockpit of the northern theater, as the British intended to attack Sackets Harbor.

8. NA, General Distribution of the Forces in Canada, 8 November 1814, RMC, CO 42/157: 335–36; General Order, Kingston, 15 October 1814, LAC, RG 8 C vol. 1172: 30, 31.

9. RMC, Papers of Major General F. W. Robinson, 22 August 1815, 263; Wellington to Bathurst, 30 October 1814, in *Report on the Manuscripts of the Earl of Bathurst*, 302.

10. Robertson to Pring, 15 September 1814, TNA, Adm 1/2737: 200, 201.

11. Pring to Yeo, 17 September 1814, TNA, Adm 1/2737: 202.

12. Pring to Yeo, 12 September 1814, in Crawford, *Naval War of 1812*, 3:612.

13. Ibid., 610.

14. Pring to Yeo, 17 September 1814, TNA, Adm 1/2737: 202.

15. Pring to Yeo, 12 September 1814, in Crawford, *Naval War of 1812*, 3:611.

16. Ibid.

17. Robertson to Pring, 12 September 1814, in Crawford, *Naval War of 1812*, 3:612.

18. Ibid., 613.

19. Ibid., 612–14.

20. Yeo to Croker, 24 September 1814, in Wood, *Select British Documents*, 3 (pt. 1): 367.

21. Ibid.

22. The Prevost–Downie correspondence included seven letters: Downie to Prevost, 1 September 1814; Downie to Prevost, 7 September; Prevost to Downie, 8 September; Downie to Prevost, 8 September; Prevost to Downie, 9 September; Downie to Prevost, 9 September; and Prevost to Downie, 10 September. See Croker to Bunbury, 18 November 1814, RMC, CO 42/158: 156.

23. Yeo to Croker, 29 September 1814, in Wood, *Select British Documents*, 3 (pt. 1): 377.

24. Ibid.

25. Sinclair to Baynes, 20 March 1815, RMC, CO 42/161: 155–56.

26. Ibid, 158.

27. Macomb to the Secretary of War, 15 September 1815, in Wood, *Select British Documents*, 3 (pt. 1): 356. There is a question of time difference in Macomb's statement, but the essential point is that the fire opened with the approach of the British flotilla.

28. Ibid.

29. Plattsburgh Court-Martial, in Wood, *Select British Documents*, 3 (pt. 1): 407; Quimby, *U.S. Army in the War of 1812*, 2:625. Prevost made no mention of these attacks in his report.

30. "No. 1: A Plan of the Situation of the British and United States Squadrons at the Time the Confiance and Linnet Anchored," TNA Adm 1/5440: 241. All the plans were drawn to the scale of one and one-half inches to the mile.

31. "No. 4: A Plan of the Situation of the British and United States Squadrons at the Time the Confiance Struck," TNA Adm 1/5440: 247. As for the range of the artillery, period sources vary somewhat in regard to the necessary elevation and range achieved. Lavery, *Nelson's Navy*, 177, provides figures based on practices with land guns.

32. Sutherland, "Civil Administration of Sir George Prevost," 139.

33. Cockburn to Sandys, 20 October 1814, in Wood, *Select British Documents*, 3 (pt. 1): 387–88.

34. Ibid., 389.

35. Ibid., 388.

36. Ibid.

37. Ibid. Arthur John Henry Somerset (1780–1816) came from an influential family whose close contacts included Wellington. One of his brothers became Lord Raglan of Crimean War fame. Between October and December 1814, Somerset, an officer in the 19th Light Dragoons, was in Montreal. A detachment of his regiment had been in the Canadas since May 1813 and had campaigned in the Niagara Peninsula and the Plattsburgh campaign. Sutherland, *His Majesty's Gentlemen*, 338. Details regarding the family history can be found at "Lord (Robert) Edward Henry Somerset," q.v., *Oxford Dictionary of National Biography*, doi:10.1093/ref:odnb /26014.

38. Robert Christie, *A History of the Late Province of Lower Canada*, vol. 2 (Montreal: Richard Worthington, 1855), 240.

39. Ibid.

40. *Montreal Herald*, 7 January 1815.

41. Newspaper clipping, "London, Tuesday, 25 October 1814," Clements Library, Brisbane Papers; emphasis in original.

42. Ibid.

43. Richard Cannon, *Historical Record of the 16th Regiment* (London: Parker, Furnivall and Parker, 1848), 29; Sutherland, *His Majesty's Gentlemen*, 380, 390.

44. *Veritas* was the pen name of Montreal merchant John Richardson, who despised Prevost over his support of French interests. His identity remained unknown for some years. *Nerva* was the pen name for Justice Samuel Gale from Montreal. Gale wrote an allegory of Prevost's actions using Ireland in place of the Canadas. Henry Scadding, "The Letters of Veritas," *Canadian Monthly and National Review* 9, no. 2 (1876): 93, 94.

45. Extract from a letter in a Halifax Paper, of the 1st of October 1814, in Wood, *Select British Documents*, 3 (pt. 1): 391, 392, 393.

46. Prevost to Bathurst, 22 September 1814, in Wood, *Select British Documents*, 3 (pt. 1): 364.

47. Ibid., 365.

48. Ibid., 364, 365.

49. Ibid., 364.

50. Prevost to Drummond, 16 September 1814, in Crawford, *Naval War of 1812*, 3:616.

51. [Stephen Sewell], "Particulars of the Late Disastrous Affair on Lake Champlain," *Montreal Herald*, 17 September 1814, in Byron N. Clark, ed., *A List of Pensioners of the War of 1812* (Burlington, Vt., and Boston: Research Publication Co., 1904), 50; *New York Spectator*, 3 October 1814, 1. Despite denying that he had no hand in authoring several articles that were critical of Prevost's wartime leadership, Sewell, a prominent Montreal

landowner, lawyer, and officeholder, was suspected of being the culprit; he was first suspended and then dismissed as solicitor general for his actions. See "Sewell (Sewall), Stephen," q.v., *Canadian Dictionary of Biography On line*, http://www.biographi.ca/009004-119.01-e.php?BioId=37247.

52. Picton to Brisbane, 31 October 1814, Clements Library, Brisbane Papers.

53. Ibid.

54. Wellington to Bathurst, 30 October 1814, in HMC, *Report of the Manuscripts of Earl Bathurst* (London: His Majesty's Stationery Office, 1923), 302.

55. Coore to Yeo, *Montreal Gazette*, 26 February 1815.

56. The Battle of Plattsburgh (Written by a Staff Officer from the Peninsula), in HMC, *Report of the Manuscripts of Earl Bathurst*, 286, 290.

57. Liverpool to Wellington, 18 November 1814, in Wellington, *SD* 9:437.

58. Ibid.

59. On 18 November 1814, John Barrow, the Second Secretary of the Admiralty, sent Yeo's letter to Henry Bunbury, the undersecretary of state (War) and one of Bathurst's key subordinates. Barrow to Bunbury, 18 November 1814, RMC, CO 42:129: 156.

60. The Battle of Plattsburgh (Written by a Staff Officer from the Peninsula), in HMC, *Report of the Manuscripts of Earl Bathurst*, 286.

61. "Anthony Merry," q.v., *Oxford Dictionary of National Biography*, doi:10.1093/ref:odnb/37760.

62. Goulburn to Bathurst, 25 November 1814, in Wellington, *SD* 9: 453, 454.

63. Torrens to Wellington, 3 November 1814, in Wellington, *SD* 9:404.

64. Wellington to Murray, 22 December 1814, in Gurwood, *Dispatches of Duke of Wellington*, 12:224.

65. Wellington to Liverpool, 9 November 1814, in Wellington, *SD* 9:425.

66. Liverpool to Castlereagh, 4 November 1814, in Wellington, *SD* 9:405.

67. Wellington to Bathurst, 30 October 1814, in *Report on the Manuscripts of the Earl of Bathurst*, 302.

68. Liverpool to Castlereagh, 4 November 1814, in Wellington, *SD* 9:405; Wellington to Bathurst, 30 October 1814, in *Report on the Manuscripts of the Earl of Bathurst*, 302, 303.

69. Prevost to Bathurst, 20 December 1814, in Wood, *Select British Documents*, 3 (pt. 1): 393.

70. Ibid.

71. Prevost to Bathurst, 26 November 1814, RMC, CO 42/157: 360.

72. Ibid.

73. Yeo to Prevost, 26 November 1814, in Wood, *Select British Documents*, 3 (pt. 1): 394.

74. Melville to Bathurst, 2 September 1815, in *Report on the Manuscripts of Earl Bathurst*, 381.

75. Prevost to Bathurst, 18 October 1814, RMC, CO 42/157: 260; Malcomson, *Lords of the Lake*, 306, 317.

76. Richard R. Johnson, "British North America, 1760–1815," in Marshall, *Oxford History of the British Empire*, 2:390, 391; Graham, *Sea Power and British North America*, 56.

77. Prevost to Bathurst, 5 March 1815, RMC, CO 42/161: 71. Murray remained in Canada uncertain as to his employment until he replaced Drummond in Upper Canada on 4 April 1815. He left for Europe immediately upon hearing of Napoléon's escape and just missed the Battle of Waterloo.

78. Ibid., 71, 72.

79. Ibid., 73, 74.

80. Ibid., 71, 72; Prevost to Bathurst, 27 March 1815, RMC, CO 42/161: 113.

81. Barrow to Otway, 30 November 1814, TNA, Adm 2/1381: 57, 58.

82. Notes on Yeo to Croker, 29 September 1814, TNA, Adm 1/2737: 179; Lake Erie Court-Martial Papers, 9 and 16 September 1814, in Wood, *Select British Documents*, 2:306. Yeo did not receive any reprimand but was instructed to provide regular reports to the Admiralty, something he had not previously done.

83. Croker to Yeo, 12 December 1814, TNA, Adm 2/1381: 74, 75.

84. *Montreal Herald*, 11 March 1815, 3.

85. Croker to Yeo, 12 December 1814, TNA, Adm 2/1381: 69–73, 75; Malcomson, *Lords of the Lake*, 323.

86. General Order, Quebec, March 1815, in *Columbian Centinel*, Boston, 19 April 1815. The same order was also printed on 26 April 1815 in the *Hallowell Gazette*, published in Hallowell, Me.

87. Drummond to Bathurst, 5 April 1815, RMC, CO 42/162: 2.

88. *Columbian Centinel*, Boston, 19 April 1815.

89. Brenton, *Some Account of the Public Life*, 177.

90. In his final days at Quebec, Prevost received praise from the provincial government. As Prevost and his party left at 2:00 P.M. on 3 April, a guard from the 4th Battalion Royal Veteran Regiment and the 103rd Foot lined the streets, while the grand battery fired a salute. *Quebec Mercury*, 4 April 1814, 110.

91. Veritas, *Letters of Veritas*.

92. Interesting Particulars of the Late, Distressing, Humiliating and Disastrous Affair at Plattsburgh, RMC, CO 42/161: 172.

93. Prevost to Bathurst, 11 May 1815, RMC, CO 42/161: 182.

94. Ibid.

95. Ibid., 184.

96. No record of Prevost's interview with Bathurst has been uncovered either in British or Canadian archives.

97. Hitsman, *Incredible War of 1812*, 276. Prevost is incorrectly reported to have moved into Greenhill Grove, an estate he supposedly inherited from his father, Augustin Prevost. This estate, located about ten miles north of London, was purchased by Augustin in March 1781 and was originally called "Pricklers." Augustin renamed the mansion Greenhill Grove in honor of an action in Canada. Greenhill Grove was sold to a brewer by Augustin's widow in June 1790. George Prevost purchased Belmont in

January 1810 for £10,594, and it remained in the family until his wife passed away in 1821. Sir Christopher Prevost, e-mail to author, 8 March 2010. The inheritance story about Greenhill Grove appears in Lewis Butler, *King's Royal Rifle Corps*, 1:325, 326.

98. Wellington to Murray, 22 December 1814, Gurwood, *Dispatches of Duke of Wellington*, 12:224; Hitsman, *Incredible War of 1812*, 276.

99. "Captains & C appointed and reappointed," *Naval Chronicle* 34 (1815): 262.

100. Ibid. In 1813, the Royal Navy commenced reducing its establishment from 117,400 seamen and marines. By 1815, the total had been cut to 90,000. By 1816, the establishment sat at 33,000 seamen and marines, and in the following year, this was reduced to 19,000 personnel. In 1814, the navy had 644 vessels in commission, but by 1817, this figure was reduced to 124. These reductions did not affect the number of post captains on the Naval List, for although from 1815 to 1817 this number stayed steady at just above 800, there were far fewer command billets. See Clowes, *Royal Navy*, 5:9, and 6:190; David Lyon and Rif Winfield, *The Sail & Steam Navy List: All the Ships of the Royal Navy, 1815–1889* (London: Chatham Publishing, 2004), 13, 33; and Rif Winfield, *British Warships in the Age of Sail, 1793–1817* (London: Chatham Publishing, 2005), xiv.

101. Yeo would not arrive off the coast of Africa until the fall of 1816. *Naval Chronicle* 36 (July–December 1816): 346.

102. Yeo to Manners-Sutton, 26 August 1814, TNA, Adm 1/2738: 142.

103. Anne Prevost recorded her feelings on the matter in her diary, noting of Yeo's actions that "no man with a nice sense of honour would have acted in this manner." Anne Elinor Prevost Diary, LAC, MG 24 A9: 174.

104. Yeo to Croker, 5 September 1815, TNA, Adm 1/2738: 140.

105. Yeo to Manners-Sutton, 26 August 1815, TNA, Adm 1/2738: 142.

106. Ibid., 142, 143.

107. Manners-Sutton to Yeo, 27 August 1815, TNA, Adm 1/2738: 146.

108. Yeo to Croker, 5 September 1815, TNA, Adm 1/2738: 140.

109. Plattsburgh Court-Martial, in Wood, *Select British Documents*, 3 (pt. 1): 400. The court-martial was held on board HMS *Gladiator*, a 44-gun frigate that was serving as the flagship for Rear Admiral Peter Halkett, the second-in-command at Spithead. *Gladiator* never went to sea, making it an ideal platform for courts-martial. Winfield, *British Warships*, 128.

110. Plattsburgh Court-Martial, in Wood, *Select British Documents*, 3 (pt. 1): 405, 456, 457.

111. Ibid., 401, 402; Everest, *War of 1812 in the Champlain Valley*, 200, 201.

112. Robert Christie, *Memoirs of the Administration of the Colonial Government of Lower Canada by Sir James Henry Craig and Sir George Prevost* (Quebec, 1818), 216.

113. Ibid.

114. Documentation regarding this process is found in TNA, WO 81/52: 6-149; and Christie, *Colonial Government of Lower Canada*, postscript following 150 ff.

115. Yeo denied he had used his time in America immediately follow-ing the end of hostilities to collect evidence. See Yeo to Croker, 19 August 1815, TNA, Adm 1/2738: 135; and Fortescue, *History of the British Army*, 10:132.

116. Macdonough to Cadwallader Colden, 3 July 1815, in Brenton, *Some Account of the Public Life*, 164.

117. Ibid., 164, 165.

118. Ibid., 164, 165, 166.

119. Yeo to Croker, 15 September 1815, TNA, Adm 1/2378: 151, 152.

120. Ibid.

121. Ibid.

122. List of Witnesses, Royal Navy, 11 January 1816, TNA, WO 81/52: 133; Oldham to Croker, 20 December 1815, TNA, WO 81/52: 103; Yeo to Croker, 15 September 1815, TNA, Adm 1/2378: 151, 152.

123. Manners-Sutton to various, 19 December 1815, TNA, WO 81/52: 101, 102.

124. Wallaston to Coore, 14 November 1814, TNA, WO 81/52: 49.

125. Oldham to Witnesses, 17 October 1815, TNA, WO 81/25: 6, 7, 8; Manners-Sutton to Witnesses, 19 December 1815, TNA, WO 81/52: 101; Manners-Sutton to Robinson, 6 December 1814, TNA, WO 81/15: 77.

126. Wallaston to Court-Martial President and Members, 24 Novem-ber 1815, TNA, WO 81/25: 61, 62; Great Britain, War Office, *The Army List for August 1813* (London, 1813), 2.

127. John Phillipart, ed., *The Royal Military Calendar* (London: T. Egerton 1820), 2:12–14; Muir, *Britain and the Defeat of Napoleon*, 83; S. G. P. Ward, *Wellington* (London: T. Batsford, 1963), 45, 60, 68; Wallaston to Court-Martial President and Members, 24 November 1815,T NA, WO 81/25: 61, 62; Oldham to Robinson, 6 December 1815, TNA, WO 81/25: 77, 78; Oldham to Prevost, 19 December 1815, TNA, WO 81/25: 99; Oldham to Yeo, 19 De-cember 1815, TNA, WO 81/25: 99, 100; Manners-Sutton to Wellington, 26 December 1815, TNA, WO 81/25: 104.

128. The *Naval Chronicle* was a professional naval journal published between 1799 and 1819; it covered a variety of topics such as action reports, intelligence, and foreign naval developments. As such, almost every naval officer, at one time or the other, would have read it. *Naval Chronicle* 34 (1815): 290. The full text of the four charges appeared in the *Boston Weekly Messenger*, 29 November 1815.

129. There are, unfortunately, few details known of this house, which apparently was on Vere Street, London. Sir Christopher Prevost, e-mail to author, 9 April 2010. During this time, Major General Roger Sheaffe called on Prevost in London to make inquiries on behalf of John Frederick Win-slow, an officer of the 41st Foot who had resigned his commission follow-ing an incident at the officer's mess in Fort George in March 1812, where Winslow struck another officer following an argument. Prevost advised Sheaffe that while he had recommended Winslow for an ensigncy, his rec-ommendation had not been forwarded due to his being in disgrace. Sheaffe to Winslow, 8 March 1816, LAC, RG 8 C vol. 1026: 74–76; Donald E. Graves, *Fort George Historical Study* (Ottawa: Parks Canada, 1979), 102–104.

130. Other family members buried in the tomb include George's parents; his sister Mary Louisa (1781–89); his wife, Catherine Anne (Phipps) Prevost (1766–1821); George's youngest daughter, Harriet Constantia Prevost (1790–1800); George's younger brother, Major General William Augustine Prevost, C.B. (1777–1824); and Fanny Sophia (Haultain) Prevost (1778–1813), the wife of George's brother, Rear Admiral Thomas James Prevost (1771–1855). Details from the records at St. Mary the Virgin provided by Sir Christopher Prevost, 5 March 2012. Thomas Prevost remarried in 1814 and is buried at another location.

As Prevost was still on active service, his rank entitled him to a military funeral; if circumstances permitted, the service would include a party comprising three battalions of infantry, four squadrons of cavalry, and an artillery salute of three rounds fired from nine guns. Unfortunately, no account of Prevost's funeral has been found. Burnham and McGuigan, *British Army against Napoleon*, 181.

131. Dropsy, or edema as it is more commonly known today, is a symptom that occurs when the body absorbs water, causing swelling of the tissue and in the lower limbs. The inadequate flow of blood caused by an irregularity in the pumping action of the heart, known as congestive heart failure, causes the body to absorb more water to compensate for the reduced flow of fluids. Oddly enough, this is one case where the period practice of bleeding or bloodletting could have provided Prevost with some relief. Hypertension and disease, as Prevost experienced during his career, could have contributed to his decline. I am indebted to Dr. Greg Baran, a physician who also portrays a regimental surgeon from the War of 1812, for clarifying these details with the author on 1 March 2012. Downing Street to Wellington, 27 December 1815, TNA, WO 81/25: 112; Oldham to Prevost, 27 December 1815, TNA, WO 81/25: 112–13; Oldham to Croker and Witnesses, 9 January 1816, TNA, WO 81/25: 128, 129.

132. Downing Street to Wm. Prevost, [?] January 1816, TNA, WO 81/25:141.

133. "On the Court Martial held at Chelsea Hospital in February 1816 on the Conduct of Lieutenant General Sir George Prevost, Commander in Chief of His Majesty's Forces in Canada," TNA, Treasury Solicitor 11/365.

134. The extract was taken from Letter No. 9, 7 July 1815, in Veritas, *Letters of Veritas*, 144–48.

135. "Court Martial held at Chelsea Hospital," TNA Treasury Solicitor 11/365.

136. The list of wrongly recorded names includes: Major General Thomas (not Charles) Brisbane, Sir Frederick (not Francis) Robinson, and Captain Robert Nickle (not Nicoll).

137. Prevost's will, originally drafted in 1803 and with a codicil added in 1808, lists properties near Portsmouth and near London as his only assets; he bequeathed both to his wife. Will of Sir George Prevost, TNA PROB 11/1576.

138. In 1805, Prevost received a sword and service of plate valued at £1,000 from the people of Dominica and plate valued at £300 from the West India Planters and Merchants. The Patriotic Fund awarded him a sword

valued at £100 and a service of plate worth £200. In 1815, the House of Representatives in Lower Canada voted £5,000 for a service of plate, which
Prevost never received. The Legislative Council refused to approve the bill
even though it had the support of the Prince Regent. Brenton, *Some Account of the Public Life*, 33, 34, 35, 176, 177, appendixes 12, 13, and 14. For
an overview of the wealth amassed by Prevost's relatives, see Campbell,
Royal American Regiment, 27, 28, 205, 206.

139. The Letters Patent for the Prevost coat of arms were issued on 2
December 1805, Ms Grants 23/272. Patrick O'Donoghue, Bluemantle Pur-
suivant, College of Arms, London, England, e-mail to author, 23 September
2010.

140. *London Gazette*, 11 September 1816, in Brenton, *Some Account of
the Public Life*, 180. The 16th Foot was selected as Prevost had been appointed colonel of this regiment in February 1814 and still held that post at
the time of his death. See Canon, *Historical Records of the 16th*, 28, 29, 30,
44, 45.

141. Hitsman, *Incredible War of 1812*, 352n12.

EPILOGUE

1. Among these officers are Lieutenant Colonel John Harvey, who
led the raid on Stoney Creek; Lieutenant Colonel Charles Plenderleath,
who was present at Stoney Creek; Lieutenant Colonel Charles de Salaberry, commander at the Châteauguay; Lieutenant Colonel John Morrison,
who led British forces at Crysler's Farm; and Lieutenant James Fitzgibbon
of Beaver Dams fame.

2. In his study of the problems of joint command in the Canadas in
"Commodore Sir James Yeo and Governor General George Prevost: A
Study in Command Relations," Canadian historian Frederick C. Drake
was interested in the fact that despite the rupture between Prevost and
Yeo, "throughout most of the war it was the cooperation between both
men that enabled the British to retain Upper Canada." Drake considered
this a significant point as "the eighteen months of cooperation during the
war meant more than the year of recrimination after it ended." When Yeo
arrived at Kingston in 1813, "[he] had to defend Canada by cooperating
with the army . . . by providing logistical support by raiding lake bases and
disrupting his opponents' supply bases, and by keeping lines of communication open rather than by risking all in a vainglorious search for battle."
In other words, Yeo's task was to avoid battle unless absolutely necessary,
while ensuring the operational needs of the army were satisfied. See *New
Interpretations in Naval History: Selected Papers from the Eighth Naval
History Symposium*, ed. William B. Cogar (Annapolis: Naval Institute
Press, 1989), 157, 159.

3. Hall, *Wellington's Navy*, 87.

4. Brian Mark De Toy, "Sir George Cranfield Berkeley," q.v., *Oxford
Dictionary of National Biography*, doi:10.1093/ref:odnb/2213.

5. In all fairness to Yeo, Berkeley did not have to concern himself
with the construction, outfitting, and manning of his squadron to the

extent the commodore did. The Portuguese Station could also tap into the resources of the Royal Navy to a level that was impossible for Yeo.

6. Colonel John Biddulph, *The Nineteenth and Their Times* (London. John Murray, 1899), 212–13.

7. H. M. Walker, *A History of the Northumberland Fusiliers, 1674–1902* (London: John Murray, 1919), 344.

APPENDIX A

1. Fitz-Enz, *Final Invasion*.

2. Prevost is referring to members of the 10th Royal Veteran Battalion, which arrived in Canada in 1807.

3. Lieutenant Colonel Thomas Bligh St. George, who served during the Detroit campaign of 1812, was severely wounded at Frenchtown in early 1813.

4. Colonel Henry Procter arrived in Canada in 1802 and when the war broke out in June 1812, he was in command of Fort George. In the following month, Brock sent him to take command of the forces in the Western District. He became a brigadier general in February 1813 and in June, when his command was redesignated as the Right Division of the Army of Upper Canada, he was promoted to major general. In October 1813, nearly all of Procter's men were captured by the Americans at Moraviantown. For a biography of Procter, see Antal, *Wampum Denied*, 67–71, passim.

5. A captain's command consisted of a company.

6. A subaltern was a junior officer, either an ensign or a lieutenant, and would have led a detachment from a company.

7. Located in New York State. Originally established by the French, the fort was occupied by the British until 1795 when it was transferred to the United States.

8. Major Donald Macpherson, an officer with the 10th Royal Veteran Battalion, commanded at Kingston until he was transferred to Quebec in the spring of 1813.

9. An artillery brigade was formed by the union of the guns (battery) with the personnel (company). It should not be confused with the formation of the same name, which is normally a grouping of two or more infantry or cavalry regiments.

10. Embodiment involved the calling up of a militia unit for a fixed period of service, normally for the length of hostilities.

11. 10th Royal Veteran Battalion.

12. This community is now known as Sorel.

13. The term "field officer" normally refers to a major but can include someone of the rank of lieutenant colonel.

14. A casemate (note Prevost's spelling) is a vaulted chamber that gains its strength from the curved shape of its roof. Casemates are the basic elements of a fort that offer protection to its occupants.

15. Between 1808 and 1810, three line regiments were added to the establishment of the British army. Two were formed in 1808: the 102nd Regiment with the personnel from the New South Wales Corps; and the 103rd,

created from the 9th Garrison Battalion stationed in Britain. In 1810, the New Brunswick Fencibles, originally raised in 1803, were taken into the line as the 104th Foot. The significance of taking these units into the line is that it extended their terms of service—initially limited to England or the colony where they were serving—to anywhere in the world. Kevin Linch, "The Recruitment of the British Army, 1807–1815" (PhD diss., University of Leeds, 2001), 25, 25n13.

16. The Nova Scotia Fencibles were raised in 1803 for the defense of the province. In 1807, it was sent to Newfoundland and was later transferred to Quebec and then, in 1814, to Kingston. The regiment was disbanded at Halifax in 1816.

17. The Royal Newfoundland Fencibles were raised in 1803. In 1805, the unit was transferred to Nova Scotia, and in 1807, it moved to Lower Canada. In the summer of 1812, the unit arrived in Upper Canada to serve as marines on the vessels of the Provincial Marine and later the Royal Navy. Elements of the regiment were present at many actions during the war.

18. Prevost here refers to the Glengarry Light Infantry Fencibles, raised in 1812.

19. Bathurst must have meant ten, as a total of twelve battalions were sent from Wellington's army to North America. These included the following units sent to the Canadas: 1/3rd, 1/5th, 1/9th, 1/39th, 57th, 76th, 1/88th; and to the Maritime Provinces: 3/27th. Four other battalions—the 1/7th, 1/40th, 1/43rd and 3/95th—departed afterward for Louisiana.

20. In April 1814, this army consisted of a cavalry division, a light infantry division, and seven divisions of line infantry. There were a total of sixty-seven battalions in the Peninsular army, of which nine were sent to Canada, one to the Maritime Provinces, two to the Chesapeake, and four to the expedition to New Orleans.

21. These companies were Turner's, Maxwell's, and Trelawney's. Two other companies, Carmichael's and Michell's, would serve in the Chesapeake.

22. Units sent from Britain for service in the Canadas included the 4/1st, 1/27th, and 1/37th. Those units destined for the Maritime Provinces included the 7/60th and 2/93rd. The 2nd Battalion Royal Marines was assigned to the Chesapeake.

23. The battalions sent to the Chesapeake were the 1/4th and 85th from Wellington's army, the 1/21st from Gibraltar, and the 1/62nd from Genoa. Those units destined for the Maritime Provinces were the 29th from Gibraltar and the 1/62nd from Genoa.

24. Bathurst was referring to the operations conducted in Chesapeake Bay between April and September 1814 that included the occupation of Washington, the raid on the Potomac River, the attack on Baltimore, and the Battle of North Point.

25. A brigade based at Kingston in Upper Canada led by Major General Sir James Kempt was assigned for this task.

26. Lieutenant General Sir John Coape Sherbrooke (1764–1830) led the British war effort in the Maritime Provinces. While he was subordinate to

Prevost for most matters, in order to ease Prevost's span of control, most of his correspondence was directly with London.

27. The Maine expedition was conducted between July 1814 and April 1815. British forces were successful in occupying several communities and fortified points along the Maine coast until after the ratification of the Treaty of Ghent.

APPENDIX B

1. The British list is compiled from Baynes to Robinson, 10 September 1814, RMC, Papers of Major General F. P. Robinson.

2. It was usual practice in the Royal Artillery to designate companies with the name of their commander.

3. A provincial corps formed in January 1813 that was attached to the Royal Artillery in Montreal. It was disbanded in 1815.

4. All units from Wellington's Peninsular Army are designated in bold text.

5. De Meuron's was a Swiss regiment that, in 1795, entered British service. In 1813, the regiment was transferred to Canada, and in 1816, it returned to England, where it was disbanded.

6. In March 1814, the 5th Battalion Select Embodied Militia was re-formed as a light infantry unit of six companies.

7. The American list is compiled from Everest, *War of 1812 in the Champlain Valley*, 165; and Herkalo, *Battles at Plattsburgh*, 123–26.

8. This table is compiled from the Plattsburgh Court-Martial, TNA, Adm 1/5450: 78.

9. One of these long guns was mounted on a pivot.

10. A Columbiad was a smoothbore gun of American design that was similar to a carronade.

11. *Yeo* and *Prevost.*

12. *Blucher.*

13. *Wellington.*

14. *Beckwith, Murray,* and *Drummond.*

15. *Beresford, Popham, Brock (B),* and *Simcoe.*

16. The American table is compiled from the Plattsburgh Court-Martial, TNA, Adm 1/5450: 79.

17. *Allen, Borer, Burrows, Centipede, Nettle,* and *Viper.*

18. *Alwyn, Ludlow, Ballard,* and *Wilmer.*

APPENDIX D

1. Antal, *Wampum Denied*, 373.

2. Ibid.

3. Sutherland, *His Majesty's Gentlemen*, entries for Major Generals Thomas Brisbane, Henry Conran, George Glasgow, and Louis de Watteville; and Lieutenant Colonels Edward Copson, Philip Hughes, Joseph Morrison, John Murray, John O'Neil, Edward Pritchard, Charles de Salaberry, and Jonathan Yates.

4. Hitsman, *Incredible War of 1812*, 344n43.

5. Transcript of Court-Martial of Major General Henry Procter, LAC, MG 13: 2, 3.

6. Ibid., 3, 4.

7. Ibid., 4.

8. Ibid., 5.

9. Ibid., 6.

10. Antal, *Wampum Denied*, 377.

APPENDIX E

1. Wallaston to Court Martial President and Members, 24 November 1815, TNA, WO 81/25: 61, 62; War Office, *Army List for August 1813*, 2.

2. Sutton-Manners to various, 19 December 1815, WO 81/52: 101, 102.

APPENDIX F

1. "On the Court Martial held at Chelsea Hospital," TNA Treasury Solicitor 11/365.

2. Edward Brenton, Prevost's civil secretary, returned to England with Prevost in the spring of 1815.

3. In this passage, Prevost was describing the opening of the campaign and not, as is suggested here, the situation around Plattsburgh.

4. Brisbane's first name was Thomas, not Charles.

5. This passage refers to an unknown person who interviewed two of the army officers in Europe.

BIBLIOGRAPHY

ARCHIVAL SOURCES

Library and Archives Canada, Ottawa (LAC)
  Manuscript Group 24 F 18, "Four Years on the Lakes in Canada in 1813, 1814, 1815 and 1816; by a Naval Officer under the Command of the late Sir James Lucas Yeo," by David Wingfield
  Manuscript Group 24 A9, Diary of Anne Elinor Prevost
  Manuscript Group 42, Andrew Cochrane Papers
  Record Group 8, C Series, British Military Records, 1811–15
  Record Group 9, Pre-Confederation Militia Records, 1811–15
  Massey Library, the Royal Military College of Canada, Kingston (RMC)
  Colonial Office 42, Secretary of State Correspondence, In-Letters, 1807 to 1815; originals held at the National Archives, London.
  The Journals of Major-General F. W. Robinson.

McCord Museum, Montreal
  War of 1812 Papers, General Order Books

The National Archives, Kew, London (TNA)
  Admiralty 1, vol. 2737, Secretary's Department In-Letters from Captains Y
  Admiralty 1, vol. 2378, Secretary's Department In-Letters from Captains R
  Admiralty 1, vol. 5450, Admiralty and Secretariat, Papers, In-Letters, Reports of Courts-Martial, August 1815
  Admiralty 2, vol. 1376, Admiralty Out-Letters, January–May 1813
  Admiralty 2, vol. 1381, Admiralty Out-Letters, October 1814–May 1815
  Admiralty 106, Navy Board, In-Letters from Yards, Canada
  Colonial Office 43, vol. 22, Letters from Secretary of State, Lower Canada, 3 September 1801–16 September 1811
  Colonial Office 43, vol. 23, Letters from Secretary of State, Lower Canada, 22 October 1811–16 March 1816

Prerogative Court of Canterbury Wills 11, vol. 1576, Sir George Prevost, 27 January 1816

Treasury Solicitor and HM Procurator Papers, 11, vol. 365. On the Court Martial held at Chelsea Hospital in February 1816 of the Conduct of Lieutenant General Sir George Prevost, Commander in Chief of His Majesty's Forces in Canada, 1816.

War Office 6, vol. 2, Out-Letters of the Secretary of State for War and Secretary of State for War and the Colonies, 1793–1859

War Office 17, Monthly Returns of the British Army in North America

War Office 28, vol. 304, General Orders Canada, 20 February–13 October 1812

War Office 71, vol. 239, Adjutant General's Office, Courts-Martial and Proceedings, Officers, October–December 1814

War Office 81/52, Judge Advocate General's Letter Books, 1815–16

War Office 1/118, Reports on the Capture of Various Islands in the West Indies from the French

Regimental Museum, The Royal Welch Fusiliers, Caernarfon, Wales
  The Diary of Drummer Richard Bentinck, 23rd Foot

University of New Brunswick, The Loyalist Collection
  Journal of Augustine Prevost, 1774

William R. Clements Library, University of Michigan, Ann Arbor
  The Papers of Major-General Thomas Brisbane

NEWSPAPERS AND PERIODICALS

Aberdeen Journal, 1806, 1808, 1809, 1810
Boston Weekly Messenger, 1815
Caledonian Mercury, 1806, 1807, 1808
Columbian Centinel, 1815
Hallowell Gazette, 1815
Hampshire Telegraph and Sussex Chronicle, 1807, 1808
Jackson's Oxford Journal, 1805
London Gazette, 1808
Naval Chronicle, 1806, 1815, 1816
Quebec Mercury, 1811, 1814

BOOKS, ARTICLES, AND BIOGRAPHICAL ENTRIES

Abbott, John, Graeme S. Mount, and Michael J. Mulloy. *The Story of Fort St. Joseph*. Toronto: Dundurn, 2000.

Adkin, Mark. *Trafalgar Companion: The Complete Guide to History's Most Famous Sea Battle and the Life of Lord Nelson*. London: Aarum Press, 2005.

Allen, Robert S. *His Majesty's Indian Allies: British Indian Policy in the Defence of Canada, 1774–1815*. Toronto: Dundurn, 1993.

Antal, Sandy. *A Wampum Denied: Procter's War of 1812*. Ottawa: Carleton University Press, 1997.

Army Officers Awards of the Napoleonic Period. London: Savannah Paperback Classics, 2002.

Arthur, Brian. *How Britain Won the War of 1812: The Royal Navy Blockades of the United States, 1812–1815.* Woodbridge: Boydell Press, 2011.

Bamford, Andrew. "The British Army in the Low Countries, 1813–1814." The Napoleon Series. www.napoleon-series.org/military/battles/c_low countries1814.html.

Bartow, Rev. Evelyn. "The Prevost Family in America." *New York Genealogical and Biographical Record* 13, no. 1 (1862): 27–28.

Benn, Carl. *Historic Fort York, 1793–1993.* Toronto: Natural Heritage, 1993.

———. *The Iroquois in the War of 1812.* Toronto: University of Toronto Press, 1998.

Biddulph, Colonel John. *The Nineteenth and Their Times.* London: John Murray, 1899.

Black, Jeremy. *The War of 1812 in the Age of Napoleon.* Norman: University of Oklahoma Press, 2009.

Blanco, Richard L., ed. *The American Revolution: An Encyclopaedia.* 2 vols. New York: Garland Publishing, Inc., 1993.

Boscowen, Hugh. *The Capture of Louisbourg, 1758.* Norman: University of Oklahoma Press, 2011.

Bowyer-Bower, T. A. "A Pioneer of Military Education: The Royal Military Academy Chelsea, 1801–1821." *British Journal of Educational Studies* 2, no. 2 (1954): 122–32.

Brenton, E. B. *Some Account of the Public Life of Lieutenant General Sir George Prevost: Particularly of His Services in the Canadas.* London: T. Egerton, 1823.

Brisbane, Thomas Makedougall. *The Reminiscences of Major General Thomas Makedougall Brisbane.* Edinburgh: Thomas Constable, 1860.

Buckley, Roger Norman, ed. *The Napoleonic War Journal of Captain Thomas Henry Browne, 1807–1816.* London: Army Records Society, 1987.

Burke's Peerage and Gentry, 1915. London: Burke's Peerage Company, 1915. http://www.burkes-peerage.net (accessed 14 October 2009).

Burnham, Robert, and Ron McGuigan. *The British Army against Napoleon: Facts, Lists and Trivia, 1805–1815.* Barnsley, UK: Frontline Books, 2010.

Butler, Lewis. *The Annals of the King's Royal Rifle Corps.* Vol. 1, *The Royal Americans.* London: Smith, Elder & Co., 1913.

———. *The Annals of the King's Royal Rifle Corps.* Vol. 2, *The Green Jacket.* London: John Murray, 1923.

Caruana, Adrian B. *The History of English Sea Ordnance, 1523–1875.* 2 vols. Ashley Lodge, UK: Jean Boudriot Publications, 1997.

Campbell, Alexander V. *The Royal American Regiment: An Atlantic Microcosm, 1755–1772.* Norman: University of Oklahoma Press, 2010.

Cannon, Richard. *Historical Record of the Eighth, or The King's Regiment of Foot.* London: Parker, Furnivall and Parker, 1844.

———. *Historical Record of the 16th Regiment.* London: Parker, Furnivall and Parker, 1848.

Cary, A. D. L., and Stouppe McCance. *Regimental Records of the Royal Welch Fusiliers (Late the 23rd Foot).* Vol. 1, *1689–1815.* London: Foster, Groom & Company, 1929.

Christie, Robert. *The Military and Naval Operations in the Canadas, during the Late War with the United States including also The Political History of Lower Canada during the Administrations of Sir James Craig and Sir George Prevost.* Quebec: n.p., 1818.

Clark, Byron N., ed. *A List of Pensioners of the War of 1812.* Burlington, Vt., and Boston: Research Publication Co., 1904.

Clowes, William Laird. *The Royal Navy: A History from the Earliest Times to 1900.* 5 vols. London: Chatham Publishing, 1999.

Coles, Harry L. *The War of 1812.* Chicago: University of Chicago Press, 1965.

Connolly, T. W. J. *Roll of Officers of the Corps of Engineers from 1660 to 1898.* Chatham: W. & J. Mackay and Company, 1898.

Conway, Stephen. "To Subdue America: British Army Officers and the Conduct of the Revolutionary War." *William and Mary Quarterly,* 3rd ser., vol. 43, no. 3 (1986): 381–407.

Crawford, Michael J., ed. *The Naval War of 1812: A Documentary History,* vol. 3. Washington, D.C.: Naval Historical Center, 2002.

———. *Documentary History of the Campaigns upon the Niagara Frontier in 1812 to 1814.* 9 vols. Welland, Ont., 1896–1908.

———. *Documents Relating to the Invasion of Canada and the Surrender of Detroit, 1812.* Ottawa: Government Printing Bureau, 1912.

Davis, Matthew L. *The Private Journal of Aaron Burr,* vol. 1. New York: Harper and Brothers, 1838.

Drake, Frederick C. "Commodore Sir James Yeo and Governor General George Prevost: A Study in Command Relations." In *New Interpretations in Naval History: Selected Papers from the Eighth Naval History Symposium,* ed. William B. Cogar (Annapolis: Naval Institute Press, 1989), 156–74.

Dudley, William S., ed. *The Naval War of 1812: A Documentary History.* 2 vols. Washington: Naval History Center, 1985, 1992.

Duffy, Michael. *Soldiers, Sugar, and Seapower: The British Expeditions to the West Indies and the War against Revolutionary France.* Oxford: Clarendon Press, 1987.

Dunnigan, Brian Leigh. *The British Army at Mackinac, 1812–1815.* Mackinac, Mich.: Mackinac State Historic Parks, 1992.

———. *Forts within a Fort: Niagara's Redoubts.* Youngstown, N.Y.: Old Fort Niagara Association, 1989.

———. *King's Men at Mackinac: The British Garrisons, 1780–1796.* Mackinac, Mich.: Mackinac State Historic Parks, 1973.

Dupin, Charles. *A Tour through the Naval and Military Establishments of Great Britain: In the Years 1816–1820.* London: Sir Richard Phillips and Company, 1822.

Dyde, Brian. *The Empty Sleeve: The Story of the West India Regiments of the British Army.* St. John's, Antigua: Hansib Caribbean, 1997.

Edwards, Joseph Plimsoll. *The Militia of Nova Scotia, 1749–1867.* Londonderry, N.S.: n.p., 1913.

Elliott, James E. *Strange Fatality: The Battle of Stoney Creek, 1813.* Montreal: Robin Brass Studio, 2009.

Ellis, A. B. *History of the First West India Regiment.* London: Chapman and Hall Limited, 1885.

Esary, Logan. *Messages and Letters of William Henry Harrison.* 2 vols. Indianapolis: Indiana Historical Commission, 1922.

Everest, Allan S. *The War of 1812 in the Champlain Valley.* Syracuse, N.Y.: Syracuse University Press, 1981.

Fay, H. A. *Collection of Official Accounts, in detail, of all the Battles Fought by Sea and Land, between the Navy and Army of the United States and the Navy and Army of Great Britain, during the Years 1812, 13, 14, & 15.* New York: E. Conrad, 1817

Ferguson, Gillum. *Illinois in the War of 1812.* Urbana: University of Illinois Press, 2012.

Fitz-Enz, David G. *The Final Invasion: Plattsburgh, the War of 1812's Most Decisive Battle.* New York: Cooper Square Press, 2001.

Fortescue, John. *A History of the British Army.* 19 vols. London: Macmillan, 1899–1930.

Galpin, Alec R. *The War of 1812 in the Old Northwest.* Toronto: Ryerson Press, 1958.

Galpin, W. Freeman. "The American Grain Trade to the Spanish Peninsula, 1810–1814." *American Historical Review* 28 (1923): 24–44.

Gaspar, David Barry, and David Patrick Geggus. *A Turbulent Time: The French Revolution and the Great Caribbean.* Bloomington: Indiana University Press, 1997.

Gibbes, Rigaud. *Celer et Audax: A Sketch of the Services of the Fifth Battalion 60th Regiment (Rifles).* Oxford: H. Pickard Hall, 1879.

Glendining's. *Orders, Decorations, Medals and Militaria for the Campaigns 1793–1840.* London: Glendining and Co., 1991. (Catalog for sale of Prevost Army Gold Medal and swords)

Glover, Richard. *Britain at Bay: Defence against Bonaparte, 1803–1814.* London: George Allen and Unwin, 1973.

———. *Peninsular Preparation: The Reform of the British Army, 1795–1809.* Cambridge: Cambridge University Press, 1963.

Gough, Barry. *Fighting Sail on Lake Huron and Georgian Bay: The War of 1812 and Its Aftermath.* Annapolis: Naval Institute Press, 2002.

Graham, Gerald S. *Sea Power and British North America, 1783–1820.* London and Cambridge, Mass.: Harvard University Press, 1941.

Gratton, William. *Adventures of the Connaught Rangers.* 2 vols. London: Henry Colburn, 1847.

———. *Adventures with the Connaught Rangers, 1809–1814.* Edited by Charles Oman. London: Edward Arnold, 1902.

Graves, Donald E. *Field of Glory: The Battle of Crysler's Farm, 1813.* Toronto: Robin Brass Studio, 1999.

————. *Fix Bayonets! A Royal Welch Fusilier at War, 1796–1815*. Toronto: Robin Brass Studio, 2006.

————. *Fort George Historical Study*. Ottawa: Parks Canada, 1979.

————, ed. *Merry Hearts Make Light Days: The War of 1812 Journal of Lieutenant John Le Couteur, 104th Foot*. Ottawa: Carleton University Press, 1993.

————. "The Redcoats are Coming! British Troop Movements to North America in 1814." *Journal of the War of 1812* 6, no. 3 (2001): 12–18.

————. *Where Right and Glory Lead: The Battle of Lundy's Lane, 1814*. Toronto: Robin Brass Studio, 1997.

Gray, William. *Soldiers of the King: The Upper Canadian Militia, 1812–1815*. Toronto: Stoddart, 1995.

Great Britain. War Office. *The Army List for August 1813*. London, 1813.

Greusal, Joseph, ed. *Collections and Researches of the Michigan Historical Society*, vol. 15. Lansing, Mich.: Wynkoop, Hallenbeck, Crawford Co., 1909.

Grodzinski, John R. "Much to Be Desired: The Campaign Experience of British General Officers of the War of 1812." *War of 1812 Magazine*, no. 6 (September 2007), The Napoleon Series, http://www.napoleon-series.org/military/Warof1812/2007/Issue7/c_BritishGenerals.html.

Guitard, Michelle. *The Militia of the Battle of the Châteauguay: A Social History*. Ottawa: Parks Canada, 1983.

Gurwood, John, ed. *The Dispatches of Field Marshal The Duke of Wellington*. 12 vols. London: J. Murray, 1834–39.

Gwyn, Julian. *Frigates and Foremasts: The North American Squadron in Nova Scotia Waters, 1745–1815*. Vancouver: UBC Press, 2003.

Haliburton, Thomas. *An Historical and Statistical Account of Nova Scotia*. 2 vols. Halifax: Joseph Howe, 1829.

Hall, Christopher D. *British Strategy in the Napoleonic Wars, 1803–1815*. Manchester: Manchester University Press, 1999.

————. *Wellington's Navy: Sea Power and the Peninsular War, 1807–1814*. London: Chatham Publishing, 2004.

Hall, John A. *A History of the Peninsular War*. Vol. 7, *The Biographical Dictionary of British Officers Killed and Wounded, 1808–1814*. London: Greenhill Books, 1998.

Heisler, John P. *The Canals of Canada*. Ottawa: National Historic Sites, 1973.

Henige, David P. *Colonial Governors from the Fifteenth Century to the Present*. Madison: University of Wisconsin Press, 1970.

Herkalo, Keith A. *The Battles at Plattsburgh: September 11, 1814*. Plattsburgh, N.Y.: n.p., 2007.

Hickey, Donald R. *Don't Give Up the Ship! Myths of the War of 1812*. Toronto: Robin Brass Studio, 2006.

————. *The War of 1812: A Forgotten Conflict*. Urbana: University of Illinois Press, 1990.

Historical Manuscripts Commission (HMC). *Report of the Manuscripts of Earl Bathurst*. London: His Majesty's Stationery Office, 1923.

Hitsman, J. Mackay. *The Incredible War of 1812: A Military History.* Updated by Donald E. Graves. Toronto: Robin Brass Studio, 1999.

———. *Safeguarding Canada, 1763–1871.* Toronto: University of Toronto Press, 1968.

———. "Sir George Prevost's Conduct of the Canadian War of 1812." *Canadian Historical Association Report* (1962): 34–43.

Horsman, Reginald. "British Indian Policy in the Northwest, 1807–1812." *Mississippi Valley Historical Review* 45, no. 1 (1958): 51–66.

Houlding, J. A. *Fit for Service: The Training of the British Army, 1715–1795.* Oxford: Clarendon Press, 1981.

Irving, L. Homfrey. *Officers of the British Forces in Canada during the War of 1812.* Welland: Tribune Print, 1908.

Isenburg, Nancy. *Fallen Founder: The Life of Aaron Burr.* New York: Penguin Books, 2007.

James, William, *Naval Occurrences of the Late War between Great Britain and the United States.* London: T. Egerton, 1817.

Johnston, Winston. *The Glengarry Light Infantry, 1812–1816.* Charlottetown, P.E.I.: n.p., 1998.

Kennedy, Paul M. *The Rise and Fall of British Naval Mastery.* Malabar, Fla.: Robert E. Krieger Publishing Company, 1982.

Kert, Faye Margaret. *Prize and Prejudice: Privateering and Naval Prize in Atlantic Canada in the War of 1812.* St. John's, Nfld.: International Maritime Economic History Association, 1997.

Kingsford, William. *History of Canada,* vol. 8. London: Keegan, Paul, Trench, Tubner & Co., 1895.

Klinck, Carl F., and James J. Talman with Additional Notes by Carl Benn. *The Journal of Major John Norton, 1816.* Toronto: Champlain Society, 2011.

Lavery, Brian. *Nelson's Navy: The Ships, Men and Organization, 1793–1815.* Annapolis: U.S. Naval Institute, 1986.

Laws, Lt. Col. M. E. S. "The Royal Artillery at Martinique, 1809." *Journal of the Royal Artillery* 77, no. 1 (1950): 70–81.

Legget, Robert. *Ottawa River Canals and the Defence of British North America.* Toronto: University of Toronto Press, 1982.

Lipscombe, Colonel Nick. *The Peninsular War Atlas.* London: Osprey Publishing, 2010.

Lossing, Benson J. *The Pictorial Field-Book of the War of 1812.* New York: Harper and Brothers Publishers, 1896.

Lyon, David, and Rif Winfield. *The Sail & Steam Navy List: All the Ships of the Royal Navy, 1815–1889.* London: Chatham Publishing, 2004.

Mahon, John K. *The War of 1812.* Gainesville: University Press of Florida, 1972.

Malcomson, Robert. *Capital in Flames: The American Attack at York, 1813.* Montreal: Robin Brass Studio, 2008.

———. *Historical Dictionary of the War of 1812.* Latham, Md.: Scarecrow Press, 2006.

———. *Lords of the Lake: The Naval War on Lake Ontario, 1812–1814.* Toronto: Robin Brass Studio, 1998.

———, ed. *Sailors of 1812: Memoirs and Letters of Naval Officers on Lake Ontario*. Youngstown, N.Y.: Old Fort Niagara Association, 1997.

———. *A Very Brilliant Affair: The Battle of Queenston Heights, 1812*. Toronto: Robin Brass Studio, 2003.

———. *Warships of the Great Lakes, 1754–1834*. Annapolis: Naval Institute Press, 2001.

Malcomson, Thomas, and Robert Malcomson. *The Battle for Lake Erie*. St. Catharines, Ont.: Vanwell Publishing Ltd., 1990.

Marshall, P. J. *The Oxford History of the British Empire*. Vol. 2, *The Eighteenth Century*. Oxford: Oxford University Press, 2001.

McConnell, David. *British Smooth-Bore Artillery: A Technological Study*. Ottawa: Parks Canada, 1988.

McNutt, W. S. *The Atlantic Provinces: The Emergence of a Colonial Society*. Toronto: McClelland and Stewart, 1965.

Morriss, Roger. *The Foundations of British Maritime Ascendancy: Resources, Logistics and the State, 1755–1815*. Cambridge: Cambridge University Press, 2011.

Muir, Rory. *Britain and the Defeat of Napoleon, 1807–1815*. New Haven, Conn., and London: Yale University Press, 1996.

Myatt, Frederick. *Peninsular General: Sir Thomas Picton, 1758–1815*. London: David & Charles, 1980.

Nafekh, Sonia. *The Story of Isaac Brock*. Kirkland, Qc.: Nafekh Technologies Inc., 2006.

Narrative of the Capture of the United States Brig Vixen *by the British Frigate Southampton and the Subsequent Loss of Both Vessels*. New York, 1813.

Niles, Hezekiah, ed. *The Weekly Register*. Baltimore: Franklin Press, 1811–1816.

Norie, J. W. *The Naval Gazetteer, Biographer, and Chronologist; Containing a History of the Late Wars*. London: J. W. Norie & Co., 1827.

Oman, Sir Charles. *A History of the Peninsular War*. 7 vols. Oxford: Clarendon Press, 1902–14.

———. *Wellington's Army, 1809–1814*. Oxford: Clarendon Press, 1903.

Oxford Dictionary of National Biography. 60 vols. Prepared under various editors. New York: Oxford University Press, 1885–2004. Also available at http://www.oxforddnb.com/.

Philalethes [George Macdonell, pseud.]. "The Late War in Canada." *United Services Magazine*, March 1848, pt. 1.

———. "The Late War in Canada." *United Services Magazine*, June 1848, pt. 2.

Phillipart, John, ed. *The Royal Military Calendar*. 3 vols. London: T. Egerton, 1820.

Preston, Richard A. "The First Battle of Sackets Harbor." *Historic Kingston*, no. 11 (1961–62): 3–7.

———, ed. *Kingston before the War of 1812*. Toronto: Champlain Society, 1959.

[Procter, Henry]. "Campaigns in the Canadas." *Quarterly Review* 27 (1822): 405–49.

———. "Indian Warfare." In *The Lucubrations of Humphrey Ravelin, Esq.* London: W. and G. B. Whitaker, 1823. 319–59.

Quartermaster-General's Department. *British Minor Expeditions, 1746 to 1814.* London: Her Majesty's Stationery Office, 1884.

Quimby, Robert S. *The U.S. Army in the War of 1812: An Operational and Command Study.* 2 vols. Lansing: Michigan State University Press, 1998.

Raudzens, George. "'Red George' Macdonell, Military Saviour of Upper Canada?" *Ontario History* 62, no. 4 (1970): 199–212.

Reilly, Robin. *The British at the Gates: The New Orleans Campaign in the War of 1812.* Toronto: Robin Brass Studio, 2002.

Riley, Jonathon. *A Matter of Honour: The Life, Campaigns and Generalship of Sir Isaac Brock.* Montreal: Robin Brass Studio, 2011.

Rives, George Lockhart, ed. *Selections from the Correspondence of Thomas Barclay.* New York: Harper and Brothers, 1894.

Robinson, Howard. *Carrying British Mails Overseas.* London: George Allen and Unwin, 1964.

Rodger, N. A. M. *The Command of the Ocean: A Naval History of Britain, 1649–1815.* London: Allen Lane, 2004.

———, ed. *Essays in Naval History, from Medieval to Modern.* Farnham, UK: Ashgate, 2009.

Rose, J. Holland. "British West India Commerce as a Factor in the Napoleonic Wars." *Cambridge Historical Journal* 3, no 1 (1929): 34–46.

Scadding, Henry. "The Letters of Veritas." *Canadian Monthly and National Review* 9, no. 2 (1876): 89–94.

Secretary of War. *Collection of Orders, Regulations and Instructions for the Army; on Matters of Finance and Points of Discipline.* London: T. Egerton, 1807.

"Secret Reports of John Howe, I." *American Historical Review* 17, no. 1 (1911): 70–74.

"Secret Reports of John Howe, II." *American Historical Review* 17, no. 2 (1912): 332–54.

Sheppard, Charles. *Historical Account of St. Vincent.* London: W. Nichol, 1831.

Silverstone, Paul H. *The Sailing Navy, 1775–1854.* Annapolis: U.S. Naval Institute Press, 2001.

Skaggs, David Curtis. *Thomas Macdonough: Master and Commander in the Early U.S. Navy.* Annapolis: U.S. Naval Institute, 2003.

Skaggs, David Curtis, and Gerard T. Altoff. *A Signal Victory: The Lake Erie Campaign, 1812–1813.* Annapolis: Naval Institute Press, 1997.

Southey, Thomas. *Chronological History of the West Indies.* 3 vols. London: Longman, Rees, Orne and Green, 1827.

Stacey, C. P. *The Battle of Little York.* Toronto: Toronto Historical Board, 1977.

———. *Quebec, 1759: The Siege and the Battle.* Edited and with new material by Donald E. Graves. Toronto: Robin Brass Studio, 2002.

Stagg, J. C. A. *Mr. Madison's War.* Princeton, N.J.: Princeton University Press, 1983.

―――. *The War of 1812: Conflict for a Continent*. Cambridge: Cambridge University Press, 2012.

Stanley, George F. G. *The War of 1812: Land Operations*. Toronto: Macmillan of Canada, 1983.

Stewart, James. *Report of Cases Argued and Determined in the Court of Vice-Admiralty at Halifax, Nova Scotia*. London: J. Butterworth and Son, 1814.

Stuart, George, comp. *Reports of Cases Argued and Determined in the Courts of King's Bench and in the Provincial Court of Appeals of Lower Canada with a few of the more important Cases of the Court of Vice Admiralty*. Quebec: Neilson & Cowan, 1834.

Sullivan, Nell Jane Barnett, and David Kendall Martin. *A History of the Town of Chazy, Clinton County, New York*. Burlington, Vt.: George Little Press, 1970.

Sutherland, Stuart. *His Majesty's Gentlemen: A Directory of British Regular Army Officers in the War of 1812*. Toronto: ISER Publications, 2001.

Thwaites, Reuben. *Collections of the State Historical Society of Wisconsin*, vol. 12. Madison: Democrat Printing Company, 1892.

Troxler, Carole Watterson. "Refuge, Resistance and Reward: The Southern Loyalist's Claim on East Florida." *Journal of Southern History* 44, no. 4 (1989): 563–96.

Tulloch, Captain M. A. "On the Sickness and Mortality among the Troops in the West Indies, Part 1." *Journal of the Statistical Society of London* 1, no. 3 (1838): 129–42.

Tupper, Ferdinand Brock, ed. *The Life and Correspondence of Major General Sir Isaac Brock, K.B.* London: Simpkin, Marshall & Company, 1845.

Turner, Wesley. *The Astonishing General: The Life and Legacy of Isaac Brock*. Toronto: Dundurn, 2011.

―――. *British Generals in the War of 1812: High Command in the Canadas*. Montreal: McGill-Queen's University Press, 1999.

―――. *The War of 1812: The War Both Sides Won*. Toronto: Dundurn, 1990.

Veritas [John Richardson, pseud.]. *The Letters of Veritas, Re-Published from the Montreal Herald; Containing a Succinct Narrative of the Military Administration of Sir George Prevost during His Command in the Canadas*. Montreal: W. Gray, July 1815.

Walker, H. M. *A History of the Northumberland Fusiliers, 1674–1902*. London: John Murray, 1919.

Wallace, Nesbit Willoughby. *A Regimental Chronicle and List of Officers of the 60th or the King's Royal Rifle Corps*. London: Harrison, 1879.

Ward, S. G. P. *Wellington*. London: T. Batsford, 1963.

―――. *Wellington's Headquarters: A Study of the Administrative Problems in the Peninsula, 1809–1814*. Oxford: Oxford University Press, 1957.

Wellington, Second Duke of, ed. *Supplementary Dispatches, Correspondence and Memoranda of Field Marshal, The Duke of Wellington*. 15 vols. London: John Murray, 1858–72.

Wheater, W. *Historical Records of the Seventh or Royal Regiment of Fusiliers*. Leeds: n.p., 1875.

White, Patrick C. T. *A Nation on Trial. America and the War of 1812*. New York: John Wiley & Sons, 1965.

Wilder, Patrick A. *The Battle of Sackets Harbour, 1813*. Baltimore: Nautical and Aviation Publishing Company, 1994.

Winfield, Rif. *British Warships in the Age of Sail, 1793–1817*. London: Chatham Publishing, 2005.

Wohler, J. Patrick *Charles de Salaberry: Soldier of the Empire, Defender of Quebec*. Toronto: Dundurn, 1984.

Wood, Captain J. H. "Extracts from the Diary of Captain, afterwards Colonel J. H. Wood, R.A.: Plattsburgh, 1814." *Women's Canadian Historical Society of Toronto* 5 (1905): 10–16.

Wood, William, ed. *Select British Documents of the Canadian War of 1812*. 4 vols. Toronto: Champlain Society, 1920–28.

THESES, DISSERTATIONS, AND OTHER UNPUBLISHED MATERIAL

Armit, W. B. "Halifax 1749–1906: Soldiers Who Founded and Garrisoned a Famous City." Photocopy, ca. 1958.

Chartrand, René, and Donald E. Graves. "The United States Army of the War of 1812: A Handbook." Photocopy, unpublished manuscript, n.d. [ca. July 1986].

Graves, Donald E. *The Attack on Sackets Harbor, 29 May 1813: The British/Canadian Side*. Ottawa: Directorate of History, ca. 1991.

———. "'The Finest Army Ever to Campaign on American Soil'?: The Organization, Strength, Composition, and Losses of British Land Forces during the Plattsburgh Campaign, September 1814." Unpublished paper in author's possession.

Grodzinski, John R. "The Vigilant Superintendence of the Whole District: The War of 1812 on the Upper St Lawrence." Master's thesis, Royal Military College of Canada, 2002.

Hooper, Thomas. *The Royal Navy Station at Ile-aux-Noix*. Ottawa: Parks Canada, 1967.

Hyatt, A. M. J. "The Defence of Upper Canada in 1812." Master's thesis, Carleton University, 1961.

Knight, Roger. "The Dockyards in England at the Time of the American War of Independence." PhD diss., University of London, 1972.

Linch, Kevin. "The Recruitment of the British Army, 1807–1815." PhD diss., University of Leeds, 2001.

Redgrave, Toby. "Wellington's Logistical Arrangements in the Peninsular War, 1809–1814." PhD diss., King's College, University of London, 1979.

Romans, Mark. "Professionalism and the Development of Military Intelligence in Wellington's Army, 1809–1814." PhD diss., University of Southampton, 2005.

Steppler, Glenn A. "A Duty Troublesome beyond Measure: Logistical Considerations in the Canadian War of 1812." Master's thesis, McGill University, 1974.

Sutherland, Maxwell. "The Civil Administration of Sir George Prevost, 1811–1815: A Study in Conciliation." Master's thesis, Queen's University, 1959.

Trenholm, Donald T. "The Military Defence of Nova Scotia during the French and American Wars (1789–1815)." Master's thesis, Mount Allison University, 1939.

Wilder, Patrick. "'We Will Not Conquer Canada This Year': The Battle of Sacket's Harbor." Unpublished manuscript in the author's possession.

Wilson, David. "Government Dockyard Workers in Portsmouth, 1793–1815." PhD diss., University of Warwick, 1975.

INDEX